AGRO BASED PLANTATION CULTIVATION AND FARMING HAND BOOK

WITH DIRECTORY OF AGRICULTURAL EQUIPMENTS & IMPLEMENTS

A complete enclopaedia on Agro Based Plantation Cultivation and Farming which deals with new technologies, processing, methods and project profiles with directory of of Agricultural Equipment and Implements. The book is covering with the 19 detailed chapters including a directory section. The Chapters included in this book are Banana Cultivation, Bee Keeping, Coconut Plantation, Dairy Farming, Eucalyptus Plantation, Floriculture (Cut-Flower), Ginger Cultivation, Goat Farming, Mushroom Cultivation, Orchard, Papaya Cultivation, Piggery Farming, Poultry Farm, Rabbit Farm, Sheep Farming, Tea Plantation, Teak Tree Plantation & Tissue Cultrure.

Written By:

EIRI CONSULTANTS & ENGINEERS

&

Compiled By

SUDHIR GUPTA

A WORLD RENOWNED CONSULTANTS WORKING OVER 20 YEARS.

ENGINEERS INDIA RESEARCH INSTITUTE

4449, Nai Sarak , Main Road, New Delhi -110 006 (INDIA)

Tel : 291 8117, 291 6431, 292 0361 • Fax : 91-11- 291 6431

PRINTED & PUBLISHED BY

ENGINEERS INDIA RESEARCH INSTITUTE
Regd. Office : 4449, Nai Sarak , Main Road, New Delhi -110 006 (INDIA)
Tel : 291 8117, 291 6431, 292 0361 • Fax : 91-11- 291 6431

DISTRIBUTED BY

SMALL INDUSTRY RESEARCH INSTITUTE

New Delhi (INDIA)

ISBN : 81- 86732- 14 - 4
Printed in New Delhi (INDIA)

Rs. 475

Printed & Published by **Sudhir Gupta** for **"Engineers India Research Institute"** and Laser Type Set by **Puneet Malhotra** at Engineers India Research Institute, and printed at **'Sanjeev Offset Printer , Krishan Nagar, Delhi - 51**

Preface

Agro Based Plantation Cultivation & Farming Hand Book

Agro Based Plantation Cultivation & Farming Industries are now-a-days flourishing and also having a bright future scope. The book which is in your hand on Agro Based Plantation Cultivation & Farming Hand Book is potentially useful book. Agro Based industry is the largest determinant of gross national production in our country.

India is home to an enormous variety & range of fruits & vegetables. Popular Indian fruits are the Mango, Banana, Papaya, Orange, Mosambi, Grapes, Apple, PineApple, Sapota, Lichi, Walnut and Guava. Grapes are an important item of export from India.

The vegetables grown in the country include the Potato, Onion, Garlic, Lady Finger, Tomato, Brinjal, Peas, Beans, Celery, Cabbage, Cauliflower, etc. India's vegetables are popular in the middle east and south east asian markets. Tea is an important item which is fluently exported to many overseas countries. Tissue Culture and Cut-Flowers (Floriculture) are the another products which are having good demand in overseas countries now a days. Like these, Mushroom Cultivation, Coconut Cultivation & Banana cultivation are having great demand in india as well also having an export demand. Poultry Farm, Piggery Farm, Rabbit Farm, Sheep Farm & Dairy Farming are now on the progressive side in an Indian market.

The book, in your hand, deals with the 19 exclusive detailed chapters. Each chapter is described with the best available datas and all the chapters described in the book are so detailed that a new entrepreneur as well as an established industrialist need not to consult with any other such book. The Major Chapters are : Banana Ciltivation, Bee Keeping, Coconut Plantation, Dairy Farming, Eucalyptus Plantation, Floriculture (Cut-Flower), Ginger Cultivation, Goat Farming, Mushroom Cultivation, Orchard, Papaya Cultivation, Piggery Farming, Poultry Farm, Rabbit Farm, Sheep Farming, Tea Plantation, Teak Tree Plantation & Tissue Culture.

Director
ENGINEERS INDIA RESEARCH INSTITUTE
Nai Sarak, New Delhi.
Fax : 91-11-291 6431

CONTENTS AND SUBJECT INDEX

Chapters **Page No.**

Banana Cultivation **1 - 25**

- INTRODUCTION 1
- VARIETIES 2
- PROPAGATION 6
- FERTILIZER APPLICATION 8
- CULTURAL PRACTICES 9
- CROP ROTATION 10
- DISEASES CONTROL 11
- PEST CONTROL 16
- FLOWERING & FRUITING 18
- MARKETING & STORAGE 19
- USES & COMPOSITION 20
- COMPOSITION OF BANANA FRUIT 21
- PLANT ECONOMICS OF BANANA POWDER 22
- PLANT ECONOMICS OF BANANA & ITS BYE - PRODUCTS 24

Bee Keeping **26 - 41**

- INTRODUCTION 26
- CATCHING THE STRAY SWARM 27
- PURCHASE OF PACKAGE BEES 30
- DIVISION OF EXISTING COLONY 31
- METHODS OF UNITING COLONIES 37
- LAYING OUT OF APIARY 38
- CONCLUSION 39
- PLANT ECONOMICS OF BEE KEEPING 40

Coconut Plantation/Cultivation **42 - 75**

- INTRODUCTION 42
- CLIMATE 43
- VARIETIES 44
- HYBRID PALMS 46
- PLANTING MATERIAL 47
- SELECTION & PREPARATION OF NURSERY 47
- LAND PREPARATION 49
- FERTILIZER APPLICATIONS 50
- IRRIGATION & SOIL MOISTURE CONSERVATION 52
- INSECTS PESTS 53
- DISEASES 55
- HARVESTING 58
- YIELD 58
- PROCESSING 59

- ECONOMICS OF COCONUT PLANTATION 59
- COCONUT EXPORTER 59
- PLANT ECONOMICS OF COCONUT OIL FROM COPRA 60
- PLANT ECONOMICS OF COCONUT PROCESSING COMPLEX 62
- PLANT ECONOMICS OF DESICCATED COCONUT POWDER FROM COCONUT 65
- PLANT ECONOMICS OF ACTIVATED CARBON 67
- PLANT ECONOMICS OF COCONUT WATER 69
- PLANT ECONOMICS OF DEHYDRATED COCONUT MILK POWDER 71
- PLANT ECONOMICS OF COCONUT SHELL POWDER 74

Dairy Farming 76 - 90

- INTRODUCTION 76
- BREEDS 77
- YIELDS 78
- USES AND APPLICATIONS OF MILK 78
- DISEASES 79
- SUPPLIERS OF CATTLES 79
- COMPOSITION OF CATTLE FEED 80
- COMPOSITION OF MILK 80
- MANUFACTURING PROCESS 81
- ADDRESSESOF PLANT & MACHINERY SUPPLIERS 83
- PLANT ECONOMICS OF DAIRY FARM 04
- IMPORTANT ADDRESSES 86
- INSTITUTIONS EDUCATIONAL AND RESEARCH 87
- NATIONAL DAIRY DEVELOPMENT BOARD 90

Eucalyptus Tree Plantation/Cultivation 91 - 101

- INTRODUCTION 91
- GROWTH HABBIT 92
- SOIL AND CLIMATE 92
- SEEDS AND STORAGE 93
- PLANTING TECHNIQUES 94
- SPACING 96
- GROWTH AND YIELD 97
- ECONOMICS OF PLANTATIONS 99

FIXED COST
RECURRING EXPENSES
RETURNS

Floriculture (Cut-Flowers) 102 - 143

- INTRODUCTION 102
- CLIMATE 102
- SOIL 103
- LAYOUT OF BEDS 103
- GROWTH AND FLOWERING 103
- PROPAGATION 106
- ROOT STOCKS 109
- PREPARATION OF BEDS 111
- CULTIVATION 112
- PRUNING OF ESTABLISHED ROSE PLANTS 114
- IRRIGATION 119

- DISEASES AND PESTS 120
- HARVESTING AND POST HARVEST HANDLING 124
  HARVESTING
  PACKAGING
  YIELD
- IMPORTANCE AND USES 125
- CUT-FLOWERS 127
- PERFUMED AND ALLIED PRODUCTS 127
  ROSE OIL (ROSE PERFUME)
  ROSE WATER
  GULKAND
  PANKHURI
  GUL-ROGHAN
- OTHER USES 129
- LAND DEVELOPMENT FOR FLORICULTURE PROJECT 129
- LAND SELECTION 130
- LAND DEVELOPMENT 131
- PRESENTLY GROWERS/SUPPLIERS OF FLORICULTURE 133
- IMPORTERS OF PLANTING MATERIAL, BULBS ETC. 135
- SUPPLIERS OF IMPORTANT MACHINES & ACCESSORIES 135
- CUT-FLOWERS IMPORTERS 137
- PLANT ECONOMICS OF FLORICULTURE 138
- PLANT ECONOMICS OF ROSE PLANTATION & ROSE OIL 142

Ginger Cultivation **144 - 162**

- INTRODUCTION 144
- SOIL 144
- CLIMATE 145
- LAND PREPARATION 145
- VARIETIES 145
- MANURES AND FERTILIZERS 149
- SOWING OR PROPAGATION 150
- MULCHING 150
- IRRIGATION 151
- WEED CONTROL 151
- DISEASES CONTROL 151
- PEST CONTROL 152
- HARVESTING & YIELD 152
- DRYING OF GINGER 153
- GRADING OF DRIED GINGER 155
- STORAGE OF SEED RHIZOME 155
- UNFAVOURABLE CLIMATE 156
- USES AND IMPORTANCE 156
- ECONOMICS OF CULTIVATION 157
- PLANT ECONOMICS OF GINGER OIL 158
- PLANT ECONOMICS OF DRY GINGER FROM GREEN GINGER 160

Goat Farming **163-194**

- INTRODUCTION 163
- ORIGIN 163
- DISTRIBUTION 164
- IMPORTANCE OF GOAT IN RURAL DEVELOPMENT 165
- BEHAVIOUR OF GOAT 167
  GRAZING BEHAVIOUR
  INDIVIDUAL RECOGNITION IN GOATS

AGONISTIC BEHAVIOUR
DOMINANCE - SUBORDINATION BEHAVIOUR
MATERNAL BEHAVIOUR
SLEEP
GOAT PRODUCTION SYSTEM 168
EXTENSIVE GRAZING
SEDENTARY FAMILY HERBS
INTENSIVE COMMERCIAL PRODUCTION
- IMPORTANT BREEDS OF GOAT 169
- FEED INGREDIENTS 172
- FEED STUFFS FOR GOAT 173
- CREEP FEEDING 175
- GROWER'S RATION 176
- FINISHER RATION 176
- ESTABLISHING A GOAT FARM 177
- ECONOMICS OF GOAT REARING 179
- ECONOMICS OF GOAT KEEPING 181
- HOUSING & CONTROLLING METHODS OF GOAT 184
- BUILDING FOR GOAT FARM 186
- PLANT ECONOMICS OF GOAT & SHEEP FARMING 191
- PLANT ECONOMICS OF GOAT BREEDING FARMING 193

Mushroom Cultivation/Growing 195 - 211

- INTRODUCTION 195
- MUSHROOM CULTIVATION IN INDIA 196
- WHITE BUTTON MUSHROOM 196
- COMPOSTING 197
- SPAWNING 198
- CASING 198
- CROPPING & HARVESTING 199
- DISEASES 199
- PRESERVATION 200
- PADDY STRAW MUSHROOM 202
- OYSTER MUSHROOM 203
- EDULIS MUSHROOM 204
- CONCLUSION 205
- CONSULTANTS FOR MUSHROOM PROJECTS 206
- IMPORTANT ADDRESSES 206
- IMPORTERS OF MUSHROOM 206
- PLANT ECONOMICS OF MUSHROOM CULTIVATION 209

Establishing An Orchard 212 - 225

- INTRODUCTION 212
- SITE SELECTION 212
- ASSESSMENT OF RESOURCES 213
- PRELIMINARY OPERATIONS 215
- PLANNING THE ORCHARD 215
- PLANNING SYSTEMS 218
- PURCHASING SAPLINGS FROM NURSERY 219
- PLANTING 220

Papaya Cultivation 226-246

INTRODUCTION 226

- CLIMATE 227
- SOIL 227
- VARIETIES 227
- PROPAGATION 230
- FERTILIZER APPLICATION 232
- IRRIGATION 232
- THINNING OF FRUITS 233
- PLANT PRODUCTION MEASURES 233
- PROBLEMS OF UNFAVOURABLE CLIMATIC CONDITIONS 238
- FLOWERING AND FRUITING 238
- MATURITY 238
- HARVESTING & YIELD 239
- STORAGE AND RIPENING 239
- USES 240
- EXTRATION OF PAPAIN 242
- ECONOMICS OF CULTIVATION 242
- PLANT ECONOMICS OF PAPAYA CULTIVATION AND PAPAIN 243
- PLANT ECONOMICS OF PAPAYA CULTIVATION 245

Piggery Farming **247-263**

- TERMS USED IN PIG PRODUCTION 247
- CONSTRAINT OF PIG RAISING 250
- SYSTEMS OF PIG HOUSING 250
- CONSTRUCTION DETAILS 255
- CATEGORY-WISE HOUSING REQUIREMENTS 258
- STANDARD GROWER RATION FOR PIG 260
- IMPORTANT ADDRESSES 261
- PLANT ECONOMICS OF PIGGERY FARM 262

Poultry Farm **264-284**

- HOW TO START A POULTRY FARM 264
- SALIENT POINTS OF WHITE LEG HORN 267
- MEAT TYPE BREEDS 268
- BROILERS FARMS 270
- PLANNING AND LAYOUT OF POULTRY FARM 272
- HOUSING PRINCIPLES AND CONSTRUCTION 273
- REQUIREMENTS OF THE POULTRY HOUSE 274
- ADDITIONAL REQUIREMENT FOR LAYERS HOUSES 276
- ADDITIONAL REQUIREMENT FOR BROILER FARM 277
- IMPORTANT ADDRESSES 278
- PLANT ECONOMICS OF POULTRY AND BROILER FARM 279
- PLANT ECONOMICS OF POULTRY FARMING 282

Rabbit Farm **285-300**

- INTRODUCTION 285
- PHYSIOLOGY AND HABITAT 286
- ADVANTAGES AND RABBIT REARING 289
- PROBLEMS OF RABBIT REARING 290
- RABBIT PRODUCTION SYSTEMS 290
- RABBIT BYE-PRODUCTS AND THEIR USE 292
- BREEDS OF RABBIT 292
- COMMON BREED AND VARIETIES OF RABBIT 293
- PLANT ECONOMICS OF RABBIT FARMING 295
- PLANT ECONOMICS OF ANGORA RABBIT 298

Sheep Farming 301 - 314

- INTRODUCTION 301
- ORIGIN AND DISTRIBUTION 302
- SHEEP CHARACTERISTICS 303
- SHEEP BREEDS OF INDIA 305
- RECENT DEVELOPMENTS 305
- SHEEP HUSBANDRY IN INDIA 306
- PLANT ECONOMICS OF CHICKEN/MUTTON (SHEEP MEAT) 309
- PLANT ECONOMICS OF GOAT AND SHEEP FARMING 312

Tea Plantation/Cultivation 315 - 335

- INTRODUCTION 315
- CLIMATE 316
- SOIL 316
- PROPAGATION 317
- NURSERY MANAGEMENT 318
- LAND PREPARATION 318
- COMMON MALADIES IN TEA NURSERY 319
- TRANSPLANTING 320
- SHADE TREES AND THEIR MANAGEMENT 320
- SPACING 321
- MANURES AND FERTILIZERS 321
- MULCHING 324
- TRAINING AND PRUNING 324
- IRRIGATION AND WATER MANAGEMENT 324
- WEED CONTROL 326
- DISEASES AND PESTS 326
- HARVESTING 331
- YIELD 332
- PROCESSING 332
- PLANT ECONOMICS OF TEA PLANTATION 333
- IMPORTERS OF TEA 335

Teak Tree Plantation 336 - 357

- TIME TABLE OF PLANTATION WORK 336
- PROBLEMS OF PURE TEA PLANTATION & REMEDIAL MEASURES 338
- MIXTURES 342
- PLANTATION METHOD OF TEAK 348
- IMPORTANT ADDRESSES 350
- PLANT ECONOMICS OF TEAK TREE PLANTATION 351
- PLANT ECONOMICS OF TEAK TREE PLANTATION 354

Tissue Culture 358 - 370

- REQUIREMENTS 359
- PROCEDURE 360
- PROTOCOL FOR CRYO PRESERVATION 362
- CONCLUSIONS 364
- IMPORATNT ADDRESSES 364
- PLANT ECONOMICS OF TISSUE CULTURE 368

Directory of Agricultural Equipment & Implements 371 - 378

Chapter - 1

Banana Cultivation

INTRODUCTION

The banana is considered to be one of the most primitive cultivatedtropical fruits in India which ranks next only to mango in area and a production. It is not only the staple food of millions of people, but also the most important commercial fruit of the tropical areas of the world now. The cultivated banana is botanically named as Musa paradisiaca belonging to the family Musaceae. It is believed to have originated in the hot tropical regions of south east Asia. It is extensively grown in many countries like Mexico, Egypt, Israel, South Africa, Indonesia, Philippines, Brazil, and Sri Lanka. Next to Brazil, India is the second largest banana producing country in the world. The chief banana growing states in India are: Maharashtra, karnataka, Kerala, Tamil Nadu, Andhra Pradesh, Orissa, Bihar, West Bengal and Assam. Banana occupies an area of about 2.83 lakh hectares with an annual production of 46.26 lakh tonnes.

Banana is a rich source of energy in the form of sugars and starch, available almost throughout the year and is the cheapest fruit in India. Almost all the parts of a banana plant are useful and today, it is the leading tropical fruit in the world market with a highly organised and developed industry.

CLIMATE

Banana is essentially a tropical plant requiring a warm humid climate,but it is adapted to a wide range of climatic conditions ranging from wet tropical to dry sub-tropical. it can grow successfully from sea level to an altitude of 1500 metres. Temperature plays an important role as the rate of new leaf formation and fruit growth is largely governed by it. It grows well at a temperature range of 10° to 40°C. However, a mean temperature of 26.7°C and 100 mm of rain per month are considered satisfactory. Frequent rains and humid weather are preferable.

Low temperature, frost and wind storm are the limiting factors in successful banana cultivation. Low temperature below 10°C is harmful and repeated occurrence of cold waves during the winter seriously interferes with the normal growth of the plant. Storms and winds are also very hazardous and sometimes result in complete uprooting of orbreakageof the pseudostem.Hot winds during summer months shed and desiccate the leaves.

SOIL

Banana requires a well drained, rich in organic matter and moisture retehtive soil for its proper growth. Depth and drainage of soil are the two most important criteria which need attention while selecting soil for banana cultivation. The soil should be well drained and at least 3' ft. deep. Thus deep, well drained, friable, loamy soil with adequate organic matter is ideal for its cultivation. It can grow in variety of soil types such as alluvial soil, black loam, sandy loam and lateritic soil. it can grow well in slightly alkaline soils but salinity above 0.05 % is injurious.

VARIETIES

More than 300 varieties of banana are known in India. Banana can be grouped into five main categories:

(i) **Desert banana:** This group consists of table varieties for consumption as such, after they are ripe, eg. Champa, Rasthali,Robusta, Dwarf Cavendish, etc.

(ii) **Culinary bananas:** These bananas can be used only aftercooking, such as Monthan, Bankel

(iii) Varieties suitable for making chips, e.g.; Nendran.
(iv) Varieties for jam making e.g.; Virupakshi.
(v) Varieties fit for making powders (baby food), e.g; Kunnan.

Varieties commonly grown in different regions are given below :

(i) **Western and Central India:** Basrai, Harichal, etc.
(ii) **Southern India:** Poovan, Dwarf Cavendish, Robusta, Nendran, Rasthali,Chakrakeli, Virupakshi, monthan.
(iii) **Eastern India:** Kabuli, Champa, Kothia, Batheesa, Martaman and AmritSagar.
(iv) **Northern India:** Champa, Rasthali, Bankel, Bathesa and Kothia.

Description of some of the major cultivars of India is given:

1. Poovan

This is an important table variety of West bengal, Tamil Nadu and Kerala. The plant is hardy and can grow vigorously under ratooning system of cultivation. The distinguishing characters of the plant is the rose pink colour of the outer side of the midrib when young, heavy bunches with closely packed fruits hand down vertically. It is hardy and can withstand moisturestress. Thebunch is medium to large sized, fruit is small, yellow skinned, firm fleshe and of poor quality. it has a good keeping quality and can be easily transported to distant markets. It is resistant to Panama wilt and bunchy top diseases. The duration varies from 11 to 14 months.

2. Bontha

Bontha is a leading commercial culinary banana variety of India, particularly of Andhra Pradesh. The plant is hardy and drought resistant. It bears a pendulous bunch with a markedly long peduncle. Fruits are long with good firth in the middle, plump, angulate, straight with blunt or knobbed apex. Rind is thick and green. The bunch contains large fruits in the proximal upper hands but with smaller fruits in the lower hand. Unripe fruits are used for making chips. It is resistant to leafspot but is susceptible to Panama disease

3. Dwarf Cavendish

Dwarf Cavendish, also called Basrai, is a leading commercial variety of Maharashtra and important commercial cultivar of Gujarat and West Bengal. The plants are dwarf and thus less prone to storm damage. The plants show good response to heavy manuring, thus give heavy yield with proper manuring and orchard management practices. The bunches are large sized, compact with good grade fruits. The fruits are large and good in quality and turn yellow on ripening in winter but remain green during the summer months. It has a poor keeping quality and the fruits easily get bruised and damaged during transportation unless handled carefully. It is resistant to Panama wilt but susceptible to bunchy top disease. The duration is 10-12 months in Tamil Nadu and 16 months under Poona conditions. Dwarf Cavendish is an important banana in international trade.

4. Robusta (Giant Cavendish)

Robusta is a semi tall sport of Dwarf Cavendish. It is grown mostly in Tamil Nadu and some parts of Andhra Pradesh and Maharashtra. Fruits are large, skin thick, greenish to dull yellow, pulp sweet and delicious. Fruits have a better keeping quality in parts of Kerala replacing 'Nendran' by virtue of its heavier bunch weight. It is a heavy yielder and requires support or staking. This variety is used for large scale export

5. Rasthali

This is another commercial cultivar grown widely in West Bengal, Andhra Pradesh, Tamil Nadu and Karnataka. Rasthali is the choicest table variety of West Bengal. Fruits are medium sized and similar to that of Poovan in appearance. Skin thin, yellow in colour, flesh firm and sweet with a pleasant aroma, Due to its better root system, it can resist strong wind better than other varieties. Its susceptibility to wilt, and easy dropping of fruits from the bunch and formation of hard lump in the pulp are the main drawbacks. The duration is from 15 to 16 months from planting to maturity.

6. Virupakshi

Virupakshi is a famous perennial banana grown in the Palni hills of Tamil Nadu. It is very much liked for its good flavour and keeping quality.

It is grown in the Palni hills (at lower elevations) as a rainfed crop mostly mixed with coffee. It is a vigorous and hardy banana though not a heavy yielder. Only when cultivated in higher elevations, Virupakshi has the characteristic flavour, which is not found in the fruits grown in the plains. In the mixed cultivation, it fits in well as a shade plant for young coffee plants. It is resistant to leaf spot desease but susceptible to bunchy top which is affecting its production.

7. Nendran

Nendran is an important commercial cultivar in Kerala and, to some extent, Tamil Nadu. It is also used as a culinary variety. Nendran bananas are moderately vigorous with slender angular, pointed fruits with starchy flesh even when they are ripe. They are resistant to Panama wilt and leaf spot diseases but very susceptible to attack by borers. The fruits are relatively longer and thicker than most other bananas. The duration is 11-12 months after planting.

8. Safed Velchi

This is a variety with good quality fruits and is under stray cultivation throughout South India and Maharashtra. It is grown as an intercrop in coconut and arecanut plantations. The plants of this variety are medium sized with yellowish pseudostem having reddish petiole margin. The fruits are small, firm fleshed and sweet. The duration is about 13 months.

9. Lal Kela

The variety is grown throughout the world. In India, this variety is grown in Bombay region of Maharashtra. The colour of the pseudostem, petiole, midrib and fruit rind is purplish red. The fruit is of good size and has a strong flavour. The rind is thick and during ripening colour changes from red to orange yellow. It is a long duration variety and takes about 18 months from planting to harvest.

10. Kunnan

This is a superior dessert variety of Kerala. Plants are medium sized and fruit have thin rind. flesh in firm and it tastes well. The fruits are irregularly curved with unusually long apex.

11. Amrit Sagar

This is considered as the choicest variety of India and grown in West Bengal. The plant is medium sized and delicate in nature. Fruit size is good with a good taste, and the rind in medium thick.

12. Chakarakeli

This is considered to be a choice variety of Andhra Pradesh. Plant are slender and medium sized with petiole borders open and prominently red. The fruit has a characteristic curvature with a prominent apex. The rind is thick, pulp yellowish and very tasty.

13. Gros Michel

This variety ranks first among the dessert banana varieties of the world. This is a recent introduction into southern India. It is suitable for cultivation only under garden land conditions because its cultural requirement are very high. Therefore, cultivators are not attracted to this variety. However, it produces heavy symmetrical bunches that permit unpacked transport. It is also susceptible to Panama wilt disease.

14. Giant Governor

Its cultivation is becoming popular in West Bengal. The plant is medium dwarf, fruits large, greenish to dull yellow in colour, flesh firm and sweet. This variety is susceptible to leaf spot disease but resistant to panama wilt.

PROPAGATION

Banana is vegetatively propagated by means of suckers, whole or bits of rhizomes of the parent plant or daughter suckers with at least one sprouting bud.

A. Selection of planting material

There are two kinds of suckers in banana viz. sword suckers and water suckers. Sword suckers have a well developed based with narrow sword shaped leaf blades in the early stages, whereas water suckers are small, undersized suckers with broad leaves of superficial origin. Healthy sword sucker of 3-4 months old is the best planting material because it is more vigorous, grows faster and comes to bearing earlier. For quick multiplication of a variety, rhizome bits cut from a healthy unbranched rhizome after trimming roots, each with a germinating eye centrally placed can be used. Preferably it should be of a good size to ensure the reserve food for early growth. The daughter rhizomes of Dwarf Cavendish bananas can be stored for two months after harvest of the bunch and keeping them in shape covered with dry banana leaves. In Kerala, rhizomes of 'Nendran' are sun dried for 2-3 days after smearing with cowdung paste and ashes. Then they are stored in shade for a month before planting.

B. Preparation of land

The land should be deeply ploughed, harrowed and levelled properly. Pits of 0.6m X 0.6m size are dug, so that the suckers are planted with rhizome 9 to 12 inches below the soil surface. The land is manure early before planting, using upto 100 tonnes of farmyard mânure per hectare. Green manuring the land with leguminous crops before planting is advisable to increase the soil fertility.

C. Planting

Planting may be done throughout the year except in severe winter and during heavy rains. However, February April, August and October are the best months for banana planting. The distance of planting varies according to the height and spread of the variety, soil fertility, topography and the growth shown in particular locality. A spacing of 2.7m X 3.0m for tall varieties and 1.8m X 1.8m for dwarf varieties are found most suitable. Dense planting with closer spacing besides controlling weeds and providing protection against windstorm gives a good return provides proper management practices are followed. High profit from banana cultivation can be taken without ratooning the crop through higher plant population (10,000 plants/ha) i.e. 1m X 1m spacing. For planting, healthy sword suckers preferably of 3 ft. height should be selected. all their leaves and roots are removed and generally 2/3rd of their pseudostem is also cut off. The pseudostem of the suckers is cut off close to the bulb. These bulbs are planted with the heart bud pointing up.

To prevent the attack of nematodes and stem weevil, the bulb or corm should be dipped in clay slurry and Furadan @ 20 to 30 g. per sucker should be sprinkled over, depending upon the size of the bulb.

Planting is done either on flat land or trenches. The basal portion of the suckers is covered with soil firmly packed and irrigated immediately. After planting one or two irrigations may be given at 4-5 days interval. The land is cultivated and earthing up of the plants is done when suckers begin sprouting. This is especially important in the shallow planted dormant bulbs of Basrai. The site for banana planting should be provided with a wind break.

FERTILIZER APPLICATION

Banana being a heavy feeder needs fertilizers in large qualities. Banana responds well to nitrogen application, and top dressing with oil cakes and sulphate of ammonia to individual plants during the first six months, gives good result. Compost or farmyard manure 15-20 kg. per pit along with 250 g. superphosphate and 250 g. of muriate of potash should be applied and thoroughly mixed with the pit soil. Nitrogen should be applied in small doses at short intervals while pnosphorus at planting time and potash at two split doses, one at planting time and another at the time of initiation of flowers. The nutrient requirement varies from place to place and variety to variety. The general recommendations on the nutrient requirement of banana in different states of India are given in the table.

Recommendations about N, P_2O_5 and K_2O requirements of banana.

S.No.	State	Rate	N	P2O5	K20
1.	Tamil Nadu	kg/ha	110	35	330
2.	Kerala	g/plant	225	225	225
3.	Karnataka	kg/ha	336	224	224
4.	Maharashtra	kg/ha	350	—	175
5.	Goa	g/plant	400	200	400

Application of manures and fertilizers in banana should be done before planting in the pit for initiation of growth and also before initiation of inflorescence. **In wet land area, best results from fertilizer applications are obtained when they are grown in split doses as indicated below:**

1st dose - 40 - 50 days after planting
2nd dose - 70 - 80 days after planting
3rd dose - 110- 120 days after planting

DESUCKERING

When the plants start growing, a number of side suckers spront from the rhizome of banana plant which compete with fruiting and should be removed. This operation of removal of unwanted suckers of banana is known as desuckering. This can be done by cutting the suckers at ground level with a crowbar having chisel like end and then pour 2 to 3 drops of kerosene oil in the central core to kill the growing point of pseudostem. The desuckering of the sprouted suckers should be continued till the emergence of the spathe in the main plant. After flowering, one sucker is allowed to grown and at maturity of fruits, another suckers is allowed to grow. In general not more than two suckers per clump should be retained at any time.

WEED CONTROL

Regular weeding is essential in the early stages of growth of banaan plant. It can be done manually by giving four spadings a year. Using mulches like paddy straw also suppresses the growth of weeds. Weedicides such as diuron and Gramazone have also been effective in controlling the weeds in Banana. Diuron @ 3 kg/ha (3 kg of Diuron in 1,200 litres of water) is sparyed before the weeds emerge and when the plants are 1-2 month old. Apary of Gramaxone @ 1.5 l/ha (1.50 litres in 1,200 litres of water) is given after six months of Diuron spray, when the weeds are 5-6 cm. tall.

CULTURAL PRACTICES

1. Earthing up

Earthing up should be done one in 2-3 months preferably during the rainy season to provide drainage, avoid waterlogging at the base of the plants and to prevent soil erosion from the basins.

2. Propping

Banana plants are provided with supports of bamboo or casuarina poles which becomes essentila at the time of bunch emergence. It prevents the uprooting of the bunch and loss due to wind.

3. Tipping of floral parts

The tipping or removal of withered floral parts by hand, has proved effective in controlling the fruit tip disease and also in increasing attractiveness of the bunches. This can be done between 8-12 days after buch emergence.

4. Trashing

Dried and decayed leaves and other plant parts should be removed as and when they appear to keep the plantation clean and avoid the incidence of pests and diseases.

5. Mettacking

Mettacking is the process of removing harvested plants. Bunches mature in 110 to 130 days after flowering dpending upon the cultivars.

6. Mulching

To conserve soil moisture and to avoid water loss, mulching with dry banana leaves and wheat or paddy straw in the basins of banana has been found to be effective.

CROP ROTATION

Perennial crop of banana by ratooning can be obtained from the same field for several years. Normally, a plantation is retained for about 3-5 years. The land vacated by a perennial plantation should be rejuvenated for about a couple of years by planting less exhasuting annual crops which don not require irrigation. Banana field can be rotated with paddy, sugarcane, cereals, cotton, tapioca, sweet potato, groundnut and ragi. Basari Dwarf is always planted for one crop only on a new piece of land which has been under a dry rainfed cereal crop in the previous year. Similarly, variety Nendran is planted afresh on a new piece of land on which banana has not been grown for at least three years.

INTER CROPPING

Intercrops can be grown easily at the early stage of growth in banana plantation. Banana itself serves as a good intercrop in coconut, and arecanut plantations. Vegetables like brinjal, colocasia, yam, dioscorea, chilli, cauliflower, radish, cabbage, cucurbitaceous vegetables and okra can be grown as intercrop. Banana is also grown as a shade plant for coffee, cocoa, rubber, orange and young mango trees.

DISEASES CONTROL

Banana is infected by many diseases. For convenience, these have been categorise into fungal, bacterial and viral disease.

A. Fungal diseases

1. Leaf spot or Sigatoka disease

It is caused by Mycosphaerella musicola. The disease is common and is distirbuted thoughout the banana growing areas of the world.

Symptoms

The first symptoms appear on leaves with the appearance of light yellowish spots which later on enlarge. The centre of the spot dries, become light grey, but a narrow dark brown margin persists giving it an eye spot appearance. Sometimes the entire leaf is affected and is seen hanging down. In case of severed infection, the bunches are smaller, fingers are undersized, immature and angular and may fall down from the pseudostem due to rotting of its stalk. Spread of disease is favoured by warm rainy or humid weather.

Control

(a) Improve drainage, control weeds, remove suckers and adopt correct spacing of the varieties. Apply fertilizers in optimum dosage. Remove infected leaves and trash.

(b) Spraying of Dithane M-45 (0.2%) or Dithane M-45+ mineral oil or Benlate+ mineral oil give the best control, followed by the Bordeaux mixture (5:5:50) at an interval of 15 days.

2. Cigar end rot

Its causal organism is Verticillium theobromae. The disease is transmitted by air-borne spores found in the debris of the banana field.

Symptoms

A black necrosis develops from the perianth and spreads into the tips of immature fingers. The necrotic tissues get covered with gungus and resemble the greyish ash of the cigar end. The pulp tissue undergoes a dry rot, very characteristic of the pathogen and is reduced to a dry fibrous conditions. Black pitting and spotting of the fruits also occur.

Control

Effective control is achieve dby application of Benlate and MBC (methyl-2, benzimidazole carbonate) at 0.05% concentration

3. Main stalk rot

A black soft rot begins at the proximal end of the main stalk of the bunch. Affected parts shrivel and dry up. In severe infection, premature ripening of fruit occurs. Rot generally occurs due to sun scald.

Control

(a) Protect the stalk with the last spathe leaf at the curvature from sunscald.

(b) Spraying of Dithane M-45 or Dithane Z-78 controls the disease.

3. Panama wilt

Panama wilt is cause by Fusarium oxysporum var, cubense. it is a soil borne disease and is more serious in poorly drained soil. it is the most destructive disease attacking the plant at any stage of its growth.

Symptoms

External symptoms of the disease consist of successive wilting or drying up of the leaves.Sudden yellowing of lower leaves including petiole is observed which late on is seen hanging withere around the pscudostem. yellowish to reddish streaks are noticed with intensification of colour towards the rhizome. Where a bunch of fruit has been formed, the fruits become bottle necked. Such fruits mature unevenly and too rapidly.

Control

(a) Use disease free suckers for planting.
(b) Uproot and burn the infected plants.
(c) Flooding of the filed for a minimum period of siz months and then crop rotation with paddy for 3-4 years is also recommended.
(d) Drenching of pits with Vapam 850 g in 100 litres of water a month before planting helps in eradication of inoculum.
(e) In the infected soil, mix quick lime @ 1 part of lime to 3 parts of soil.
(f) Diping of suckers in Bavistin or JK Stein (0.1%) solutions before planting followed by drenching of plants is also recommended.

B. Bacterial disease

1. Bacterial soft rot

This is a minor bacterial disease caused by Erwinia spp. It affects the rhizome and pseudostem.

Symptoms

Rotting of the centre or a portion of the rhizome occurs emitting a foul smell. The rotting progresses up the pseudostem causing internal decay, often with vascular discolouration. Yellowing and wilting of the leaves also occurs.

Control

Soil drenching with bleahing powder is beneficial.

2. Bacterial wilt or Moko disease

Its casual organism is Pseudomonas solanacearum.

Symptoms

The presence of yelow fingers in an otherwise green stem often indicates the presence of Moko disease. When young leaves are infected they become pale green or yellow and collpase near the junction of the lamina. Fruit rot, fruit stalk vascular discolouration, wilted or blackened regrowth of suckers, blackened and dead male flowers, buds etc. are some characteristic symptoms of this disease.

Control

(a) Completely destroy the diseased plant and uproot the neighbouring healthy plants which may have contacted the diseases.

(b) Insects transmitting the disease can be controlled by removing them from the main axis before the bunch matures.

(c) Herbicides, eg. 2,4-D and 2,4,5-T can be used to kill the infected plants.

(d) Dieldrin spray onto a mat wil prevent insects transmitting the diseases to the unaffected plants.

C. Viral diseases

1. Bunchy top

Bunchy top is one of the most destructive viral disease, transmitted to healthy plants by the aphid (Pentalonia nigronervosa). It is widely spread in Karnataka, Tamil Nadu, Kerala and Maharashtra. Dwarf bananas are very susceptible to the disease.

Symptoms

The leaves of a badly infected plants are bunched together at the top. forming a rosette. Margins of the leaf are wavy and slightly rolled upwards. The infected plants remain markedly stunted and don not produce any bunch of commericail value. The presence of uninterrupted dark green streaks along the secondary veins of the lamina or petole is a characteristic symptom of the buncy top.

Control

(a) Spary kerosene oil till it reaches the psudostem, on day before roguing the infected plant to kill the aphid.
(b) Spary the neighbouring bananas plants upto a distance of 50 ft. with Rogor (0.05%) or Metasystox (0.05%) to kill aphid and avoid the spread of the disease.
(c) Uproot the plants from the base and chop the pseudostem into small pieces and burn or bury them in a pit.

2. Mosaic or infectious chlorosis

This disease is cause by strains of cucumber mosaic virus transmitted by aphids. It is endemic in western India.

Symptoms

The most characteristic symptom is the chlorotic or yellowish green patches or the mottling over the entire surface of young leaves. As the disease progresses, leaves emerge misshapen. Leaf margin is irregularly wavy, often with blotches or necrotic tissue and the lamina is reduced in width. Leaf veins thicken abnormally and become prominent. Leaf sheaths also pull away from the pseudostem easily. Bunches when formed are misshapen, hand horizontally and consists of merely tow or three fingers in most severe cases.

Control

(a) Dry heat treatment at 40°C for a dya is useful in curing infected rhi zomes.

(b) Grow resistant varieties and species like Athiya Kol, Karu Bale, M. Balbisiana, M. coccinia, M. acuminata, etc.

PEST CONTROL

A. Insect pests

Insects are the common pests attacking the banana plantations. Some of these major pests include rhizome weevil, pseudostem weevil, flea bectle, and aphid.

1. Flea beetle

Two species of flea bettles viz. Nodostoma subcastatum and N. Viridipennis are reported on banana from India. The adult bettle feeds on the unfolded tender leaves and fruits. These appear around April-may and are active till September-October. The central top whorl leaves are worst affected. The fruits become unmarketable due to the feeding injury made by the pests.

Control

(a) Clean cultivation and phytosanitation measures should be adopted.
(b) Spraying of 0.05% Endosulphan or 0.1% carbaryl mmediately after emergence of new foliage and during fruiting period at an internval of 15 days is effective in controlling the pest.

2. Rhizome weevil

The larva or grub of banana weevil, borer (Cosmopolitus sordidis) makes tunnel into the rhizome to fruit stalk. Injury to the crom prevents the flow of nourishment to the plant and the leaves turn yellow, wither and die prematurely.

Control

(a) Dip the plant material in Monocrotophos (0.1%) solution be fore planting.
(b) Dust BHC 10% @ 20 g. plant on the surface of the pseudostem

and mix them in the soil.

3. Pseudostem weevil

This is another serious and specific pest of banana common in Assam, West Bengal, Bihar, Delhi and Uttar Pradesh. The grub feeds on the leaf sheath and bores into the pseudostem. The pseudostem thus damaged becomes weak and starts rotting. The pest is active during the summer and monssoon seasons.

Control

(a) Uproot and burn the infested plants.
(b) In the initial stage of infestation, insert aluminium phosphate tablets @ three tablets of 0.5 geach per pseudostem.

4. Aphid

Aphids are serious pests of banana which act as vector of the virus causing bunchy top disease. They are commonly spread in eastern and southern parts of the country. They are seen aggregated under the outer leaf base on pseudostem and around the cronw of the plants.

Control

(a) Remove and destroy the virus affected plants.
(b) Spary 0.03% phosphamidon or Dichlorvos to kill the aphids.

B. Nematodes

Two species of important and destructive nematodes viz. burrowing nematode (Radopholus similus) and spiral nematode (Helicotylenchus multicinctus) restrict the cultivation of banana in almost all the nanan growing regions of the world. These attack the roots and rhizomes of the banana plant causing extensive root necrosis and ultimately affecting the entire plant. The affected plants do not repond to fertilizers, irrigation of cultural practices as a result of which retarded growth, yellowing nematode causes diseases like rhizome rot, root rot, balck head, toppling diesease and decline.

Control

(a) Dip the banana suckers in mud slurry (made by mixing 40 litres of clay in 50 litres of water) and sprinkle with carbofuran @ 1.2 g (a.i) or Aldicarb @ 1.0 g (a.i) per sucker. The suckers should be dried in shade and used for planting.

(b) Disinfect the suckers after paring by dipping them in a hot waterbath at 55°C for 10 minutes.

(c) Plant certified nematode free setts obtained eithr by heat treatment, paring or selection.

(d) Crop rotation should be followed by planting sugarcane after the destruction of he infected plants, which eliminates the nematodes after 10 weeks.

(e) Soil application of Aldicarb or Carbofuran @ 2 kg (a.i) per ha is useful.

(f) Grow nematode resistant varieteis for eg. "Bodles Altaport" (a cross between "Gros Michel" and "pisang LIlin").

FLOWERING AND FRUITING

Under favourable conditions banana plant normally starts flowering in 9-10 months after planting and takes 3-4 months for bunch maturity. The inflorescence consists of different type of flowers i.e. female, male and hermaphrodite in the same floral stalk. The inflorescence initiation takes place from the hear of the pseudostems. The basal nodes of the inflorescence bear female (pistillate) flowers and the upper node bear made (staminate) flowers. The common type of inflorescence is the one in which the basal protion bears pistillate flowers which develop into fruits followed by decidurous staminate flowers, e. "Poovan", Monthan, etc. In another group, the whole inflorescence bear pistillate flowers, which develop into fruits, eg. Thattila Kunnan, Aiyiranka, Rasthali etc. In an other group, the basal flowers develop into fruits followed by persistant male flowersconsisting of green rudimentary ovaries with persistant perianth and bracts, eg. Dwarf Cavendish, Nendran, etc. Pollination is mainly by bees and birds which visit the flowers for nectar. The fruit of the banana is either seeded or vegetatively parthenocarpic i.e. develops without pollination. The vast majority of edible bananas are parthenocarpic.

HARVESTING AND YIELD

When picked green at full maturity, banana fruits give the best ripening result. Therefore, they are harvested at this stage. There are a few maturity standards such as drying off top leaves, changing in colour of the fruit from deep green to lighter green, shedding of the floral end of the fruit by slight brush with the hand, and whne the ridges on the surface of the skin change from angular to round after attainment of 3/4th full stage. Number of days from emergence of inflorescence or shooting (i.e. 90 to 120 days banana takes to mature after shooting) and pulp to skin ration are also good indications of banana maturity. Pulp to skin ration varies from variety to vareity, eg. Dwarf Cavendish bananas at three quarters full manturity shows a pulp/skin ration of 1.35 to 1.40.

Generally the dwarf varieties are ready for harvesting within 11 to 14 months after planting, while tall varieties take about 14 to 16 months to be harvested. For harvesting, the bunch is cut by a sharp sickle from the plant, leaving 30-40 cm of the fruit stalk to serve as a handle. The bunches should no be cut until they are just ready to be transported.

The yield varies depednign upon the variety, plant density soil fertility and cultural practices. The fruit yield is roughly 25-50 tonnes per ha on an average, 18 to 25 tonnes/ha in the case of tall varieties like Champa and Martaman and 50-65 tonnes/ha in the case of robusta. However, a good bunch will contain 190-200 fingers on an average.

MARKETING AND STORAGE

Before taking to markets, grading fruits is necessary. Grading in banana is done according to size, number of fingers, ripening and maturity stages and general appearance of the fingers. Immediate markeing of banana fruits my not be possible and, as such, storage of fruits may beocme necessary.

At room temperature, benana harvested at three-fourth maturity can be stored well for 5 to 7 days. However, they can be stored at 13°C temperature with a relative humidity of 85 to 95% for about three weeks. The storage life of banaan can be prolonged by usnign sealedl polythene bags containing ethylene absorbene like purafil (potassium permanganate absorber on an inert material). A prestorage dip in E9267 emulsifiable mineral oil at

0.4% has been found effective in reducing fruit decay and also prolonging storage life.

ARTIFICIAL RIPENING

Banana is ripened artifically by several method sin different parts of the country. Fruits for local consumption are ripened by hanging the bunches in a shady place. Smoking with straw, leaves and cowdung is done in a close chamber with bunches arranged in a heap for 18-24 hours in summer and 48 hours in winter to induce ripening in Maharashtra and Tamil Nadu. Ripening by covering the bunches with funny sacks and applying ethylene at a concentration of one part per thousand helps in initiating ripening of banana. Commercially, ripening of banana is initiated by using various chemical substances such as 2,4-D (2,4 dichlorophenoxy acetic acid) @ 1000 ppm for 10 seconds. Calcium carbide is another chemical used for the large scale artificial ripeining of banana fruits.

USES AND COMPOSITION

Banana is the cheapest and most nourishing of all fruits. It has got a number of uses. Almost all the parts of banana are useful in some or other ways. Various industrial and medicinal uses of banana re summarised here.

A. Industrial Importance

1. Banana is used in the processing industry to prepare products such as banana pulp, canned slices, jam, flakes, juice, banana figs, chips, fruit bar, powder etc.
2. It is a flourishing industry in certain areas of Tamil Nadu where banana is cultivated exclusively for leaves to make dinner plates and wrapping material.
3. Banana sheaths and leave are used for making crude ropes.
4. Starch is manufature from the pseudostem.
5. Used in the food industry, eg. for preparing babyfood from Kunnan and Nendran varieties.
6. Unripe banana fruits as well as the inner core of the pseudostem are used for cooking as vegetable.
7. Used in the manufature of beer and (pure and denatured) alcohol.
8. Yeast of good quality can be made out of banana flour which can replace malt in breweries.

9. The juice from the pseudostem can be used in dyeing industry.
10. Fibre production and paper making from fibre are commercial possibilities.
11. Banana is used as feed for cattle and pigs in some countries.
12. It is one of the largest single trade itmes in International fruit trade.

B. Medicinal values

1. Banana flour made into gruel and dilute with milk is good for patients suffering from gastritis.
2. Banana ash is rich in alkaline salts and, therefore, checks acidity in stomach, heart burn and colic panins.
3. Ripe fruits taken with tamarind and salt are said to control dysentery.
4. Fruits of 'Poovan' are believed to be good even for diabetics.
5. Ulcers are cured by smearing a paste of aromatic and sweet fruits of Devakadali variety of banana.
6. Ayurvedic medicines are prepared from ripe banana fruits.

Composition of banana fruit

S.No.	Components	Amount
1.	Moisture	70%
2.	Carbohydrate	27.0%
3.	Crude fibre	0.5%
4.	Protein	1.2%
5.	Fat	0.3%
6.	Ash	0.9%
7.	Phosphorus	290.0 ppm
8.	Calcium	80.0 ppm
9.	Iron	6.0 ppm
10.	B-Carotene	0.5 ppm
11.	Riboflavin	0.5 ppm
12.	Niacin	7.0 ppm
13.	Ascorbic acid	120.0

ECONOMICS OF CULTIVATION

Cultivation of banana is a highly paying agricultural venture. Generally, a farmer can generate Rs.35 to 40 thousand from one hectare of banana plantation. However, the net profit is highly varying from reqion to region depending on the soil and climatic conditions, varietal suitability, protection of plantation from attack of insect pests and diseases, availability of producgtion inputs, etc. .

PLANT ECONOMICS OF BANANA POWDER

Rated Plant Capacity = 5000,00 KGS/DAY

COST OF LAND & BUILDING

(Area Required 500 sq.mt. **Rs. 3,90,000.00**

PLANT & MACHINERY

1. Drying Chamber
2. Hot air supplier
3. Washing and boiling tank
4. Pulveriser
5. Vibrating Screen
6. Sulphur house
7. Misceilaneous Equipment like wooden trolleys, weighing machine, Aluminium vessel etc.

TOTAL **Rs. 2,52,000.00**

OTHER FIXED ASSETS **Rs. 80,000.00**

FIXED CAPITAL

1.	LAND & BUILDING	Rs.	3,90,000.00
2.	PLANT & MACHINERY	Rs.	2,52,000.00
3.	OTHER FIXED ASSETS	Rs.	80,000.00
	TOTAL	**Rs.**	**7,22,000.00**

LIST OF RAW MATERIALS

1. Fully matured but slightly unripe banana 60 MT
2. Sulphur, and other necessary chemicals
3. Containers

TOTAL WORKING CAPITAL/MONTH

1.	RAW MATERIAL	Rs.	1,28,000.00
2.	SALARY & WAGES	Rs.	27,720.00
3.	UTILITIES & OVERHEADS	Rs.	32,600.00
	TOTAL	**Rs.**	**1,88,320.00**

TOTAL CAPITAL INVESTMENT

TOTAL FIXED CAPITAL	Rs.	7,22,000.00
TOTAL WORKING CAPITAL FOR 3 MONTHS	Rs.	5,64,960.00
TOTAL	**Rs.**	**12,86,960.00**

TURN OVER/ANNUM

By selling of 150 MT of Banana Powder **Rs. 37,50,000.00**

PROFIT = RECEIPTS - COST OF PRODUCTION =11,16,553.80

PROFIT SALES RATIO = Profit / Sales x 100 = 29.77 %

RATE OF RETURN = Operating profit / T.C.I x 100 = 86.76 %

BREAK EVEN POINT (B.E.P) = 37.26 %

PLANT ECONOMICS OF BANANA & ITS BYE PRODUCTS

Plant capacity = 40.00 MT/day

LAND & BUILDING

(Total Land area in 10000 sq.mts.)	**Rs.**	**78,40,000.00**

PLANT & MACHINERY

Total cost of Plant & Machinery	**Rs.**	**13,29,00,000.00**

OTHER FIXED ASSETS	**Rs.**	**10,00,000.00**

FIXED CAPITAL

1.	LAND & BUILIDING	Rs.	78,40,000.00
2.	PLANT & MACHINERY	Rs.	13,29,00,000.00
3.	OTHER FIXED ASSETS	Rs.	10,00,000.00
	TOTAL	**Rs.**	**14,17,40,000.00**

WORKING CAPITAL REQUIREMENT/MONTH

RAW MATERIALS

2500 Tonnes of Banana Bark and Banana Skin, 125 Tonnes of Chlorine, Soda Ash 100 MT, Other Chemicals such as Rosin, Starch, Alum, Sulphur dioxide, Greva Bananas 100 tonnes, Vegetable oils)	**Rs.**	**59,65,000.00**

TOTAL WORKING CAPITAL/MONTH

1.	RAW MATERIAL	Rs.	59,65,000.00
2.	SALARY &WAGES	Rs.	1,18,125.00
3.	UTILITIES & OVERHEADS	Rs.	1,02,000.00
	TOTAL	**Rs.**	**61,85,125.00**

TOTAL CAPITAL INVESTMENT Rs. 16,02,95,375.00

TURN OVER/ANNUM

1. By sale of 12000 MT of Paper
2. By sale of 1800 MT of Chips
3. By sale of 2400 MT of Powder

TOTAL Rs. 19,44,00,000.00

PROFIT SALES RATIO = Profit / Sales x 100= 26.39 %

RATE OF RETURN = Operating profit / T.C.I x 100 = 32.00 %

BREAK EVEN POINT (B.E.P) = 57.69 %

Chapter - 2

Bee Keeping

Introduction

Anyone who want to start beekeeping has to first acquire few beehives and set them in a properly planned lay out. The hives can be secured by :

(1) Catching a story swam
(2) Purchasing package bees
(3) Dividing the existing bee colonies. All these methods require specific knowledge and skills different from each other.

Hiving is done often along with the acquisition of a stray swarm. Hence the methods of hiving are explained first. The colonies are placed in a lay out design following a certain principles.

Hiving the Swarm

The collected swarm can be hived, by any one method out of two methods of hiving explained below. i.e.

(1) Slow method of hiving
(2) Quick method of hiving.

1. SLOW METHOD

A hive is set up on the proper site in the apiary. Its brood chamber is filled with frames of comb-foundation. A board is set against the entrance sloping down to the ground and covered with a white cloth. Then a handful of bees are put into the hive and the inner cover of the box is placed on it. The rest of the bees of the swarm are shaken from the basket on to the sloping board. The instinct of the swarm is to move upward into the darkness of a cavity (here the cavity is the hive). Therefore, the bees start going upward until they find entrance to the hive. At this point, bees start to fan and send a scent. When the scent reaches the rest of the bees they all begin to move towards entrance. The whole swarm takes few hours to go inside the hive. The bees should be liberally fed with sugar syrup to make them settle down to work. After a week colony should be examined for newly formed brood.

2. QUICK METHOD

This method of hiving the bees, takes only a few minutes. A hive is set up as explained above. But the frames of foundation are not put into the brood chamber but are kept within easy reach. The entrance of the hive is completely closed, the main part of swarm bee cluster is then poured into the brood chamber. The remainder bees sticking to baskets are thrown in by knocking and shaking the basket. The bees are now in a heap at the bottom of the brood chamber. The frames of foundation are now gently put in the hive over the bee cluster. As the bees climb up on the foundation the frame will slowly sink into place. They are then adjusted into the correct spacing. The bees should be provided with sugar syrup, in ample quantity. The crown broad (top cover) is put in its place and the entrance hole for bees is opened up. Always give the swarm a full box of frames of foundation. If the box is partially filled the bees will make their own wild comb. Examine the bee colony after a week, for new formed brood by the queen.

CATCHING THE STRAY SWARM

Many swarms, during early honey flow period of the locality, are found settled on places which are least visited by man. Such swarms (bee colonies) are called stray swarms. Therefore, to acquire stray swarms in the nearby locality is the least expensive method. They are settled on a thin tree branch, in an inaccessible or accessible place, in the wall or wood log or sometimes hovering in air.

1. USING A BOX OR BASKET

An unwanted swarm, settled on a thick tree branch or underside of the roof, can be collected by placing a basket or a small box open on one side, near the cluster of bees and moving the bees gently into it with a leafy twig or by hand. Light smoke produced from cow-dung cake can be used to make the bee enter the basket. When few bees have moved into the basket, the rest will gradually follow them. If the basket has to be carried to some distance, it should be covered with a piece of perforated cloth or mosquito net. The swarm is usually hived during late hours in the afternoon. Meantime, a thin sugar syrup should be sprinkled over the bees.

2. CUTTING SWARM BRANCHES

The thin branches carrying the swarm is gently and carefully cut with a secateur. The cut branch is wrapped lightly with a piece of mosquito net or a similar perforated cloth , before carrying it to some distance. Then captured swarms are hived.

3. ACCESSIBLE SWARMS

When a swarm is found on a place where it is possible to carry the beehive then it can be caught direct into the hive by applying quick method of hiving in the late afternoon hours. Then these hives are carried to proper site in the evening after closing the entrance hole.

4. INACCESSIBLE SWARM

When a swarm is settled on the top of the tree on small twigs or on the side of a hill slope the working man cannot get access to it from any side. Such swarms are disturbed by spraying water with the help of a sprayer or syringe, till the swarm is resettled on an approachable site. The swarm is caught in a usual way in the basket and hived.

5. SWARMS IN THE WALL

For such swarms, there are two methods to collect the bees. If the swarm is settled in such a way that the wall can be opened by taking out a few bricks, to approach the swarm. Then it can be shifted to the modern hive, before peak honey flow season. The technique of shifting the wall-hive to modern hive consists of giving a few puffs of smoke to the bees. The surrounding area is cleaned. The modern hive is placed near the entrance on one side or below it. With judicious smoking and a brush made from grass,the combs are cleaned of bees. The cleaned combs are cut from their attachments to the wall and mounted on frames and tied with pieces of string. The frames with tied combs are placed in the new hive. Any big chunks of honey should not be tied to the frames,but fed to the bees subsequently. All the bees are transferred to the new hive, with the help of hands or a cup. During the whole process, carefully spot out the queen and keep it in a queen cage and release at the entrance of the new hive so that she may enter it. The hive is closed and carried to proper site in the evening. Examine the bee after a week. Make sure that colonies get ample quality of the sugar syrup for a few days.

When the bees have settled in a wall in such a way it can not be opened, the only way to transfer bees is by fixing a one-way bee escape at the entrance, closing all chinks and crevices and placing the hive with some brood frames and a queen in queen case near the entrance of the colony from another colony. In this way bees can come out of the wall-hive, but can not enter back into it and make a cluster near the wall entrance for sometime, and finally are lift with no other alternatives except to enter the hive, just lying nearby. It takes about 2-3 weeks to complete transfer of wall-cavity hive into new hive.

6. SWARMS IN HOLLOW WOOD

When the bees are settled in the hollow of an old tree which can be cut or some old hive which can be mould to one side, the technique to transfer colony from old hive to new hive consists of moving the wooden log or hive to one side and placing the new hive in its place. The entrance of new hive must be in the same direction. Then the old-hive is opened or wood log is cut opened. The bees are smoked out and floor of the old hive are cleaned off the bees. The old hives are cleaned off the bees and turned upside down so that the hive becomes free from bees. The brood combs of the old hives are cut and fixed on the frames to be kept in the new hive. These frames with brood are kept into the new hive. Bee cluster lying on the ground is poured into the new hive with the help of a cup or by hands. The flying bees and bees gone out will join the new hive through the entrance being in the same direction.

The transfer of bees is generally carried in the late afternoon and new hive is taken to new place late in the evening, when all the bees have returned home. The bees are fed with sugar syrup to make them settle comfortably. After a week the colony is examined for brood health.

7. HOVERING SWARMS

Sometimes hovering swarms appear near the will established apiary of the locality. These swarms are available during the beginning period of pasturage flow, when the bee colony divides itself into severaldaughter colonies. About 30-70% worker bees with old queen leave the colony before 5-6 days the new daughter-queen comes out of its queen cell. This bee swarm on its way to new place can be artificially made to settle on a nearby shelter by spraying water. The settled swarm is captured and hived.

PURCHASE OF PACKAGE BEES

Package bees are bees produced for sale. Well established bee farms sell bees in package boxes, which are easy for transportation. The boxes have wire screen on two opposite sides, contain one kilograms of adult bees, without brood or combs, with or without queen. A mated queen in queen cage is supplied with bees, so that receiver can be certain that she is present. Package bees are produced in areas where there is an abundance of pollens and a long sustained nectar flow.

The package bees are installed in the new bees within 36-48 hours after they are packed. Bees are fed sugar syrup on arrival. The ideal situation to install package colony is when it is cool or there is a light rain spell, during peak pasturage flow season. This keep the flying of bees to a minimum. Mostly this is done in the late afternoon hours.

A modern hive is set up on the chosen site. Its brood chamber is filled with frames of comb foundations. The closure of the package box is removed and bees are shaken on the top of combs in the new hive. The bees get their way on various frames within an hour.

The queen sent in the packages is usually a young mated queen. During transport, the bees in the packages accept the new queen. Therefore, some beekeepers release the queen directly from the queen cage into the hive. But the preferred method is to remove much of the sugar candy in the queen cage and to place the cage on the bottom board or in between frames in such a manner that on the queen will change out of its cage after the bees have settled.

New installed package bees should be fed combs of honey or sugar syrup immediately. Package colonies are checked two or three times after installation, at about weekly intervals, both for food and brood.

DIVISION OF EXISTING COLONY

Another technique for acquiring a new bee colony is by making division of the one strong existing colony at the farm.

This can be done by any one methods described here for division of a colony:

(A) Simple division
(B) Artificial swarming
(C) Mixing extraframes from colonies likely to swarm
(D) Uniting weak colonies.

A. SIMPLE DIVISION

An existing colony is divided into two colonies, each containing more or less equal number of bees, without paying any attention to which part the queen goes. This method is more successful, if done at the outset of a good pollen and nectar flow. The incoming food stimulates new colonies to feed the larvae in queen cell better. It further takes 20-25 days for eggs to become foragers. The simple division of colony can be done in any of the following ways. The care is taken that each daughter has eggs or one day old larvae, from which it may develop a new queen and there are sufficient bees to keep the brood warm and healthy.

The simple division of a colony can be done in two ways:

(1) By separation of chambers.
(2) By separation of frames.

1. Separation of chambers

One may divide a hive by separating its various chambers into a separate colony, by placing them on a new site with new bottom and cover.

2. Separation of frames

One may divide all the fames with brood and bees, equally in two or more colonies and keeping them in separate chambers with bottom. Usually one frame with brood and three frames with bees are placed in each new colony. Rest of the space is filled with new frames with fitted comb foundation. Colonies are fed properly.

B. ARTIFICIAL DIVISION

Artificial division of a honey bee colony requires the skill of finding queen and queen cells. A populous colony, during honey flow season, is divided into two or many parts, in such a way that one daughter colony gets the mother queen, while another gets only the developing brood. This can be done in various ways which are described here.

1. Bifurcation

The mother colony is divided into two hives, taking care that one daughter colony gets the mother queen and is installed on the same site, while the second colony gets the developing brood and is shifted to new site. This is done by displacing the mother colony to one side on the original site about 60 cm away. A new hive with the frames of drawn comb-foundation is now placed at the original site. Two frames full of honey, pollen, capped or uncapped brood along with bees and the mother queen are placed in this hive. Destroy all developing queen cells on these two frames. A light artificial feeding is given and five is closed for a week. After a week again queen cell, if any found on these frames is destroyed. The colony is checked for new brood development. This establishes one daughter colony.

The remaining part of the mother colony consisting of various frames of brood, honey,bees, and many developing queen cells are thoroughly examined to select a best queen cell. The selected queen cell is about 25-29 mm in length. Queen cell longer than this are often diseased or contain a larvae which has already died. The surface of the cell should be very rough with ridges of wax marking out a type of cellular pattern. Smooth cells usually produce queens of an inferior quality,light in weight and having a smaller number of ovarioles than usual for their strain. The queen cell meant for retention should have developed from the queen cup, and not from worker cells. The queen cell are often made at the bottom of the frame. The best queen cells is one that is found on the side of the comb.

Before any queen cell is finally selected, the end of it should be scrapped with the finger nail, to make sure that the queen has not already emerged and the lid had been replaced. A slightest tough will remove the lid if the cell is vacant. After confirming that the selected queen cell has the developing queen in it, destroy all other queen cells. The hive is closed after giving artificial feeding and carried to new site in the apiary, which should be about 30 metres away from the original site. A weekly check is maintained to destroy any left or newly developed queen cell or emergency queen cell from workers larvae. After about 3-5 weeks, colony is checked for new developing brood produced by a new young mated queen.

2. Multifold division

Mother colony is divided into a number of daughter colonies when it is desired to increase the number of colonies for sale or increase in size of the apiary.

The method consists of following steps:

(a) First the mother colony is divided into a number of specially prepared small bee hives called nuclei. Each nucleus hive gets two frames of brood, honey,adult bees and one selected developing queen cell, with a frame of drawn comb-foundation. The mother queen is kept aside.

(b) These nuclei are closed at the bee entrance and from the top with wire gauze. They are placed in a cool, dark room for about two days.

(c) The bees are transferred to actual bee-hive installed at new sites in the apiary. The rest of the hive is filled with frames.

(d) Each daughter hive is checked to ensure it has a developing queen cell. If not, it is provided with a ripe queen cell in queen cell protector or a virgin queen or a mated queen or the mother queen in a queen introducing cage. These hives are fed sugar syrup and closed for two weeks.

(e) Each hive is checked to ensure that new queen has emerged

,mated and laying eggs, by looking at the new brood. This confirms the establishment of the new colony.

3. Damaree techniques

The Damaree technique consists of multiplication of the existing colony into two or many hives. It is suggested for those apiaries, which maintain multistory hives. This system allows to separate mother queen and brood into different boxes. The new colonies can be separated from each other partially or completely, but in each case boxes are still placed one above the other with super in between, on the same pile.

The system consists of following:

(a) In a multistoried hive, all the bees are in contact with each other and queen is confined by an excluder to brood chamber. A new box is placed over the top of the hive and a few frames with brood, honey and bees without queen are shifted to this box. The new chamber is separated from the rest of the colony by solid or perforated board. A separate entrance on the opposite side to the bottom hive is provided.

(b) After two days, the top box is checked for developing queen cell and if not found then it is provided from outside in queen cell cage. It ripe into queen which later mates and begins to lay eggs.

(c) These bee colonies retain sufficient common smell or odour and live like good friends. Such colonies can be reunited by removing the board separating them. The two queens fight and the young, vigorous queen remains and controls the beg united colony.

4. Harsh technique

Harsh technique of the multiplication of existing bee colony is based upon the natural instinct of worker bees to develop an emergency queen cell from the worker cell containing a day old larvave in a hopeless colony, which is queenless and has no chance of developing queen cell.

The technique consists of following steps:

(a) A populous mother colony is divided into two or many parts,in such a way that one part gets the mother queen and installed in the same site.

(b) The daughter colonies, each having two or more frames of young brood,honey,adult bees,without any queen or queen cell.

(c) This artificially created condition of queenlessness induces the worker bees to develop an emergency queen cell to maintain the viability of the colony. They build it from a normal worker cell containing young larvae less than 36 hours old. They feed the larva royal jelly in great quantity. of the emergency queens is normally satisfactory,provided it has developed from a very young larva. The queens from old larvae are of poor value.

(d) A frequent check and feeding the colony is required for asufficient long time period of 30-40 days, before the new queen is able to lay eggs, and further it takes 20-25 days to workers to becomes foragers. The presence of new brood and pollen confirms the establishment of the new colony.

C. MIXING EXTRA FRAMES

Sometimes, the bee colonies, during peak honey flow season start rearing brood at a rate faster than normal. This leads to swarming instinct. To save the colony from swarming, without disrupting much honey flow and without affecting thestrength of the bee coloniessome frames are taken out from each such colony and mixed into a new hive to establish a new colony.

This involves following steps:

(1) The mother colonies are smoked judiciously.

(2) One or two frames with capped brood along with adhering young bees are taken out from each such colony.

(3) The collected frames frames from several different hives are placed into a new hive, in a new site. The bees after a little fight get aquainted.

(4) A ripe queen cell in a queen protector or a queen in an queen introducing cage is put in the new hive and released after two or three days.

(5) The hive is checked after two weeks to examine the working of queen.

D. UNITING WEA COLONIES

The weak colonies are generally affected by insects, pests and diseases. It is, therefore, necessary demanding to unite two or more weak colonies in one functional strong colony.

There are a number of situations in which union of weak colonies becomes a necessity. They are:

(a) colonies with and without queen
(b) colonies with queen
(c) stray swarm with working colony
(d) queenless colonies
(e) laying worker colony with normal colony.

The general methods of uniting colonies are described in details in section V in this booklet though the procedures involved in each case are described here.

(a) Colonies with and without queen

Uniting of two colonies is done late in the afternoon. The bees of both colonies are heavily smoked. This forces the bees to suck the stored honey and become well fed. The frames of the two colonies are intermixed by arranging them alternatively. The bees area is sprayed with sugar syrup containing oil of peppermint or wheat flour. The hive is closed. The work of the queen is checked after 3-4 days. The hive is cleaned and closed. The work of the queen is checked after feeding sugar syrup.

(b) Colonies with queen

The colonies to be united are brought slowly close to each other, by shifting about two metres closer every day during night.If the quality of the queen in each colony is known from the colony record, the better queen is retained in its colony, while other queen is collected in queen case and reared separately or the colony is made queenless. Now the two colonies can be united as explained above.

Another way to unite two colonies with their queens is to keep them close to each other or to smoke heavily both colonies . Intermix, their frames on a new hive. The combs with bees of one colony should alternate with combs of smoke again in the new nive, spray sugar syrup scented with oil of peppermint or wheat flour and close the hive for a week. The younger and more vigorous queen defeats the old and weak queen. The colony can be checked after one weak.

(c) Stray swarm with working colony

Often small truant swarm from outside is caught and it is desired to unite it to an established colony. The swarm and the colony should be smoked heavily and the former should be dumped into the latter. More smoke should be blown into the hive. The sugar syrup scented with oil of peppermint is sprinkled over them. Close the hive for a week. The work of the surviving queen may be checked up after a week.

(d) Queenless colonies

The queenless colonies are smoked heavily and their combs are intermixed by arranging combs alternately. A ripe queen cell in a queen cell protector or a virgin queen or a mated queen in a queen introducing cage is given to the hive and released after 2-3 days. The hive is examined after a week for queen's working.

(e) Laying worker colony with normal colony

To unite or absorb bees from laying worker colonies is to divide their frames with brood and bees to several strong normal colonies, after smoking. Give one or two frames from such colonies to each normal colony, there is a danger of the later queen being killed by the former. Smoke or spray scented sugar syrup and close the hive. Examine after a week.

VI. METHODS OF UNITING COLONIES

The main problem in uniting weak colonies is that each colony has its own peculiar odour and the bees of two different colonies usually fight. Therefore, it is necessary either to blend the odours of the two colonies clowly or to suppress both odours or various odours by a stronger odour, before they could be united into one colony successfully.

The two methods of uniting weak colonies are:

(1) Slow odour blending
(2) Suppressing odours.

1. Slow odour blending

The method is also called news paper plan. The colonies to be united should be brought nearer to each other by moving them closer. about 1-2 metres every day,so that the field bees are not drifted to previous site. When the colonies are sufficiently close, one colony is placed over the other colony, by separating them with perforated news paper. The bees knaw through the sheet and intermix in about two days.

2. Suppressing odours

This is also called smoking method. When colonies to be exited have been brought close to each other, as explained above the bees in all the colonies are smoked heavily and the colonies are united into a new hive. The sugar syrup scented with oil of peppermint or wheat flour should be sprinkled over the bees and hive is closed and open to examine only after 3-4 days.

LAYING OUT OF APIARY

An apiary is place where a group of beehives are placed for honey production. The arrangement of these hives is called layout of an apiary.

Some of the important steps to be followed during the layout of an apiary are stated here.

(1) Select a location where bee pasturage will be available in plenty.

(2) Acquire the desired number of bee hives, approximately 40-50 per apiary, keeping distance between two adjacent apiaries (about 2-3km) so that forage gatherers get enough pasturage.

(3) Place the hives in a circle, facing in or out, giving a different approach angle for each hive. This reduces the chances of bees entering into the wrong colony while returning from a flight.

(4) Beehives should be placed in such a way that it reduces the amount of walking by the beekeeper. When he is inspecting the colonies.The space between two beehives must not be less than three metres.

(5) The location of the apiary must have good source of water in the vicinity because bees collect large quantities of water which they use tocool the hive when it is warm and to dilute the feed they give to their larvae.

(6) A dry location that gets maximum of sunlight will reduce the incidence of diseases like nosema, which generally occurs frequently under wet location. A location under the shade of the tree is considered to be the best for a beehive.

(7) An apiary in a region of prolonged dearth period, requires a seasonal migration (shifting place) of beehives to some suitable areas. There fore, the apiary must be well connected with roads and transport facilities.After arranging a suitable site for each hive, the bee-keeper should arrange for bee-colonies in a well planned lay out so that man agement becomes easy.

CONCLUSION

The techniques of acquiring a swarm should be first understood by a bee-keeper before he can actually practice them. Because the technique vary with types of swarm and place where they are found. Similarly the general principles for laying out an apiary should be followed for successful bee keeping.

PLANT ECONOMICS OF BEE KEEPING

Rated Plant capacity = 60,000 KGS/ANNUM

LAND & BUILDING

Land Area reqd. 1 Acre	Rs.	5,00,000.00

PLANT & MACHINERY

Bee Hives, Bee Colonies,
Bee Hives stand (Wooden),
Feeding pots, Comb foundation,
Crude honey extractor,
Migration Card, Misc. Viz. smoker,
queen excluder sieve storage tank etc.

TOTAL	**Rs.**	**15,20,000.00**
OTHER FIXED ASSETS	Rs.	70,000.00
FIXED CAPITAL	Rs.	20,90,000.00

WORKING CAPITAL REQUIREMENT/ANNUM

RAW MATERIALS

Frames for Bee Keeping, Sugar	Rs.	14,10,000.00

TOTAL WORKING CAPITAL/ANNUM

1. RAW MATERIAL	Rs.	14,10,000.00
2. SALARY & WAGES	Rs.	6,61,500.00
3. UTILITIES & OVERHEADS	Rs.	81,000.00
TOTAL	**Rs.**	**22,24,531.25**
COST OF PROJECT	Rs.	22,24,531.00
TOTAL CAPITAL INVESTMENT	Rs.	26,28.125.00

COST OF PRODUCTION/ANNUM Rs. 28,27;343,75.00

TURN OVER/ANNUM

Receipt By sale of Crude Honey Rs. 33,60,000.00

PROFIT = RECEIPTS - COST OF PRODUCTION

PROFIT SALES RATIO = Profit / Sales x 100 = 15.85 %

RATE OF RETURN = Operating profit / T.C.I x 100 = 20.27%

BREAK EVEN POINT (B.E.P.) = 64.60 %

Chapter - 3

Coconut Plantation/Cultivation

INTRODUCTION

The coconut palm is one of the most useful plants in the world. It is grown in more than 80 countries of the world. The botanical name of the coconut palm is Cocos nucifera and it belongs to the family palmeae.

A. ORIGIN AND DISTRIBUTION

Though there are many theories on the origin and dispersal of the coconut palm, Malaysia or Indonesia are the most likely places of its origin. It is believed that the coconut was introduced to India about 3000 years back. The major coconut growing countries of the world are found in Asia, Oceania, West Indies, Central and South America, East and West Africa.

India, with a total annual production of 5,734 million nuts from 108.3 million hectares area ranks third in the world coconut production. Coconut is not grown in all the states of the country but is confined to the coastal states like Kerala, Tamil Nadu, Karnataka, Andhra Pradesh, Maharashtra, Orissa and West Bengal. Even among the coastal states, there is an imbalance in the distribution of the crop. As such, about 65% of the total coconut area is concentrated in Kerala with 58.7% of the total coconut production of the country.

B. ECONOMIC IMPORTANCE

Coconut is mainly cultivated for the nuts from which two important commercial products, Copra and fibre are obtained. Copra yields oil and oilcake. The trunk of the mature plant is used as timber for constructing houses and plaited leaves are used for thatching houses, fencing, etc. The unopened spathe is tapped for toddy. This toddy can be converted into jaggery, sugar and vinegar. Water from tender coconut is very refreshing, delicious and highly nutritious. The coconut shell is largely used as a fuel for the production of charcoal. Thus every part of this palm is useful in one way or another.

C. CHIEF CHARACTERISTICS OF COCONUT PALM

The coconut palm is tall and stately in appearance and attains a height of about 15 to 30 meters when fully mature. The trunk is characteristically unbranched and topped by a crown of large pinnate leaves. An adult palm usually carries 30 to 40 peripinnate leaves in its crown. The life span of the leaf from its emergence to shedding, is about 2.5 to 3 years and a new leaf appears in the crown every three or four weeks in a healthy palm. On an average, the palm produces about 12 leaves annually.

The coconut palm has no tap root, but has a thick growth of string like root system emanating from the blunt bottom of the stem. The number of roots produced by a fully grown tree ranges from 1500 to 8000 depending on the soil condition.

The inflorescence develops within a strong, tough pointed double sheath called spathe. When the spathe is fully grown the entire structure collectively called "spadix", would be about 1 to 1.2 m in length and 14 to 16 cm in diameter. The inflorescence bears 30 to 35 flower bearing spikelets densely set with male flowers. The male flowers may number about 250-300 per spikelet. The female flowers are found at the base of the spikelet and each spikelet may carry only one or a few female flowers.

CLIMATE

Coconut is essentially a crop of the humid tropics. Although it is mainly grown in the coastal plains, it is possible to grow even at elevations of 600 to 900 metres above the sea level in areas near equator. A rainfall of 100 to 225 cm per annum evenly distributed throughout the year, appears to be most congenial. The palm can stand even higher rainfall, provided the soil is well drained.

The optimum mean annual temperature for its best growth and maximum yield is about 27° Centigrade. A hot humid climate is also good for the growth of the coconut palm.

SOIL

The coconut palm adapts itself remarkably well and thrives in almost all types of well-drained tropical soil such as coastal sand, red loam, laterite, alluvial and the reclaimed soil of the marshy low-land.

VARIETIES

There are only two distinct varieties/groups of coconut, the tall and the dwarf. Dwarf varieties take 6 to 7 years. The tall variety is extensively cultivated in all the coconut tracts of the world. It will grow upto a height of about 15 to 18 meters. The crown will have 25 to 40 fronds (an often large, finely divided leaf). It is a comparatively hardy type, late bearing and lives upto ripe age of 80 to 90 years. The tall variety is largely cross pollinated and its copra, oil and fibre are of good quality. The nuts mature within a period of 12 months after pollination.

The production characteristics of few tall varieties of coconut are given in the following Table :-

Performance of few tall varieties of coconut

Variety	Yearly yield of nut pet palm	Mean Copra per nut (g)	Annual out turn of copra per palm (kg.)	Nuts required for 1 tonne of copra	oil per centage
Lakshadweep Ordinary	9.2	180	16.6	5560	72
Philippines	86	224	19.4	4465	69
Jawa	69	246	16.9	4065	70
Cochin China	66	234	15.49	4275	66
New Guini	70	231	16.1	4330	66
Lakshadweep	140	81	11.3	14,500	75
Micro Coastal Indigenous	62	171	10.6	5850	71
Kappadom	46	308	14.1	3250	70

Dwarf variety of coconut is characterised by its short stature and earliness in bearing. In India, two important dwarf types commonly found are "Choughat Dwarf Green" and "Dwarf Orange".

Following are the few characteristics of the dwarf varieties given in the following given Table

Some important characteristics of the dwarf types

Characteristics	Dwarf green	Dwarf orange
Age at first flowering in years	3	4
Number of leaves on the crown	26	28
Annual yield of nuts	66	90.8
Copra content per nut in year	92.14	99.23
Calculated annual yield of copra per tree in kg.	6.081	9.010
Percentage of oil in copra	73.54	66.13

A. HYBRID PALMS

In inter-varietal crosses involving the tall variety as the female and the dwarf variety as the male, the seedlings exhibit hybrid vigour which becomes manifest in the nursery in the vegetative characteristics such as height, girth at collar and number of leaves. The seedlings on planting have a rapid growth rate with a higher rate of leaf production, shorter prebearing period, high bearing capacity and economic nut characteristics.

The inter-varietal hybrids produced for commercial plantings are the Tall x Dwarf and Dwarf x Tall with different parental combinations.

1. TALL x DWARF (TxD) HYBRIDS

In the T x D hybrid, the ordinary tall is the female parent and the dwarf the male parent. T x D hybrids possess desirable characteristics like early bearing, ability to give the normal yield even in the first year of bearing and higher productivity than any of the parental types.

2. DWARF x TALL (DXT) HYBRIDS

The Dwarf x Tall hybrid is more vigorous than TxD hybrid. It comes to bearing in four to five years after planting and out-yields the ordinary tall.

PLANTING MATERIAL

Since coconut is a cross pollinated perennial crop, which can be propagated only through seeds, selection of the planting material is of vital importance. The selection has to be made at the mother-palm level and at the seedling stage.

A. SELECTION OF MOTHER PALMS

Select mother palm having the following characteristics:

1. Regular bearing habit and yielding not less than 80 nuts per annum.
2. Age 20 years or more (5 years after reaching maturity falls the bearing capacity)
3. About 30-40 fully opened leaves with short petioles and wide leaf base firmly attached to the stem.
4. Bearing at least 12 bunches of nuts with a strong bunch stalks.
5. Husked nuts should weigh not less than 600 grm.
6. Bearing nuts of medium size and oblong shape.
7. Mean copra content of 150 g per nut or more.

B. COLLECTION AND STORAGE OF SEEDNUTS

Collect mature nuts (above 11 months old) during the period from December to May. Lowering of bunches by means of ropes may be done when the palms are tall and ground is hard. Store seednuts in shade for a minimum period of 60 days prior to sowing in the nursery. For storage, arrange the seednuts with the stalkend up over 8 cm layer of sand in the shed and cover with sand to prevent drying of nut water. Up to five layers of nuts can be arranged one over the other.

SELECTION AND PREPARATION OF NURSERY

Nursery site should be well-drained and with adequate light. In open areas provide shade during summer. Prepare beds of 1.5m width and of convenient length with 75cm space between beds. Treat beds. Treat beds with Aldrin or BHC 5% or 10% dust at the rate of 12 g/sq m. if soil is not sandy, to prevent termite attack.

A. PLANTING AND SPACING OF NUTS

At the time of planting, the seednuts should be checked further and the nuts in which water has dried up or kernel rotted should be discarded. Among the many pre-sowing treatments recommended for reducing the period of germination, simply soaking the seednuts in water for two weeks prior to sowing has been found to be very effective. The nuts are placed in the nursery either vertically with the stalk end up or horizontally. Horizontal planting with the widest of the three segments placed upper most has been found to give a higher percentage of early and total germination and vigorous seedling with thicker girth at the collar region.

Plant the seednuts in the trenches 25 to 30 cm deep at a spacing of 30 cm (between rows) x 30 cm (between nuts) at 4-5 rows per bed and cover with soil so that the top portion of husk alone is visible.

B. CARE AND MANAGEMENT OF NURSERY

Provide protective fencing to the nursery if it is located in an open area. If the nursery soil is sandy, provide mulching immediately after assertion of monsoon rains.

Irrigate the nursery once in two days during summer months by pot irrigation or through other methods such as sprinkler irrigation.

The nursery site should always be kept free of weeds. If termite attack is noticed, remove soil in the affected area up to a depth of about 15 cm and dust soil and nuts with BHC or Aldrin. Periodical spray of 1% Bordeaux mixture or any other copper fungicides is effective to prevent other infection.

C. SELECTION OF SEEDLINGS

Make rigorous selection and select only good quality seedlings (9-12 months old) based on the following characteristics.

1. Early germination, rapid growth and seedling vigour.
2. Having 6-8 leaves for 10-12 months old seedlings and minimum 4 leaves for 9 months old seedlings.
3. About 10-12 cm girth at collar region.
4. Early splitting of leaves.

5. Green colour of leaves.

Remove seednuts which do not germinate within 6 months after sowing. Only 60-65% of ideal seedlings are available even in a well managed nursery.

D. REMOVAL OF SEEDLINGS

Removal of seedlings from the nursery is done by lifting them with spade and cutting the roots. Keep the seedlings in shade and do not expose them to sun. Never lift the seedlings from the soil by pulling through the leaves or stem.

LAND PREPARATION

The area proposed for the plantation should be cleared and planting holes marked out at the appropriate places. The initial preparation of the land will, however, depend upon the topography, soil type and the ground water level.

On slopes and in areas of undulating terrain, prepare the land by contour terracing or bunding. In low lying areas form mounds to a height of at least 1 metre above water level.

The clearing and leveling of land have to be done before preparing the pits or before transplanting seedlings. The depth of the pits depend upon the soil type and water table. In the sandy loam soil with a low water table, the planting pits of the size 1 m x 1 m x 1 m are generally recommended. In laterite soil with underlying rock, pits of 1.2 m x 1.2 m x 1.2 m size are prepared. In sandy soils, the size of pits may be 0.75 m x 0.75 m x 0.75 m. Burial of two layers of husks in the floor of the pits will be useful for moisture conservation. After arranging each layer, sprinkle BHC 10% on the husk to prevent the termites.

SPACING

Spacing depends upon the planting system, soil type, etc. In general, a spacing of 7.5 m to 9 m, accommodating 177 to 124 palms per hectare is adopted under the square system of planting. The triangular method accommodates 20 to 25 more palms per hectare. In the hedge system of planting a spacing of 5 to 5.5 m along the row (South to North) and 9 to 10 m between the row is given.

TIME OF PLANTING

In general, planting the seedling during May with the on set of pre-monsoon shower is ideal.

AFTER-CARE OF YOUNG PLANTATIONS

Sufficient attention will have to be paid to young palms in the early years of their growth. The transplanted seedlings should be shaded and irrigated properly during summer. For the first two years from planting, irrigate at the rate of 45 litres of water per seedlings, once in 4 days, during summer months.

WEEDING

It is equally important to keep down the weed growth around the seedlings. A circle of about 1 to 2 metre radius should always be kept free of weeds and this area is mulched with the dried weeds or any other organic mulches. As the palm grows, the size of the circle can be increased or the entire garden ploughed or dug up.

GAP FILLING

At the end of the first year, the gap caused by the loss of seedlings should be filled up. Similarly all the unhealthy and defective seedlings should be replaced by fresh planting. The process may have to be continued up to five years after plantation.

FERTILIZER APPLICATIONS

The coconut palm removes large quantities of nutrients from the soil continuously. This progressive removal of nutrients eventually depletes the soil of its nutrient resources unless replenished through a sustained programme of balancd manuring.

To ensure quick growth and early bearing. it is necessary to apply the complete nitrogen, phosphorus and potash (NPK) fertilizers from the early stage. The first dose of fertilizers should be applied three months after planting. The scheduled dose of NPK recommended for young palm is given in following ***Recommendation in ..... Table.***

The recommended dose of fertilizers is 500 g of N, 300 g of P^2O^5 (phosphorus) and 1200 g of K^2O (potash) per palm per year for the ordinary tall varieties. Hybrids and high yielding varieties should be fertilized with 1000 g of N, 500 gm of P^2O^5 and 2,000 g of k^2O. Table shows the recommended doses of fertilizer for an adult palm.

Fertilizers may be applied in two split doses. After the occurrence of summer showers (April-June), one third dose of fertilizers is spread around the palm within a radius of 1.8 m and raked in.

Circular basins, 1-8 m in radius and 25 cm in depth, may be dug in July - August and the green leaf manure or compost is applied and partially covered. The remaining two-third dose of the fertilizers may be spread over the green-leaf manure or compost in the first week of September and basins are closed. Under irrigated conditions and in areas with assured supply of moisture throughout the year, the annual dose of fertilizer may be applied every three months in equal split doses.

Table

Recommendation in terms of commonly available

Time of application of fertilizers	Hybrid and high yielding variety											
	April-May						Aug-Sept					
	N	U	P	RP	K	MOP	N	U	P	RP	K	MOP
3 months after planting							110	240	54	190	228	380
First year	110	240	54	190	228	380	220	480	103	340	444	740
Second year	220	480	103	370	444	740	446	970	206	740	888	1480
Thisr year	331	720	157	560	666	1110	667	1450	310	1110	1332	2220

U-Urea *(N-46%)*
RP-Rock phosphate *(P-28.4%)*
MOP-Muriate of potash *(K2-60%)*

In addition to the recommended levels of fertilizers, 1.0 kg..of dolomite or 1.0 kg. of lime with 0.5 kg. of magnesium sulphate per palm per year may be applied in acidic soils. Dolomite or lime may be broadcast in April-May in the basins and incorporated into the soil by forkjing. Magnesium sulphate can be applied along with other fertilizers in the basins in September.

IRRIGATION AND SOIL MOISTURE CONSERVATION

The coconut palm responds well to summer irrigation. Under west-coast conditions, 2 cm irrigation once in 5 days during December to February and once in 4 days during March to May have been found to be deneficial in sandy loam soils. Where basin irrigation is practiced, 200 litres/ palm once in 4 days will be beneficial. In areas where water is scarce, drip irrigation system can be adopted. The requires only 30 litres of water per day per palm. An increase of 50 to 100% in the yield of nuts can be obtained by giving summer irrigation.

Addition of coconut pith/coir dust as a mulch at 25 kg./palm basin or mulching with husk with the convez side upwards will help in conserving soil moisture.

INTERCROPPING

A variety of intercrops can be frown in coconut field. Important once are given below.

Cereals	-	Rice, maize
Legumes & pulses	-	Groundnut, horsegram and cowpea
Tubers	-	Tapioca, sweet potato, yam and colocasia.
Spices and and condiments	-	Ginger, turmeric, chilies, pepper clove.
Fruit plants	-	Banana, pineapple, papaya
Beverage crops	-	Cocoa
Fodder grasses	-	Hybrid Napier, Guinea grass.

These crops are to be adequately and separately manured in addition to the manures applied to the coconut palms.

INSECT PESTS

The coconut palm is susceptible to many insects and reduce the yield considerably. Some of the important insects are described here.

1. RHINOCEROS BEETLE.

This is perhaps, the most serious pest of the coconut palm and is found in all the coconut growing countries.

The adult beetle bores through the soft tissues of the bud by cutting and chewing the tender unopened leaves and inflorescence. The affected leaves, on emergence, will give a characteristic fan-like appearance where the leaflets are cut off in the same place on both sides of the leaf stalk. Sometimes the beetles have also been found boring into the soft tissues of the tender nuts.

CONTROL

(a) Hook out the beetles from attached palms by using beetle hook.
(b) Fill up the top most leaf axils around the spindle with a mixture of BHC 5% DP or Chlordane 5% DP and sand in the proportion of 1:2.
(c) Treat manure pits and other possible breeding sites with BHC or Carbaryl to control grubs. Uses 58 g of BHC in the required quantity of water to spray 1 W.M. of the breeding material.

2. RED PALM WEEVIL

Unlike the rhinoceros beetle, the adult of this insect is not capable of causing any damage to the palm.

The diagnostic symptoms are presence of hole on the stem, oozing out of viscous brown fluid and extrusion of chewed up fibers through the hole, longitudinal splitting of leaf base and wilting of central shoot. Sometimes the gnawing sound produced by the feeding grubs inside will also be audible.

CONTROL

(a) Leaf axil filling as suggested under rhinoceros beetle will be useful against the red palm weevil also.

(b) Avoid making steps on the tree trunks.

(c) Inject attacked palms with Pyrocone E 2/20 or Carbaryl at 1% concentration (Pyrocone 10 ml. or 20 g of Carbaryl 50%, wp in 1 litre of water/palm).

(d) When the pest infestation is through the crown, clean the crown and pour the insecticidal suspension.

3. LEAF EATING CATERPILLAR

Leaf eating caterpillar is another serious pest of coconut in coastal and brackish water tracks.

The caterpillars live on the under suface of leaflet inside silken galleries and feed voraciously on the chlorophyll containing functional tissues. This affects the health of the palm adversely and results in reduction of yield.

CONTROL

Spraying of infested of infested palms on the lower surface of leaves with Dichloros (0.02%) or BHC 0.2% would give satisfactory control. The treatment may be done at quarterly intervals in March, June, September and December.

4. COCK CHAFER BEETLE

The larvae of the cockchafer beetle which are popularly known as white grubs cause damage to the coconut palm. These soil inhibiting white grubs feed on the roots of coconut palm. The attacked palms turn pale yellow and there is considerable reduction in yield. In severe attack, the immature nuts fall off. When the attack is on the young palms, the growth will be stunted and flowering delayed.

CONTROL

1. Plough or dig the infested soil and expose the pest to the attack of natural enemies like birds, cats, dogs, etc.
2. Apply Heptachlor @ 1.4 kg. ai/ha (28 kg. of 55 DP) during April-May, after the receipt of pre-monsoon shower. Second

application is to be given during the month of September.

5. CORIED BUG

This bug has become a serious problem in many parts of Kerala.It causes damage to the buttons and tender nuts. Nuts are shed in severe cases of infestation. Even those nuts which are retained in the bunches become deformed with the characteristic clevices on the hus just below the perianth. There will also be gummy exudation from such clevice.

CONTROL

Spraying Carbaryl or BHC or Endosulfan 0.1% on the unopened spathes and bunches will control the pest.Apart from these major insects, there are some other insects which attack the coconut palm. Mealy bug and termites are the two more important pests among them. The mealy bug can be controlled by two sprays with 0.1% Fenitrothion or Monocrotophos. The termites can be controlled with 0.1% BHC or Chlordane spray.

Rats damages tender nuts and cause severe losses in many places. Shed tender nuts with characteristic holes can be located at the base of the affected palms. Rats can be controlled by providing mechanical barriers, Poison baits and traps.

DISEASES

The important diseases affecting coconut are:

1. BUD ROT

It is a very serious disease of coconut. The earliest symptoms of this disease is the yellowing of one or two younger leaves surrounding the spindle. The spindle withers and drop down. The tender leaf base and soft tissues of the crown rot into a slimy mass of decayed material giving out a foul smell. The disease proves fatal if not checked at the early stage. Young palms are more susceptible than older ones particularly during monsoon season.

CONTROL

1. In early stages of the disease (when the heart leaf starts withering) cut and remove all affected tissues of the crown and apply Bordeaux Paste and project it from rain till normal shoot emerges.
2. Burn all disease affected tissues removed from the palm.
3. Spray 1% Bordeaux mixture on spindle leaves and crown of disease affected as well as neighbouring palms, as a prophylactic measure.

2. LEAF ROT

The main symptoms of leaf rot disease are blackening and shrivelling up of distal ends of the leaflets in the central spindle and younger leaves. Later the affected portion breaks off in bits. The tree gradually weakens and the yeild is reduced considerably.

CONTROL

Spray crown and leaves with 1% Bordeaux mixture or 0.5% Copper Oxychloride formulations or 0.4% Mancozeb in January, April-May and September. While spraying, care is taken to spray the spindle leaf.

3. ROOT (WILT) DISEASE

The root (wilt) disease has been prevalent in Kerala for nearly 100 years and is believed to have made its appearance after the great flood of 1982.

The important symptoms of the disease are abnormal bending or ribbing of the leaflets, termed as flacidity, and general yellowing and marginal necrosis of the leaflets. The leaflets also curve inwardly so that the whole frond develops a cuplike appearance. Abnormal shedding of buttons of immature nuts is also noticed.

CONTROL

Since the disease is not lethal but debilitating and no curative control measures are known at present, the approach should be to manage the disease in the already infected plantations. The following measures are recommended.

1. Removal of disease affected palms from the areas of sparse incidence. In areas of heavy incidence of disease, all the heavily infected and unproductuve palms (those yielding less than 10 nuts per palm per year) should be eradicated.
2. Replanting with recommended hybrids or high yielding varieties such as West Coast Tall or Chandrakalpa is suggested.
3. Application of NPK fertilizers, magnesium sulphate and organic manures at recommended dose should be followed.
4. Growing green manure crops in the basins and appropriate inter and mixed crops is also advisable.
5. Irrigation during the summer months is necessary.

4. STEM BLEEDING

Symptoms of stem bleeding appear as exudation of reddish brown liquid through the growth cracks at about 2-3 feet above ground level and bleeding patches higher up in the trunk. The tissues beneath the bleeding points dcay, the palm is reduced in size and yield declines. The disease may prove fatal also.

CONTROL

1. Remove completely affected tissues by chiseling and thereafter dress the wounds with hot coaltar or Bordeaux past. Avoid any mechanical injury to the stems.
2. Improve general conditions of plantation through proper manuring, soil management and other cultural practices.

5. MAHALI OR FRUIT ROT AND NUT FALL

Shedding of female flowers (buttons) and immature nuts are the symptoms of this disease. Water soaked lesions appear on the young fruits or buttons near the stalk. Later these lesions develop into a decay of the underlying tissues.

CONTROL

Spray 1% Bordeaux mixture or copper oxychloride preparations (0.5%) on the crown of palms once before the monsoon and once or twice later on at intervals of 40 days.

6. TANJORE WILT

The disease was first noticed in the coastal areas of Thanjavur district. Decay of root system, flaccidity of spindle laeves, browning of outer leaves, arrested fruit set and appearance of bleeding patches on the stem are the main symptoms of this disease. The internal tissues are dissolved and disintegrated, emitting a bad smell.

CONTROL

1. Apply organic manures @ 50 kg./palm.
2. Apply neemacake @ 5 kg./palm per year.
3. Reduce fertilizer application to 1/4th of the recommended dose in disease affected areas.
4. Drench the basins with 40 litres of 1% Bordeaux misture to soak the soil upto 15 cm depth at quarterly intervals.
5. Avoid flood irrigation in order to prevent the possible spread of the pathogen through soil.

HARVESTING

The coconut palm is unique in that once it attains bearing stage it continues to bear a bunch of nuts at every leaf axil almost at monthly intervals all the year round and throughout its life extending over 45 or 60 years. Generally, harvesting is done once in every 45 or 60 days. Tender nuts for a delicious soft drink are harvested at the age of six to seven months. Nuts for making copra and good quality fibre are harvested at the age of about 11 months.

YIELD

By proper manuring and cultivation, an average yirld or 60 to 100 nuts per palm can be obtained from the tall variety under rainfed conditions. Under irrigated conditions, 80 to 120 nuts are available from a palm. From a weli maintained one hectare of coconut farm the average yield of 10.000 to 14,000 nuts are available per year.

STORAGE

After harvest, the usual practice is to store the nuts in heaps under shade for a few days. This type of storing has following advantages.

1. Harvesting becomes easier.
2. Shelling is cleaner and easier.
3. The moisture content of the meat i.e. (the edible part of the nut) decreases and the thickness of meat layer increases. Consequently, the yield of copra and oil increases.
4. The quality of copra produced is also superior to that of unstored nuts.

PROCESSING

The main product obtained from coconut is copra or the dried kernel of the nut. The 'cup' copra is prepared by splitting the husked nut into two hales and drying them in the sun. After drying for a day or two, the kernel gets detached from the shell or, if necessary it is removed from the shell. The drying is continued for another four or five days. The oil is extracted from this copra.

ECONOMICS OF COCONUT PLANTATION

Coconut is a profitable crop and each part of the palm can gain income to the farmer. Today, copra and coconut oil are traditional commodities in the world markets for oilseeds, oils and fats. Due to a large population and excess domestic consumption our exports are confined to coir and its products domestic market of coconut contributes Rs. 30,000 million. But not all products of the coconut are fully utilised in the country. Therefore, there is a great need to take up its cultivation.

COCONUT EXPORTER

Coconut Development Board
P.O.Box 1021, Cochin-682011
Kerala
Tel : 91- 484 - 360737
Fax : 91 - 484 - 360737

PLANT ECONOMICS OF COCONUT OIL FROM COPRA

Plant capacity = 10.00 TON/day

LAND & BUILDING

(Land area required 2000 sq.m.)	**Rs.**	**12,90,000.00**

PLANT & MACHINERY

(Copra grinders , Oil Screw Presses,Oil Gutters (M.S) Settling Tank (M.S) Filter Press,Rotary Oil Pump, Filtered Oil Tank	Rs.	1,25,000.00
Air Compressor, Various Jigs, Fixture, pipings, Conveyors & elevators	Rs.	4,00,000.00
Boiler, Various measuring instruments, weighing scales etc		
TOTAL	**Rs.**	**16,75,000.00**

OTHER FIXED ASSETS	**Rs.**	**3,57,500.00**

FIXED CAPITAL

1.	LAND & BUILDING	Rs.	12,90,000.00
2.	PLANT & MACHINERY	Rs.	16,75,000.00
3.	OTHER FIXED ASSETS	Rs.	3,57,500.00
	TOTAL	**Rs.**	**33,22,500.00**

WORKING CAPITAL REQUIREMENT/MONTH

RAW MATERIALS

Copra, Filter cloth, Sulphuric acid,
Solvent (I.P.A.)Charcoal bags
Drums for packing,

TOTAL	**Rs.**	**44,84,565.00**

TOTAL WORKING CAPITAL/MONTH

1. RAW MATERIAL	Rs.	44,84,565.00
2. SALARY & WAGES	Rs.	1,59,250.00
3. UTILITIES & OVERHEADS	Rs.	2,12,000.00
TOTAL	**Rs.**	**48,55,815.00**

TOTAL CAPITAL INVESTMENT

TOTAL FIXED CAPITAL	Rs.	33,22,500.00
TOTAL WORKING CAPITAL FOR 3 MONTHS	Rs.	1,45,67,445.00
TOTAL	**Rs.**	**1,78,89,945.00**

TURN OVER/ANNUM

Oil (0.6 wt of copra) 1,800 tonnes
Cake (0.40 of wt of copra) 1200 tonnes

TOTAL	**Rs.**	**7,10,40,000.00**

PROFIT = RECEIPTS - COST OF PRODUCTION = 11.74 %

RATE OF RETURN = Operating profit / T.C.I x 100 = 46.61 %

BREAK EVEN POINT (B.E.P) = 42.70 %

PLANT ECONOMICS OF COCONUT PROCESSING COMPLEX

Plant capacity = 92.55 MT/day

LAND & BUILDING

(Land 8 acres) **Rs. 2,11,10,000.00**

PLANT & MACHINERY

(Coconut husk removing machine,
Coconut breaking machine continuous,
Coconut kernel shreddler,
Coconut grating machine fine type,
Continuous conveyer belt dryer with,
Automatic sieving machine,
Automatic desicated powder,
Quality and laboratory testing,
Coconut milk, m.beverage & m.powder,
Water heating tank (s.s.), Long strainer,
Coconut milk storage tank ,
Coconut milk pasteuriser (PHE),
Milk chiller, Milk beverage making tank (s.s),
Automatic weighing, filling,Cream separator
centrifuge type, Cream pasteuriser,
Refrigeration machine , Cream filling in moulds
by weighing,Coconut cream slabs wrapping,
Conveyor belts (s.s), Vacuum pan evaporation,,
Double drum drier, Micro pulveriser
S.S. Sieving machine, Coconut powder automatic
weighing,Oil section, Plate and frame filter press,
seaming machine, Continuous conveyor belt dryer,
Hammer mill, Pulveriser, Sieving machine,
Activated Carbon Section :Mixing machine
with Z-type blade, Pneumatic type powder
elevator, Drying chamber continuous type with,
Conveyor belt, bucket elevator, Activated
chamber, Cooling chamber with continuous
conveyer belt,Washing conveyer belt with

dilute, Pulverising machine, Vibrating screens, Automatic, weighing, filling, Quality testing and laboratory, Coconut Coir Section ,Coir Crushing Machine, Coir fibre extraction, Coconut water processing stainless steel storage Vacuum type deaerator, Candle filter, Botling machine (automatic), Bottle washing machine and, Conveyor belt, Coconut water pasteuriser (P.H.E), Testing equipments, Pumps, valves, tanks, pipelines, Conveyer belt, bucket elevator, Boiler,

TOTAL **Rs. 2,88,80,000.00**

OTHER FIXED ASSETS **Rs. 1,47,00,000.00**

FIXED CAPITAL

1.	LAND & BUILDING	Rs. 2,11,10,000.00
2.	PLANT & MACHINERY	Rs. 2,88,80,000.00
3.	OTHER FIXED ASSETS	Rs. 1,47,00,000.00
	TOTAL	**Rs. 6,46,90,000.00**

RAW MATERIALS

Coconut , Chemicals as ZnCl2, HCL, milk,Packaging materials

TOTAL **Rs. 2,16,00,000.00**

TOTAL WORKING CAPITAL/MONTH

1.	RAW MATERIAL	Rs.	2,16,00,000.00
2.	SALARY & WAGES	Rs.	5,58,500.00
3.	UTILITIES & OVERHEADS	Rs.	4,62,000.00
	TOTAL	**Rs.**	**2,26,20,500.00**

COST OF PROJECT **Rs. 8,16,55,375.00**

TURN OVER/ANNUM

1. By sale of Desicated Coconut Powder 1500 MT
2. Coconut Water 9000 MT
3. Coconut Oil 240 MT
4. Coconut Milk liquid 900 MT
5. Coconut Milk beverage 525 MT
6. Skimmed Milk Powder 1050 MT
7. Coconut Cream 2100 MT
8. Coconut Flour 4950 MT
9. Paring Oil 330 MT
10. Coir 4920 MT
11. Coconut Shell Powder 1500 MT/day
12. Activated Carbon 750 MT

TOTAL **Rs. 40,19,10,000.00**

PROFIT SALES RATIO = Profit / Sales x 100 = 24.91 %

RATE OF RETURN = Operating profit / T.C.I x 100 = 75.53 %

BREAK EVEN POINT (B.E.P) = 26.04 %

PLANT ECONOMICS OF DESICCATED COCONUT POWDER FROM COCONUT

Plant Capacity = 200.00 KGS/day

LAND & BUILDING *(Land area reqd. 1200 Sq.mt.)*	**Rs.**	**13,50,00,000.00**
PLANT & MACHINERY	**Rs.**	**2,91,000.00**
OTHER FIXED ASSETS	**Rs.**	**2,05,000.00**

TOTAL FIXED CAPITAL

1. LAND & BUILDING	Rs.	13,50,000.00
2. PLANT & MACHINERY	Rs.	2,91,000.00
3. OTHER FIXED ASSETS	Rs.	2,05,000.00
TOTAL	**Rs.**	**18,46,000.00**

WORKING CAPITAL REQUIREMENT/MONTH

RAW MATERIALS

(Coconuts, Packing material for packing)

TOTAL	**Rs.**	**94,000.00**

TOTAL WORKING CAPITAL/MONTH

1. RAW MATERIAL	Rs.	94,000.00
2. SALARY & WAGES	Rs.	37,560.00
3. UTILITIES & OVERHEADS	Rs.	27,550.00
TOTAL	**Rs.**	**1,59,110.00**

TOTAL CAPITAL INVESTMENT

TOTAL FIXED CAPITAL	Rs.	18,46,000.00
TOTAL WORKING CAPITAL FOR 3 MONTHS	Rs.	4,77,330.00
TOTAL	**Rs.**	**23,23,330.00**

TURN OVER/ANNUM

1. By sale of 60 MT of 60,000 kgs of Coconut Powder
2. By sale of oil
3. By sale of unprocessed coir 21.8 MT
4. By sale of coir dust 5.45 MT
5. By sale of Broken shell 21.8 MT
6. By sale of poonac 100 kg.

TOTAL **Rs. 30,19,550.00**

PROFIT = RECEIPTS - COST OF PRODUCTION = 5,76,980.55

PROFIT SALES RATIO = Profit / Sales x 100 = 19.11 %

RATE OF RETURN = Operating profit / T.C.I x 100 = 24.83 %

BREAK EVEN POINT (B.E.P) = 59.45 %

PLANT ECONOMICS OF ACTIVATED CARBON

Plant capacity = `1.00 MT./day

LAND & BUILDING
(Land required 500 sq.mt) **Rs. 11,25,000.00**

PLANT & MACHINERY

(Viberating Screens, Mild Steel Retorts,
Furnace for retorts Activation chamber,
Drier, Boiler, Pelletizing machine,.
Other misc. like conveyors pipes

TOTAL Rs. 4,05,000.00

OTHER FIXED ASSETS Rs. 20,000.00

FIXED CAPITAL

1.	LAND & BUILDING	Rs.	11,25,000.00
2.	PLANT & MACHINERY	Rs.	4,05,000.00
3.	OTHER FIXED ASSETS	Rs.	20,000.00
	TOTAL	**Rs.**	**15,50,000.00**

WORKING CAPITAL REQUIREMENT/MONTH

RAW MATERIALS

(Coconut shell, Carbon dioxide (pure),
Packing material,

TOTAL Rs. 58,500.00

TOTAL WORKING CAPITAL/MONTH

1.	RAW MATERIAL	Rs.	58,500.00
2.	SALARY & WAGES	Rs.	67,375.00
3.	ÚTILITIES & OVERHEADS	Rs.	26,700.00
	TOTAL	**Rs.**	**1,52,575.00**

TOTAL CAPITAL INVESTMENT Rs. 20,07,725.00

TURN OVER/ANNUM

By Sale of 300 M.T. of Activated Carbon Rs. 30,00,000.00

PROFIT SALES RATIO = Profit / Sales x 100 = 18.84 %

RATE OF RETURN = Operating profit / T.C.I x 100 = 28.16 %

BREAK EVEN POINT (B.E.P) = 65.12 %

PLANT ECONOMICS OF COCONUT WATER

Plant capacity = 4,50,00,000 No. Bottles,

LAND & BUILDING
(Land 8 Acres) **Rs. 1,14,10,000.00**

PLANT & MACHINERY

Coconut husk removing machine,
Coconut breaking machine continuous,
hydraulic press, Coconut water processing
stainless steel storage tank, Small s.s. tank,
Vaccum type deaerator,Candle filter,
Botling machine (automatic),
Bottling washing machine and
sterilising machine,Conveyor belt,
Coconut water pasteuriser (P.H.E),
Testing equipments,Pumps, valves,
tanks, pipelines, Boiler

TOTAL **Rs. 81,55,000.00**

OTHER FIXED ASSETS **Rs. 1,74,50,000.00**

FIXED CAPITAL

WORKING CAPITAL REQUIREMENT/MONTH

RAW MATERIALS

(Green Coconut 50 Lakhs pieces,
Chemicals preservatives, and other
miscellaneous, Packing materials
5 of raw materias,

TOTAL **Rs. 84,25,000.00**

TOTAL WORKING CAPITAL/MONTH

1.	RAW MATERIAL	Rs.	84,25,000.00
2.	SALARY & WAGES	Rs.	3,08,880.00
3.	UTILITIES & OVERHEADS	Rs.	3,07,000.00
	TOTAL	**Rs.**	**90,40,880.00**

COST OF PROJECT **Rs. 4,37,95,660.00**

TOTAL CAPITAL INVESTMENT **Rs. 6,41,37,640.00**

COST OF PRODUCTION/ANNUM **Rs. 12,26,99,735.20**

TURN OVER/ANNUM

1. By Sale of 4,50,00,000 No. Bottles
2. By Sale of Coconut Husk 300,00,000 Kgs.

TOTAL **Rs. 16,50,00,000.00**

PROFIT = RECEIPTS - COST OF PRODUCTION

PROFIT SALES RATIO = Profit / Sales x 100 = 25.64 %

RATE OF RETURN = Operating profit / T.C.I x 100 = 65.95 %

BREAK EVEN POINT (B.E.P) = 28.87 %

PLANT ECONOMICS OF DEHYDRATED COCONUT MILK POWDER

Plant capacity = 6700.00 KGS./day

LAND & BUILDING

(Land 2.5 acres.) **Rs. 1,63,00,000.00**

PLANT & MACHINERY

Coconut husk removing machine, Coconut breaking machine continuous hydraulic press type, Coconut Kernel Shreddler, Coconut grating machine fine type, Dehydrated Coconut milk powder, Water heating tank, Screw Type Extracter, Long Strainer (S.S) with bottom milk collecting trays, Coconut milk storage tank (S.S.), Coconut milk pasteuriser (PHE), Spray Drier,Automatic Weighing, Filling,Sealing, Cream Separator Centrifuge type,Cream Pasteuriser, Refrigeration machine, Cream filling in moulds by weighing filling machine, Coconut cream slabs wrapping -machine, Conveyor belts, Vacuum Pan Evaporator, Coconut water processing stainless steel storage tank, Small S. S. tank, Vacuum type deaerator, Candle Filter, Bottling machine (automatic), Bottle Washing machine and sterilising machine, Conveyor belt, Coconut Water Pasteuriser (P.H.E.), Quality and laboratory Testing, Pumps, valves, tanks, pipelines fitting, Conveyor belt, bucket elevator, Boiler

TOTAL **Rs. 2,01,10,000.00**

OTHER FIXED ASSETS **Rs. 78,00,000.00**

FIXED CAPITAL

1. LAND & BUILDING	Rs.	1,63,00,000.00
2. PLANT & MACHINERY	Rs.	2,01,10,000.00
3. OTHER FIXED ASSETS	Rs.	78,00,000.00
TOTAL	**Rs.**	**4,42,10,000.00**

WORKING CAPITAL REQUIREMENT/MONTH

RAW MATERIALS

Coconut 50 lakhs pieces, Milk, Preservatives, and other, miscellaneous Chemicals, Packaging materials, Bottles, Container etc. 20% of raw materials

TOTAL **Rs. 2,15,00,000.00**

TOTAL WORKING CAPITAL/MONTH

1. RAW MATERIAL	Rs.	2,15,00,000.00
2. SALARY & WAGES	Rs.	3,48,750.00
3. UTILITIES & OVERHEADS	Rs.	5,56,600.00
TOTAL	**Rs.**	**2,24,05,350.00**

TOTAL CAPITAL INVESTMENT **Rs. 11,14,26,050.00**

TURN OVER/ANNUM

1. *RECEIPT BY SALE OF :*
   Dehydrated (skimmed) Coconut Milk
2. Coconut Cream 3150 MT.
3. Coconut Water 90,00,000 litres.
4. Coconut Husk 4920 MT.

TOTAL **Rs. 33,41,40,000.00**

PROFIT = RECEIPTS - COST OF PRODUCTION = 3,80,75,350.50

PROFIT SALES RATIO = Profit / Sales x 100 = 11.40 %

RATE OF RETURN = Operating profit / T.C.I x 100 = 34.17 %

BREAK EVEN POINT (B.E.P) = 45.31 %

PLANT ECONOMICS OF COCONUT SHELL POWDER

Plant capacity = 1.00 MT/day

LAND & BUILDING

(Area Required 400 Sq. Mt.)	**Rs.**	**2,60,000.00**

PLANT & MACHINERY

Coarse Crusher, Hammer mill,
Pulverizer, H.P. motor & starter
Screen of 20 mesh, 60 mesh,
80 mesh, 160 mesh & 200 mesh
size with motorstarter, Bag filter

TOTAL	**Rs.**	**3,70,000.00**
OTHER FIXED ASSETS	**Rs.**	**70,000.00**

FIXED CAPITAL

1. LAND & BUILDING	Rs.	2,60,000.00
2. PLANT & MACHINERY	Rs.	3,70,000.00
3. OTHER FIXED ASSETS	Rs.	70,000.00
TOTAL	**Rs.**	**7,00,000.00**

WORKING CAPITAL REQUIREMENT/MONTH

RAW MATERIALS

Coconut shell	**Rs.**	**60,000.00**

TOTAL WORKING CAPITAL/MONTH

1.	RAW MATERIAL	Rs.	60,000.00
2.	SALARY & WAGES	Rs.	21,875.00
3.	UTILITIES & OVERHEADS	Rs.	13,040.00
	TOTAL	**Rs.**	**94,915.00**

TOTAL CAPITAL INVESTMENT

TOTAL FIXED CAPITAL	Rs.	7,00,000.00
TOTAL WORKING CAPITAL FOR 3 MONTHS	Rs.	2,84,745.00
TOTAL	**Rs.**	**9,84,745.00**

TURN OVER/ANNUM

By sale of 300 MT of Coconut Shell	**Rs.**	**21,00,000.00**

PROFIT = RECEIPTS - COST OF PRODUCTION = 6,58,516.08

PROFIT SALES RATIO = Profit / Sales x 100 = 31.36 %

RATE OF RETURN = Operating profit / T.C.I x 100 = 66.87 %

BREAK EVEN POINT (B.E.P) = 41.65 %

Chapter - 4

DAIRY FARMING

INTRODUCTION

More than Five percent of the world's milk comes from Buffalloes. Buffalloes milk is used in much the same way as cow's milk. It is high in fats and total solid, which gives it a rich flavour. Many people prefer it to cow's milk and are willing to pay more for it. In India, where in Mumbai area alone an estimated 10,000 new born calves starved to death each year through lack of milk. The demand for Buffallo milk in India (About 60% of the milk consumed over 80% in some states) is reflected in the prices paid for a litre of milk; about 130 paisa for cow's milk compared with about 200 paisa for buffallo milk Twelve of the Eighteen major breeds of buffallo are kept primarily for milk production (although male may be used for traction & all animals are eventually used for meat.) The main milk breeds of India & Pakistan are the murrah, Nile/Ravi,Surti, Mehsana, Nagpur, & Jafarabad.

The domesticated water buffallo is one of the gentlist of all farm animals. Despite an intimidating appearance it is more like a house hold pat-sociable, gentle, and serve. In rural Asia the care of buffalloes is after turned over to small boys & girls aged about 4 to 9.

Another belief is that the buffallo is exclusively a tropical animal. River type buffalloes, However, have been used to pull snow plows during Bulgarian winter.

Buffallo milk has a higher content of both butter fat and non fat-solids than cows milk does. Throughout much India it is in such demand that Cow's milk is sometimes hard to sell.

Breeds

The major genetic division of the buffallo are the swamp Buffallo of the eastern half of the Asia, which has swept back horns and the river buffalo of the western half of Asia which usually has the curled horns. There is also the mediterranean buffalo, which is of the river type but has been isolated for so long that it has developed some unique characteristics.

Although there is only one breed of swamp buffallo, certain sub-groups seem to have specific inherited characteristics. Swamp buffalloes range from 250 kg for some small animals in China, 200-300 kg in Berma ąnd 500-600 kgs in Laos. Only in India and Pakistan are there well defined breeds with standard qualities. There are eighteen (18) river buffallo breeds in south asia which are further classified as the Murrah, Gujrat, Uttar Pradesh, Central Indian & South Indian breeds. These are the five groups and main breeds :

Groups	Breeds
Murrah	Murrah,Nili/Ravi, Kundi
Gujrat	Surti, Mehsana, Jafarabadi
Uttar Pradesh	Bhadawari, Tarai,
Central Indian	Nagpuri,Manda, Pandharpuri,
Sambal pur, Jerangi, Kala Handi,	
South Indian	Toda, south Kanara,

The best known breeds are Murrah Nili/Ravi, Surti, Jafarabadi, Mehsana, & Nagpuri.

Genetics

The swamp buffalo has forty eight chromosomes, the river buffallo fifty similar in the two types and they cross breeds to produce fertile hy-brid progeny. Cattle however, have sixty (60) chromosomes and although mating between cattle & buffaloes is common, hy-brids from the union are unlikely to occur.

Individual buffaloes show large variation in milk yield, conformation, horn shape, colour,meal production, temparament, growth rate, & other characteristics.

The large bulls that would be best for breeding purposes are often being selected as draft animals and Castrated, or sent to slaughter or shot by hunters.

YIELDS

In countries like India & Egypt, the milk yield of buffaloes is generally higher (680-800kg) than for local cattle (360-500 kg). However since selection for exceptional, large variations in yield occur between individual animals and milk production of dairy buffaloes falls short of its potential. Indian Government forms, average yields for milking buffaloes range from 4-7 kg per day in lactations averaging 285 days, Daily yields of 12 kg have been reported for some Bulgarian buffalo cows & and a daily production of over 20 kg has been reported for some remarkable animals in India. A peak milk yield of 31.5 kg/day has been recorded from a champion Murrah buffalo in the All India Milk yield competition conducted by Govt. of India.

DAIRY MANAGEMENT

The characteristics of the dairy buffalo so closely approximate those of the dairy cow that successful methods of breeding, husbandary and feeding for milk production for the cow can be applied equally to the dairy buffalo. Buffaloes however have not been breed for uniform udders and it is more difficult to milk them by machine.

USES & APPLICATIONS OF MILK

Buffalo milk can provide a wide variety of products : butter, butteroil (Clarified butter or ghee) soft and hard cheeses, condensed or evaporated milk, Ice-cream, Yogurt and buttermilk. It is of great economic importance in India in preparing tonned milk- a mixture of buffalo milk and milk made by reconstituting skim milk powder.

The richness of buffalow milk makes it highly suitable for processing.

To produce 1 kg of cow's milk but only 5 kg of buffalo milk. To produce 1 kg of butter requires 14 kg of cow's milk but only 10 kg of buffaloes milk. Because of these high yields, processors appreciated the value of buffallo milk. Buffallo cheese is pure white. Cheese are becoming increasingly popular throughout the world. Demand is rising at a rate that is among the highest for any food product cheese offers particular benefit to areas where refrigeration is not widely available where transporting high protein foods to remote areas is difficult and where seasonal fluetnations affect milk supplies.

DISEASES

Newborn buffalo calves, like bovine calves, can succumb in large numbers to viruses, bacteria, and poor nutrition. This is largely due to poor management during the calf's first 2 months of life. For example, villagers in some countries often sell the valuable buffalo milk, thus depriving the calves.

Buffalo calf losses are often similar to those of the cattle around them, but the animal's proclivity for wallowing exposes calves to waterborne diseases.

SUPPLIERS OF CATTLES

M/s. Haryana Dairy Development Co-op Federation Ltd.,
Bhiwani, (Haryana)

M/s. Govt. of Jammu and Kashmir,
Animal Husbandary Deptt,
Cattle Breeding Farms,
Beli Charana, Jammu Cantt.

M/s. Govt. Of Punjab,
Animal Husbandary Deptt.,
Cattle Breeding Farms - Mattewara,
Ludhiana (PB).

M/s. Indian Agricultural Research Intitute,
Pusa, New Delhi - 110 012.

COMPOSITION OF CATTLE FEED

There is no definite composition to Buffalo feed compound but in general practice the following composition is followed :-

Ground nut Cake	25%
Wheat bran	27%
Grain Husk	15%
Maize	30%
Mineral	1%
Salt	2%

COMPOSTION OF MILK

COMPOSITION

Buffalo milk contains less water, more fat,slightly more lactose,and more protein than cow's milk. It seems thicker than cow's milk because it generally contains more than 16 percent total solid compared with 12-14 percent for cow's milk. Although the butterfat content is usually 6-8 percent, it can go much higher in the milk of some well fed dairy buffaloes and in the milk of Swamp buffaloes (which are not normally used for milking). Cow's milk butterfat content is usually between 3 and 5 percent.

Because of its high butterfat content, buffalo milk has considerably higher energy value than cow's milk. Phospholipids are lower but cholesterol and saturated fatty acids are higher in buffalo milk. Studies have shown that digestibility is not adversely affected by this. Because of the high fat content, the buffalo's total fat yield per lactation compares favourably with that of improved breeds of dairy cattle, it is much higher than that of indigenous cows.

Normally the protein in buffalo milk contains more casein and slightly more albumin and globulin than cow's milk. Several researchers have claimed that the biological value of buffalo milk protein is higher than that of cow's milk, but this has not yet been proved conclusively.

COMPARATIVE GROSS COMPOSITION (IN PERCENT) OF BUFFALO AND COW'S MILK

Total	Solid	Fat	Protein	Lactose
River buffalo	17.96	7.45	4.36	4.83
Swamp buffalo	18.34	8.95	4.13	4.78
Friesian Cow	12.15	3.60	3.25	4.60
Native Cow	13.45	4.97	3.18	4.59

NOTE

In general, buffalo milk is conderably higher in total solids, fat, and protein than milk from improved or native cows. Buffalo milk is slightly higher in lactose.

Source

R.E. McDowell, Department of Animal Science, Cornell University.

MANUFACTURING PROCESS

The manufacturing process for Dairy milk is started with the milking buffaloes by hand (at small scale) & milking buffaloess by machine (at large scale).The process is given here with :-

MILKING BUFFALOES BY HAND

The profitable operation of a dairy herd depends in a large part upon how well you milk your buffaloes. You can do everything else carefully and well, but if you do not milk your buffaloes properly, you can never be successful in dairying. Poor milking habits cause low production, mastitis, & poor quality milk. An important part of milking buffaloes is to produce the cleanest possible milk. Milk must be low in sediment.

Although machine milking is rapidly replacing hand milking, many dairymen still use the latter. In milking by hand. buffaloes must be carefully prepared to produce high quality milk.

COOLING & STORING MILK

The careless handling of milk between milking & delivering to the plant can cause high bacteria counts to develop in the milk thus a mechanical cooler is employed for the purpose. Whole of the milk should be stored at 50°F to prevent spoilage. Storage Tanks made of stainless steel are employed for storing the raw milk.

FILTERATION

The cold raw milk is filtered, however, it can be fitlered before cooling & storing in tank, but the precaution is to be taken at this stage so that no foreign matters or undesired materials may be carried on.

HOMOGENIZATION

Filtered milk is fed into homigenizer. Homogenization is the process by which the milk is emulsified and are further divided to produce a more stable emulsion that will not separate on standing. The fat is emulsified with liquid part of milk that are water mostly. Hence, to prevent sedimentation of fat in milk. This homogenization process is done. By this way high quality homogenized milk is produced.

CLARIFICATION

The milk is passed through a clarifier as it leaves the homogenizer. Cold milk clarification is preferred to hot milk. This clarification operation can be perform before homogenization. But the complete clarification can be achieved at this stage.

PASTEURIZATION

In this process, the clarified milk is fed to pasteurizer and heated to the required temperature & held there during the holding period (usually at 145°F & for at least 30 minutes). Vat pasteurizer with jackets & agitators is employed for the pasteurization.

REFRIGERATION OR FREEZING SYSTEM

After the complete processing of milk it is to be stored in a cold upto chilling condition so that no unwanted micro-organisms/pathogenic organism can be developed in the processed milk. It is stored until delivered for distribution i.e. for packing in Cans or pouches.

TESTING

The testing of milk is an essential for the quality control purposes. However, testing may be done prior to storage under freezing condition. But it is better to test the final product before packing.

PACKING

There are two methods adopted from packing milk. Firstly packed or stored in aluminium milk cans for distribution. Secondly milk packed in plastic pouches of capacity 1/2 kg, 1 kg, & 2 kgs packs.

ADDRESSES OF PLANT & MACHINERY SUPPLIERS

MILK STORAGE TANKS

M/s. Dany Dairy and Food Engineers
Private Limited,
7/4 km. Stone Debradun Road,
P.B. No. 115,
SAHARANPUR - 247001

PLANT ECONOMICS OF

Rated Plant capacity = DAIRY FARM(1200 LTR./DAY)

LAND & BUILDING

(Total Land required 2000 sq.m) Rs. 21,80,000.00

PLANT & MACHINERY

Steam boiler,Homogenizer complete with accessory,Refrigeration system consists of air compressor, refrigerants & cerenlating tube tank
Pasteurizer with cooling arrangement
Filter (ordinary),Pouch making, filling & sealing M/c,complete automatic with printing ,arrangement
Milk reception tank (Stainless 20000 steel make)
Milk Cans (Aluminium)
Dies, Buffalloes Kundi 100 Nos.
Misc. other equipments such as Laboratory & testing equipments

TOTAL Rs. 17,17,000.00

OTHER FIXED ASSETS Rs. 4,20,000.00

FIXED CAPITAL

1.	LAND & BUILDING	Rs. 21,80,000.00
2.	PLANT & MACHINERY	Rs. 17,17,000.00
3.	OTHER FIXED ASSETS	Rs. 4,20,000.00
	TOTAL	**Rs. 43,17,000.00**

WORKING CAPITAL REQUIREMENT/MONTH

LIST OF RAW MATERIALS

Raw Material for Buffaloes feed
green fodder/Cattle feed
Health expenses (medicines) etc.
Raw material for pouch Polythene sheet
Misc. other items such as
printing ink etc.

TOTAL WORKING CAPITAL/MONTH

1.	RAW MATERIAL	Rs.	59,500.00
2.	SALARY & WAGES	Rs.	38,750.00
3.	UTILITIES & OVERHEADS	Rs.	15,200.00
	TOTAL	**Rs.**	**1,13,450.00**

TOTAL CAPITAL INVESTMENT

TOTAL FIXED CAPITAL	Rs.	43,17,000.00
TOTAL WORKING CAPITAL FOR 3 MONTHS	Rs.	3,40,350.00
TOTAL	**Rs.**	**46,57,350.00**

TURN OVER/ANNUM

By sale of 1200 x 365 litres of Milk (Dairy Farming)	Rs.	52,56,000.00

PROFIT = RECEIPTS - COST OF PRODUCTION = Rs.23,72,383.00

PROFIT SALES RATIO = Profit / Sales x 100 = 45.14 %

RATE OF RETURN = Operating profit / T.C.I x 100 = 50.94 %

BREAK EVEN POINT (B.E.P) = 42.88 %

IMPORTANT ADDRESSES

Alfa Laval (India) Limited
Div - Tetra Pak Processing
Dapodi, Pune
Tel : 0212 - 776321, 773253
Fax : 0212 - 779479
(Tetra Pak's processing & packaging protect the natural good ness and quality of milk over a long period making extensive distribution possible without refrigeration. Aseptically packed milk can be conveniently had without boiling again.)

Project Engineering Services
C-3/3, Rajouri Garden,
Post Box No. 6561, New Delhi - 110 027.
Tel : 5417510, 8 - 340642
Fax : 5419768
(Stainless Steel Flow Equipments For Dairy)

E.N. Project and Engineering Industries Private Ltd.
Office : FA-357, Mansrover Garden,
New Delhi - 110015
Tel : 5412736
(Manufacturers & Suppliers of Milk Tankers, Pasteurizers, Silos, Chillers, Cream Tanks, Ghee Boilers etc. on turn key basis.)

Khambete Kothari
Cans & Allied Products Pvt. Ltd.
Jalgaon- 425 003 (M.S.)
Tel : 24750
(Light Weight Durable & Hygenic Can)

Mojj Engineering Systems Pvt. Ltd.
81-B/15, M.I.D.C., Bhosari,
Pune - 411 026
Tel : 91 - 212 - 790360
Fax : 91 - 212 - 792836
(Offers Milk Powder Plant, Instant Milk Powder Plants,Cheese Plants, Casein Plants & Other Milk Projects)

Samarpan Fabricators Limited
Plot A, 182/A, 183, Road 16/Z, Wagle,
Industrial Estate, Thane,
Mumbai - 400 604.
Tel : 5320029, 70373/0822. (Off.)
0730/1842 (Fact.)
Fax : 91 - 22 - 5320033
(Packaging Machine, Automatic Form Fills Seal M/C.)

Mysore Feeds Limited
Regd. Office : 283/284, Old Tharagupet,
Bangalore - 560 053.
Tel : 2861471/2872215
Fax : 2874175
Factory : Nayandahalli, Mysore Road,
Bangalore-560 039.
Tel : 8600008/8600290
Fax : 8600840
(Milk Can Brand Cattle Feed)

R.M.C. Packaging Systems Pvt. Ltd.
25 A & B, Electronic Complex, Kushaiguda,
Hyderabad - 500 762. (A.P.)
Tel : 622556, 824308.

Chadha sales Pvt. Ltd.
Dairy Equipment Engineers
137, Rajendra Market,
Tis Hazari,
Delhi-110 054
Tel:2922290/2944840/2511416
Fax: 011-2914211
(Aluminium Alloys Milk Cans)

INSTITUTIONS EDUCATIONAL & RESEARCH

College of Veterinary
Rajendra Nagar,
Hyderabad-500 030 (A.P.)
Tel : (040)245164

Andhre Pradesh State Meat & Poultry
Development Corpopration Ltd. (MAPDEC)
Shanti Nagar,
Hyderabad - 500 028 (A.P.)
Tel : (040)36681, 221580

Bihar Veterinary College,
Patna - 800 014 (Bihar)
Tel : 222231

Farmers Training Centre (Kisan Vidyapith)
Samastipur Distt.,
Pusa - 847423 (Bihar)

Action for Food Production (AFPRO)
25-IA, Institutional Area, Pankha Road,
D Block, Janak Puri,
New Delhi - 110 058
Tel : 5555412, 5553652
Fax : 011- 5500343

Indian Agricultural Statiatics Reasearch Institute (IASRI)
Library Avenue, Pusa,
New Delhi - 110 012
Tel : (011)587121

Indian Council of Agricultural Reasearch (ICAR)
Krishi Bhawan, Dr. Rajendra Prasad Road,
New Delhi - 110 001
Tel : (011)388991

College of Veterniary Science & Animal Husbandry
Anand Campus, Kheda Distt.,
Anand - 388110(Gujarat)
Tel : (02692) 23486

Tata Marginal Farm Management Institute
Tata Baug, Lunsikui,
Navsari - 396445 (Gujarat)
Tel : 3948

College of Animal Sciences
Hissar - 125004 (Haryana)
Tel : (01662) 73721

Krishi Gyan Kendras (Vet & Anim Ses)
HAU Farm, Near Dist. Court,
Bhiwani.(Haryana)

Central Institute For Research On Buffaloes
Sirsa Road,
Haryana - 125001.
Tel : 4513, 4170, 5148

Indian Vaterinary Research Institute (IVRI)
Regional Research Station, c/o HP Krishi
Vishvavidyalaya,
Palampur - 176061(H.P.)
Tel : 30526

Central Food Technological Research Institute (CFTRI)
Cheluvamba Mansion,
Mysore - 570013 (Karnataka)
Tel : (0821)22660

Central Institute of Agricultural Engineering (ICAR)
Nabibagh, Berasia Road,
Bhopal - 462018(M.P.)
Tel : (0755)530980 - 987

Baif Reasearch Institute Of Cattle & Agricultural Development
P O.Uruli Kancha,
Distt. Pune - 412202(Maharashtra)
Tel : (0212) 816248

Orrisa Veterniary College
Estd. 1955, Orrisa ,
Veterinary College,
Bhubaneswar - 751003.(Orrisa)
Tel : 400732
Fax : 0674 - 407780

State Animal Health Institute
Ladowali Road,
Jalandhar. (Punjab)

College of Dairy Science Udaipur
College of Dairy Sci., University Campus,
Udaipur,
Rajasthan - 313001
Tel : 412719

Training Institute for Training Of Veterinary
P.O. & Distt, Midnapur - 721101
Tel : 62506

NATIONAL DAIRY DEVELOPMENT BOARD (NDDB)

Head Office
PB No. 40, Anand - 388 001
Tel : (02692) 40148/40149, 40157/40159

Western Region
PB No. 9074
Western Express Highway Goregaon (East)
Bombay - 400 063
Tel : (022) 8402869/8403512/8403689
Fax : 022 - 8402122

Northern Region
PB No. 4906
Safdarjang Enclave,
New Delhi-110 029
Tel : (011) 6875847/6877851,603398/603453
Fax : 011-688366

Chapter - 5

Eucalyptus Tree Cultivation/Plantation

I. Introduction

Eucalyptus tree was introduced in india from Australia about 200 years ago. During 18th century a few trees were planted in the Nilgris hills of Tamilnadu. Around 1956, a hybrid Eucalyptus, known as " Mysore gum " became more popular in Mysore. Large scale plantations of this species were taken up in Uttar Pradesh. Eucalyptus grandis which was first introduced in Kerala for afforesting the grass lands of high ranges, has emerged as the most important species for pulp-wood plantations in kerala. The other Eucalyptus species that are grown in India are E.citriodra, E.citriodra, E.globlus and E.grandis.

Over 6 million hectares of eucalyptus plantations have been established throughout the world in more than 60 countries.Another 50 countries have small scale plantations either for trial or for ornamental purposes. Brazil is the leading country in eucalyptus planting in the world with an area of 10,52,000 hectares under eucalyptus plantations. Other important countries are Argentina, Cameroons, Chile, China, Cuba, Cypress, Equador, France. America. India. Iraq, Israel, Italy, Japan, Kenya, Russia, New Zealand, United Kingdom. spain etc. Total area planted under Eucalyptus in our country is about 7-8 lakh hectares. It is grown in different parts of the country viz. Punjab, Haryana. Andhra Pradesh,Karnataka, Tamilnadu,

Kerala, U.P., Bihar, West Bengal, Madhya Pradesh and Maharashtra.

II. Growth Habit

Eucalyptus trees are evergreen trees, new leaves appear as the old ones are shed. It has no well defined season of growth and continue to grow in all seasons. It attains a height of about 30 mts. and more with a straight clean bole. They have the ability to colonize bare ground without shelter. Some of the species occuring in extremely dry areas are no higher than shrubs. The shrubs namely, E. erythrandra, E.burdethiana and E.mitrata are 6-8 mts. tall with a voluminous root system. Many of these species, when cultivated under more favourable conditions,develop into small trees.

There is a great variation in the height of various Eucalyptus species of tree habit in their homeland and ranging from 20-114 mts. and girth upto 3-4 mts.

In India, the successful Eucalyptus are generally moderately large trees and attain a height of 30-45 mts. and diameter of 1-2 metres. The trunk of the tree is generally straight and constitute half of the total height.

In India, the oldest plantation of E.globulus contains trees upto 45 mts. in height and 5-6 mts. In girth while in Kodaikanal the tree measures only 37 mts. in height and has a girth of 9.6 mts. A number of eucalyptus species have an effective subterranean protective organ known as "diagnotuber" enabling the trees to produce new shoots if the arieal parts are destroyed. Other growth habits which have made eucaluptus so popular are indefinite shoots and naked buds which permit the plant to grow indefinitely and to produce new orders of branches as long as favourable conditions exist for growth. In the axil of each leaf there is a naked bud, which is a growing tip that can immediatly produce a branch of next order. A pad of meristematic tissue at the base of each naked bud can produce several auxiliary shoots in the event of the original being destroyed. These small eye shaped structures are seen on the main stem and branches of the tree.

III. Soil and Climate

Eucalyptus flourishes from coastel areas to areas situated at an altitude of 200 mts. and climate varying from tropical to warm temperate and annual rainfall ranging from 400-4000 millimeteres. It can grow in a wide variety of soil conditions but reqires deep, fertile, well draimed soils with adequate moisture for best growth. It is not suitable for steep hill slopes, dry and water logged areas. It staganates on poor heavy and sandy soils if not irrigated. Highly alkaline saline soils, clay and kankar (calcareous) pan are also limiting factors. Eucalyptus show a tremendous variation in size at maturity perphaps the greatest in the plant kingdom. they vary from dwarf multistemmed trees called " mallees" to mountain giants towering over 100 mts. in to the air, their atraight trunks, branches for over 30 mts. The smaliest eucalyptus are found with regions with poor soils and arid climates. The giant trees occur in high rainfall areas with deep and fertile soils.

IV. Seeds and Storage

Eucalyptus regenerate by seed. Lately, vegetative multiplication of superior clonal material of specially bred and selected eucalyptus is recieving special attention to achieve very high yields of 50-60 cubic meteres per hectare per year. Eucalyptus are quite, stable and genetic breakdown in them do not occur.

The choice of trees for seed collection depends primarily on the purpose for which the seeds are being collected. Seeds may be required for afforestation programmes, for trials or for research purposes. The usual principle of selection of trees is that the seeds should be collected from trees showing a high degree of desireable characteristics such as rapid growth, good form, high yield etc.

For most of the species, the period between flowering and seed maturation is long enough to give the collecter time to prepare for seed collection. This interval varies from 6 to 16 months for different species.

Eucalyptus seed usually mature when the fruits become brown and hard. In some instances seeds are viable before they have fully matured i.e. when seed coat is relatively soft and light in colour.

The maturity of seed can be tested by a transverse cut through the fruit ex. with secateus; if the seeds are mature they will be seen as white embryos within dark seed coats, and brown will also be present towards the top of the capsule.

From a single mature tree about 1-2.5 Kg. of seed can be collected.

On an average from one kilogram of E.tereticornis 25000-30,000 healthy plants can be grown.

V. Planting Techniques

Eucalyptus Plantations require well drained, deep and fertile soils. Sandy soils may be good, provided facility of adequate irrigation is available. Choice of proper species for a particular type of site is also an important factor for the success of an eucalyptus plantation. Specific sites suitable for different species are given in the following table

Table 1: Site charateristics for different species

S.No.	Species	Site charateristics
1.	Eucalyptus hybrid	Gently slopy areas and well drained plains,drier localities, wasteland,farm bunds, agricultural fields
2.	Eucalyptus tereticornis	Hills and plains, mined out areas, refactory sites.
3.	E.citiriodora	Hills upto 1200 mts.
4.	E.grandis	Plateau, plains, high rainfall areas
5.	E.globulus	Hilly areas above 1200 mts. but with no snow fall.
6.	E.microtheca	Plains, alkaline soil areas with precariously low rainfall.
7.	E. melanopholia	Plains areas having drough problems
8.	E.saligna E.rudis E.rostrata.	Plains

Barren areas cover saline and alkaline tracts, sandy areas with low nutritional status and extremely low and erratic rainfall. Eucalyptus comaldulensis can be planted in these areas.

In Ravine areas, E.tereticornis and E.comaldulensis are grown. Grass land and barren treeless areas can be planted with E.grandis and E.tereticornis.

For planting, pits with 30 x 30 x 30 x 30 cms are to be dug fairly in advance of planting, except in coastel areas. While digging the pits, the soil of the top half of the pits is to be kept seperately. The planting can be done in different systems that are given below.

1. Block planting

Eucalyptus are planted in blocks either in existing blanks or on sites containing vegetation. Plantations are carried out both manually and by mechanised means. The site is made into ridges of 20-30 cms. high which are made at 4 mts. interval and planting is carried out over these ridges. The inter spaces are leased for agriculture. Till two years intercultivation can be done.

In manual planting, pits of 30 x 30 x 30 cms. or 45 x 45 x 45 cms. or 60 x 60 x 60 cms can be dug depending on the soil and irrigation facilities. In waterlogged areas, planting on raised mounds upto one metre high is done in certain areas in punjab, Haryana, and Uttar pradesh, usually in multiple rows along roads.

2. Row Planting

Row plantations are carried out along roads, canal banks and Railway lines. Along roads eucalyptus are planted behind first row of shade trees. The first row is located at a distance of 9 mts. from the road along National Highway and 7.5 mts. along other roads. The rows are planted at 1 x 1 mts. to 3 x 2 mts. spacing, depending on local practice. In the railway lands, the first row of plants is located not nearer than 5 mts. from the centre of the railway track. In case of canals, the first row is located about one metre, away from the outer edge of the service road.

3. Line planting

Eucalyptus are being planted increasingly along with boundaries of cultivated fields in single rows. Spacing of 0.5 mts. -4 mts. is maintained. A spacing of 1.5 mts. for field boundaries and for wind breaks. Where plants are desired, to be kept for 20 years, or more, a spacing of 4 mts. is desireable.

They have branch shedding habit so these should not be planted near building an along transmission lines. They are good plants for tall hedges if they are regularly pruned with a spacing of 1.5 metres.

In Gujrat, a spacing of 1 x 1 mt. spacing and 2 x 2 mt. spacing in Andhra pradesh are being adopted. The Eucalyptus seedlings should be planted soon after the regular monsoon sets in. It should be completed with in 3rd week from the start of the regular monsoon rains. On the coastel sands, planting should commence two weeks after the monsoon starts. More details about spacing are as folows.

VI. Spacing

In crops such as Eucaluptus which are harvested at short rotations, correct spacing plays a vital role, in increasing their productivity. Spacing will depend on the objective of planting, the soil type, moisture regime, the percentage of bark, density of wood and several other factors.

The volume per tree is significantly correlated to the spacing as the average diameter is directly related to the spacing between plants. In general, the total volume production decreases as spacing is increased. Experiments proved that closest spacing gioves highest volume production but at higher rotation of about 10 years, a very close spacing does not give because of less survivals. A summary of the results obtained from various trials in terms of diameter and volume (under bark volume) production under selected spacements at the age of 6 years has been presented in the following years:

Table 2: Different recommended spacings in Eucaluptus

Spacing daimeter	Average (cu.mts)	Volume/ha (%)	Survival(nits) (cms)
1 x 1	9	148	56
1.4 x 1.4	9	80	65
2 x 2	10	36	63
2.45 x 2.45	11	50	73
3 x 3	13	60	91
1 x 2	10	132	78
1 x 3	10	119	75
1 x 4	12	112	83
1 x 5	13	115	93
1 x 6	14	106	86
2 x 0.5	8	114	58
2 x 1.5	10	81	71
2 x 2.5	11	66	81
2 x 3	12	74	85
3 x 0.3	10	288	80
3 x 0.6	10	152	88

The indication from these trials is that when production of higher diameter classes is taken into consideration. close spacings still give high volume production at the age of 6 years, but wider spacing of 5-6 sq. mts. per plant show an incresing in volume production at higher ages of 8 to 10 years.

VII. Growth and Yield

The eucalyptus plantation show great variations in the height and diameter growth of trees. Very often the biggest tree from a plantation will be more than 4-5 times bigger than that of the smallest one. In agroforestry systems, eucalyptus grows to a height of about 12 mts. and 40-45 cms girth bat the age of 3 years.

Application of fertilizers have shown great response to height and diameter increament. An average yield of 63.5, 25.0 and 11.9 tonnes per hectare respectively for E.globulus, E.grandis and E. tereticornis in different states are given in following table.

Table 3: Volume of 8 year old E.tereticornis(m3/ha over bark)

State	Volume over bark(m3/ha)	
	Maximum	Minimum
Uttar Pradesh	228.7	11.9
Andhra Pradesh	76.57	37.45
West Bengal	59.72	58 15
Bihar	98.57	27.87
Madhya Pradesh	35.55	30.98
Tamilnadu	325.23	18.35
Kerala	100.13	51.43
Karnataka (Mysore)	205.1	16.81

Table 4: Biomass estimation for some of the Eucalyptus Ecosystem

S.No.	Species	Age (yr.)	Total biomass (t/ha)
1.	Eucalyptus hybrid(U.P.)	5	68.4
		10	141.6
		12	178.5
		16	194.6
2.	E.hybrid (Karnataka)	5	5.6
		6	25.5
		7	21.3
		8	25.2
		10	27.1
3.	E.hybrid (Bihar)	3	11.9
		5	26.1
4.	E. hybrid (haryana)	4	20.1
		6	34.6
		8	88.7
		10	137.7
5.	E.tereticornis (U.P.)	5	81.1
		9	196.7
6.	E.globulus (Tamilnadu)	5	38.1
		7	142.7
		9	139.0
		16	220.4
7.	E.grandis (Kerala)	3	64.8
		5	112.5
		7	110.0
		9	207.6
		11	300.6

VIII Economics of Plantations

Economics of Eucaluptus plantations has been estimated on the average basis such as average site quality, average spacing, average inputs, average yield etc.

For estimating the returns from a commercial operation of eucaluptus plantations a farm of about 25 acres is an ideal one. About 2000 trees per acre in the configuration of 2 x 1 mt is expected to be quite productive. In a cycle of 6 years each tree should grow to weigh about 100-150 kgs.which should fetch about Rs.55/- cut and delievered at buyer's place. After providing for cutting an dtransportation changes, it should ahve a net realisation of rs. 40 per tree.

A. Fixed costs

Fixed expenses in taking up eucalyptus plantations are given here. Costs of various operations may be variable depending on the prevailing conditions.

a.	25 acres of land @ 5,000/acre including conveyance charges	Rs.	1,25,000.00
b.	Cost of preparing land for plantation @ Rs. 1000/acre	Rs.	25000.00
c.	Planting, fencing, hedges, gate and a room.	Rs.	75,000.00
d.	Tubewell, power connection, agricultural implements and irrigation channels	Rs.	1,00,000.00
e.	Construction of labour huts.	Rs.	25,000.00
f.	Cost of plants @ Rs. 0.5/ in plant	Rs.	25,000.00
g.	Pit digging, manure, insecticide and planting @ Rs. 1.25 plant	Rs.	62,500.00
h.	Consulting charges @ 1 plant	Rs.	50,000.00
i.	Other miscellaneous fixed expenses	Rs.	20.000.00
	Total	Rs.	5,07,500.00

B. Recurring expenses

The recurring expenses would vary from year to year. These would be more during first 2-3 years and subsequently reduce over the 18 years period.

On an average, total recurring expenses for the first 6 years period are given here.

a.	Weeding	Rs.	15,000.00
b.	Irrigation and maintenance of channels (about 65 irrigations @ Rs. 2000/- irrigation)	Rs.	1,35,000.00
c.	Insecticides for first 2 years @ Rs. 200/-acre	Rs.	5,000.00
d.	Manuring	Rs.	5,000.00
e.	Watchman @ Rs. 500/- per month for 2 persons	Rs.	72,000.00
f.	Other miscellaneous expenses @ Rs.5000/- year for 6 years	Rs.	30,000.00
g.	Opportunity cost of fixed cost @ 15 % for 6 years	Rs.	4,50,000.00
	Total	Rs.	7,12,000.00

C. Returns

a.	Number of plantations @ Rs.2000/-are		50,000 trees
b.	Matured trees after accounting for 20 % mortality		40,000 trees
c.	Sales realisation @ Rs. 40/- per tree (40,000 x 40)	Rs.	1,60,000.00
d.	Total profit (16,00,000- 7,12,000)	Rs.	8,88,000.00
e.	Profit per year	Rs.	1,48,000.00

Assuming that the increase in cost of inputs would be offset by increased prices of eucalyptus wood and therefore workimg out the profitability for next 12 years, the net returns workout as follows

a.	Interest for 12 years @ 15 %	Rs.	9,00,000.00
b.	Other recurring expenses	Rs.	2,00,000.00
	Total	Rs.	11,00,000.00
c.	Sales Realisation @ 40/- tree for two crops	Rs.	32,000,00.00
d.	Profit over 12 years period	Rs.	21,00,000.00
e.	Profit per year	Rs.	1,75,000.00

Likewise a profit of Rs. 1,48,000/- per year is shown during the first 6 years and a profit of 1,75,00,00/- year has been shown during the next 12 years. On an average, it calaulates 1.6 lakhs per year of 18 years which is quite attractive. In case intercropping is resorted in the initial years, the profitability would be even better.

Chapter - 6

Floriculture (Cut-Flower)

INTRODUCTION

The rose has been loved and cherished from very ancient times. In modern age, its importance has become still greater because rose breeders have been increasing its range of colours while at the same time adding valuable characters like disease resistance and a longer period of flowering. It is a versatile plant and the fantastically large number of types available is one of the reason for its great popularity. There are now roses for every purpose and even the person with only a tiny plot of land will find there are varieties available to him which will provide a welcome splash of colour to a wall or furnish quantities of exquisite cut flowers. Now-a-days, roses are grown throughout the country and perhaps no flower is more loved in India. The rose is valued for purposes of worship and for making garlands in our country. Recently the Rose Society of India has laid out a beautiful National Rose Garden in New Delhi.

CLIMATE

The climate conditions of India re well suited to rose cultivation. Rose need bright sunshine and free ventilation. Sunshine for six hours is idea for better growth and flowering.

In the northern plains, roses flower best during winter whereas in the temperate hilly regions of the Himalayas in summer. Western part of India have excellent agro-climatic conditions for rose growing. The plains of eastern India are also suitable for the cultivation of many rose cultivars. Bangalore has mild climate where roses can be grown for flowers throughout the year.

SOIL

Although any soil is good for rose cultivation provided it has proper drainage, the ideal soil should be medium loam having sufficient organic matter, pH or 6.0 - 7.5. The land where th external drainage is poor and water stagnates during monsoon should not be selected for rose growing. In every heavy soils, gravel and sand may be mixed into the bed to allow drainage. The land with high water-table is not suitable for rose beds.

LAYOUT OF BEDS

The plan of rose garden and design of the beds should be simple and informal. Rose beds may be of various design, depending upon the liking of the grower. However, rectangular beds are advantageous for maintenance. The width of the beds should be such that operations like weeding, hoeing, forking, cutting of flowers etc, can be done from both the side of the bed, without stepping into the bed. A plot size of 6.0 X 1.2 m or 6.0 X 1.65 m is suggested for better management of rose plants. The length can be increased to a limited extent depending upon the specific situations.

GROWTH AND FLOWERING

Factors like genetic or inherent factors, climatic or environmental factors such as light, temperature, moisture, aeration and managemental factors like nutrition and soil conditions influence growth and flowering.

A. Genetic factors

Like other plants, growth and flowering behaviour of roses is governed by genetic factors. The range of variability in roses is very great. There are tall cultivars growing several metres high and are suitable for planting in backdrop and as hedges. On the other hand, miniature roses with dwarf habit and producing small flowers are also available. Several cultivars are bushy in nature while many are climbers and ramblers. A wide choice of cultivars with long sturdy stems having nice flower forms suitable for cut-flowers are also available today. Similarly, there are cultivars blooming in different periods and producing varied yield and quality of flowers. Some possess high quality perfume.

B. Environmental factors

Along with genetic factors, environmental factors play an important role on growth and flowering.

1. Light

Light is one of the most important factors influencing the growth and flowering of roses. This may vary with intensity, duration and quality of light. The total plant weight may be reduced by the decrease in light intensity, and the number of flowers produced increases with increased radiation.

Plants growing under shade produce leaves with low chlorophyll content. However, because of high light intensity and the consistent rise in temperature, summer grower apply a light shading material on the roof of the glasshouse. Colour of rose flowers is also influenced by the high intensity of light. The influence of duration of light is most marked and spectacular on growth and in inducing of suppressing flowering.

2. Temperature

Temperature affects the quantity and quality of the plant and the flower. At a night temperature of 15.5°C the quality and quantity of roses produced are considered to be satisfactory. Low temperature also brings about the development of pigment in the leaves stems or flowers. The stem and flower buds needs an exposure to cool temperature for their expansion. Winter chilling is necessary for flower bud formation.

3. Humidity

Humidity plays an important role in the incidence of pests and diseases affecting the growth and flowering. Certain disease like mildew's are associated with high relative humidity. Its importance, however, lies in the internal water conditions of the plants. By maintaining reasonably high humidity, the internal deficiency of water will be less. Enlargement of cells is caused by water and, therefore, we should the loss of water from the plants so that leaves and flowers would be larger and stems longer.

4. Aeration

Proper soil aeration and an exchange of air in greenhouse are also desirable for the normal growth and development. Compact soils have restricted aeration which impede the activity of roots affecting the plant growth. Air circulation ensures an adequate supply of carbon dioxide and oxygen for physiological processes occuring in the plant and also reduces the relative humidity which may cause serious infections. Carbon di-oxide is an important factor in photosynthesis in increasing the stem length and dry matter.

C. Plant management practices

Pruning, pinching, disbudding, deshooting, defoliation and deflowering are the plant management practices done for rose cultivation.

1. Pruning

Pruning is an important operation regulating the growth and flowering of roses. Prunng in roses is explained in detail the cultivation section. Following are some other plant management practices which influence the vegetative growth and production of flowers.

2. Pinching

Removal of a part of terminal growing portion of stem is called pinching. It reduces the plant height but promotes auxiliary branching and also prevents maturity of flower but.

3. Disbudding

Removal of undesirable buds is known as disbudding. Keeping only the central bud and removal of others cause development of a quality bloom.

4. Deshooting

Deshooting is generally followed in Hybrid Tea roses. Young vegetative shoots developing from the axils of leaves of basal and lateral shoots are removed to allow only one terminal shoot. In several rose cultivars such side shoots develop from the eyes down the stem below the terminal flower bud. If these shoots are not inched off at the initial stage, plants become much branched and produce a number of small flowers.

5. Defoliation

Although defoliated plants produced about twice as many shoots as undefoliated, many of them are blind and the total number of flowers is less. Complete defoliation causes atrophy of almost all flower buds. Removal of only mature leaves causes about 50% blindness. Removal of only young leaves, however does not cause blindness.

Leaf removal on dormant shoots results in the production of short and non-flowering shoots, Removal of the upper-most leaf at the time of pinching results in highly significant increase in flower production. Leaf removal from semi mature shoots is more effective on flower production than from young shoots. Flower quality, is also not reduced by this practice.

6. Delflowering

Removal of faded flowers is called deflowering. If the spend blooms are not removed in time, there is a chance of developing fruit bearing seeds. Once the hips are formed and reach the advance stage of development, growth and flowering are severely reduced during the season. Cutting of faded flowers forces strong laterals which produces a good quality flower.

PROPAGATION

Among propagation methods, budding is most popular in our country because it produces better quality flowers and faster growth of plants. Other methods like, seed propagation, layering, grafting are also important.

1. Budding

Budding is the most popular and successful method for multiplying roses. It provides larger number of plants than cuttings, layering or grafting, as a single shoot of the desired scion furnishes a number of buds for budding. Shield or T-budding is the method ordinarily used. On the selected rootstocks, the buds are inserted into a T-shaped incision and then tied with suitable wrapping material. It takes 3-4 weeks for the buds to unite. The side branches of the stocks are removed which compete with the scion for supply of nutrients and water.

2. Grafting

Inarching or grafting is another method of propagating roses but the cost of a grafted plant in the long run may be higher than that of budded plant. The rootstocks are raised in small pots or polythene bags. The scions are selected scion shoots. The scion shoot should be of medium texture, free from pests and diseases and 1-3 eyes in length. Larger scions are not recommended. A strip of bark, about 3 cm long with a part of wood, is removed from the stock as well as from the scion, and the latter is attached properly on to the stock and wrapped. After union the scion shoot is cut below the graft and the rootstock above the graft union.

3. LAYERING

a. Ground layering

It is performed by bending shoots to the ground and covering it with soil, leaving the terminal and exposed. A wooden peg or stone and a bamboo stick can be used to hold the bent shoot and exposed shoot in their position. Rooting at nodes usually takes place in a month or so and the layered shoot is detached 15-20 days after root formation.

b. Air layering

It consists of removing a ring of bark, about 2.5 cm long, from around the shoot to be rooted and covering it with a rooting medium. The use of damp sphagnum moss around the ringed portion and covering with polythene film have been found beneficial. Application of some root promoting substances may further improve the root formation in air layers.

4. Cutting

Propagation of roses by cuttings is normally done to raise stocks for grafting or budding. Climber, Rambler, polyantha and Miniature roses respond quite well to this method. Although cuttings are almost always prepared from shoots, root cuttings have also been found to form shoots and ultimately a new plant.

a. Root-cutting

Some rose species like *Rosa blanda, R. nitida* and R. *Virginiana* can be propagated by root-cuttings. The cuttings should be taken from young and healthy plants and it is important to maintain polarity when planting. The proximal end (nearest to the crown of the plant) of root piece should always be up. The cuttings should be inserted vertically with the uppermost level of the rooting media.

b. Stem-cutting

Raising plants by stem-cuttings is one of the least expensive and easiest method of rose multiplication. Usually, stem cuttings give satisfactory results when rooted during the period from late June to November. Cuttings should normally be taken during the monsoon or spring. Each shoot should be cut clean just below the node and lower leaves removed.

Sand is the best rooting medium but vermiculite or perlite also gives satisfactory results. Addition of peat moss to the sane in proper proportions is useful as it increases the water-holding capacity of the medium. In case of Miniature roses, a mixture of perlite and peat moss in the ratio of 1:1 is good for rooting of cuttings. The cuttings are usually planted 3 cm apart in a row and 8 cm between rows and watered as per the need. Within a moth or so, roots and shoots will develop from the cutting and in about a fortnight; the plants may be transplanted in another well prepared bed or in pots.

Regeneration of rose plants from cuttings is influenced by various factors such as type of cuttings, treatment of cuttings, the age and physiological conditions of the stock plant, type of wood selected for cuttings and environmental conditions during rooting. Hardwood cuttings are widely used in the propagation of rose rootstocks. Cultivars of Miniature roses are easily propagated by cuttings of soft-wood or semi-hardwood under mist. Hardwood cuttings taken from basal and mid portion of the shoot shows much better rooting than those taken from apical cuttings.

5. Seed propagation

This method of propagation if generally adopted by breeders for developing new cultivars with desirable characters. When the fruits are fully ripe, they are harvested and thoroughly dried before the extraction of seeds. Most rose seeds when mature are in a resting condition requiring an after-ripening period before germination. Stratification of seeds at 1.6 - 4.4°C is required after harvest. Stratification of 6 weeks is sufficient for *Rosa multiflora, R. rugos* and *R. hugonis* require 4 - 6 months, and R. blanda requires 10 months. Warm stratification followed by cold stratification has also been found beneficial in *Rosa canina* seeds which requires warm treatment at 26.6°C for 2 months followed by 3 months at 4.4°C for better germination. Hybrid rose seeds usually respond best to a stratification temperature of 1-4.4°C for 69-90 days.

Clean seeds are sown about 5 cm apart in pans or in small plots to raise the seedlings. Soil used for this purpose should be prepared by adding a good quality of well rotten farm yard manure. Though the time of sowing mainly depends upon temperature, sowing in the months of October-November is idea in most of the places. Seeds may take several weeks to germinate. Germination is probably prevented in rose seeds by inhibitators occuring in the seed coat, as well as by the mechanical restriction imposed by the massive pericarp. The stage of hi-ripeness is an important factor effecting germination. Temperature is another very important factors influencing the germination. Treatment of seeds with sulphuric acid and for 1-2 hours before sowing was fond to improves the germination.

Rose seedlings tend to flower even when they are very small and this exhaust themselves. Therefore, the flower buds should be pinched off as soon as they appear, until the plants are reasonably large and sturdy. It is important to keep the seedlings growing continuously without any check in development. A continuous moisture and nutrient supply, control of weeds and of diseases and pests contribute to successful seedling growth.

ROOT STOCKS

For grafting or budding, proper selection of rootstock is of immense importance. Rootstocks are known to impart marked effects on the vigorous, precosity, productivity, quality of flowers, longevity of bushes, disease resistance, adaptability to soil climatic conditions etc, and therefore, it is necessary to choose the most suitable rootstocks for budding or grafting roses. The rootstock should have the following qualities.

i. It should produce fibrous root system.
ii. It can easily be propagated from cuttings.
iii. It should have vigorous growth habit, be healthy and resistant to diseases and frost.
iv. Plants should have uniform growth.
v. It should have a bark, thick enough to hold the bud firmly and provide sap to the budded plant.
vi. It should be reasonably free from suckers.
vii. It should support the budded plant for a long time.
viii. It should withstand a wide range of soils and climatic conditions.

Some of the commonly used rootstocks are given here :

a. ***Rosa barboniana*** **(Edward rose)**

It is one of the most popular stock and used extensively in the northern plains of India. Plants are hardy, vigorous, propagated easily by cuttings, provide straight stems of suitable length and is found useful for budding standards.

b. ***Rosa canina*** **(Dog rose)**

It is usually propagate by seed since the cuttings do not root easily. However, the seeds are difficult to germinate. The prominent thorns make it difficult to handle. It also tends to produce sucker.

c. ***Rosa indica***

This is a large climbing shrub and is used extensively as rootstock for greenhouse forcing roses. It is easily propagated from cuttings and under suitable conditions produces a large symmetrical root system. It is well adapted to both excessively dry or wet soil conditions and can withstand high soil pH. Since it is not cold hardy, it should be used only in areas with mild winters. Plants raised on this rootstock are vigorous and produce flower with longer stems. The rootstock is also quite tolerant to powdery mildew and insect pests. In India, it has been recommended for northern plains.

d. ***Rosa laxa***

This is well adapted to rich heavy soils and plants budded on it have vigorous growth. It can be propagated both by seed and cutting and have a very good root system.

e. ***Rosa manetti***

This ia a very old stock used for propagating dwarf roses and for planting in sandy soils. It is easily propagated from cuttings, produces plants of moderate vigour, and is resistant to some s trains of verticillium wilt. This rootstock has, however, proved unsuitable for the production of cut flowers in greenhouse.

f. ***Rosa multiflora***

This is a widely used rootstock for outdoor roses. Several strains are available, some giving better bud unions and bud development than others. Cuttings of this species root easily, develop a vigorous, nematode resistant root system, and do not sucker excessively. It is adaptable to a wide range of soil and climatic conditions. In India, it does well in Bihar, Bengal and in the hills when used as rootstocks.

PREPARATION OF BEDS

Preparation of soil is the key to success with roses. It should be rich, porous and well drained. The initial preparation of rose beds should preferably be started during summer season, so that soil gets exposed to sun and air and during the monsoon it gets a chance to settle down before planting. The area selected for rose growing should be cleaned of weeds. According to the plan, the borders of the proposed beds should be properly marked.

If the soil is light, sandy and stony, the top 30. The dug up soil is heaped on the ground com of the soil in the bed should be dug up to make trench. The dug up soil is heaped on the ground. The next 30 cm of soil in trench should be dug as deep as possible, and properly pulverized and levelled in the trench itself. After that about half portion of the dug out soil, heaped on the ground surface, should be returned to the trench. This layer needs manuring with organic manure @ 50-60 tonnes/ha or FYM or compost. The remaining portion of the dug out soil should be returned to the trench. Application of superphosphate @ 30 kg/ha, and Aldrin or BHC (5% dust) @ 100 kg/ha is done, and the beds are irrigated thoroughly.

On the other hand, if the soil is heavy it would be necessary to dig out the second 30 cm layer of the soil and heap on the ground surface. The next layer of the soil should de deeply dug, pulverized and levelled. The second layer of soil after it it pulverized and sun-dried, should be returned to the trench and manured with organic manure @ 50 tonnes/has. The remaining operations will be similar as in the case of sandy soil.

CULTIVATION

Planting, pruning, application of manures and fertilizers, irrigation, weed control are some of the cultivation practices that are described here.

A. Planting

Few important preliminaries for planting are given here:

1. Cut away all immature, dead or diseased shoots and snags. Also as far as possible, each shoot to the next outward growing bud should be cut.
2. Remove all suckers growing below the point of union.
3. Reduce the possibility of loss of moisture, leaves including dried and yellow one should be remôve.
4. If the roses are with shrivelled bark, immersing of the plant in water for 24 hours is necessary to plump them.
5. Inmerse each plant in a suspension of one gram blitox in one litre of water to lesson the risk of attack of fungi.

At the planting time beds should be thoroughly prepared. At the planting time the soil should neither be too wet nor too dry. At each marked spot, a hole measuring 20-30 cm in diameter na d30 cm deep should be dug, and the plant with earthball should be lowered into the hole. Then the soil around the plant should be pressed firm to avoid air pockets in the soil. The bed after planting should be thoroughly irrigated.

If the rose plants, are with bare roots, the roots along with stem up to the bud union should be dipped in water for about 6 hours before planting, to restore the loss of moisture during transit period.

Planting should be done with the bud union 2.5-5.0 cm above th soil level. Roses can be planted any time except in very hot summer and during heavy rains when the soil is very wet. The suitable time for planting roses in most plains of India is during September-October and in the hill it is during October-November or February-March. In general a spacing of 60-75 cm between plants and rows is suggested.

B. Pruning

Pruning refers to the removal of certain portion of a plant. It is an important operation for maintenance of flariferousness and flower quality along with vigour of rose plants. The practice of rose pruning consists of two operations.

i. Thinning out, i.e. removal of old, weak, dry, twigs and diseased stem and branches from the point of start, and
ii. Shortening of stems, which aims at cutting down of last years growth to a desirable height.

1. Pruning time

The best time of pruning is the period plant is at dormant or near dormant stage. Pruning time will depend entirely on the climatic conditions of the region. The most usual time for pruning is during October-November after the rains are well over and the cold season is approaching. In Banagalore and around the coastal towns of Madras and Bombay pruning is practised twice in the months of November and June for winter season and monsoon season blooms. Pruning in the hills by the end of March or April.

2. Where and how to prune

While pruning a plant a cut has been made at about half-a-centimeter above a vigorous bud and the cut should be slightly slanting, sharp and clean.

All wounds are dressed with cane scaler to protect against attack of fungus and caneboring insects. The cut surface may be painted with fungicide or chaubattia paint (prepared by mixing 4 parts of red lead, 4 parts of copper carbonate, 5 parts of linseed oil, and a small quantity of BHC). Spraying of insecticides like rogor or malathion immediately after pruning.

3. Types of pruning

Depending upon the extent and level of shortening, there are 3 types of pruning light, moderate and hard. In light pruning, the healthy shoots, left after thinning of diseased and unwanted portion, are cut. Moderate pruning is done by cutting back the ripe main and lateral shoots of the previous years growth at about half the length of the growth. Hard pruning consists of keeping only 3 or 4 shoots of the last year and heading back at about 3 or 4 eyes from the base.

As preliminary to the main pruning operation, all weak, diseased, dead and slender growing and overlapping branches are to be completely removed. In the remaining healthy growing shoots, the amount of pruning largely depends upon clutivar and class of rose, the health and vigour of the plant, space provided for each plant, fertility of soil and the desired flower quality etc. Generally, strong and sturdy plants are pruned lightly moderate growers moderately and weak plants relatively hard. If the soil is sandy, and the nutrient level in the soil is not high, pruning should be light. In case of heavy and fertile soils, pruning may be a little harder. Hard pruning is also advisable to obtain blooms with longer stems.

4. Pruning of one-year old plants

Rose plants should never be pruned until they are properly established and adapted to the new environment. In the first year of planting, the pruning is done of weak, dead and crowded branches to give a definite shape to the plants. The real pruning starts in the second year of the growth of plants. viz. Hybrid Tea and Floribunda groups.

Climbing and rambling do not require any pruning except the removal of weak, unhealthy, deed and interlaced twigs. the polyanthas are pruned lightly whereas the miniatures are not pruned.

5. Pruning of established rose plants

i. Hybrid teas

The established Hybrid Teas, should have all dead, weak damaged and crossing shoots removed from their point of origin, leaving only 4 or 5 healthy basal shoots. It has been observed that hard pruning, reduces the number of flowers per bush but increases the flower size and the length of stem.

ii. Floribundas

The main object of pruning roses of this class is the production of abundant flowers with mass effect in the bed. It is necessary to remove the mass of twiggy growth at the ends of main stems and extra growths should be trimmed. Thus or moderate pruning is the general recommendation for floribundas.

iii. Polyanthas

The primary objects of pruning roses of this group are to obtain large number of flowers and to give a good shape to the plant. Thinning of dead, weak and overcrowded shoots and tripping of the end of branches that have already flowered are all that is really necessary.

iv. Miniatures

Miniatures roses are generally not pruned except the removal of dead, diseased and overcrowding branches. Some of the older stems may also be pruned to make a well balanced compact bush which is the most desirable character of this class.

v. Climbers and ramblers

The hybrid tea climbers hardly need and pruning because it is desirable to promoted of the lateral and side branches to bear flowers. The best flowers are produced on the short branches that emerge form older canes. So they require only removal of tips. The climbing Floribunda, Polyanthers and some shrubs of the Hybrid Musk group only bloom in the new wood.

vi. Standard

Standards which are generally hybrid teas or floribundas do not need drastic pruning. Growth which comes in the way of its main stem, should be removed to give symmetry to the plant.

vii. Shrubs

In general, the majority will not need any pruning but they may be cut back to keep them in shape. The weak and dead shoots should also be removed.

viii. Species of roses

Rose species and their allies also need no pruning. Once established growing strongly, the dad and weak growth of the plants should be removed entirely from the base in the first year itself.

`1. Manures

Organic manures like FYM, oil cakes, bone meal etc. are very essential which supply plant nutrients and maintains a good soil structure. Green manuring with sunnhemp and *dhaincha* can also be practised. For the light soils, cattle manure and for the heavy soils horse or pig manure are best suited.

a. Rate of application

Sandy soils need heavier and more frequent application of organic manure than heavier soils. Application of well decomposed cowdung of FYM @ 8-10 kg/plant (4.5 tonnes/ha) has been found useful for the growth and flowering of roses.

b. Time and method of application

The bulky organic manures in order of preference may by FYM, compost, cow dung slurry form bioags plants, cattle dung and activated sludge. Oil cakes and droppings of poultry, sheep or goat (@ 1 litre/plant) may be used for supplemental manuring. The quality of these manures is smaller than in the basic manuring. Basic manuring in case of new planting should be done at the time of preparation of rose beds.

Supplementary manuring should be done after the first flush of blowing is over and there is pause for the next flush. The manure should be spread in a band around each rose plant, at least 20-30 cm away from the stem or between the rows of plants.

c. Liquid manures

Manures are decomposed in water so that plant nutrients from complex organic forms are converted to simple soluble forms. the liquid when applied to the soil reaches the plant roots directly and provides them with nutrient elements in readily utalizable forms. Excreta of animals and oil cakes after rotting are also used as liquid manure. The diluted liquid becomes lighter than that of tea liquor. The liquid (about 1 litre) is put around each plant, about 20-25 cm away from the stem. The soil should be moist at the time of liquid manuring. The application may be repeated at an interval of 5-7 days till the flower buds start opening.

2. Inorganic fertilizers

For sustained production and maintenance of proper plant health it is essential to apply fertilizers to roses. Urea, single superphosphate and both potassium sulphat and muriate of potash are the widely used fertilizers. The most common practice is to apply these fertilizers mixed to the soil in certain proportions, known as fertilizer mixtures. Micronutrients are usually supplied through foliar sprays.

a. Fertilizer rates

For improving the growth and flowering of roses, some formulae of the mixtures are given here.

		(by weight)
i)	Groundnut cake	5 kg
	Bonemeal	6 kg
	Ammoniumphosphate	2 kg
	Ammoniumsulphate	1 kg
	Single superphosphate	2 kg
	Potassium sulphate	1 kg
ii)	Nitrate of potash	6 parts
	Ammonium sulphate	2
	Superphosphate	16 parts
	Sulphate of potash	8 parts
	Magnesium sulphate	2
	Iron phosphate	1/2
	This mixture is applied @ 50	100 g/plant.

b. Time and method of application

Fertilizers are applied in three split doses and application should be made when there is sufficient moisture in the the soil. Normally, the first application of the mixture is given about 15 days after pruning when the new growth has started. After the first flush is over the second does of fertilizer mixture is applied.

The method of application varies according to plant density and size of the plants. If the plant density is low, the requisite quantity of fertilizers mixture can be applied in a continuous band around the plant, 20-25 cm away from the stem. If the plant population is fairly large, the fertilizer dose should be fixed according to smaller units and place in continuous band in between the rows of plants, also between the plants and edges of the borders. The applied fertilizers incorporated into the soil but should not be deep.

c. Liquid fertilizers

A solution prepared by dissolving 0.680 gm KNO_3, 340 gm ammonium sulphate and 170 gm potassium phosphate in 432 litres of water and applied at the rate of half gallon per plant three times a week for a month and thereafter once a week before slow, produced outstanding blooms suitable for exhibition. Another solution prepared by dissolving ammonium sulphate, 56.6 gm superphosphate and 28.3 gm sulphate in 36 litres of water and applied at 9 litres per plant is also found very useful to improve the quality of flowers.

The advantage of the this method is that the nutrients in solution reach the plant roots immediately for utilization. the disadvantages are the extra cost of application, the risk of toxicity and fixation of phosphates to soil, rendering it unavailable to plants. As a regular feeding of rose plants this practice seems unnecessary.

d. Foliar feeding

This is an excellent supplement to root feeding because the leaves can directly absorb the nutrients. It minimizes the amounts of fertilizer mixture used. The concentration of solution should not be very high (not more than 0.3%) it damages the leaves.

For supply of macronutrients, the composition of the spray solution should be 7 gm oz potassium sulphate, 14 gm ammonium sulphate, 28.3 gm potassium nitrate in 36 litres of water and is applied @ 1.36 g/litre. Good results can also be obtained by using ammonium phosphate and potassium nitrate in equal proportions by weight, and applying the mixture @ 2.5 g/litre of water.

In case of micronutrient deficiency foliar application of a solution prepared from the mixture containing 15 g manganese sulphate, 20 g magnesium sulphate, 10 g chelated iron and 5g borax @ 2g/litre has been found very effective for obtaining brighter colour in flowers and foliage.

e. Combination of organic and inorganic manures

A pot mixture of 14 kg castor-cake, 9,5 kg finely powdered charcoal, 226 gm superphosphate, 113.2 gm carbonate of potash, 113.2 gm nitrate of soda, 283 gm leaf mould and 45.5 kg loamy soil is helpful for obtaining increased yield of flowers.

D. Irrigation

Adequate soil moisture at all stages of vegetative growth and flowering is essential for the rose plants to meet the water loss through transplantation and evaporation from soil. Water requirement also depends upon the size of the plant and the growth period.

In lighter soil more frequent irrigation is required than that in heavy soil. Rose beds can be watered once a week or 10 days in winter and twice a week during summer season.

E. Mulching

Mulching conserve soil moisture, supply humus making material and suppress weeds resulting in improved growth and flowering. Mulches also keep the soil some what cooler in summer.

Among the substances used for mulching, well rotten garden compost, FYM, Peat, straw sawdust, ground or whole corn cobs and other similar materials make satisfactory mulches. Mulches can be applied soon after the newly benched plants are established and growing satisfactorily.

F. Hoeing

Light hoeing is a very effective way to keep the soil porous so that light, air and water may reach the roots better to improve moisture retention capacity and to keep rose beds free from weeds. Roses are shallow rooted plants and roots of established plants tend to grow near the surface. Therefore, shallow hoeing is preferred.

G. Weed Control

Weeds pose a very serious problem in rose cultivation as they not only consume water and nutrients from the soil but also act as hosts for a number of diseases and pests. Manual weed control is effective it done frequently. Chemical weed control is comparatively economical, convenient and efficient in eradicating weeds. Application of CMU and DCMU four to five weeks after planting in late December and early January controls all weeds, in a rose nursery.

DISEASES AND PESTS

Major diseases and pest on rose are given here.

A. Diseases

Like any other crop, roses are also prone to many diseases, some of which have been found to be very destructive. The most important diseases and the measures for their control are described here.

1. Die-back

The causal organism is a fungus namely *Diplodia rosarum*. The disease causes death of the plant from top to downwards. When plants are prunued, sometimes, blackening of twigs starts below the pruned surface which extends further down, killing the whole plant. The older plants are more prone to the attack of the disease.

Control

a. Cut the affected parts and burn it.
b. The secateur should be disinfected with spirit and the cut ends

immediately coated with a paste containing 4 parts of copper carbon ate, 4 parts of red lead, and 5 parts of linseed oil. c. Add 0.1% BHC to paste to check the digger wasp attack.

d. Grow resistant varieties like white christmas, royal ascot, blue moon and crimson glory.

2. Black spot

The disease is caused by *Diplocarpon rosae* characterized by dark brown, circular spots with fringe borders, present on both sides of leaflets. At a later stage, the leaves becomes yellow and fall. If left uncontrolled, the whole stem is defoliated and the plant becomes weak. Leaf buds and the flower buds are also affected.

Control

Since the black spot fungus is located under the protecting cuticle, no fungicide can kill it without destroying the leaf. Hence, cure of this disease is difficult and prevention seems to be the only hope. The infected leaves, as soon as they are observed should be clipped off, taken out of field and burnt. Preventive sprays of fungicides like Zineb reduce the damage to a large extent. Martin Frobrisher, Belaya, John Cabot, and Carefree Beauty are also found to be resistant to black spot disease.

3. Rose wilt

It is a viral disease caused by *Marmor flaccumfascines*. The first symptom appears in the form of recurving of leaflets at the tip of young shoots which are brittle. Defoliation may happen, with leaves turning yellow and falling off. The stem also gets infected and the whole plant dies. In epidemic form one infected plant could ruin the whole within a couple of years.

Control

Control of aphids, which transmit the disease, helps to control the infection. The affected plants should be removed and burnt.

4. Rose mosaic virus

Chlorotic areas along the midribs of the leaflets and localized distortion are the principal symptoms. Sometimes one finds ring and watermark pattern. Another strain of this virus causes brighter and light yellow patterns.

Control

Diseased plants should be destroyed and never used for propagation.

B. Pests

Rose attract a large number of pests which cause considerable damage. At almost every stage, be in the nursery or in beds, rose plants are prone to attack by various pests. Some of the commonly reported insects and other pests attacking roses are mentioned in detail here.

1. White ants

White ants also known as termites cause damage to rose plants even before they are established. Small colonies are formed inside the soil and the insects multiply very rapidly during the rainy season. The insects destroy the underground parts including the roots of the young as well as old plants. Sometimes. rose plants wither.

Control

Apply 5% BHC or Aldrin in the pits before planting roses. Drenching of rose beds with Aldrin also controls the damage in established gardens.

2. Red scales

They infest roses in the green house and in the garden and the affected branches become dry. The insects can easily be detected by the reddish brown encrustations on the lower portion of old stem and at times the younger shoots also which sucks the plant sap.

Control

The menace can be removed by rubbing the scurfy encrustations with a used tooth brush, or a cotton swab dipped in methylated spirit. Spraying the affected plants with insecticides like malathion or rogor will control the insect. Application of granular insecticides like carbofuron at 1.5 kg a.i/ha and Disulfoton and Phorate at 3.0 kg a.i./ha also gives good control of rose scales.

3. Jassids (Leaf hopper)

These are very small, light grey or pale green insects which such the cell sap from the leaves. It causes yellowing or whitening of the attacked surface, giving the plants a sickly appearance.

Control

Jassids can easily be controlled by spraying with 0.03% parathion, 0.1% Metacid or 8% Thimet as soil application. The use of 0.05% Monocrotophos is also effective in controlling jasids.

4. Red spider mite

As result of their feeding, white specks appear on the leaves and these specks coalesce and appear as white patches. Ultimately; affected leaves become mottled, turn yellow and fall. Some polyantha and floribunda roses completley lose their leaves prematurely due to the attack of this pest. The damage is more pronounced during warm and dry season.

Control

Frequent spray with sulphur helps to control this mite. Several mite-killers such as kelthane morestan, dimite, Tedion have been reported to be very effective in controlling rose mites, ml kelthane is throughly mixed with 10 m of water with 10-15 drops of any sticker and application of this chemical every 5 or 6 days may be sufficient to control the mites. Spraying the affected plants with 0.05% parathion or 0.1% Metasystox is also suggested.

HARVESTING AND POST-HARVEST HANDLING

Time and stage of harvesting, stòring and transportation of the flowers are the important aspects to be considered.

A. Harvesting

The stage at which flower should be cut, either for decoration or for despatch, is the tight-bud stage when the buds show full colour but the petals have not yet started unfolding. If harvested at this stage, they last longer and retain colour and freshness during transportation. If a flower bud of red cultivar cut at a little earlier stage it s fails to open later. Pink and red cultivars should be allowed to develop to a stage where one or two of the outer petals begin to unfurl. Loose flowers, used for making garlands, preparing perfumes etc. are harvested only when they are fully open and collected in large open baskets.

The flowers should be cut in the early morning before sunrise or late in the afternoon when the sun is about to set as to avoid damage of buds due to high temperature during the day. Late harvest results in short vase life of cut flowers and low oil content in loose flowers used for preparing perfumes. For cut flowers, stem with two, five leaflet leaves should be cut and immediately dipped into clean water up to the base of the flower buds. The delay in keeping the flowers in a bucket of water will cause air entry and result in vascular blockage. The stems should be re-cut in water about 2 cm above the previous cut end. If they are not required for immediate used, the cut-flowers along with stems dipped in water in the bucket should be stored at a cool air temperature of 4.4 - 7.2 C for about 6-12 hours to harden the buds and thus enhances their keeping quality. During winter (December-January) a shorter treatment for 6-8 hours is sufficient while a longer duration of 8-12 hours is required in March-April.

B. Packaging

The cut blooms are graded according to the length of stem and then packed in corrugated card-board boxes. The size of the box varies with the quality of roses to be packed. The inside area of the box will be cushioned with polythene or soft materials. The blooms are generally packed in bundles. The upper half of each bundle having flower buds is wrapped in a corrugated paper which is fixed with an adhesive tape. Labelled flower bundles are places opposite to another in such a way that their flower buds lace the sides of the box and their stem ends towards the centre of the box. The inside of the box is finally covered with a sheet of tissue paper before putting on the cover of the box. Along the outer edges of the box, adhesive tapes can be fixed to close it.

C. Yield

The yield of cut-flower depends on a number of factors such as type of cultivar, and cultural practices adopted from time to time. Gold strike and pink garnette, are high yielding cultivars which produces 24-28 flowers per plant. Sonora and Coral princess given low yields (15 flowers per plant per years) of 60% grade. Plant density has much influence on the yield of quality blooms per unit are. About 1,20,000 cut flowers of exportable quality from an area of one hectare is obtained by close planting and providing plastic cover over the plants during November-February. In an essential oil-bearing rose, a yield of 6977 kg petals per hectare was recorded when planting was done at 2.5 X 0.5 cm apart. One of the best methods for maximization in yield and quality of flower is through balanced application of fertilizers.

IMPORTANCE AND USES

The rose, because of its utility, occupies a pre-eminent, place amongst the flower crops and is one of the oldest of fragrant flowers to be cultivated by man. Its different types having beautiful flowers of exquisite shape, different sizes, bewitching colours and most delightful fragrance has made it an important flower or its varied used. The various ways in which rose can be used are mentioned in detail here.

A. Exhibition and decorative purposes

Varieties of roses which are most suitable to a particular type of decoration are given here.

1. Shrub or bush

Shrub or bush roses are planted in small groups at a height of 5-10 cm from the ground level to create excellent mass effect in a rose or flower garden. They may also be mixed with other plants in a shrubbery, e.g. christian, midle double delight, first prize, gladiator, kiss of fire, midle meilland, montezuma, paradise, peace and super star.

2. Standard Rose

Standard rose or tree rose, is a very important feature in the rose garden. They are allowed to form buds only at the top leaving the entire stem clear of any vegetative growth. According to their height of budding they may be full standard (1.0-1.5 metres high), half standards (45-60 cm high) or weeping standard (1.65 m or higher above the ground). Hybrid Teas and few grandiflora are suitable for making the full standard roses. Floribunda and Polyantha roses are excellent for growing as half standards. For weeping standards, climbing and rambling roses are used as the long branches of the crown may be allowed to hang down.

3. Climbers

The climbing and rambling roses can be used to cover the walls of houses or fencing or pergdas, arbours and arches. Ramblers produce flowers only once in a year and flowers are in clusters lasting for several weeks. The beautiful climbers and Ramblers like America pillar, Blaze, Delhi Pink Pearl, Don Juan, Golden showers, Lamargue, Mardan white, Mardan Pink, Marechal Neil and Royal gold add to the beauty of the garden.

4. Hedges and edges

A rose can also be used for making hedge or edge. Rose hedges except when pruned, remain full of life and colour and give protection due to the presence of thorns. Vigorous Floribundas are suitable for hedge and of necessary the plants can be planted in two rows. Some suitable cultivars are Border coral Circus, Frensham and Runiba, Climbing or rambling roses may also be used for making tall hedges. rose cultivars like coralin, Lady Reading, Magic, White Button etc. may be used for making edges.

5. Rockery

Roses may also be grown in rockeries and for this purpose hardy miniature and ponepon cultivars such as Fairy Queen and Magic may be selected.

6. Pot plants

Roses can be easily grown as pot plants in suitable containers kept both indoors as well as outdoors. For balconies and terraces which receive limited sunlight minitares and dwarf polyanthas should be selected. The cultivars like Baby Darling, Cindrella, Starina etc, are quite suitable for this purpose. Bush roses may also be grown in pots for beautifying the compounds around the building and for display in rose shows.

7. Hangers

Miniaturs can also be grown in hanging baskets and cultivars suitable for making rose hangers are climbing Miniature-Red cascade and Yellow Doll.

B. Cut-flowers

Apart from making garlands, bouquets, button-holes their use for wership in temples, rose makes one of the best cu-flowers and as such is in great demand in the internal as well as foreign markets. Germany is the biggest consumer and importer of cut-flowers. Rose cut-flowers are being exported from Maharashtra (India) to the Middle EAst countries.

Rose cut-flowers arranged in flower vases looks extremely beautiful and they have a rightful place in the scheme of interior decoration. In general, cultivars with more petallage and opening slowly with long lasting quality are chose as cut-flowers. Some of the cultivars suitable for this purpose are christian Dior, Happiness, Montezuma, Queen Elizabeth, Sea pearl and Super star. Presently cvs. Belinda, golden times, Illona, Laminuette, Montreal, Mercedes, Red success, Somia Meilland are in great demand as cut-flower in foreign markets. Two Indian or Arjuna and Raktagandha producing flowers with long stems are also suitable for cut-flowers.

C. Perfume and allied products

Oils, perfumes and other products made from rose petals are of superior quality.

1. Rose oil (Rose perfume)

Rose oil is an important commercial product obtained from rose petals. Apart from sweet fragrance it has medicinal value and is often used in Ayurveda Bulgarian rose is largely used in perfuming soaps and cosmetics. Limited quantities of the oil are used in flavouring soft drinks and alcoholic liquors. Rose oil has antibacterial property. The commonly grown rose species for rose oil are Rosa damascena, R. borbonians, R. centifolia, R. alba and R. Gallica. In India, R. damascena and R. borborniane are cultivated fro rose oil.

Though France, Cyprus, Greece, India, Italy, Morocco and the USA are import countries producing rose oil, Bulgaria is a major producer an exporter of rose and the rose perfumery. The oil is extracted by steam distillation and its quality depends much and cultivars and stage of picking. Generally 1 kg oil is obtained from 3,000-4,000 kg petals. Among the different species, R. Damascena gives the maximum oil yield, R. borboniana and R. tepltiz are also good. The principal constitutents of normal rose oil are I-citronellol (40-65%), Geraniol, nerol 1-linalool, phenyl ethyl alcohol, small quantities of esters, nonyl aldehyde, citral, engenol sesquiter penes and the vaxy constituent stearoptene.

To obtain good quality rose oil, the flowers are to be harvested early in the morning, as the percentage of valatile oil decreases with the advancing day.

2. Rose water

Rose water is also an important commercial product obtained form rose petals. It is used as a perfume and in medicines and confectionary. It has the property of cooling the body and is often used in eye lotion and eye drops for its soothing qualities. It is also used in drinking water and social occasions. The roses used for preparing oil are also used for making rose water.

3. Gulkand

Rose petals are also preserved for direct consumption by making gulkand which is prepared by pounding equal proportions of petals and white sugar. It is considered both a tonic and taxative. Rose damascens, R. chinem's,

R. Gallica, R. ponifera and some other scented roses e.g. Edouard are used for preparing gulkand.

4. Pankhuri

Dried rose petals are known as 'pankhuri' which is occasionally used for preparing sweetened cold drinks.

5. Gul-roghan

It is a rose hair oil prepared from rose petals by enflurage with wet sesamum seeds.

D. Source of vitamins

Rose hips are a very good source so ascorbic acid, i.e. vitamin C. Every 100 g of rose hips syrup contains 150 mg of ascorbic acid as compared with only 50 mg present in fresh orange juice, 20 mg in tomatoes and 5 mg in apples. The ascorbic acid content, however, varies with species and some of th promising vitamin C bearing species are *R. rugosa, R. ambhyotta, R. aciculari R. davaricas, R. pendulian, R. glauca* and *R. canina.* Apart from Vitamin C, the hips of *R. roxburghil, R. acicularis, R. rugosa, R. davurica* and some of the spices are found to contain vitamins, Ai, B2, K and E.

E. Other Uses

In Europe, roses are used for making pot-pouri, conserves, rose vinegar and rose petal wine, Jams, jellies and syrups have been made for centuries in Bulgaria and exported. Rose aids in digestion and has certain curative properties. In Czechoslovakia, fruits of wild roses are used for preparing a hot drink like tea and a popular wind. in America, bushes of *R. multiflora* are utilized as shock absorber or crash barrier.

LAND DEVELOPMENT FOR FLOURICULTURE PROJECT

Cultivation of flowers for exports is gaining momentum in our country. This is basically due to the benefits of high density planting controlled conditions planting controlled conditions made available by the Greenhouse, proper monitoring of irrigation, fertigation and pest control etc.

This gives a quality yield with quantitative results.

As in any other industry, here the degree for success is substantially depentent on the quality of the technical input going into it. This has to be tailored to suit the needs of the Plants and the Climatic condotions of the place the project is located in. Many times it is heared that quite a few projects are suffereing due to ill designed and unsuitable nature of these elements. As in any other industry the infrastructure in such projects is subjected to a lot of wear and tear by the vagaries of the weathers as well as the day to day use of the equipment.As none of the projects woulds like to spend their time or money on repairing or restructuring the infrastructure, it would make sense to absorb the more information and selecting the right equipment before on such an activity. As one sets about setting such a project, he has to select land, select the infrastructure, appoint consultants, collaborators etc. As one goes about this job, he meets a myarid of suoppliers and a vast product range to select from. From the day one begins land selection, he meets hordes of experts and agents, each emphasizing as to why his proposal is the best buy and reasoning why. One also is going to run into a flock of suppliers of varoius infrastructural elements needed for such a project. However at the end of the implementation, mopst of the projects have a lot to complain about. Looking at say,selection of the Greenhouses for example, these are availble from Rs. 300/- to Rs. 700/- per sq. mt. More baffling is the fact the some of the expensive ones weren the ones to be heavily damaged when hit by heavy winds last season.

Serializing chronologically, the begining of the project activities is land selection and next one is land development.

LAND SELECTION:

Regular aspects which are looked into, when the land hunt begins include a motorable access, availability of a dependable water source of adequate capacity at a reasonable distance, availability of electric power on site, soil conditions which suit the Agricultural expert's needs etc.Getting a piece of land with all these attributes at a reasonable price and a clear title is easier said rhan done. Here are the other essentials one has to look at in the matter of Land selection.

A. Geometrical shape of the land:

If one could not get rectangular plot with a correct orientation,there is no bother a all. However since most of the shapes of land resemble starfishes than squares, this is a very relevant aspects in land selection. For the project, the quantum of area that can be brought under Greenhouse Cultivation is tantamount. Hence a smaller plot may yield more area under Greenhouses than a larger plot which is not in a correct shape
and orientation.

B. LEVELS OR CONTOURS OF THE LAND :

The land in question has to be level in where the Greenhouses are proposed. The undulasting shape of land can be brought to be desired shape cutting and filling, in other words dressing land by use of Earth moving equipment. Since the cost of land development is a variable figure, it will burden the project to that extent.

C. Cost of approach:

Most of the lands for such activities have to procure access from the main road. A road needs to be constructed to have motorable access upto the land. This needs to be accounted in the land cost.

LAND DEVELOPMENT:

After procuring the land, and preparation of a suitable layout, one should begin with Land Development. The process of land development includes operation of cutting and filling till a dressed shape of the land is achieved which which in technical terms is called the formation level. One of the basic essentials in the land selection should be the soil content. The operation of the land development can be persued more conveniently when there is sufficient soil to enable devrelopment. Rock outcrops if any, have to be blasted or chiseled in this operation. Blasting activity to the extent necessary for the entire project should be finished off before construction of the Greenhouses. There have been reports about Greenhouses of the first phase of some projects getting damaged by the flying splinters, when blasting was done for the subsequent phases.

The developed or dressed land has shops in two directions:

(i) Slope along the guters.
(ii) Slope across the gutters.

While slope along the gutters is mandatory, the slope across can after the development cost. The illustration-1 shows a line sketch of a general arrangement of Playhouses both of imported and local makes on a developed land.

ILLUSTRATION - 1

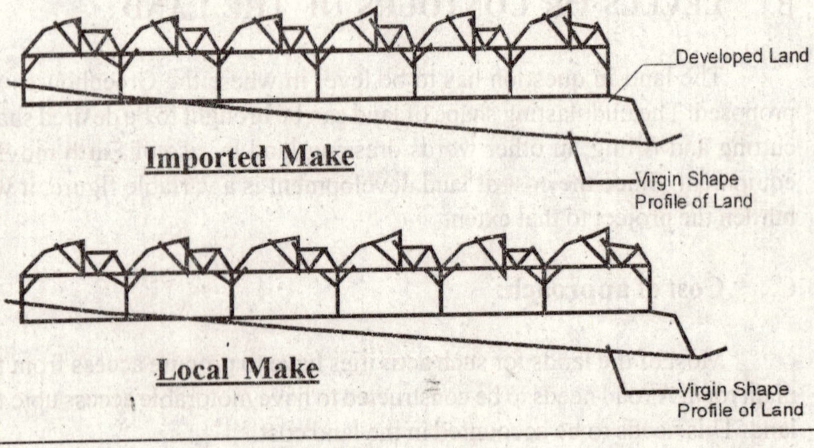

It has been seen that generally the imported makes of Greenhouses require more earthwork than their local counterparts. While every thing is right and fine for a flat or level land, tackling a sloping land with economy of development cost is a technical challange. It is essential for the Greenhouse makers to come up with arangements which will not increase the project cost on this account.

Excessive land development can cause land slides as is shown in illustration -2. To prevent this, one may have to go for the construction of a retaining wall. A term like cost of developped land needs to be developped which will include the basic price of land, the cost of approach road, the cost of land development and the cost of construction of retaining walls if any. This divided by the area that can come under Greenhouse cultivation is really the rate what matters most of the promoter and the project. Promoters must seek technical assistance from this stage onwards to be able to get right proposal on hand.

ILLUSTRATION - 2

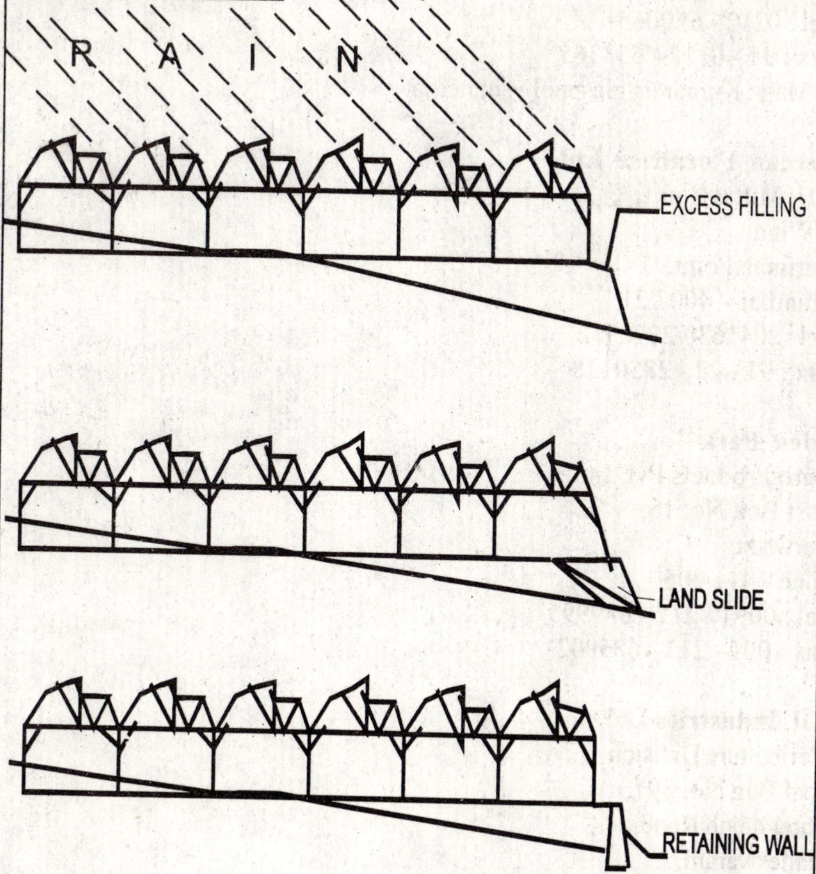

Presently Growers/Suppliers of Floriculture (Cut-Flowers)

A.H.M. Witmer,
Prem Villa
347, 14th Main,
Raj Mahal Vilas Extn.
Bangalore - 560 080
Tel/Fax : 080 - 3440164
E-Mail : moerheim @ giasbg01.vsnl.net.in.

Kumar Gentech & Tissue Culture Co.
783, Bhawani Peth,
Pune - 411 042
Tel : 0212 - 650065
Fax : 91 - 0212 - 653365
E-Mail : Kumar @ giaspnol.vsnl.net.in.

Deccan Florabase Ltd.
103, Mittal Court,
B Wing,
Nariman Point,
Mumbai - 400 021
Tel : 2041630/2870332
Fax : 91 - 22 - 2850138

Eden Park
Agro Products Pvt. Ltd.
Post Box No. 15,
Yerwada,
Pune - 411 006
Tel : 0091 - 212 - 689995
Fax : 009 - 212 - 685002

IDL Industries Ltd.
Floriculture Division
Post Bag No. 397,
Chowdaiah Road,
Malleswaram,
Bangalore - 56003
Tel/Fax : 91(08)8461537 (India)
Pager No. : 9628 - 801905.

Sachin Floritech Limited
305,Vijay Apartments,
Dharam Karan Road,
Ameerpet,
Hyderabad - 500 016 (A.P.,India)
Tel : 91 - 40 - 291190
Fax : 91 - 40 - 293557

IMPORTERS OF PLANTING MATERIAL, BULBS ETC

Westend Marketing Co.
219, Ist Floor, 4th Cross,
Lalbagh Road,
Bangalore - 569 927
Tel : 080 - 2225746, 2239708
Fax: 91 - 80 - 2225746

SUPPLIERS OF IMPORTANT MACHINES & OTHER ACCESSORIES

Creative Plastics
Gala Compound,
Haji Bapu Road,
Malad (East),
Mumbai - 400 097
Tel : 022 - 840 9368
Fax : 8431209
(Poly Film & Grippers with Accessories)

B & V Agro Irrigation Co.
410, AGH Chambers,
379/81, Narshi Natha Street,
Masjid Bunder,
Mumbai - 400 009.
Tel : 343 65 75/ 344 95 68
Fax : 3451058
(Agro Shade Net)

Doulatram Agro-Tech Pvt. Ltd.
L.R.E.W., ' Empire House',
3rd Floor,
214, A K Nayak Marg,
Fort,
Mumbai - 400 001
Tel: 022-2063228
Fax: 122-2069709
(Knitted Shade Cloth For Plant Protection)

Kumar Gentech & Tissue Culture Co.
783, Bhawani Peth,
Pune - 411 042
Tel : 0212 - 650065
Fax : 91 - 0212 - 653365
E-Mail : Kumar @ giaspnol.vsnl.net.in.
(Florist Gerbera Hilverda Carnation Flamingo Flower Bulbs Greenhouses)

Sundeep Enterprises
67/8/D-3, MICD,
Chinchwad, Pune - 411 019
Tel : 770542, 760768
Fax : 0212 - 770534
(Best Quality Export Boxes in Micro & Narrow Broad Flute Corrugated Boxes for Fresh Flowers)

Jet Air Freight
Trupti Apartments, Unit No. 4
Koldongari Lane - 2, Andheri East,
Mumbai - 69
Tel : 8365458, 8346984
Fax : 8351015
(International Freight Forwarders Specialising In Export of Fresh Flowers)

Thakur Floriculture
Village Ladpur
Post - Khatoli,
Distt.Muzaffar Nagar (U.P.),
Tel : 01316 - 73974
(Suppliers of Gladiolus, Tube Rose Seeds)

Garden Aids
1099/13, Hari Singh Nalwa Street,
Karol Bagh,
New Delhi - 110 005
Tel : 011 - 5724554, 6521529.
(Flower Seeds, Flowering Bulbs, Garden Accessories , A Complete Rangew Of Rain Bird Sprinklers & Manures)

Anand Body Builders
B-14, Nizammudin East,
New Delhi - 110 013
Tel : 4692116/4601503
(Refrigerated Vans/ Trucks, Insulated Vans/Trucks, Cold Boxes, Cold Rooms & Specialised Containers)

Malmo Exim Ltd.
B-13, Acme Estate, Sewree (East),
Mumbai - 400 015
Tel : 4131111, 4151111, 4133132
Fax : 4152222, 4135719
(Agro Net)

CUT FLOWER IMPORTERS

BAARDSE b.v.
P.O. Box 1007
1430 BA Alasmeer, Netherland
Tel. : (31) 2977- 515 51
Fax. : (31) 2977- 280 63

FLORIMEX b.v.
Zwarteweg 149
1431 VL Alasmeer,Netherland
Tel. : (31) 2977 - 255 55
Fax. : (31) 2977 - 417 01

Floratex GmbH
Flughafen - Gebanude 458
D - 6000 Frankfurt/Main 75
Germany.

PLANT ECONOMICS OF FLORICULTURE [CUT-FLOWER ROSE WITH GREEN HOUSE TECHNY.]

Plant capacity = 22,40,000/annum

LAND & BUILDING

(Land 10 Acre)	Rs.	76,39,000.00

PLANT & MACHINERY

(Water Storage tank (PVC tank), Pipes and fitting with water system, Drip irrigation, Water pump 5 HP motor, Central Air conditioning System for Rose Flower Storage Shed ,Air Cooler, Air heating System with hot air blower, Air Dehumidifier, Small equipments for cutting of branches, pesticide sprayers, scissors and others (lot), Tractor with complete accessories, Refrigerated Van, Conveyor belt Automatic flower wrapping machine & carton filling sealing equipment with complete accessories

TOTAL	**Rs.**	**48,45,000.00**
OTHER FIXED ASSETS	**Rs.**	**17,00,000.00**

FIXED CAPITAL

1.	LAND & BUILDING	Rs.	76,39,000.00
2.	PLANT & MACHINERY	Rs.	48,45,000.00
3.	OTHER FIXED ASSETS	Rs.	17,00,000.00
	TOTAL	**Rs.**	**1,41,84,000.00**

WORKING CAPITAL REQUIREMENT/ANNUM

RAW MATERIALS

(Rose Plants from Nursery,
Manure, cowdung of animals,
Chemicals, Pesticides, fertilizers,
Packing baskets with polythene,
Miscellaneous

TOTAL	**Rs.**	**7,46,500.00**

TOTAL WORKING CAPITAL/ANNUM

1.	RAW MATERIAL	Rs.	7,46,500.00
2.	SALARY & WAGES	Rs.	14,97,000.00
3.	UTILITIES & OVERHEADS	Rs.	6,40,000.00
	TOTAL	**Rs.**	**28,83,500.00**

COST OF PROJECT	Rs.	1,43,64,218.75
TOTAL CAPITAL INVESTMENT	Rs.	1,49,04,875.00
COST OF PRODUCTION/ANNUM	Rs.	71,31,662.50

TURN OVER/ANNUM

By sale of Cut flower (Rose)

TOTAL	**Rs.**	**1,34,40,000.00**

PROFIT = RECEIPTS - COST OF PRODUCTION

PROFIT SALES RATIO = Profit / Sales x 100 = 46.94 %

RATE OF RETURN = Operating profit / T.C.I x 100 = 42.32 %

BREAK EVEN POINT (B.E.P) = 44.72

PLANT ECONOMICS OF CUT FLOWER - FLORICULTURE

Plant capacity = 5,00,000 CUT ROSE FLOWER/ANNUM

LAND & BUILDING		
(Total land required is one Acre.)	**Rs.**	**7,79,000.00**
PLANT & MACHINERY		
(Water pump Pipes & fitting, Air condition, Water tanks, Water tank, Temperature Insulation with thermocole sheet for maruti van, Air Cooler, Small equipments for cutting,)		
TOTAL	**Rs.**	**2,65,000.00**
OTHER FIXED ASSETS	**Rs.**	**1,35,000.00**
FIXED CAPITAL	**Rs.**	**11,79,000.00**
RAW MATERIALS		
(Nursery Plants of Rose, Manure (Cowdung and other animals), Chemicals,pesticides,fertilizers, Flower Pot for Green House, Packing basket with polyethene , Miscellaneous	**Rs.**	**30,000.00**
TOTAL	**Rs.**	**2,70,000.00**

TOTAL WORKING CAPITAL/ANNUM

1.	RAW MATERIAL	Rs.	2,70,000.00
2.	SALARY & WAGES	Rs.	4,63,500.00
3.	UTILITIES & OVERHEADS	Rs.	1,90,000.00
	TOTAL	**Rs.**	**9,23,500.00**

COST OF PROJECT	**Rs.**	**12,36,718.75**
TOTAL CAPITAL INVESTMENT	**Rs.**	**14,09,875.00**
TURN OVER/ANNUM (By sale of 5,00,000 Pc. Cut Flower)		
TOTAL	**Rs.**	**25,00,000.00**

PROFIT = RECEIPTS - COST OF PRODUCTION

PROFIT SALES RATIO = Profit / Sales x 100 = 45.58 %

RATE OF RETURN = Operating profit / T.C.I x 100 = 80.82 %

BREAK EVEN POINT (B.E.P) = 38.00 %

PLANT ECONOMICS OF ROSE PLANTATION & ROSE OIL EXTRACTION

Plant capacity = 400.00 ML/day

LAND & BUILDING

[Land 11 acres (10 acre for cultivation), 1 acre for processing]	Rs.	**10,72,500.00**

PLANT & MACHINERY

(Tin lined copper vessel,
Coal fired oven of clay brick,
Condenser S.S.lined,
Water circulation pump,
Cylindrical S.S. collecting vessel, Laboratory equipment,
Water storage tank, Tube well pumps Pipes, & fittings, pumps,
storage,stainer,

TOTAL	**Rs.**	**7,60,000.00**
OTHER FIXED ASSETS	**Rs.**	**5,95,000.00**

FIXED CAPITAL

1. LAND & BUILDING	Rs.	10,72,500.00
2. PLANT & MACHINERY	Rs.	7,60,000.00
3. OTHER FIXED ASSETS	Rs.	5,95,000.00
TOTAL	**Rs.**	**24,27,500.00**

WORKING CAPITAL REQUIREMENT/ANNUM

RAW MATERIALS

(Manures, pesticides,
chemicals, Rose flower from outer sources
Packaging bottles, caps, cartons

TOTAL	**Rs.**	**12,40,000.00**

TOTAL WORKING CAPITAL/ANNUM

1. RAW MATERIAL	Rs.	12,40,000.00
2. SALARY & WAGES	Rs.	1,00,000.00
3. UTILITIES & OVERHEADS	Rs.	1,92,500.00
TOTAL	**Rs.**	**15,32,500.00**

COST OF PROJECT	**Rs.**	**25,23,281.25**
TOTAL CAPITAL INVESTMENT	**Rs.**	**28,10,625.00**
COST OF PRODUCTION/ANNUM	**Rs.**	**20,95,737.50**

TURN OVER/ANNUM

1. By sale of 18 Kgs of rose oil
2. By sale of rose water 10000 litres

TOTAL	**Rs.**	**27,20,000.00**

PROFIT = RECEIPTS - COST OF PRODUCTION

PROFIT SALES RATIO = Profit / Sales x 100 = 22.95 %

RATE OF RETURN = Operating profit / T.C.I x 100 = 22.21 %

BREAK EVEN POINT (B.E.P) = 52.15 %

Chapter - 7

GINGER CULTIVATION

INTRODUCTION

Ginger (Zingiber officinale) is a herbaceous perennial plant in nature but is generally grown as an annual crop. It is mainly grown for its underground root like stem which are aromatic and used both as a spice and medicine. It is native of South-East Asia and is cultivated in Jamaica, Nigeria, Syria, Brazil, China, Japan and Indonesia. India produces 50% of the world production of ginger. It is cultivated in almost all the tropical and sub-tropical parts of India, especially in Kerala, Karnataka, Tamil Nadu, West Bengal, Bihar, Himachal Pradesh, Uttar Pradesh and Maharashtra. It is exported mainly to middle east countries.

SOIL

Ginger thrives well on a variety of soils. provided sufficiently well distributed rainfall or irrigation and adequate drainage facilities are available. A deep well drained friable loam, rich in humus, is ideal soil for its cultivation. It thrives well in sandy loam to loam soils with sufficient organic matter. it does not withstand waterlogging and should not be grown in low lying fields. It grows well on red laterite soils. but cannot be grown successfully on alluvial soils.

CLIMATE

The agro-climatic conditions for growing ginger are idea in the Eastern Ghat. It grows well in areas where rainfall is heavy, in tropical and sub-tropical zones. It requires warm and humid climate for its proper growth and development. In hills, it can be grown up to an elevation of 1500 metres from sea level. The optimum temperature range for its growth is from 24°C to 28°C. It rs on the rhizome size i.e. if the same variety is grown in plain, the rhizomes are reduced in their size to a greater extent and vice versa.

LAND PREPARATION

Ginger rhizomes require a fine tilth of soil for their normal development of shape and size. In hard soils rhizomes are often malformed. Therefore, it is essential that the land should be thoroughly ploughed by giving 4-6 ploughing in March-April to obtain deep fine tilth after harrowing and planking. During the last ploughing farmyard manure is mixed with the soil. The land is divided into raised beds, one meter wide and of convenient length varying from three to six metres and 15 cm high, with a spacing of 30 cm between beds for drainage channels. In hill regions the beds are to be formed along the contours.

VARIETIES

The choice of variety is an important aspect in cultivation of ginger. The variety having high dry rhizome with less fiber and high recovery of oil and oleoresin are preferred for local as well as in foreign markets.

1. PGS-19

This variety is recommended for cultivation at high altitudes like Pattangi (Semiliguda) in Orissa. It produces reddish bright rhizome and matures in 218 days, with 23.5% dry ginger recovery, 10% oleoresin, 2% essential oil and 3.8% crude fibre contents. It yield about 11.5 tonnes rhizome per hectare.

2. PGS-37

It is recommended for Orissa for Eastern Ghat high land zones. It is known by the name "Suprabha". It produces bright glazy rhizomes and matures in 229 days. It contains 20.5% dry recovery, 8.9% oleoresin, 1.9% essential oil and 4.4% crude fibre contents. It yields about 16.5 tonnes rhizomes per hectare.

3. Kundali Local

This variety is a local variety. It is recommended for Orissa. It matures in more than 229 days. It produces reddish bright rhizomes. Its dry recovery is 18.5%, oleoresin 8% essential oil 1.6% and crude fibre 3.9 per cent. It is highly susceptible to soft rot disease. It yields about 8.5 tonnes rhizomes.

4. Nadia

The variety is recommended for wide range of hilly areas of altitude about 1500 metres south as in Assam, Uttar Pradesh and Himachal Pradesh. It has yielded about 25 tonnes of green ginger per hectare in North-east region with 18% dry ginger recovery.

5. Tura

This variety is recommended for a wide range of hilly areas of North-east region. It yields about 22 tonnes of green ginger per hectare with 17% of dry ginger recovery.

6. Chekeralla

This variety is recommended for hilly regions of Uttar Pradesh. It yields about 23 tonnes of green ginger containing 17% dry matter and 19% fibre in dry ginger.

7. Khasi Local

This variety is recommended for Uttar Pradesh and other hilly regions with high humidity. It yields about 1.5 quintals green ginger with 18% dry ginger recovery.

8. Poona

This variety grows well up to an altitude of 1500 metres. It yields about 25 tonnes green ginger with 20% dry matter containing 19% fibre in dry ginger.

9. Thing Puri

This is a high yielding variety recommended for hilly regions of Uttar Pradesh. It yields about 24 tonnes of green ginger with 20% dry matter and containing 19% fibre in dry ginger.

10. Rio-de-Janeiro

This is an exotic variety which grows in a wide range of hilly climatic conditions. It has recorded high yields in North-eastern hill regions. Its average yield is 29 tonnes per hectare with 20% dry ginger recovery.

11. China

It is also an exotic variety grows well in a wide range of climatic conditions. It expressed a quite stable yield in varying climatic conditions. It yields about25 tonnes of green ginger per hectare.

12. Baharich

It grows well in tropical and sub-tropical climate. It is susceptible to soft rot disease. It yields about 20 tonnes of green ginger containing 19% dry matter and 155 fibre in dry ginger.

13. Thinglaidon

This variety grows well in hilly zones of Uttar Pradesh and yields about 25 tonnes of green ginger per hectare with 19.5% dry matter and 18% fibre in dry ginger.

14. Awoch

It is grown in hilly regions of Assam. It rhizomes are more than 10 cm in length and yields about 45 g/plant. It produces about 18 tonnes per hectare green ginger.

15. B-1

It is cultivated in Assam and the plants are 38 cm in height and produce about 41 g of green ginger per plant. It produces about 25 tonnes/ hectare.

16. Ausu

This variety is grown in Assam. The plant has 24 cm height and produces 86 g rhizome, yielding about 20-25 tonnes of green ginger per hectare.

17. Kerala Local

This variety is cultivated in Kerala. The plant is 30 cm in height and produces 80 g of rhizome, yielding about 20-25 tonnes of green ginger per hectare.

18. Wynad

This variety is grown in hilly regions of Kerala up to a height of 2000 metres. The plant is green, 30 cm in height, produces 60 g rhizome per plant and yielding about 16 tonnes of rhizome per hectare.

19. Maron

It grows in a limited area of high hills in Kerala. Its plant is 26 cm in height and produces about 50 g rhizome thus yielding about 20-22 tonnes of green ginger per hectare.

20. Himachal Selection (local)

This variety is widely grown in hilly regions of Himachal Pradesh like Shillai, Pab, Andhra, Parara and Dhaulakuan. It produces a large number of daughter rhizomes/plantlets and the size of the rhizomes is also thick and produces 86 g rhizome per plant, yielding about 25 tonnes/hectare of green ginger

21. Narasapattam

This variety grows in tropical hilly regions, yields about 19 tonnes per hectare with 22% dry matter contents and 5% crude fibre of the green ginger.

22. Karkal

This variety grows in cool humid regions. It is low yielding variety produces about 12 tonnes to green ginger per hectare with 25% dry matter and 8% of crude fibre contents of the green ginger.

23. Vengara

It is a low yielding variety which responds well to a wide range of agro-climatic conditions. It yields about 10 tonnes per hectare with 25% dry ginger and 5% of crude fibre. It is used in preparing flavouring drinks.

24. Ernad Majeri

It grows in wide range of agro-climatic conditions, yields 12 tonnes of green ginger per hectare with 21% dry matter and 2.4% crude fibre. It is a good variety for home consumption.

25. Burdwan

It grows in warm humid climates. Its rhizomes are attractive reddish brown in colour. It yields about 15 tonnes per hectare with 22% dry ginger and 2% crude fibre content. It is good variety for consumption.

MANURES AND FERTILIZERS

Ginger is a nutrient exhausting crop which requires a good quality of manures and fertilizers for high economic returns. About 50 tonnes of well decomposed farmyard manure should be applied at the time of land preparation and about 80 kg nitrogen., 50 kg phosphorus and 50 kg potash per hectare should also be added. The one third of nitrogen and full doses of phosphorus and potash are applied at the time of sowing and the rest of nitrogen should be applied in two equal doses at the intervals of two months from planting. The irrigated crop is given a top dressing with farmyard manure or oil cakes, particularly in northern India. In Maharashtra, castor cake at the rate 30-40 quintals per hectare is used for 2-3 top dressing.

SOWING OR PROPAGATION

Important aspects of ginger sowing are described below.

1. Seed Treatment

Seed rhizomes weighing 30-60 g each with two sprouting buds are to be treated with 0.3% Dithane M-45 solution for a period of 20-30 minutes, to protect against the soft rot disease. Seed can be treated with Bavistin 0.05% solution.

2. Seed rate and spacing

On an average 15-20 quintals of seed rhizomes are required for one hectare planting. These are planted by keeping a distance of 20-25 cm between plants to the depth of 4-5 cm in the moist soil. Higher seed rate is used for planting at higher altitudes.

3. Planting time and method

In the hilly regions, the best time of planting is March-April, while in plains ginger can be planted even up to May. Late sowing gives poor yields and more sun burn. Planting can be done on flat land or on raised bed. In high rainfall areas it is advised to plant on raised beds, which will provide proper drainage to the excessive water. In less rainfall areas, planting should be done on flat land which will help in moisture conservation. On hilly slopes planting should be done on contour lines. Seed rhizomes are sown with the help of seed-drill in lines.

MULCHING

Mulching can be done soon after sowing with 203 cm thick layer of well decomposed farmyard manure (FYM) @ 10 tonnes per hectare. Mulching with tree leaves and harrowing the field also protect soil moisture and enhance the uniform germination. Mulching also protects the seeds from the direct sun and increases humus in the soil. Seeds of cluster bean, pigeon pea or castor are sown on irrigation channels to shade the ginger plants.

IRRIGATION

The seed rhizome sprouts within a fortnight. The beds should not be irrigated before sprouting. After germination a mild irrigation is given if required in the absence of rains. After this the field should be given thorough drying period for a week or so. Then the crop requires a regular irrigations at an interval of a fortnight followed by weeding and hoeing. Frequent irrigation is necessary where soil has less water retention capacity. However, during rainy season there is no need of irrigation. During later stages, when rhizome formation is taking place, dry weather conditions are found to be congenial.

WEED CONTROL

There is luxuriant growth of weeds in the hilly areas because of heavy rainfall. Therefore, the field should be kept free of weeds by hoeing with the help of khurpi of hand hoe or spade. Normally tow thorough hoeings and one earthing up are sufficient for removing the weeds.

DISEASE CONTROL

Ginger in India is mainly attacked by two diseases viz. soft rot and leaf spot. These diseases are described below.

1. Rhizome rot or soft rot

The disease is caused by Pythium aphanidermatum. The affected rhizomes become soft and pulpy and on pressing it collapses very easily. Due to rotting of internal tissue. Leaves of affected plants become yellow and have water soaked areas that rot at the basal portion and shoots finally wilt and collapse.

Control

1. Use disease free seed rhizomes.
2. Treat the rhizome with Dithane M-45 or Dithane Z-78 (0.25%) for 30 minutes before storage as well as before sowing.
3. Drench the affected plants immediately with 0.3% Blitox-50 as soon as the initial symptoms of leaf yellowing are detected.

2. Leaf spot

This disease is caused by Phyllosticta zingiberi and Lep-topharic spp. Irregular linear spots with whitish centres spotted with black dot like structures and brown margins appear on leaves.

Control

Spray 4:4:50 Bordeaux mixture or Dithane Z-78 or Dithane M-45 at the rate of 0.25 per cent, at fortnightly intervals as soon as disease symptoms appear.

PEST CONTROL

There are a few pests which attack the ginger plant. They are described here.

1. Stem borer

Ginger stem borer is a serious pest of the crop.

Control

Spray 0-1% Malathion 3-4 times at one month interval from the second month of planting.

2. Parrots

Parrots are the biggest enemies of gingers. They peck at the new shoots. the protect, a scare crow helps to keep away the parrots.

HARVESTING AND YIELD

On maturity, the crop attains yellowish colour. It takes about 8-10 months of mature. The leaves and pseudostems begin to dry. Rhizomes are lifted either with a digging fork or with spades. If there is demand of green ginger in he market, it can be harvested at early stage. After harvesting, the rhizomes are to be freed from roots and soil and dried under shade for 2-3 days.A yield of 18-26 tonnes per hectare can be obtained depending upon climatic conditions and cultural operation adopted.

CROP ROTATIONS

In irrigated lands, ginger is rotated with betelvine, plantain, tumeric, onion, garlic, chilli, sugarcane, maize, ragi and groundnut. Under rainfed conditions it may be grown once in three or four years in rotation with tapioca, sweet potato, yam, chilli and dry land paddy.

MIXED CROPPING

Ginger is mostly grown as mixed crop with shade giving plants like banana, pigeon pea, tree-castor and cluster bean. Ginger is grown as intercrop in the field of coconut, coffee and orange plantations on the west coast areas. At higher altitudes in Himachal Pradesh, tomato and chilli are grown as intercrops with ginger.

DRYING OF GINGER

The dried ginger is mainly prepared and supplied to the world market. The process of preparing dry ginger after harvesting involves the following steps.

1. Selection of variety for cultivation, having some intrinsic properties for chemical and physical characteristics and its suitability for drying.
2. Selection of medium sized rhizomes for drying, which have developed a full aroma, flavour and pungency. Large-sized rhizomes are not suitable for drying because of high moisture and fibre contents which cause difficulty in drying and frequently become wrinkled on drying and contain below standard contents of volatile oil.
3. Separation of segmented rhizomes into uniform sized groups for proper drying.
4. Curing by keeping them in shade for drying for 3-4 days or at a desirable temperature and relative humidity. curing heals the cuts and scratches on the surface of the rhizome and prolongs its storage and processing life by checking damage by fungus growth.
5. Trimming the cured rhizomes with the help of sharp knife and removing the undesirable parts like roots, stems, scales, etc. and retaining only the healthy rhizomes.
6. Washing of the trimmed ginger should be done in clean running water to remove soil and other undesirable matter adhered to the rhizomes in between fingers and fingerlings.

7. Killing the rhizome by immersing the living cells/rhizomes in boiling water for about 10 minutes, before drying.
8. Peeling or scrapping the skin can be done by many ways as follows :

   a. Peeling with bamboo knife about 10 cm long with wooden handle are used to peel the skin in such a way that it does not destroy the cells below it, which are delicate and contain much of the essential oil. For manual peeling only that much quantity of fresh rhizomes is harvested which can be peeled on the same day. One person can peel upto 20 kg of fresh rhizome per day. Peeling rhizomes are washed in fresh water and allowed to remain in water overnight.
   b. Peeling by Sukhjhol method is followed in some areas of Sirmaur (H.P.). In this method the healthy rhizomes are sorted and exposed to sun for 6-7 days. The sun-dried side cut ginger along with a few pointed sharp stones are filled in the bamboo baskets. The basket is tied with ropes fixed on poles and constantly shaken till peeling process is completed. Peeled rhizomes are spread on floor for 2-3 days for partial dehydra tion. The whole process is repeated till the outer skin is removed completely. It is then dried again in the sun for reducing moisture content. Usually 7-8 drying cycles are accomplished to process takes 20-30 days. Two persons can peel about 1.5 quintals of fresh ginger in eight hours.
   c. Peeling by Punjhole method is followed in Paunta (H.P.). The fresh rhizomes are immersed in water by keeping in bamboo basket, followed by rubbing by feet in the same basket. This helps in removing the outer skin of rhizomes. This is then washed properly and exposed to sun for about a week. Meanwhile the side branches over the rhizomes are clipped off with the help of knife after the first drying is over. The subsequent shaking and drying are done in the same manner as in Sukhjhol method.
   d. Peeling by mechanical method has now been introduced for processing ginger. Both manually operated as well as power driven machines are available for peeling the fresh rhizomes. Two persons can peel 8-10 quintals of ginger in 8 hours by manually operated machine, while electricity driven machine can peel about 25-30 quintals of ginger in 8 hours.
9. Liming normally improves the appearance i.e. colour and attractiveness and keeping quality of the ginger. The peeled ginger is

placed in quick lime water, 8-10 g lime dissolved in one litre of water, for a period of six hours before drying. The lime treated ginger is like most in the local as well as international market and brings premium prices.

10. The peeled rhizomes are dried in the sun by spreading in layer for 6-8 days, with frequent turning every day till minimum 7% moisture is left.
11. Fumigation with sulphur dioxide for six hours is given to the dried ginger rhizomes before storage or marketing.

GRADING OF DRIED GINGER

Grading is done normally by the traders in the local market for dried ginger. There are no standard grade specifications notified by the Directorate of Marketing and Inspections, Government of India. The trader grade the dry ginger on the basis of chemical analysis, size, shape, dry matter and fibre contents into following grades.

1. Gala, containing least fibre
2. Gatti
3. Darah
4. Chouga, containing highest fibre contents.

In case of grocery trade for domestic culinary consumption the appearance is the primary quality determinant, while for industrial use essential oil or oleoresin preparations are of utmost improtance. The dried ginger is evaluated on the basis of aroma, flavour, volatile oil contents and pungency level.

STORAGE OF SEED RHIZOME

Seed rhizome required for coming season plantation is stored by some special techniques to conserve its moisture to protect it form rotting and to maintain its vigour in sprouting for 4-5 months of off-season period.

1. Storage in field

A part of the field with ginger crop is allowed to remain unharvested in December. A thick layer of dry leaves is spread over the entire area to protect the seed rhizome from drying up. This is harvested in April, when required for plantation.

2. Storage in smoke houses

After harvesting the seed rhizomes are dipped in a thick solution of cow dung and then dried over bamboo mats especially fixed, sufficiently high from the ground, in a room. The room is smoked periodically once in three or four days till the rhizomes are taken out about a fortnight before planting.

3. Storage in pits

The freshly harvested rhizomes are cut into seed size pieces, each having at least 2-3 buds, weighing 25-30 gram. These seed rhizomes are treated with o.25% solution of Ceresan for 30 minutes and dried under shade to make the surface dry. These are stored in a pit, dug inside the room in layers 10-15 cm/m deep, with a small gap between rhizomes and the wooden plank, for healthy aeration during storage. A small hole is made on the plank and rest of the surface is plastered with soil and cowdung. This is the best method for preserving rhizome moisture and its vigour for sprouting.

UNFAVOURABLE CLIMATE

Excessive rainfall during germination and early period of growth is harmful and affects growth adversely. Warm and humid climate at any stage of ginger plant growth encourages the rhizome rot disease.

MEDICINAL VALUE

Ginger oil has numerous medical uses. It is used as carminative, rubefacient, stimulant, and in gastritis, dyspepsia, flatulence, etc. Its oil has a number of other uses for animal disease as stimulant, carminative, etc.

USES AND IMPORTANCE

Ginger is a commercial crop. Its dried scrapped or unscrapped rhizomes are used in production of various useful products like volatile oil, oleoresin and edible product. By steam distillation of fresh or dried rhizomes, about 203% of pale yellow viscous oil is obtained. The oil has aromatic odour. Fresh ginger yields more volatile oil than the dried ones. Ginger oleoresin or gingerine is manufactured in India by extraction of powdered dried ginger with suitable solvent like alcohol or acetone. It contains both the volatile and non-volatile oil.

Ginger is used in culinary preparations such as sauces, soups, curries and pickles. It is preserved in the form of canned rhizome. It is also used as spice in dried form. It is used as flavourant in soft drinks, liquors, in bakery products and confectionery. It is used in various food products like ginger bread, curry powder, and manufacture of certain soft drinks like ginger tonic, etc. It is also used for the manufacture of oil, essence, tinctures, oleoresins, etc. Ginger candy prepared from green or fresh ginger is favourite to many people and has great demand. Many alcoholic beverages like ginger brandy, ginger wine and ginger beer can be prepared.

ECONOMICS OF CULTIVATION

The dry ginger yield varies from 30-40 quintals per hectare. The sale rate is Rs.2000 per quintal, thus bringing about Rs. 60 to 80 thousands and if the cultivation and processing cost of Rs.25-30 thousands is deducted, a net return of Rs. 35-50 thousands per hectare is obtained which is quite lucrative.

***Note:** Junk value is calculated only on those articles which can be resold after their life span. Life span of building and machinery is 15 and 10 years, respectively.*

PLANT ECONOMICS OF GINGER OIL

Plant capacity = 200.00 Kgs/day

LAND & BUILDING

(Land area required 1400 sq.mt)	Rs.	30,10,000.00

PLANT & MACHINERY

Condenser, Storage tank,
Piping system etc., Accumulator
Pulveriser, Pumps, Electricity
Installation erection, Commissioning,
Weighing & Testing equipments

TOTAL	**Rs.**	**6,50,000.00**
OTHER FIXED ASSET	**Rs.**	**37,500.00**

FIXED CAPITAL

1. LAND & BUILDING	Rs.	30,10,000.00
2. PLANT & MACHINERY	Rs.	6,50,000.00
3. OTHER FIXED ASSETS	Rs	37,500.00
TOTAL	**Rs.**	**36,97,500.00**

WORKING CAPITAL REQUIREMENT/MONTH

RAW MATERIALS

Ginger, Lime, Nacl	**Rs.**	**3,80,600.00**

TOTAL WORKING CAPITAL/MONTH

1. RAW MATERIAL	Rs.	3,80,600.00
2. SALARY & WAGES	Rs.	80,940.00
3. UTILITIES & OVERHEADS	Rs.	80,025.00
TOTAL	**Rs.**	**5,41,565.00**

TOTAL CAPITAL INVESTMENT **Rs. 53,22,195.00**

COST OF PRODUCTION/ANNUM **Rs. 79,84,537.90**

TURN OVER/ANNUM

By sale of 6000 kg **Rs. 1,02,00,000.00**

PROFIT = RECEIPTS - COST OF PRODUCTION

PROFIT SALES RATIO = Profit / Sales x 100 = 21.72 %

RATE OF RETURN = Operating profit / T.C.I x 100 = 41.63 %

BREAK EVEN POINT (B.E.P) = 50.48 %

PLANT ECONOMICS
DRY GINGER FROM GREEN GINGER

Rated Plant capacity = *1.00 TON/day*
= *300.00TONannum*
DRY GINGER

LAND & BUILDING

(Land required 450 sq.m) **Rs. 6,90,000.00**

PLANT & MACHINERY

Tube well 2"
Concrate structure
Scalding drum heated with steam
Boiler for steam to heat dryer and
scalding drum,Laboratory equipment
Drying trays with frances & supports
of agriculture waste like leavosof
Bennana or other available source
Grinder

TOTAL **Rs. 4,95,000.00**

FIXED CAPITAL

1.	LAND & BUILDING	Rs.	6,90,000.00
2.	PLANT & MACHINERY	Rs.	4,95,000.00
3.	OTHER FIXED ASSETS	Rs.	75,000.00
	TOTAL	**Rs.**	**12,60,000.00**

WORKING CAPITAL REQUIREMENT/MONTH

RAW MATERIALS

Green Ginger	Rs.	12,60,000.00

TOTAL WORKING CAPITAL/MONTH

1. RAW MATERIAL	Rs.	12,60,000.00
2. SALARY & WAGES	Rs.	51,250.00
3. UTILITIES & OVERHEADS	Rs.	1,10,600.00
TOTAL	**Rs.**	**14,21,850.00**
WORKING CAPITAL	**Rs.**	**42,65,550.00**
MARGIN MONEY FOR W/C LOAN	**Rs.**	**10,66,387.50**

COST OF PROJECT

TOTAL FIXED CAPITAL	Rs.	12,60,000.00
MARGIN MONEY	Rs.	10,66,387.50
TOTAL	**Rs.**	**23,26,387.50**

TOTAL CAPITAL INVESTMENT

TOTAL FIXED CAPITAL	Rs.	12,60,000.00
TOTAL WORKING CAPITAL FOR 3 MONTHS	Rs.	42,65,550.00
TOTAL	**Rs.**	**55,25,550.00**

TURN OVER/ANNUM

By sales of 300 ton of DRY GINGER **Rs. 2,25,00,000.00**

PROFIT = RECEIPTS - COST OF PRODUCTION = 40,44,429.00

PROFIT SALES RATIO = Profit / Sales x 100 = 17.98 %

RATE OF RETURN = Operating profit / T.C.I x 100 = 73.20 %

BREAK EVEN POINT (B.E.P)= 34.92 %

Chapter - 8

GOAT FARMING

INTRODUCTION

The goat is a versatile animal. It is known as the 'poor man's cow' in India, and as 'wet nurse' of infants in Europe. Goats can be kept with little expense. Marginal or undulating lands unsuitable for other types of livestock may be used and any inexpensive shelter will suffice. Of all the domestic animals, the goat undoubtedly has the greatest range of adaptations. Goat thrives well on poor agricultural lands, where they browse on incidental vegetations. In arid areas where vegetation is sparse and is too steep for cultivation, goats roam more widely than other herbivores and meet their requirements from browsing on weeds neglected by others. They have a higher tolerance to feed deficient in crude protein and certain minerals.

Goat milk is cheap, wholesome, easily digestible and nutritious. It is recommended for use in dyspepsia, peptic ulcer and pyloric stenosis. It is also preferred to cow milk for liver dysfunction, jaundice, biliary disorders, acidosis and insomnia.

ORIGIN

The goat was probably the first animal to be domesticated around 9000 to 7000 BC. This long association between goat and humans indicates the variety of functions the goat can provide. Like many other domestic animals, the goat was first used for meat production, but it has also preceded the cow as a dairy animal. Goats are small, hardy animals and are easily maintained than cattle. The frequency with which goats were represented in decorative or ornamental items indicate the value place on the animal by human over a long period.

Although the origin of domestic goats has not been conclusively established on the basis of genetical studies, it nevertheless appears from comparative morphological research, supplemented to a limited extent by data from breeding experiments, that the wild Bezoar of South-west Asia can be considered as the progenitor of most domestic goats.

DISTRIBUTION

The world population of goats is about 500 million, which is approximately on third of the number of cattle of sheep. Goats are very adaptable animal and are found in many climates.

Dry tropical country is home of about half of the goats in the world. In these countries there is often not enough rain for rural people to make a living out of growing crops, and goats are able to survive on poor food and less water than cattle. In countries where there is more rain, the small size of the goat makes it a suitable animal for farmers with little land. Goats can also thrive in areas which are rocky or cold, they originally come from mountaineous countries. Very humid areas are less suitable for most dairy breeds because of an increased risk in disease. However, there are, in the humid tropics, local breeds of goats which are perfectly adapted. They produce milk although their main product is generally meat.

The countries where goat is commonly domesticated are India, Pakistan and Nigeria. In India, the population of goats has increased at the rate of almost one million per annum during the past 25 years which works out to nearly two per cent per annum and is quite high in comparison to population growth of other domesticated livestock species. The distribution of goat population is given in table ***Statewise distribution......***

Perceptible increase in the population of goat is because of its prolificacy in producing more than one young at the time of kidding and of short generation interval. Being a prolific breeder, the unique ability of the goat in kidding twice in 14 months and of producing seven female kids in eight years cannot be achieved either by a cow or buffalo in their life period.

Statewise Distribution of Goat Population in India

State	Population (in million)
Andhra Pradesh	4.88
Assam	2.00
Bihar	12.22
Gujarat	3.60
Haryana	0.68
Himachal Pradesh	1.06
Jammu & Kashmir	1.40
Karnataka	4.00
Kerala	1.58
Madhya Pradesh	7.73
Maharashtra	9.10
Orissa	4.80
Punjab	0.54
Rajasthan	12.59
Tamil Nadu	5.94
Tripura	0.44
Uttar Pradesh	11.19
West Bengal	11.91
Others	0.67
All India	95.33

IMPORTANCE OF GOAT IN RURAL DEVELOPMENT

Goat keeping has immense scope in our village. It can strengthen the economy of rural people, improve their level of nutrition and generate employment opportunities. The importance of goat in the rural economy is evidenced by its unparalleled economic traits, ability to get acclimatized under diversified agroclimatic conditions, unfastidious type in choosing of available forage, higher fertility and short generation interval.

i. Impact on rural economy

Economically goat is ideally suited for poorer rural folk especially for marginal and landless labourers by its low cost maintenance short-term return on capital with low risk capital investment, no involvement of extraneous labour, as such the entire rural family members especially women folk and children are brought out into the gamut of activity; thereby the health status is bound to improve with availability of cheap and good quality protein through goat milk and mutton. Goat thrives and add to the rural economy even in areas where it is difficult to raise cows or buffaloes. Perhaps it is the only farm livestock which fits well for effective utilization in the diverse socio-economic situations of the rural India.

ii. Impact on rural health and nutrition

The greatest value of the contribution of milk and meat is towards the impact on rural health and nutrition. The value is especially significant to the peasants who live on the poverty line and to the vulnerable groups, the pregnant and nursing mothers and the young. The supply of animal protein in the form of milk and meat, although small, represents a consistent supply. Quite often, the supply makes the difference between adequate nutrition and malnutrition to many of thee farmers, who cannot afford to buy these products or alternatively, are unable to produce these by rearing cattle and buffaloes.

iii. Impact on rural employment

To uplift the weaker section of the society, the government provides a subsidy ranging from 25% to 33.3% depending upon the eligibility under various programs like the Integrated Rural Development Project (IRDP), Special Livestock Production Programme (SLPP) and Intensive Cattle Development Project (ICDP) with proper guidance on feeding and appropriate management practices, goat keeping would ensure good profit.

Since goat keeping has a great potential in the country side, small farmers, landless labourers and other weaker sections of the society should be encouraged to keep goats. The locations of goat units should be such that there is ample facility for marketing goat products at reasonable price.

BEHAVIOUR OF GOAT

Animal behaviour is the expression of an effort to adapt or to adjust to different internal and external conditions. Observations on behaviour of goats will help the farmers to keep the animal healthy and sound. Some important behaviour of goats are explained here.

i. Grazing behaviour

In order to attain optimal efficiency for the digestion of nutrients consumed, farm animals develop distinct grazing and ingestive behaviours. Goats are very selective in their feeding and are energetic, inquisitive and versatile in the art of food gathering. They are reported to become fed up with one type of diets very soon and seek out new types of fodder etc. They eat only tender leaves of the plants leaving aside the more coarser ones.

Goats are reputed to have bitter taste receptors, so they enjoy a wide variety of bitter plants that are distasteful to other animals. Goats have higher threshold for bitter tastes than do camels. The threshold of taste discrimination is partly genetic. It also generally takes longer time to eat than sheep.

ii. Individual recognition in goats

In goats having social groups, it is important for members of the group to recognize each other and to detect the strangers. It is probably the olfaction (sense of smell) that plays an important role in individual recognition and it has unique significance among the senses in that smells often persist in an area long aft r the intruders have gone.

iii. Agonistic behaviour

The males of goat fight when they meet other strange males of the same species. Goats stand on their hind feed and swing their heads sideways as a means of striking one another as they come down.

iv. Dominance - subordination behaviour

When a young kid is born, it first shows the fighting behaviour. Its relationship with its mother is peaceful and may remain so after the animal becomes adult. Likewise, the relationship between twins or between kids born at about the same time is also peaceful. However, a kid which approaches an adult female other than the mother is almost sure to be butted away. Older males respond in the same way if kids attempt to compete with them.

v. Maternal behaviour

When the kids are born, the mother cleans the young one by licking them and encourage them to stand and to move. The bond between the mother and young depends on events presumably hormonally controlled, which transpire within a few minutes after the birth of the kid. Individual differences in temperament persist among animals reared in identical environments.

vi. Sleep

Goats have their period of inactivity scattered throughout the 24 hours but mainly during night. Goat exhibit both orthodoxical (true) and paradoxical sleep, while lying in sternal recumbancy with their heads sometimes resting on the flank. Sleeping condition lasts for 1 to 20 minutes and animal sometimes produce snoring sound depicting sound sleep.

GOAT PRODUCTION SYSTEMS

Goat rearing differs from country to country and region to region, but there are three main systems of production, which are commonly followed.

1. Extensive grazing

In this system, large herds of goats (usually more than one hundred animals) travel over large areas of land in search of feed. This is most often practiced by nomadic people in countries where there is little rainfall. The goats are mainly kept for their meat. Some milk may be taken and this often made into cheese which is easter to store and carry than milk.

2. Sedentary family herds

In this system, a small number of goats (usually more than about fifteen) is kept in one place to provide both milk and meat for a farm family. The goats are often fed on agricultural and household by-products like vegetable leaves or rice straws and are given some shelter is wet weather and at night. Tethering is also common in this system, where the movement of each goat is controlled by a rope or chain.

3. Intensive commercial production

In this system medium to large herds (25 to 200 goats) are kept to produce milk for sale. The system is common in some parts of europe but is rare in tropical countries. In an intensive sytem the goats are provided with good pasture or cultivated fodder crops and usually with cereal based concrete feed. Housing, special milking equipments and veterinary medicines are also used to help increase the production of goats.

IMPORTANT BREEDS OF GOAT

India is not only having the largest goat population in the world, but has the largest number of breeds as well. Both indigenous and exotic goats are found in India. The indigenous goats are grouped on the basis of their geographical regions which are described here.

A. Indigenous goats

These are further divided on the basis of the regions they are found in.

1. Breeds of Temperate Himalayan Region

Kashmiri and gaddi are the two main breeds of temperate Himalayan region.

a. Kashmiri

They are large, hardy goats and are found in the high hills of Kashmir and Tibet. The colour generally is white though grey and brown are not uncommon. The body is covered with fine silky hair, beneath which there is the fine fur called 'Pashmina' which is used for making Kashmir rug shawl.

b. Gaddi

The breed is found in Kangra, Kulu and Chamba regions of Himachal

Pradesh. The general colour is white. Horn are pointed at the apex. The skin is very tough and covered with long hair. They are used for transport.

2. Breeds of northern region

There are three important breeds of northern region: Jamunapari, Barbari and Beetal.

a. Jamunapari
b. Barbari
c. Beetal

3. Breeds of southern region

In southern region there are more goats than in the north Indian plains. The important breeds are: Berari, and Surti.

a. Berari

This breed is mostly found in Berari, Nagpur, Wardha and Nimar area. They are black in colour but tall in stature and yield about 0.5 kg milk per day.

b. Surti

It is a short statured breed and is generally reared in the cities. It is stall fed. About 1-2 kg. milk is yielded per day.

4. Breeds of eastern region

Only Bengal goat is worth mentioning in the eastern region.

a. Bengal goat

This breed originated in Bengal. It is a small legged and small size goat weighing about 15 kg. The skin is of superior quality and is in demand in India and abroad. It is a poor yielder. The shoulder and hip are equal in height, chest is wide and ears erect. Three colours are found namely black, brown and white.

B. Exotic goats

Some exotic breeds are also important in the economic point of view.

1. Alpine
2. Nublan
3. Saab
4. Toggenbur

A Feeding Schedule for Goat

Sl No.	Age and stage of production	Feed ingredients	Daily amount to be fed
1.	Birth to 3 days	Colostrum	Ad libitum
2.	Three days to three weeks	(i) Whole milk	450 ml
		(ii) Water, Salt	Ad libitum
3.	3 weeks to 4 months	(i) Whole milk	450 cc upto 8 weeks
	(Start minimizing milk & completely stop it when kids attain 4 months age)	(ii) Creep feed	550 g daily
		(iii) Lucern hay	Ad libitum
		(iv) Water, salt	Ad libitum
4.	Four months to pregnancy	(i) Conc. mixture	15-16% CP @ 450 g/day
		(ii) Dry conc.	15% CP @400-500 g
		(iii) Lucerne hay	Ad libitum
		(iv) Water, salt	Ad libitum
5.	Milking doe	(i) Conc. Mixture	350 g for each litre of milk
		(ii) Trace mineralised salt	1%
		(iii) Molasses	5-7% of conc.mixture
6.	Buck	(i) Only pasture	Non-breeding season
		(ii) Conc.mixture	400 g. daily at breeding season

FEED INGREDIENTS

Several feed ingredients are used to provide nutrients in the diet. Common feed ingredients supply nutrients. Some feed ingredients are used for providing only a particular nutrient, while others provide more than one nutrient. These ingredients are concentrates, roughages, feed additives, mineral supplements and vitamins.

1. Concentrates

Concentrates are low in crude fibre and high in digestible nutrients. Concentrates are also of two kinds; high energy concentrates like maize, rice, sorghum, bran, molasses, etc., while high protein concentrates are groundnut cake, cotton seed cake, soyabean meal, etc.

2. Roughages

Roughages are rich in crude fibre but contain low amounts of digestible nutrients, subabul leaves, sorghum fodder, *bajra*, rice and wheat straw, grasses like Napier, para and young pasture grasses, silage and dry hay are roughages.

3. Feed additives

Feed additives are chemicals that are added to the feed for growth promotion and diseases prevention. For example, antibiotics such as aureomycin and terramycin.

4. Mineral supplements

Salt, oyster shell, lime stone, bone meal, wood,ash etc supply minerals.

5. Vitamin supplements

Dietary requirements of goats are simple because feeds that they consume mostly supply their necessary requirements. However, Rovimix A.D. is a Vitamin supplement that can be used, if needed.

FEED STUFFS FOR GOAT

A wide variety of feed stuffs can be fed to goats. The important ones of them are described here.

1. Maize

Maize is the the most popular grain used in feed. It has 8 to 9% crude protein (C.P.) and is high in energy. Its digestibility and palatability is also high. It is rich in vitamin A and yellow pigment (carotene).

2. Sorghum

Sorghum is another source of high energy feed. Protein content ranges from 5 to 9 per cent. It can replace corn also.

3. Wheat bran

Wheat bran is a by-product of flour industry. It is contains 12 to 14% protein and 6.5% total digestible nutrients (TDN). It is a rich source of phosphorus and vitamin B complex.

4. Rice bran

Rice bran contains 12-14% protein and 12% oil. It is also rich in vitamin B complex.

5. Groundnut cake

Ground nut cake is an important source of protein. Three types of cakes are available like *Ghani*, expeller and solvent extract cake. Oil content in ghani are 10 to 12% expeller 6 to 8% and 0.5 to 0.7% solvent. The protein content varies from 48 to 50 per cent.

6. Cottonseed cake

Cotton seed cake contains 38 to 40% protein. It is rich in phosphorus but deficient in calcium.

7. By-products of legumes

By-product of legumes are obtained during pulse processing. These are known as *chunees* and are rich in protein ranging from 15 to 20 per cent. Different *chunees* are *arhar*, urad, mung, masur and gram chunees.

8. Molasses

Molasses contains 0.4% crude protein, 10% fat and 93.1% carbohydrates and 2.3% ash.

9. Subabul leaf meal

As a leaf meal, subabul contains 21% crude protein but as green roughage it contains 8% crude protein. It is a rich source of vitamin A.

10. Roughages

Nutritive value of roughages depends on whether they are green or dried, have been harvested before or after flowering or are grain by-products. Sorghum, maize, silage and grasses are the main roughages.

11. Lucerne

Lucerne is a legume (rich in protein) and is an ideal green fodder for milch goats and growing stock, kept under stall feeding. It contains 20% crude protein.

12. Napier and guinea grass

Napier and guinea grasses are perennial and drought resistant. They contain 5% crude protein.

13. Tree leaves

Goats are particularly fond of tree leave. Feeding tree leave is cheap and economical. Some important tree leaves liked by goats are *arjun, ber, pippal, babul, neem, khejri, shisham* and subabul.

CREEP FEEDING

The adult size of the goat varies from 25 kg. to 80 kg. according to breed. Therefore, depending upon the breed and the nutritional status of the pregnant doe, the birth weight of the kids varies from 1.9 to 5 kg. To obtain a faster gain in kids and to make a available goat milk for human consumption, it is required to provide goat milk for human consumption, it is required to provide them a balanced starter feed known as 'creep ration' up to 10 weeks of age.

For the first seven days the kids should be nursed by the doe with milk and colustrum. Colustrum should be fed to new born kids within 15 minutes after birth. At least for four days colustrum feeding should be carried out. Over-feeding should be avoided and good results are obtained if the frequency of feeding is four or more.

Feeding Schedule of Kids upto Weaning

Age of kids	No. of feeding per day	Dame's milk or cow milk (ml)	Green feed	Starter feed
1 to 7 days	with the dame	Dame's milk	—	—
8 to 42 days	4	100	Ad lib.	Creep ration
43 to 60 days	3	100	Ad lib.	Feed Ad lib.

Kids should be separated from their mothers from 8th day and kept on starter ration till 60th day. They should be allowed restricted suckling 2-3 times a days or should be bottle fed. with a definite allowance. Free choice legume hay, minerals and drinking water should be made available with starter ration. Feeding schedule of kids up to weaning is given in the table.

Provide a good legume hay (or fresh green grass) and calf starter along with fresh water at three to four weeks of age. Equal parts of cracked maize, crushed oats, wheat bran and 10% linseed meal may be fed as the concentrate mixture. Milk replacers may be fed after the kids reach four months age.

From four months to breeding age (one year or above), kids may be fed roughages that will provide enough nutrients for normal growth. If low quality roughages are fed, supplement the ration with a 12 to 14% protein ration used for dairy calve at the rate of 350 to 400 g daily. Do not allow growing dairy goats to become too fat. Reduce the intake of energy feeds as necessary to prevent this. Always provide clean, fresh water and minerals to kids as they grow. Commercial minerals mixture may be used.

GROWER'S RATION

Good quality roughages will provide adequate nutrition to the growers. If legumes are not available, additional concentrates will have to be provided. Quality roughages should have 20 to 25% dry matter. The average composition of grower's ratio is given in table.

FINISHER RATION

During finishing period, generally one third gain in body weight is achieved. For good carcass cereal based energy rich feeds are required to be fed. The roughage should constitute about 20 to 25% dry matter for fatty finish and 30 to 40% for lean carcass production. A complete ration providing 5-6% DCP (Digestible crude protein) and 60-65 per cent TDN (Total digestible nutrients) is quite satisfactory for finishing period.

Composition of Growers Ration per day

Body wt.	Milk (g)		Conc. mixture (g)or kid starter(g)	Green fodder (Kg)
	Morning	Evening		
2.5	200	200		
3.0	250	250		
3.5	300	300		
4.0	300	300		
5.0	300	300	50	Ad lib
6.0	350	350	100	Ad lib
7.0	350	350	150	Ad lib
8.0	300	300	200	Ad lib
10.0	150	150	350	Ad lib
15.0	100	100	350	Ad lib
20.0		350		1.5
25.0		350		2.5
30.0		350		2.0
40.0		350		2.5
50.0		400		4.0
60.0		500		5.5
70.0		500		6.0

ESTABLISHING A GOAT FARM

The first thing to remember in dairy goat keeping is that the major objective should be to handle the goat so that she will produce efficiently and profitably. Following few lines explain the factors which are to be considered while starting goat farming.

1. Where to start with

Goat is such a useful and potential animal which can be seen from sea level to the top hills of Himalayas. Goat farming can be done at any place where there are goats in the vicinity. In a home level rearing this can be kept near the house or farms whichever may be convenient for the farmer to watch out.

2. Breeds of choice

The aim of the farmer must be the prime concern while determining the type of breed to be selected. Most of the farmers look for milk and meat production. Therefore, only those breeds should be selected which are well recognised for their milk and meat producing qualities.

3. Purchase of animal

After careful selection of breeds, the question arises when to produce the animal. This mainly depends upon the climate of the locality and expected age of animal to be purchased. The maximum emphasis while purchasing the animal should be given to early breedable age. The goats should be purchased during August to October or February to March.

4. Management

Good management means the judicious combination of all the available resources and their proper utilisation to earn the maximum return on the total cost invested on goat rearing. A farmer can bring tremendous improvement by following scientific management of breeding, kidding, milking, rearing kids, heifer, adult, accounts, etc.

5. Feeding and nutrition

Feeding is the most important factor affecting the milk yield of goats. Improvement in feed quality will lead to increased milk production.

6. Housing

Goats are likely to suffer from parasite diseases under wet and dirty conditions. In hot conditions without shade the goat will lose a lot of water from her body. Both these things will lead to a loss of milk production. Therefore, housing is an important way of keeping the goat healthy and in good condition.

7. Prophylatic measures against diseases

Care of health is an important way of making sure that animals remain productivity. Every farmer should know how to recognise and, if possible, prevent and cure the most important health problems which may affect the animal. Good feeding and proper housing minimize the diseases of goat to a great extent in the village condition.

Goat keeping is not an easy task and many factors are to be considered for a successful goat rearing. Through the application of efficient management practices and the experience gained though goat rearing will enable the farmer to utilize the resources profitably and extract maximum benefit from it.

ECONOMICS OF GOAT REARING

The parameters adopted for working out the economics of a unit comprising 95 she goats and 5 bucks for one year given here. However, according to the size of the flock and number of animals, a farmer can work out his own parameters on the basis of the following points.

1. In village goats can find enough grazing throughout the year.
2. Goats are browsing rather than grazing animal, and take 80%of their total intake as browse, which they obtain from awide variety of vegetation.
3. The flock consists of 95 she goats each costing Rs. 550/- and 5 bucks each costing Rs. 650/-.
4. On an average a goat requires a covered space of one square meter and the construction cost of goat shed is Rs. 450 persquare meter.
5. A goat requires an open area 1.5 square metres and theconstruction cost of open area is Rs. 150 per square meter.
6. The space for feed and fodder storage-cum-office room is 20 square metres, and the construction cost is Rs.450 per square meter.
7. The depreciation is 15% on animals, 10% on goat house and 15% on equipments per year.
8. During the lean period 2 kg. of locally available legumebhusa should be provided per day per animal. About 2 kg. of grain fodder per animal may be provided a the time of fodder scarcity. The cost of dry fodder is Rs.50 per quintal.
9. Farmers should provide 200 g. of concentrate per kid during the fourth and fifth months (on 60 days) and 300 g. per shegoat in advanced pregnancy for two months and 500 g. per buck per day during the two breeding seasons annually. The concentrate to be fed to kids, pregnant goats and bucksduring breeding season is priced as Rs.250/-

per quintal.

10. The kid is fed milk from one teat, and the other teat is milked for sale (0.5 kg. per goat per day) for three month i.e. upto weaning.
11. The ratio of male and female kid is 1:1 and the averagenumber of kid per goat is 1.6 (as twinning is common in goats).
12. Goat produces low fat meat. The dressing varies from 44.2 to 49.5 per cent.
13. The average milk production is one litre per day per animal.
14. Goat milk is sold at the rate of Rs. 2 per litre.
15. The animals are kept in a single flock and two labourerswill suffice.
16. Generally the mortality of kid of 10%, conception rate 70%and an adult mortality five per cent.
17. All male kids when 9 to 10 months old are to be sold and notkept for breeding.
18. The age at maturity in all goats is 10 months, and thegestation period fivemonths. She goats are generally in milk when 15-16 months old.The lactation length is 6-7 months with a dry period of 2-3 months if she goat is bred after three months of kidding.
19. Expenditure on veterinary aid, etc. is partly compensated by the sale of manure.
20. Goat can be bred at about one year of age, but they must attain weight of about 30 kg. A goat can be bred thrice in two years period. Males should not be used for breeding before they are one year old.

By mobilizing the production potential of goat in a shorter time with low cost technology goat-keeping in rural parts of India will be a complimentary animal husbandry system to crop production and will constitute a special function in the integrated rural development. The following table explains the details of the economics of goat keeping.

Economics of
Goat-Keeping (95 she-goats and 5 bucks)

1. Fixed capital of non-recurring expenditure **(In Rs.)**

a. Animals

i.	Cost of 95 she-goats just kidded @ Rs.550 per she-goat	52,250
ii.	Cost of 5 bucks @ 650 per buck	3,250
	Total	55,500

Note: Investors/Entrepreneurs are requested to modify the rates of above mentioned animals. We hereby provide rough estimates rates of animals/ raw materials etc.

b. Buildings

i.	Goat house for 100 goats, covered space required at the rate of one square meter per goat	45,000
ii.	Open area for 100 goats, open space required at the rate of 1.5 square metres per goat	22,500
iii.	Kid pens for 140 kids, space required at the rate 0.56 sq. metres per kid	37,800
iv.	Kidding pen, one room 1 sq. m X 1 sq. m	4,500
v.	Two sick animal rooms, each 1 sq. m X 1 sq. m	4,500
vi.	Milk recording room 1 sq. m X 1 sq. m	4,500
vii.	Space for feed and fodder storage cum office room, 20 sq. metre	9,000
		1,27,80

c. Equipment

cost of appliances, weighing balance, milk weighing balance, milk pails, buckets and nipple feed for kids and other equipment	2,000
Total fixed capital invesment (a+b+c)	1,85,300

2. Fixed cost or overhead cost per year

a.	Depreciation on cost of animal @ 15%	8,325
b.	Depreciation on cost of buildings @ 10%	12,780
c.	Depreciation on cost of equipments @ 15%	300
	Total operating fixed cost per year	21,405

3. Working capital or recurring expenditure

i.	Cost of dry fodder for 100 animals for 60 days @ 2 kg per animal per day, i.e. total 120 quintals of fodder @ Rs. 50 per quintal	6,000
ii.	Cost of dry fodder for 138 kids for 60 days @ 1.5 kg per kid per day, i.e. total 124 quintals fodder @ Rs. 50 per quintal	6,200
iii.	Cost of feeding for 67 pregnant does @ 300gms. per pregnant doe per day for 60 days, i.e. total 12 quintals (considering 70% conception rate)	3,000
iv.	Cost of feeding for 138 kids @ 200 gms per kid per day for 4th and 5th months of age, i.e. total 16.60 quintals of feed @ Rs. 250 per quintal (Considering 1.6 as kidding average and excluding 10% mortality)	4,150
v.	Cost of feeding for 5 bucks @ 500 g per buck per day for 120 days, i.e. total 3 quintals of feed @ 250 per quintal	750
vi.	Veterinary aid, etc. for 100 goats @ Rs.15 per goat	1,500
vii.	Veterinary aid, etc. for 138 kids @ Rs.10 per kid	1,380
viii.	Cost of 2 labourers @ Rs. 500 per month per labourer for one year	12,000

ix.	Incidental charges	1,520
	Total recurring expenditure per year	36,500
	(add due to adult mortality @ 5%)	2,750
	Total recurring expenditure per year	39,250

4. Operational expenditure per year

Total operating fixed cost per year	21,405
Total recurring expenditure per year	39,250
Total operational cost per year	60,655
Total operational cost excluding depreciation on animals, building and equipments	39,250

5. Income

1.	Sale of milk for first 90 days @ 0.5 ltr. per goat per day, i.e. total 4,275 ltrs. milk @ Rs.2 per ltr.	8,550
2.	Sale of milk for next 100 days @ 1.00 ltr. per goat per day, i.e. total 10,450 ltrs. milk @ Rs.2 per ltr.	20,900
3.	Sale of 67 kids at the age of 9-10 months @ Rs.425 each	28,475
4.	Sale of 60 bunnies at one year of age (retaining 10 for replacement) @ Rs.450 each	27,000
5.	Sale of 11 culled animals (10 females and 1 male) @ Rs. 600 each	6,600
	Gross Returns	91,525

6. Profit

Particulars	Including depreciation (Rs.)	Excluding depreciation (Rs.)
Gross returns	91,5,259	1,525
Total operational cost	60,655	39,250
Profit per year	30,870	52,275
Profit per animal per year	308.70	522.70
Input output ratio	1:1.50	1:2.33

HOUSING AND CONTROLLING METHODS OF GOAT

Housing is also an important way of controlling the goat. The other methods of control commonly used are herding, tethering and fencing. Control methods also help to prevent the loss of goats by theft, by attacks from wild animals or by the goats wandering off. General needs of goats for shelter, design of actual goat house, tethering, and fencing are the points to be considered when planning to house and control goats.

A. General need of goats for shelter

The following are the important aspects which need to be considered when planning a goat house.

1. The house must provide shade whole day and also protection from heavy rains. This can be achieved by having a large roof overhanging the side of the building.
2. The house must be free from droughts. In colder climate, the side facing cold winds should have preventive structure.
3. At high altitudes where the climate is cold, bedding materials such as straws or dry grasses should be provided and the house should have durable wall on every side.
4. The house must be built in such a way that goats do not injure themselves on sharp points or edges. Goats will often try to escape from their buildings and does may suffer damage to the udder in the process. For this reason, barbed wire should never be used and care

must be taken that there are no nails or broken pieces of wood sticking out.

5. All doorways must be spacious enough for a pregnant doe to easily go through.
6. The design of the building should make feeding and cleaning easy. If does are kept in individual pens, the farmer should be able to give feed without entering each pen.
7. The building should have good ventilation and lighting. This will help to prevent disease.
8. The floors of the goat house should be dry and well drained. Goats do not like cold or wet floors which may cause illness. For this the floors are raised above the ground to keep them dry. In some places floors are kept sloping to provide drainage or are covered with bedding which is regularly replaced.
9. Bamboo, thatch and rammed earth are often used as local construct ing material for goat houses.
10. There must be enough space for all the goats in the building to move about and lie down in comfort. The space needed will depend on the size of the goats, adult does usually need 2.0-2.5 square metres. Moreover bucks will need more and young kids will need less space.

B. Design of goat houses

There are two designs of goat houses:

(1) Ground Level House

(2) Raised Level House.

1. Ground level house

This kind of house is suitable for cold areas. The house is built with a rammed earth floor and brick wall is 1.5 m high. The roof which is raised in the centre, is made up of thatched straw. Ventilation is by a gap of about 20 cm. between the top of the walls and the roof. It has a central passage.

On both sides of the central passage does are kept in individual pens. Each pen is about one metre by three metres size. The front of the pen is made of wood and has also a hinged gate for entrance. The gate also has a rack in which hay or green feed is placed and also a hook which holds water bucket.

To keep the does in individual pens are not essential but they make sure that each doe gets the correct amount of feed.

2. Raised level house

This kind of house is best for humid climate and is suited for less than 5 to 6 goats. The house is made of bamboo rails and has no solid sides. The floor is also made of bamboo and is raised about one metre off the ground by wooden stills. Dung and urine falls through gaps in the floor. A ramp allows the goats to enter the house. The roof is made up of any thatching material and should extend to the side of the house up to one metre height. The goats need not have individual pens and they share a rack of food and water container.

C. Tethering

Tethering is a very common method of controlling, used by farmers keeping a small number of goats. Each goat wears a collar and this is attached to a rope or chain. At the other end of the rope or chain is a part fixed into the ground. Several times a day when the goat has eaten all the food upto its reach the post is moved to new area for fresh browsing.

Tethering requires little effort by the farmer but it needs to be done carefully to prevent injury.

D. Fencing

It is not generally a suitable method to control goats. Because goats can jump great heights, fences will have to be at least 1.5 metre high. They will also have to be made of strongly wood or a fine wire mesh because goats will try hard to get through any small space. This makes fencing very expensive.

In Europe and some other parts of the world, electric fencing is used. This is also expensive but it usually successful.

BUILDING FOR GOAT FARM

Building are necessary for goat keeping. Goats are reared for milk, meat or both. To get maximum production proper accommodation is necessary. Following are the common types of sheds for goats.

1. General flock shed

Adult breeding ewes or nannies are housed in this shed. Each shed should accommodate about 60 ewes or nannies. The shed should be 3 meter high and should have moorum or brick on edge floor. In low lying and moist areas the floors should preferably be elevated and in colder regions they may be made of wood.

2. Shed for ram or buck

Rams or bucks are housed individually in these sheds. Wooden partitions can be raised in a bigger shed to partition it into stalls.

3. Lambing or kidding shed

These are the maternity pens, pregnant ewes or nannies are housed individually in these sheds. These sheds shall be made drought free. In northern parts of the country some warning device like a room heater should be installed in maternity pens, so that new born kids or lambs are protected from cold during winter.

4. Sick animal shed

These sheds are mainly for sick animals which are made away from other sheds. The average size of the shed is about 3 X 2 X 3 metres.

5. Shearing room

This is the place where goats are shorn. This room should be well lit by having large glass windows all around. The floors should be cement paved smooth.

6. Accessory buildings

Next to the shearing room there shall be a wool store for storing wool and shearing equipments. This room should have clean smooth floors and walls lined with glazed tiles upto a height of 1.5 metres. The room should be dust and damp proof. There should be three windows on three sides of the room. There should also be space for weighting machine, stores for concentrates mixture, medicines, farm equipment etc. and sheds for hay straw storage.

7. Building for milch goats

Larger milch goat farms are rarely seen in this country, though all over the country people do keep one or two milch goats for family requirements. When a few goats are kept, all that is required for them is a simple shelter under which are provided a water trough and feed manger, the sizes the latter depending on the number of animals housed.

The milch goats should be housed in one shed divided in to a number of stalls, one stall for each doe. This facilities milking and stall feeding of goats individually. The stalls may be arranged in to rows with a passage in between them. The dimensions of each stall should be 0.8 m. wide and 1.2 m. long. The length of the shed depends on the number of milch goats kept. There should be partitions between stalls made of brick work or stone slabs or iron tubing. Sometimes a small milk room is constructed at one end of the milch goat shed. This is analogous to milk houses on dairy farms.

8. 'Lean-to' type shed

The cheapest form of building is the 'lean to type' shed located against the side of an existing building. Such a shed for two goats should be 1.5 m. wide and 3.0 m. long. This length provides 0.3 m. for the manger and 1.2 m. for the goats; the remaining 1.5 m. space is sufficient for two milking does with a stub wall between them.

The height of the nearest wall should be 2.3 m. and on the lower side 1.7 m. giving a slope of 0.6 to the roof, which may be tiled or thatched. An open framed window and door of proper size should be provided on the lower side. Arrangements for storing hay or dried feed can be made over head.

A goat, when reared singly, can be housed in any building provided it is dry, free from drought and well ventilated. The space allowed should be 1.8 X 1.8 m. A plain board 28 cm. wide and 2.5 cm. thick with two circular holes sufficiently large for receiving two small galvanized iron pails, may be used in place of the manger of a trough for food. It should be raised 50 to 60 cm. height from the floor, supported on wooden or iron brackets fixed to the wall. These pails, one for water and the other for food are preferred by the manager, as the residue of feed can be easily removed.

Stilted housing is common in Assam, Kerala and Orissa which are areas of heavy rainfall under the humid climate or in temperate cold climate. The floor of the pen is raised to about 1.5 m. above the ground level. This facilitates easy cleaning and collecting of the dung and urine. The buildings are often constructed from bamboo and the roofs are thatched.

In tropics because of high temperature, heavy rainfall and infestation of diseases, the goat houses are build above ground level. This done for good ventilation and heavy rain splashes.

9. Space for goats in stanchions and confinement

The size of the stanchion where the goat is kept should be 0.75 m. wide and 1.2 m. long. Goats kept longer in a pen should have a floor space of two square metre.

The buck should be housed separately. A single stall measuring 2.4 X 2.0 m with the usual fitting for food and water would be suitable for the bucks. Two buck's should not be kept together, particularly during the breeding season because they might fight and injure each other. Kids should be provided with separate loose stalls away from adult females. The walls and doors of these stalls should be about 1.3 m. high. A box barrel or a log is provided for exercise. One stall measuring 1.8 sq. m. can accommodate upto 10 kids. Such loose stalls are also suitable for goats at the time of kidding. All stalls should be provided with an enclosure in which the animals can be let loose housing system reduce for the housing cost and labour.

An enclosure measuring 12 X 18 m. is adequate for 100 to 120 goats. Such an enclosure or exercise paddock should be properly fenced with strong woven wire which should not enough space at the bottom. The exercise paddocks should be made bigger than the enclosures and should have some shade trees, if the stock is to be maintained constantly in confinement. Barbed wire should not be used so as to avoid injury to the udder, teats and body. It will be good if a box of 1 X 1 m. and 60 cm high and a stationery steel drum or a log of 30 cm X 2.4 cm size is provided for their exercise.

10. Segregation shed

When the herd is large, provision for a small segregation shed about 3.6 X 5 m. is very desirable. It should be built in the farthest corner of the farm and provided with a well fenced yard; it should be divided into two or three sections. Each yard should have a separate watering arrangement.

11. Hay racks

Goats are very wasteful and refuse to eat what has dropped on the ground. Hay racks are very helpful for feeding. Th bars of bay racks should not be more than 5 cm. apart and there should be a wooden board fixed about 15 cm below the rack to collect the feed from the rack while the goat is feeding.

12. Urine collection tank

Usually people who rear goat do not bother to collect and use goat urine and allow them to get soaked into the soil around the housing. This creates in-sanitary condition. Hence arrangements such as a small non-permeable collection tank made of any convenient material should be made along with housing. Urine can be used as an excellent manure.

13. Composting

The waste from goat house like dropping, trampled grass, straw etc. are precious organic materials which, if composted properly can be used as a manure for one's own use or for sale. There are a number of methods of composting.

PLANT ECONOMICS OF GOAT AND SHEEP FARMING

Plant capacity =120000 LT.GOAT MILK/YEAR

LAND & BUILDING	Rs. 8,90,000.00

PLANT & MACHINERY

Milk tank, Milk Cans (Made of Aluminium), First Aid isntrumentsLaboratory & Testing Equipments, Ordinary Filter, Feeding Equipments Viz. Hay racks &feed trough etc. Misc. Equipments.	Rs. 20,000.00
TOTAL	**Rs. 2,10,000.00**

OTHER FIXED ASSETS	Rs. 10,44,000.00

FIXED CAPITAL

1. LAND & BUILDING	Rs. 8,90,000.00
2. PLANT & MACHINERY	Rs. 2,10,000.00
3. OTHER FIXED ASSETS	Rs. 10,44,000.00
TOTAL	**Rs. 21,44,000.00**

WORKING CAPITAL REQUIREMENT/MONTH

RAW MATERIALS

Cattle Feed Green Fodder /Concentrate, Health Expenses medicines etc.	
TOTAL	**Rs. 1,00,000.00**

TOTAL WORKING CAPITAL/MONTH

1.	RAW MATERIAL	Rs.	1,00,000.00
2.	SALARY & WAGES	Rs.	41,880.00
3.	UTILITIES & OVERHEADS	Rs.	34,500.00
	TOTAL	Rs.	1,76,380.00

TOTAL CAPITAL INVESTMENT **Rs. 26,73,140.00**

COST OF PRODUCTION/ANNUM **Rs. 26,87,075.20**

TURN OVER/ANNUM **Rs. 50,95,000.00**

PROFIT = RECEIPTS - COST OF PRODUCTION = 47.26 %

RATE OF RETURN = Operating profit / T.C.I x 100 = 90.08 %

BREAK EVEN POINT (B.E.P) = 28.02 %

PLANT ECONOMICS OF GOAT BREEDING FARMING (FOR MUTTON PURPOSES)

Plant capacity = 25.00 NOS/day

LAND & BUILDING

1. *Open land 2 Acres (8080 sq.mts.)*
2. *Closed Area 2000 sq.mts.*

TOTAL	**Rs.**	**28,00,000.00**

PLANT & MACHINERY

Water pump 3 HP motor,
Water tank (Sintex),
Utensils, equipments trolleys, and others,
Electrical fittings, fixtures etc,Other equipments,
medical equipments,laboratory equipments

TOTAL	**Rs.**	**5,65,000.00**

OTHER FIXED ASSETS	**Rs.**	**64,25,000.00**

FIXED CAPITAL

1. LAND & BUILDING	Rs.	28,00,000.00
2. PLANT & MACHINERY	Rs.	5,65,000.00
3. OTHER FIXED ASSETS	Rs.	64,25,000.00
TOTAL	**Rs.**	**97,90,000.00**

WORKING CAPITAL REQUIREMENT/MONTH

RAW MATERIALS

(Feed, Green Fodder/Concentrate,
Health expenses medicines & others

TOTAL	**Rs.**	**45,000.00**

TOTAL WORKING CAPITAL/MONTH

1. RAW MATERIAL	Rs.	45,000.00
2. SALARY & WAGES	Rs.	45,960.00
3. UTILITIES & OVERHEADS	Rs.	23,750.00
TOTAL	**Rs.**	**1,14,710.00**

COST OF PROJECT	**Rs.**	**98,76,032.50**
TOTAL CAPITAL INVESTMENT	**Rs.**	**1,01,34,130.00**
COST OF PRODUCTION/ANNUM	**Rs.**	**39,08,278.60**

TURN OVER/ANNUM

1. By sale of Goat (for slaughter-purpose).
2. By sale of manure

TOTAL	**Rs.**	**91,00,000.00**

PROFIT = RECEIPTS - COST OF PRODUCTION

PROFIT SALES RATIO = Profit / Sales x 100 = 57.05 %

RATE OF RETURN = Operating profit / T.C.I x 100 = 51.23 %

BREAK EVEN POINT (B.E.P) = 35.57 %

Chapter - 9

Mushroom Cultivation/Growing

I. INTRODUCTION

The use of mushroom as human food dates back to time immemorial. Today with the development of better technologies and greater realisation of their nutritive values, mushrooms has come to occupy an important place in food habits of people in several parts of the world. Commercial cultivation of mushrooms started in Europe at the turn of this century. With all the increasing scientific research in the biology of mushrooms and more improvised techniques for growing them, mushroom cultivation has almost become an industry in several countries like USA, UK, France and Netherlands. With all their historical background and nutritive importance, it is unfortunate that in India mushrooms have not caught the imagination of the people at large to become an important food item. Perhaps the reasons for their not being taken up widely is their non-availability at low prices for the common man and also due to lack of knowledge of their cultivation methods. Hence, it is necessary that a large number of people are made aware of the simple methods required for successful cultivation of edible mushrooms.

II. MUSHROOM CULTIVATION IN INDIA

Although the methods of mushroom cultivation were known to people in the various countries, its cultivation practices were not well known in our country till recently. Because of its fine characteristics, the mushroom is now being cultivated on a commercial scale in many countries.

Mushrooms grow in every country on all types of soils. They appear in all seasons, chiefly during the rainy weather, where ever organic matter or its decomposition products are available. Plant residues, by suitable treatment, can be converted into substrates for the cultivation of mushrooms. There are two main systems of growing mushrooms. One is shelf system and the other one of tray system. Both are equally popular. They can be grown in polythene bags also, when the space is restricted. Mushrooms that are cultivated in India are white button mushroom (Agaricus bisporus), paddy straw mushroom (Volvariella volvacea) and oyster mushroom (Plrutoyud-sajol-caju).

In the north India, the climatic conditions prevailing during different seasons can be exploited for growing mushrooms throughout the year. For this a year-wise mushroom production schedule has been suggested:

Mid-November to mid-March : white button mushroom

February to mid-September : Paddy straw mushroom

Commercially mushrooms are grown indoors. It has been observed that the location for growing mushrooms should not be too moist. The best way of mushroom growing should be a place where there is a good and fresh water supply, availability of the fertilisers for making compost and a good market for the disposal of the mushroom.

III. WHITE-BUTTON MUSHROOM

White-button mushroom (Agaricus bisporus) is the most popular and economically sown to grow and is extensively cultivated throughout the world. However, due to its low temperature requirement, its cultivation is restricted to the cool climatic areas and to the winter in the plains of northern India.

It can be grown anywhere if the essential conditions are obtained or controlled. These conditions include-temperature remoisture, ventilation and food spawn. The temperature requirement for the spread of the mycelium or the vegetative growth is 22 to 25°C. For the reproductive stage the temperature requirement is 14 to 18°C. Within the limits prescribed, the temperature should be uniform throughout the growth of the crop. If it is too cold the development of the spawn will be retarded. A high temperature will favour the development of moulds and bacteria, which will soon destroy the spawn or crop.

Moisture is an important factor in the cultivation of the mushroom and needs careful application. The mushroom requires an atmosphere nearly saturated with moisture, get the direct application of water on the beds is more or less harmful direct application of water on the beds is more or less harmful to the growing crop. Good aeration is essential for a healthy crop, because ventilation is one of the important factors governing the mushroom production. Good ventilation is responsible for the maintenance of congenial environmental conditions and also for the removal of toxic gas by the introduction of adequate fresh air. Good spawn is also very much essential. Spawn is merely the mycelium from a deleted mushroom grown in some convenient medium and it is the strain of mushroom selected which decides the types of mushroom the spawn will produce.

For the cultivation of white button mushroom (Agaricus Bisporus) the following steps should be kept in mind. These include compost and methods of composting, spawn and methods of spawning, casing and harvesting.

A. COMPOSTING

Compost is the substrate on which mushroom grows. The biochemical activities of a number of micro-organisms make the substrate selective for the growth of mushroom, Agaricus (white button mushroom). The process of compost making is known as composting is defined as indefinite microbial degradation of organic wastes. The process of composting involves microbial decomposition of the organic materials, synthesis of microbial proteins and conditioning of the fibrous material to absorb and retain moisture.

By composting we kill all the harmful organisms present in the manure and transform the medium being used into one which would be more suitable for mushroom growth. Compost is prepared by mixing wheat straw or paddy straw with a number of organic or inorganic fertilisers in fixed proportion. Horse manure and chicken manure can also be used besides wheat straw and paddy straw. Composting yard should be given in order to allow uniform fermentation. While turning is going on watering should be done to make the pile moist in an even manner.

A good compost should be brown with a distinct but inoffensive smell. There should be no smell of ammonia. When squeezed in the hand no water should trickle down, yet it should be moist. When rubbed between the fingers there should be no feel of greasiness. The entire compost will be placed in controlled environment. By raising the temperature of this environment to 54,4°C by peak heating for one week in order to kill all insect pests and fungal parasites is called pasteurization which may not be possible under normal environmental conditions. This is the second phase of composting. After composting the spawn will be introduced into the compost and the process is called spawning.

B. SPAWNING

Spawn is the mushroom seed, comparable to the vegetative seed in crop plants. It is merely the vegetative mycelium from a selected mushroom grown in a convenient medium, and the particular strain of mushroom cultivation and its yield depend to a large extent on the purity and quality of the spawn used. The success of mushroom cultivation and its yield depend to a large extent on the purity and quality of the spawn used. The amount of spawn should be sufficient to help rapid and vigorous coverage of the beds with the organism. It must be sufficient to fight successfully against any other organism that are always present in manure and to overcome any slightly adverse conditions of moisture or consistency that are present. When conditions are ideal in the beds, less spawn is needed.

C. CASING

Casing means covering the compost with a thin layer of soil or soil-like material after the spawn has spread in the compost. Casing is done due to some reasons like, it helps to give support to the mushroom. Casing soil provides humidity as it can hold water for a longer period. Casing prevents quick drying of the spawned compost and, therefore, it helps better spawn growth. Casing helps to regulate the temperature. Sudden reduction of temperature also encourages fruiting, soil loses moisture by evaporation and after each watering a cool layer is provided.

A good and ideal casing material should have good water holding capacity, otherwise the water will go straight to the compost and the surface of the compost will become water logged and will cause damage to the spawn. It should absorb water quickly and should release it slowly. It should have good aeration capacity, that is, it should be quite porous so that exchange of gases can take place easily. The texture of the casing material should be such that it should not be altered by watering. It should be free from disease organisms, insects and undecomposed vegetable matter.

Soil has been recognised as the universal casing material. Soil contains many micro-organisms. To use it as a casing material it should be sterilised in such a way that harmful micro-organisms are killed and the useful ones remain. Sterilisation of the casing materials done either by chemicals or by heating. Sterilisation under pressure is not advisiable as the beneficial micro-organisms are also killed and leave the soil more susceptible to re-infection.

D. CROPPING AND HARVESTING

Excessive humidity during the cropping will result in heavy concentration of carbon-di-oxide. The more the volume of mushrooms grown in a room the more will be the need of fresh air, a more carbon-di-oxide will be formed. The greater the humidity and higher the temperature, the more are the changes of pests and diseases. It is, therefore, essential to keep the temperature low. Apart from regular spraying of insecticides, efforts should be made to keep the circulation of fresh air around the beds Mushrooms mostly appear in "flushes" and at temperature of 68° F, it generally takes 7 to 8 days to come to the button stage from the first appearance of the formation of a pin head. The humidity of the mushroom house will determine whether there is any need of watering the bed. While watering, gentle spraying is essential, otherwise the casing soil will get disturbed. The duration of cropping varies with circumstances.

E. DISEASES

Mushrooms are subject to many fungal, bacterial and viral diseases. Even a little carelessness in the different steps during cultivation can play a disturbing role in the mushroom growth. Improper pasturisation of compost and casing soil can be the major source of diseases. Once the disease is introduced in the farm the secondary infections can be carried out by different agencies such as air, water, machines and workers. The important fungal, bacterial and viral diseases with symptoms, causal organisms and control should be well understood. The important diseases are soft mildew or cobweb, brown plaster mould, white plaster mould, olive green mould, inky cap, green mould, truffle disease, bubble disease brown spot disease, bacterial blotch, and viral diseases. The important insect pests are sciarids, phorids, spring tails, cecid, mites and nematodes.

F. PRESERVATION

Mushrooms, like fruits and vegetables are highly perishable. The demand for mushrooms never coincides with the supply, the day when there is good production the demand may low and vice-versa. To prevent such a glut in the fresh market it is necessary to preserve them. Mushrooms require a great deal of attention during storage, marketing and processing at the post harvest stage. Discoloration, weight and flavour loss are some of the problems. Mushrooms stored at 21P°C remained whiter than those stored at 1°C or 11°C, but they mature at a mush faster rate.The loss of whiteness during storage is a complex process. It was found that the mushrooms stored at 21°C hardened at a faster rate than mushrooms stored at 11°C or 1° centigrade. Chemical action plays a great role in the toughening process. Toughening and the degree of maturity were greatest at 21° centigrade. Different methods are given here to increase the shelf-life of white button mushrooms.

1. STORAGE IN FRESH CONDITIONS

Mushrooms have a high rate of respiration and hence proper attention should be given during storage. Vacuum cooling also helps in increasing the shelf life. In this case mushrooms are packed in a film which is punctured to allow evaporation from the mushrooms. The punctured hole is covered with a small piece of sticking tape after vacuum cooling, to stop the gas flow and to allow the over-wrap to function properly. In South India fresh mushrooms are sent to other places by packing in polythene bags and these are kept in paper lined bamboo baskets or in corrugated cardboard.

2. CONTROLLED ATMOSPHERE

Shelf-life of fresh mushrooms in increased in a controlled atmosphere consisting of 9 percent oxygen and 25 percent carbon-di-oxide. Partial evacuation followed by flushing with carbon-monoxide and storage at low temperature, can also extend the storage life upto 20 days.

3. GAMMA RADIATION

Shelf-life of mushroom can be increased upto 10 days by giving gamma radiation and storing mushroom at 15o centigrade.

4. FREEZE DRYING

Freeze drying is done by immersing the sliced mushroom in a solution of 0.05% sodium meta-bisulphite and 2 percent salt for about 30 minutes. These are then blanched in boiling water for 2 minutes. The frozen mushrooms are dried to a moisture content of 3 percent in freeze drier and packed in cans under vacuum.

5. STEEPING

Edible mushrooms have been steeped in a solution of 2.5% salt, 0.2% citric acid, 0.1% ascorbic acid, sodium bicarbonate, potassium metabisulphite, which can preserve the mushrooms upto ten days without any microbial spoilage.

6. DEHYDRATION

For dehydration purpose, mushrooms are harvested at a mature stage. These can be dried in the sun or in mechanical dehydrator at 60-70°C. Dried mushrooms can be stored for 6-7 months and better reconstituted by immersing in a solution of sugar and ascorbic acid.

7. CANNING

Canners prefer mushrooms to be picked up at an early stage. Fresh mushrooms are dipped in boiling water for two to three minutes and put in cold water. Blanching is necessary to control discolouration. Blanched and cooled mushrooms are filled in cans. Brine solutions (2% common salt + 2% sugar + 0.3% citric acid) is boiled and filtered and added into the cans. The cans are sterilised with boiling water at 85°C and later they are wiped dry and kept in cool dry place.

IV. PADDY STRAW MUSHROOM

Paddy straw mushroom (Volvariella species) is cultivated in the tropical climates of India. Even then it is less attractive commercially owing to very low yield per unit weight of the substrate and an extremely short shelf life. But, as a kitchen-garden crop it is preferred because it is very delicious and also very delicious and also very nutritious.

The cultivation of this mushroom was first tried at Coimbatore and since then its cultivation has been taken over at other places also. It grows at high temperature between 30 and 45°C. It can therefore, also be cultivated during the summer months. A variety of materials have been tried for cultivation, for example, cotton waste, paddy straw etc. In India, three species of Volvariella are grown, namely V.diplasia, V.volvacia and V.esulenta. Volvariella volvacea is the most commonly grown mushroom out of this species.

A. CULTIVATION

Paddy straw (Volvariella species) which is to be used should be uncrumpled, not very leafy, not more than one year old and preferably should be hand threshed. It should be stored at a proper place so that it does not get wet during rain. Paddy straw is made into bundles. The bundles are soaked in water for 18 to 24 hours. Soaking can be done in small tanks and the bundles should be completely immersed in water. The bundles are taken out and excess water drained off. The bundles are arranged such that they make one layer on which small bits of spawn are placed 3 to 4 inches inside the margin, leaving a space of 5to 5.5 cm from each other. A small quantity of arhar or gram dal powder is sprinkled over the spawn bits. Each layer is spawned in the same way. Finally the last layer is spawned all over and covered with a thin layer of loose straw and the bed is pressed down. The bed is covered with a polythene sheet. Watering depends upon the humidity of the air. Mostly no watering is required for the first 3 or 4 days. Watering of the beds and temperature within the beds are very important factors for the yield of paddy straw mushroom.

The bed temperature should remain between 30 and 35°C after spawning. The temperature should not go below 30°C during the growing period. Small buttons start appearing 7 to 10 days after spawning. At that time the polythene sheet should be removed from the bed. They remain in the button stage for 4 to 5 days and then grow into full size. Picking is done by gently twisting the fruiting bodies. Different methods are used for cultivation by different workers. Spawning the different layers of the bed is an influencing factor in straw mushroom production. Spacing between the spawn bits also influences the yield. Smaller spacing (5 cm) between small spawn bits (10 mm) and larger spacing (10 cm) between large spawn bits (100 mm) gives better yield.

Volvariella species can also be grown in winter. The only care taken is to maintain the temperature is low, the bed temperature will also be low. Hence, bed temperature is increased by incorporating the leaf materials which can be used fresh or partially dried. The bed is compacted and covered with transparent polythene sheet.

B. PRESERVATION

Paddy straw mushroom has very little shelf life. It is consumed fresh but it can preserved either by dehydration or by canning. Fresh mushroom must be consumed immediately after harvest. It if is preserved at a low temperature (10 to 15°C) it can be kept well for about 48 hours. If the mushrooms are immersed in 10 percent brine solution followed by drying in the air they can be preserved for one week. Drying is done either in the sun or at a temperature of 55 to 60°C. Fresh mushrooms are reduced to one eighth their original weight after dehydration. Dried mushrooms can absorb water from the atmosphere, so they should be packed either in aluminium foil or in polythene bags. If they are not dried properly they give a fowl smell, which however, goes off during cooking.

V. OYSTER MUSHROOM

The oyster mushroom (Pleurotus species) needs moderate temperatures of 22-28°C for its growth. It grows under natural conditions on trees or dead woody branches of trees. This mushroom is also known as "Dhingri". It is used in the preparation of many delicious dishes. In India, the following species of Pleurotus genus have been cultivated so far Pleurotus ostreatus, Pleurotus flabettatus, Pleurotus sajor caju, Pleurotus eryrgil, Pleurotus sapidus, Pleurotus cornucopiae. The cultivation of Pleurotus flabellatus has been tried on wheat, ragi and rice straw. The highest yield was obtained on rice straw.

A. CULTIVATION

There are several methods of cultivation of Pleurotus species with only little difference or modification. Dried paddy straw was chopped into 1 to 2 cm long bits and soaked in water overnight. Excess water is drained off and horse gram powder and spawn were added and mixed with the foregoing mix (substrate) and kept in a room at 21 to 31°C with sufficient light and ventilation. The mycelium took 11 to 14 days to permeate the substrate in the bags. During the period the temperature of the substrate varied between 32 and 36°C and later became almost constant at 25 to 28°C with the appearance of mushroom pins on the upper side. The polythene bags were cut open on the sides without disturbing the bed, which had become quite compact by them. Water should be, sprayed over it twice in a day. In 3 to 4 days, the crop started coming up. The beds, in bags as well as on the circular stands, were placed in a well-ventilated room with normal conditions of temperatures, relative humidity and light. The temperature range is 20 to 32°C with relative humidity 35 to 75 percent. The mushrooms are harvested from the 4th day onwards. Supplementation of mushroom beds with cotton seed powder after the spawn seen, increases the yield by 85 percent. This also improves the texture and flavour of the mushroom.

Oyster mushroom is grown on paddy straw and some other agro-residues. It can be grown in a thatched hut, polythene bag and a mud/ pucca house.

VI. EDULIS MUSHROOM

Agaricus bitorquis is a new species of mushrooms also known as "Edulis" and grown at a higher temperature and higher carbon-di-oxide concentration. It has a better shelf life as compared to Agaricus bisporus. The difference with Agaricus bisporus is that the first flush in Agaricus bitorquis comes a little later and also the intervals between the flushes are more. The first generally appears between 22 to 26 days after casing and the second flush comes in the interval of 10 to 12 days. The compost which is used for the cultivation of Agaricus bisporus can be used for the cultivation of Agricus bitorquis.

A. SPAWNING

The rate and method of spawning is the same as that of

A. Bisporus.

The mycelium of Agaricus bitorguis grows at a higher temperature. The average bed temperature during the mycelium growth should be about 30°C and the growing room should be ventilated as little as possible. The mycelium of Agaricus bitorquis dies off after prolonged exposure to temperature above 34°C. After 12 to 14 days of spawning the casing can be done. As the mycelium of Agaricus bitorquis is finer the compost at casing time will look less white than that of Agaricus bisporus. A few weeks after casing the compost turns extremely white. The same sterilised casing material as that of Agaricus bisporus can be used for Agaricus bitorquis. After 10 to 12 days when the mycelium has reached. The casing soil, the temperature should be lowered. By starting the ventilation, the temperature can be brought down to 25°C. It is believed that the requirement of fresh air for Agaricus bitorquis is less than that of Agaricus bisporus. During growth, due to less ventilation, evaporation may be less. For this the moisture of casing layers should be regularly checked as high temperature and high humidity may be conducive to many diseases such as bacterial spot and blotches which may cause heavy damage. If the cut surface of the stem turns brown and if many pin heads die it shows that the casing layer is too wet.

B. HARVESTING

As the time period between the button and open stage is quite short, it is advisable to pick the mushroom at the proper time. As the mushroom requires high concentration of carbon-di-oxide and high temperature for its growth, one feels inconvenient at the harvesting time, so before and during picking, ventilation and circulation be temporarily raised. Hence, we see that the temperature requirement of Agaricus bitoquis is high.

In general, it can be said that stagnation, damp air, with temperature above 15°C to 16°C encourage the infection, so the gorwers are mostly in a fix, as increasing the ventilation will cause scaling and a higher humidity will promote the bacterial infection.

VII. CONCLUSION

Increase in population is creating an alarming situation in the food problem in India. Malnutrition in terms of "protein" deficiency is becoming major health hazard in the developing countries. It is unfortunate to realise that mushrooms did not receive universal acceptance over the years since a number of naturally growing mushrooms are poisonous. Today the concept has changed because the cultivated edible species of mushrooms are totally safe for human consumption. Mushroom farming is becoming successful because of its very low inputs. In India, mushroom growing can be highly rewarding because of a variable climate. The technology can be profitably considered in areas where land is a limiting factor and agricultural residues are abundantly available. The cultivation of three types of mushrooms, white button (Agaricus bisporus), paddy straw (Volvariella spp) and dhingri (Pleurotus spp.) which can be grown at different temperature in different seasons, should be intensified, thus making mushroom a year round crop.

CONSULTANTS FOR MUSHROOM PROJECTS

A.M International,
Jain Hills,
Shirsoli Road,
Jalgaon - 425 001.
Tel : 257 - 220033/37
Fax : 91 - 257 - 221133

IMPORTANT ADRESSES

Blue Star Limited
13, Community centre,
New Friends Colony,
New Delhi.
Tel : 6834262, 6911660.
Fax : 6841485, 6834957.
(Cold Room / Deep Freezers)

IMPORTERS OF MUSHROOM

Blue Prince Mushroom
Station Road,
Rustington,
Littlehampton BN 16 3RF, U.K.
Tel : 0044 - 903 - 775 - 111
Fax : 0044 - 903 - 787 - 022.

Fitch & Sons,
Wandlee House, Riverside Drive
Mitcham CR4 4BU, U.K.
Tel : 0044 - 71 - 720 - 1660
Fax : 0044 - 81 - 640 - 4621

Middlebrook Mushrooms Ltd.
Great Bowden Road
Market Harborough LE16 7DE, U.K.
Tel : 0044 - 858 - 410 - 451
Fax : 0044 - 858 - 410 - 197

R.H.M. Foods Ltd.
10, Victoria Road,
London NW10 6NU, U.K.
Tel : 0044 - 81 - 965 - 6565
Fax : 0044 - 81 - 965 - 6565

Baxters of Speyside Ltd.
Fochabers, NR Elgin IV32 7LD,U.K.
Tel : 0044 - 343 - 820 - 293
Fax : 0044 - 81 - 688 - 8652

Brook Bonds Foods Ltd.
Leon House, High Street,
Croydon CR9 1JQ,U.K.
Tel : 0044 - 81 - 686 - 8899
Fax : 0044 - 81- 688 - 8652

Aquaferme SPRL
Rue De Maou 60,
6721 Anlier Habay, Belgium.
Tel : 0032 - 63 - 422 - 149/422167
Fax : 0032 - 63 - 423 - 408

Delimex
Park Tremeland 59,
3120 Tremelo, Belgium.
Tel : 0032 - 16 - 531739
Fax : 0032 - 16 - 531759

L.DE Schouwer & Co.
Verdunstraat 395,
1130, FHarren Brussels, Belgium.
Tel : 0032 - 2 - 2152576
Fax : 0032 - 2 - 2418560

Champix Sprl
50 Allee Verte,
B-1210 Brussels, Belgium.
Tel : 0032 - 2 - 21 - 58986
Fax : 0032 - 2- 2158592.

Desmet A. BVBA
Leopold III Laan 40,
B-8749,
Warengem Beveren,
Belgium.
Tel : 0032 - 56 - 714958.

Gowa BVBA
20,Obeekstraat,
Heusden Zolder 3550,Belgium.
Tel : 0032 - 3 - 8872031.
Fax : 0032 - 3 - 8876097.

Aarts Conserven B.V.
Houthuizer weg 20,
5973 RG Lottum,
The Netherlands,
Tel : 0031 - 77 - 661404,
Fax : 0031 - 77 - 661440

Coencn's Conserven B.V.
P.O.Box 6055,
5960 AB Horst (L),
Industriestraat 7,
596 Y PG Horst (L),
The Netherlands.
Tel : 0031 - 4709 - 3241.
Fax : 0031 - 4709 - 6935

Nenk Van Den Bergh B.V.
P.O.Box 254180 BA Waardenburg
Steenweg 73 A 4181 AK Waardenburg,
The Netherlands.
Tel : 0031 - 4181 - 2515
Fax : 0031 - 4181 - 2460

PLANT ECONOMICS OF MUSHROOM CULTIVATION

Rated Plant capacity = 600.00 TON/annum MUSHROOMS AND ITS PRODUCTS

LAND & BUILDING

Land 2 Acres (8080 Sq.mts) Rs. 69,20,000.00

LIST OF PLANT & MACHINERY

(Washing tank (SS) ,Vacuum drier
Steam Jacketed Kettle ,Boiler Steam
Can seamer (Automatic) ,Blender
Boiling Water bath ,Fruit Pulper
Autoclave for can sterilisation
P.P. Sealer,Black Polyethene trays
and shelves ,Spray gun with
motorised pump & Heat Convectors
Device for compressing and levelling
the fertilized soil in trays and
harvesting m/c,Cooler for air cooling ,
Weighing scale weighing, Laboratory tesing
equipments, Air ionizer,Process control
equipments and instrumentation.
Conveyor belt, Bucket elevators etc
Miscellaneous equipments
Deep freezing unit with complete
accessories & equipments,Automatic
packaging m/c. weighing filling &
sealing & pouch packaging etc.

FIXED CAPITAL

1. LAND & BUILDING	Rs.	69,20,000.00
2. PLANT & MACHINERY	Rs.	1,65,92,000.00
3. OTHER FIXED ASSETS	Rs.	39,00,000.00
TOTAL	**Rs.**	**2,74,12,000.00**

WORKING CAPITAL REQUIREMENT/MONTH

LIST OF RAW MATERIALS

Spawn (vegetable myceliun)gray
Compost fertiltzer of standard
Paddy Straw & Wheat Straw
Carbendazine solution & Benomyl
PVC films/bags to Store harvested
mushroom Spices, Oil, Vinegar
and other Tin Cans
(1 lb. capacity)

TOTAL WORKING CAPITAL/MONTH

1. RAW MATERIAL	Rs.	15,78,000.00
2. SALARY & WAGES	Rs.	1,72,800.00
3. UTILITIES & OVERHEADS	Rs.	56,500.00
TOTAL	**Rs.**	**18,07,300.00**

COST OF PROJECT

TOTAL FIXED CAPITAL	Rs.	2,74,12,000.00
MARGIN MONEY	Rs.	13,55,475.00
TOTAL	**Rs.**	**2,87,67,475.00**

TOTAL CAPITAL INVESTMENT

TOTAL FIXED CAPITAL	Rs.	2,74,12,000.00
TOTAL WORKING CAPITAL FOR 3 MONTHS	Rs.	54,21,900.00
TOTAL	**Rs.**	**3,28,33,900.00**

TURN OVER/ANNUM

By Sale of 3,78,450 Kgs. of Canned Mushrooms
By Sale of Dehydrated Mushroom
By Sale of Mushroom Pickles

TOTAL **Rs. 4,18,65,300.00**

PROFIT = RECEIPTS - COST OF PRODUCTION

PROFIT SALES RATIO = Profit / Sales x 100 = 23.20 %

RATE OF RETURN = Operating profit / T.C.I x 100 = 29.59 %

BREAK EVEN POINT = 54.34 %

Chapter - 10

Establishing An Orchard

INTRODUCTION

Establishment of an orchard is a long term investment deserving careful planning and management. Any initial mistake in the selection of site, planting distance, varieties, cultural practices, procedures in raising nursery or in the management practices can considerably reduce the returns from orchard.

SITE SELECTION

Selection of site is important for orchard establishments as most fruit trees are perennial. Climate and soil are the chief natural factors on which success or failure of the orchard depend. In the selection of site, the following aspects should be carefully considered:

1. Regular transportation facilities;
2. Good marketing facilities;
3. Sufficient irrigation facilities;
4. Availability of sufficient labour and experienced fruit growers;
5. Easy availability of farm inputs like manures, fertilizers, seedlings, implements, instruments, tools etc;
6. Safe distance from any badly diseased plantations;

7. Proximity of owner's house to orchard for effective supervision;
8. Presence of fruit based industries to ensure a steady market for products;
9. Avoidance of waterlogged area or provision for good drainage and
10. Possibility of locating the orchard, if possible, close to horticultural research stations, agricultural colleges, district farms and demonstration farm from where advice of experts is available.

ASSESSMENT OF RESOURCES

Selection of site should be followed by a detailed assessment of its resources namely Land, Climate, Location, Soil, Vegetation, Water Source, Power, Availability of labour, Marketing facilities, Availability of inputs, Storage facilities, Processing facilities, Credit/banking facilities and Cooperative support. The following are some of the important factors to be considered for assessment.

1. Land

Area, topography, direction of slope,drainage point, whether hilly, slopy, levelled or rocky.

2. Climate

Tropical, subtropical, temperate, humid, dry, amount of rainfall.

3. Location

Closeness to road, river, streams, market, village, town, city, transport and communication facilities, agricultural universities, research stations, demonstration farm, seed farm, horticultural departmental offices.

4. Soil

Clay, clay-loam, loam, sandy, sandy- loam, fertile, depth of soil, organic matter content, erodee/not eroded.

5. **Vegetation**

Thick, moderate, scanty and variety of vegetation.

6. **Water Source**

Whether there is any water sources in theland, ground water table.

7. **Power**

Electricity, diesel, animal.

8. **Availability of labour**

Sufficient/not sufficient.

9. **Marketing facilities**

Sufficient/not sufficient.

10. **Availability of inputs such as fertilizer, pesticides and medicines**

Available/not available

11. **Storage facilities**

Available/not available

12. **Processing facilities**

Available/not available

13. **Credit/banking**

Available/not available

14. Cooperative Support :

Available/not available

Preliminary Operations

After selecting a site, a few village operations have to be done on the land. These operations improve the physical, chemical and biological conditions of the soil. Some of the main operations are described.

1. Clearing the land

All undesirable vegetations in the field (such as trees, shrubs, bushes, grasses and parasitic plants) should be cleared off.

2. Ploughing or digging the land

It is highly advantageous to plough or dig the land to loosen the compactness of soil and to bury leaves and other plant residues. It will make the soil conditions more favourable to plant growth by improving the water holding capacity of the soil. If possible, levelling of the land should also be carried out.

3. Levelling the land

Levelling involves considerable shifting of soil and, therefore, is an expensive process. This is practised mainly in undulated site. The site is divided into sections and levelled sectionwise.

PLANNING THE ORCHARD

Before undertaking the actual planting it is worthwhile to prepare a plan according to scale on paper for the orchard showing the alignment of farm roads or paths, buildings, irrigation channels, fruit trees grown in different sections, drainage channels and locations of hedges and windbreaks.

A. Roads and Buildings

The main road of the orchard should be connected to village road. This road, as far as possible, should be in the centre of the orchard.

Sub-roads can also be constructed perpendicular to the main road. These sub-roads can lead to different sections in the orchard. The width of the main road can be 2 to 3m depending on several factors like size of farm, mode of transport and the volume of farm products. The roads should be given a mild slope to drain out water.

Buildings are mainly constructed for keeping the implements, storing the produce, keeping the records, etc. Watchman's residence can also be constructed at a convenient place in the orchard. These buildings can be constructed at one place so as to reduce the construction cost. For effective supervision, it can be built in the centre and near the main path of the orchard. The land required for construction should be left unplanted even if the construction is delayed.

B. Irrigation Facilities

Adequate irrigation facility is one of the main farm inputs for production. This can be made available by digging well(s) or through government irrigation channels.

If a well is the source of irrigation, it should be dug before planting as the trees require water as soon as they are planted. The water from the well should be delivered, as far as possible, at the highest point to facilitate easy distribution at less cost. The main channel is fed with water from the main source. If necessary, sub-channels can also be constructed to carry water to different blocks. Usually, the width of the main channel is 1.5 metre and of the sub-channel 0.75 metre. However, it varies with size of the orchard and the number of trees one wants to irrigate.

C. Fencing

To prevent destruction of the trees by cattle and to protect the orchard from treespassers, it is necessary to provide some kind of fencing on all sides of the orchard. This should be done preferably before planting the fruit trees. While planning for fencing, it should be remembered that the fencing should be as economical as possible both in terms of expense and land use.

Types of fencing:

There are four types of fencing.

1. Barbed wire fencing

The most common type of fencing, though expensive, is barbed wire fencing. The wires having iron thorns do not allow anybody to enter the orchard easily. Wire fencing occupies less space compared to other types of fencing.

2. Wall fencing

Wall fencing is of different types e.g; mud wall, concrete wall, stone wall, brick wall, etc. The height may vary from orchard to orchard and also from place to place. However, a wall of five feet around the orchard is considered ideal.

3. Wood wall fencing

It is just like a stone wall fencing except that in place of stones, wooden logs are used. This fencing is practised where wood is cheap, specially, in the case of orchards located near the forest. However, such fencing is discouraged in view of the disappearing forests.

4. Trees, bush & shrub fencing

This is also known as live fencing. These types of fencing occupy a lot of space but they provide good protection and also beauty to the orchard. The plants chosen for the hedge should be fast and thick growing and also strong and thorny. The living fence needs much care and management.

D. Wind breaks

A windbreak consists of one to three rows of tall trees planted closely together around the orchard against the direction of the wind or at suitable intervals in the orchard to give effective protection to the fruit trees against strong and desiccating winds. The main functions of windbreaks are:

1. They reduce the wind velocity and minimise the damage to fruit trees;
2. They minimise the adverse effects of high and low temperatures on

plants;

3. Fruit set better in the orchard, as conditions are more favourable for pollination. There is less dropping or rubbing of fruits; and
4. Water loss due to evaporation of soil moisture is reduced to a great extent.

The windbreaks are raised by planting trees like eucalyptus in one row along with a second parallel row of slow growing, dense crowned evergreen trees such as tamarind, jackfruit, shisham, mango, jamun and ber.

Planting Systems

Commonly, there are five systems of orchard planting. They are: Square system, Rectangular system, quincunx or diagonal system, Hexagonal system and Contour system. A brief explanation of these systems are given below.

1. Square system

Square system of planting is the simplest and the most convenient among the planting systems. Trees are set at the corners of a square formed by intersecting lengthwise parallel lines with crosswire parallel lines. In square system, plant to plant distance is the same as row to row distance.

2. Rectangular system

The method is similar in all respects to square system except that plant to plant distance is less than row to row spacing.

3. Quincunx or diagonal system

The quincunx or diagonal system is same as square system, but with the addition of a tree in the centre of each square. In this case, the number of trees are almost double of that in square system. The central tree is usually not a permanent tree and is planted just to fill the central place to serve as an additional source of income till the main trees come into bearing.

4. Hexagonal system

The hexagonal system is also known as equilateral triangle system as the trees are planted at the corners of equilateral triangles. In this system, the distance between the rows is 86 per cent of plant to plant distance.

5. Contour system

Contour is an imaginary line across a slope joining the points at same elevation. The system is only meant for hilly tracts. Contour lines are marked using a dumpy level or any other suitable instrument and trees are planted on them at the required distance. This controls the soil erosion.

Purchasing Saplings from Nursery

After preparing the layout plan, the grower must place his order for planting material well in advance. The factors to be considered while purchasing plants are :

(1) Age and grade of trees
(2) Source of supply

1. Age and grade of trees

The age of trees is always estimated on the basis of the age of scion (the aerial portion of a plant which is being propogated by grafting on another plant). Fruit trees, one or two years old , are ready for planting. Neither older trees not too young trees should be purchased since they don't establish themselves easily.

Along with age, the size of the tree in terms of diameter of the trunk should also be considered. The optimum diameter ranges between 1.5 to 3 cm. for most of the plants.

As far as possible, purchase only those trees which are propogated from selected strains or variety , which had consistently shown execellent performance.

2. Source of supply

It is always advisable to purchase trees from a nursery of established reputation, preferbaly from one on the approved lists of the department of agriculture of the state.The fruit grower himself (if necessary accompanied by an experienced person) should visit nursery to buy the plants.

The plants may be purchased from a nearby nursery. It is essential to inspect all the stock carefully before purchase. Reject all the diseased plants as they are likely to transfer the diseases to the healthy plants.

If the plants received are deciduous (a tree which sheds its leaves every year at the end of the growing season), they should be planted with in 48 hours. They should be stored in a cool place under shade and should be watered till they are planted.

Fruits plants propogated vegetatively (i.e. through grafting, budding, layering, etc) are true to parent plant as a reult it is possible to obtain uniformity in growth, yield and quality of fruits.

PLANTING

A. SEASON

The season of planting varies with different fruits and local conditions. In india , there are two seasons of planting :

(i) Monsoon (June to August)
(ii) Spring (February to March).

The monsoon season is considered to be ideal time for planting evergreen fruit trees like citrus, mango and guava. If irrigation is assured spiring season is the best time for planting.

B. SELECTION OF PLANT MATERIAL

Quality of the produce and the ultimate success of the orchard depend upon the planting material selected at the time of establishment of the orchard. The following points should be kept in mind while selecting plant material:

1. Select vigorous, healthy and well growing plants;
2. Plants should be free from pests and diseases;
3. Plants which are one year old and of medium size (0.75 to1.0 metre height) are ideal for planting;
4. Avoid very old and very young plants as plant mortality is high in such

plants;

5. Select plants of known origin or parentage;
6. Select a variety with good bearing and assured market;
7. Choose one or two varieties keeping in mind the uniformity in their growth and yield;
8. Purchase atleast 20% more plants considering the possible casualities;
9. Plants should have a sufficient ball of earth to protect their roots or they should be the ones growing in polythene bags.

C. Distance

The planting distance (space between plant to plant) varies with the kind of fruit trees, size at maturity, fertility of soil, rainfall or availability of irrigation water and other agro climatic factors.

For proper development and better yield, the fruit trees must be spaced accurately. The two important factors which determine the spacing of fruit plants are:

(i) Natural habit of the plant,
(ii) Soil and climatic conditions.

Trees with a naturally big spread such as mango, jackfruit and litchi need larger space than trees such as *santra, musambi,* guava, peaches and plum. Grafted or budded trees in general being smaller than trees raised from seeds require less spacing. Trees of the same kind grow better and bigger in a favourable agro-climatic and soil conditions than the trees growing in unfavourable conditions. The former obviously require more spacing than the latter.

Table 1 provides the normal planting distance for the most common fruit trees.

Table 1 - Planting distance for common fruit trees

	Name	Distance (metres)
1.	Almond	6-8
2.	Apricot	6-8
3.	Apple	8-9
4.	Avocado	8-9
5.	Banana	1-2.5
6.	Ber	11-12
7.	Bread fruit	12
8.	Cashew nut	7-8
9.	Cherry	10-12
10.	Custard apple	5 - 6
11.	Date palm	11-12
12.	Fig	3-4.5
13.	Grape	2.5-4
14.	Grape fruit	6-8
15.	Guava	6-8
16.	Hazel nut	2-3
17.	Jackfruit	10-12
18.	Jamun	10-12
19.	Japanese persimmon	7-8
20.	Kagzi lime	5-6
21.	Karonda	2-3
22.	Lemon	5-6
23.	Litchi	9-12
24.	Loquat	7-9
25.	Mandarin	4.5-6
26.	Mango	12
27.	Mangosteen	9-11
28.	Mulberry	6-8
29.	Papaya	2.5-3
30.	Passion fruit	3-4
31.	Peach	6-8
32.	Pear	4-5
33.	Pecan nut	12
34.	Phalsa	5-6
35.	Pineapple	1-2
36.	Plum	5-6
37.	Pomegranate	5-6
38.	Pumelo	5-8
39.	Santra	6-8
40.	Sapota	8.5-10
41.	Strawberry	0.8-1.0
42.	Sweet orange	6-8
43.	Walnut	12

The distances are determined based on the crown's growth of various fruit trees under normal soil and climatic conditions. The branches of trees when fully grown should not overlap each other. Hence, the tree to tree spacing is equal to the diametre of the crown of a full grown tree.

D. Disadvantages of close-planting

1. Close planting results in over-crowding.
2. When trees are planted too close to each other, their roots become entangled and compete for nutrients. Consequently trees grow poorly.
3. Closely planted trees do not get sufficient light and air.
4. When there is scarcity of water the closely planted trees suffer more.
5. Due to inadequate growth and development, the yield of closely planted trees will be low.
6. Inadequacy of light in thickly planted orchards results in poor development of fruit colour.
7. Close planting hinders proper cultural operations.
8. Closely planted trees naturally tend to grow tall and slender making pruning, spraying and harvesting difficult.

E. Digging of pits

The plot where the trees are to be planted should be laid out by marking the position of fruit trees by fixing pegs.

1. Time of digging

If planting is to be done at the onset of monsoon, the pits should be preferably dug during the end of previous monsoon or in winter. In heavy rainfalls, planting can be done after the monsoon so that the young plants are not affected by water-logging.

2. Size and soil mixture for preparation of pit

Size of the pit varies with the root system of the fruit plants. In general, pits having 1 X 1 X 1 metre size are dug for planting of fruit trees. These pits are exposed to sunlight for fifteen days. The pits are then filled with a mixture of soil and well prepared farm yard manure.

Farm yard manure should be well decomposed. A mixture of three baskets of farm yard manure, on basket of sand and enough top soil dug out from the pit should be used to fill two third of the pit. This mixture can be added with 50g of BHC (10%) dust and 250g of single superphosphate. Mix the entire material thoroughly and fill 2/3 of the pit.

3. Materials for digging

The implements and materials required for digging and filling the pits are:

(a) Pick axe,
(b) Spade,
(c) Basket,
(d) Farmyard manure,
(e) Measuring tape,
(f) BHC powder (10%)
(g) Single super phosphate (SSP)
(h) Rope,
(i) Sand,
(j) Pegs and stakes.

4. Procedure for digging

The following procedure is adopted for digging the pits:

a. Measure the area;
b. Locate the spots for digging pits with the help of pegs;
c. Dig one cubic metre size pits using pick axe, spade, etc;
d. Dig the pits preferably at least 3-4 weeks before planting;
e. Mix the dug out surface soil with three baskets of farm yard manure and one basket of sand;
f. Spread 50gm BHC (10%) dust and 250gm of single super phosphate over the soil - FYM - sand heap;
g. Mix the entire material thoroughly; and
h. Put the soil mixture into the pit and fill upto 2/3 of its height.

F. Procedure of Planting

The planting, with its root intact within the mud ball, should be placed in the middle of the pit. Soil should be put in the pit from all sides making it a little higher than the ground level. While planting, care should be taken to keep the graft or land joint well above the surface of the soil. The plant should be planted as deep as they stood in the nursery. For better contact of root with the soil around, the soil should be pressed well and irrigated immediately. The plant should be staked with any support to protect them from being damaged by strong winds.

Chapter - 11

Papaya Cultivation

INTRODUCTION

Papaya (*Carica papaya*) belonging to the family Caricaceae was introduced in India in 16th century by the Portugese. It is one of the few plants which produces fruits throughout the year. It owes its popularity to various simple reasons like, it requires less area per tree, comes to fruiting in a year, easy to cultivate provides per hectare income next only to banana and has high nutritive and medicinal value.

Papaya is a native of tropical America. It is now grown in all the tropical and sub-tropical countries, e.g. Australia, Hawaii, Taiwan, Peurto Rico, Peru, Florida, Texas, California in the USA, various of Central and South Africa, Pakistan, Bangladesh and India. In our country papaya is chiefly cultivated in Assam, Andhra Pradesh, Uttar Pradesh and Tamil Nadu. In India, about 17,000 hectares of land is under papaya cultivation.

At a time, a tree can yield 100 fruits, each weighing about 1 kg. Regular consumption of papaya can ensure a good supply of vitamin A and C, which are essential for good health. Moreover it is a cheap fruit available in all seasons, in all places to all the people.

CLIMATE

Papaya requires a warm and humid climate and can be cultivated up to an elevation of about 1000 metres. Though a tropical plant, papaya does well even in warm sub-tropical climate. It grows and fruits well where the summer temperature does not get below 5°C. It is very sensitive to frost, strong winds and water stagnation. It requires annual rainfall of about 1500 mm. Dry climate accompanied with the little rainfall is favorable to add sweetness to the fruit. High humidity is unfavourable as the fruit quality becomes inferior.

SOIL

It can grow in a wide range of soil provided the soil is well drained and aerated. A rich well-drained sandy loam soil is the best for papaya cultivation. It cannot stand high water table and water logging conditions. Like all other fruit trees, it grows well in deep, rich alluvial soil on the banks and deltas of big rivers of India. It can also grow well in the medium black soils of the Deacon-plateau as well as in the literate soils of the Western Ghats. Papaya does not thrive well in calcareous and stony soil since they contain little organic matter. Acidic soils (below pH 5) are not suitable for the successful cultivation of papaya.

VARIETIES

A large number of varieties or types are found in papaya due to its propagation by seed and cross-pollinated nature, resulting in wide variation of varieties. However, true to the type have also been evolved. Description of some of the important varieties is given below.

1. Washington

Washington is one of the oldest variety of papaya in the world. This is a popular variety of western India. The fruit is round to ovate in shape, medium to large in size and the fruit pulp is sweet with desirable flavor. It can be used for planting in home gardens as well as for commercial purpose.

2. Honey Dew

Honey Dew is best suited for cultivation in northern India. Trees are of medium height bearing fruits low on trunk. Fruits are elongated with few seeds, having good taste and flavor. It is a prolific bearer. It is also known as Madhu Bindu due to high percentage of fruit sugar.

3. Coorg Honey Dew

It is a chance seedling of Honey Dew variety. It produces only hermaphrodite and female flowers. NO male plants are found. The fruits are oblong and the flesh is thick with good flavor. It is a dwarf and prolific bearer.

4. CO-1

It is a selection from the progeny of the variety 'Ranchi'. Plants are dwarf with fruits round or oval in shape with golden yellow skin and orange coloured flesh.

5. CO-2

This variety was developed by selection from a local variety at Coimbatore. The plant is medium to tall, fruits are ovate in shape, large in size and skin is yellowish green. it is good table variety and one of the best varieties for papain extraction.

6. CO-3

This is a hybrid between CO-2 and Sunrise Solo. It bears hermaphrodite and female flowers only (gynodioecious). The fruit is medium sized, red in colour and good for table purpose. It has a good keeping quality.

7. CO-4

This is a hybrid between CO-1 and Washington. The plant is dioecious, very dwarf and high yielding. it is suitable for home gardens both as an ornamental tree and for obtaining fruits. Fruit is large, flesh thick yellow with purple tinge, sweet in taste and has good keeping quality.

8. Pusa Delicious

This also a gynodioecious variety. Fruit is medium sized, with deep orange colour flesh and has an excellent flavour.

9. Pusa Majesty

This is also gynodioecius line. Fruits are medium in size and round. It is good for table purpose and has a good keeping quality, less prone to damages during transportation and storage. It is tolerant to viral diseases and is the best papain yielder.

10. Pusa Giant

This is a dioecious variety. The plant is very vigorous and withstands strong wind and storms. Fruits have attractive big size and are borne at 1 m. height from the ground. It can be used for vegetable and canning industry.

11. Pusa Dwarf

Pusa Dwarf is the most suitable variety for high density orcharding, nutrition garden and kitchen garden. It is dioecious variety and is a heavy yielder. The plant is dwarf in stature and bears fruit very low (20-30 cm. above ground level). Fruits are oval in shape and medium size.

12. Pusa Nanha

This variety has been developed through mutation breeding. Plants are very dwarf bearing fruits at 30 cm above ground level. Fruits are oval in shape and medium sized. Suitable for roof gardening. Tolerant to strong winds.

13. Pusa Nahi

Pusa Nahi is an extremely dwarf variety of about 1 m height. It bears fruits at ground level and is suitable for home gardens. Duration-one moth earlier than other varieties.

14. Solo

Solo is a famous variety of Hawai island. Fruits are small, deeply ribbed, pear shaped, flesh yellow orange with good keeping quality. The fruit is of excellent quality weighing about 1 kg. The variety produces hermaphrodite and pistillate flowers (female) in a 2:1 ratio.

15. Plant Papaya - 1,2,3

These are selections relaeased from G.B. Pant Agriculture University. They are now recommended for commerçial cultivation.

PROPAGATION

Papaya is normally propagated by seed. Due to its cross pollinated nature, the purity of varieties has to be maintained carefully. Therefore, pure seeds should be obtained from a reliable source.

1. Selection of seed

Select the seeds from plants which are healthy and vigorous, and bear good quality fruits, having thick flesh with attractive size, colour, and shape. Seeds used for raising the seedlings should be fresh as they lose their viability within 45 days. The seeds should be rubbed with wood ash and dried before storage. They can be stored for months retaining their viability, if they are kept in clean and air-tight bottles. Storage of seeds at 10°C is also effective for maintaining seed viability.

2. Preparation of nursery bed

The site selected for seed bed is well dug or ploughed and kept as such for a week or two. The seed bed should be well raised (about 15 cm. above ground level) for effective drainage and of 2 m X 1 m size. Application of two baskets of silt and one basket each of leaf-mould and farmyard manure (FYM), spread equally on the top soil encourages good growth of seedlings is from middle of June to the end of October. Treat the seeds with either Agrosan G.N. or Thiram @ of 1 g/250 g of seeds. The treated seeds are sown 2-4 cm. deep and 5 cm. apart, in rows 15 cm. apart. The seedbed is immediately watered after sowing of seed. The watering should be given daily except during rains. About 250 g. seeds are sufficient to raise seedlings for one hectare. Seeds start germinating within 15-20 days.

3. Aftercare and transplanting of seedlings

Seedlings are ready for transplanting in the main field when they are about 60 days old or have attained a height of 15-20 cm. To prevent the damping-off of seedlings after emergence, drenching the nursery bed with 0.2% Captan (200 g. in 100 ltrs. of water) carried out. This practice can be repeated after 4 days, if necessary.

4. Raising the seedlings in polythene bags

Papaya seedlings are very delicate and care is needed in digging them out and transplanting them. Seedlings raised in polythene bags can stand transplanting better than those raised in seed beds. Perforated polythene bags (20 X 15 cm. size with 150 gauge thickness) can be used as containers. Four to five seeds are sown in each bags filled with a mixture of sieved soil, FYM and sand in equal proportion. After germination, only one seedling is retained. They should be treated with Captan 0.2% after their emergence in polythene bags and can be transplanted into the pits by just removing the lower polythene layer.

5. Land preparation for planting

The site selected for planting the seedlings should be well prepared through repeated ploughing and harrowing and finally levelled pits of 1/2 X 1/2 X 1/2 m are dug at 1.8 m. distance. The pits are exposed to the sun and filled back with top soil and two of three baskets of farmyard manure @ 36-45 kg. and bonemeal @ 1.36 kg per pit. The filled up pits are marked by small pegs and left over till the planting season.

6. Planting

The best season for planting papaya is the beginning of monsoon. However, planting can be done any time from June to November. To obtain high proportion of female trees, 3 seedlings are planted in each pit, 25 cm. apart in a triangular fashion. Seedlings should be planted with an earth ball around roots and leaves cut back. When plants flower, the sex can be identified leaving the healthy appearing female in the pit. In deoecious varieties such as CO-1 or CO-2, a ratio of one male to every 10 female trees, well distributed in the field, should be retained for good pollination. for gynodioecious varieties, where no male plants are found, eg. Coorg Honey Dew, Solo, CO-3, Pusa Delicious and Pusa Majesty, only one seedling is planted per pit, since the chances of getting a male tree is too obscure and only hermaphrodite trees serve as pollen source. Planting should be done in the evening or in a cloudy day and the field should be watered regularly atleast twice a day until the seedlings are well established. They should be protected from excessive sunlight and heat by shading.

FERTILIZER APPLICATION

Papaya is a heavy feeder fruit crop. In order to maintain a continuous supply of fruits, it is important to provide it with an adequate amount of fertilizers at frequent intervals. It is also necessary to have a balanced C/N (Carbon:nitrogen) ratio for proper fruiting. The following dose of manures and fertilizers per plant has been recommended to obtain the maximum fruit yield.

1. **Organic manures (basal dose)**

   (a) Compost-20 kg.
   (b) Cake-1 kg,
   (c) Sterrameal or rallies meal 1 kg.

2. **Inorganic fertilizers (top dressing)**

   (a) Nitrogen-200-250 kg,
   (b) Phosphorus-200-25- g,
   (c) Potassium 250-500 g.

This dose makes a good balance between vegetative growth and fruiting. The above fertilizer dose should be applied in six split applications, once in tow months commencing from the second month of planting. The fertilizer should be put in the irrigation ring and mixed thoroughly with the soil. Application of excess nitrogen, which is a common practice among the farmers should be avoided as it increased vegetative growth and leads to poor fruiting.

IRRIGATION

Papaya responds well to better water management by rapid development of fruit and supply of fruits regularly. Regular irrigation helps in fruit development and induces the tree to bear a number of fruits with larger size. Irrigation may be given once in 8-10 days in winter and 6 days in summer. Plants should be irrigated soon after manuring. However, excessive water leads to water-logging conditions, which are very harmful for the plants. The ring system of irrigation is better than the bed or basin system as it prevents collar rot disease. Trenches may be dug between plant rows during monsoon to avoid water stagnation in the field.

THINNING OF FRUITS

Thinning of fruits becomes essential in papaya when several fruits set in a cluster instead of a single fruit at each node. The operation is performed immediately after fruit set and involves thinning or removal of the fruit clusters, leaving not more than two fruits at each node. This prevents the damages of fruits due to over-crowding and their competition for nutrients and fruit drop.

PLANT PROTECTION MEASURES

Plant protection includes the disease control, pest control, weed control and protection from unfavourable environmental conditions.

A. Disease control

Among the diseases, the fungal diseases and the viral diseases are prevalent.

1. Fungal diseases

Some of the important fungal diseases are discussed here.

a. Collar rot or stem rot

This is a serious disease that occurs in the nursery as well as main field. Its casual organism is *Pythium aphanidermatum*.

Symptoms:

Water soaked lesions appear on the bark just above the ground level. Simultaneouly the terminal leaves turn yellow, and finally drop down. Fruits also shrivel and drop off. Roots deteriorate and decay. Stem is girdled at the base.

Control

i. Use well drained field for papaya plantation.
ii. Badly affected plant should be uprooted and burnt.
iii. Waterlogging should be avoided.
iv. Spraying of 1% Bordeaux mixture or any copper oxychloride @ 2 g. per litre of water will check further spread of the disease.

b. Root rot

Its casual organism is *Phytophthora palmivora*. However, this disease of the young seedings in the nursery is caused by *Rhizoctonia solani* and *Fusarium spp*. The disease occurs in damp climate of heavy rainfall area where water stagnates in the subsoil.

Symptoms

The top roots become rotten due to stagnation of water in the subsoil and uptake of nutrients by the fibrous roots is interrupted, resulting in very poor fruiting or no fruiting at all.

Control: In the nursery the disease can be controlled by:

i. seed treatment with fungicides like Captan and Ceresan;
ii. sterilization of nursery beds by burning with dried leaves:
iii. spraying of 40% formaldehyde two weeks before sowing; and
iv. application of 100 g. $CuSO_4$ and 1 kg lime along with organic manures in the pits as a basal dose.

c. Powdery mildew

Symptoms

White powdery growth appears on both the surfaces of leaves and white stranded patches appear on the fruits. Young infected leaves dry up prematurely and drop down, which results in severe yield reduction. Disease ia favoured by high humidity, moderate temperature and cloudy weather and is a serious disease in south India.

Control

Spraying Sulfex (0.2%) or Bavistin (0.1%) is effective.

d. Anthracnose

Symptoms

The disease affects both the leaves and the fruits. In the initial stage, fruits show spots which first appear as brown superficial discolouration of the skin. Later on, these spots turn into circular, slightly sunken areas. Gradually the lesions join together and sparse mycelial growth often appears on the margins of such spots. Infection at early stage of fruit growth results in mummification and deformation. Necrotic spots are produced on leaves and stems. The diseases is favoured by wet weather conditions.

Control

Field spraying of Bavistin or Topsin-M (0.1%) at 20 days intervals or Dithane M-45 or Daconil (0.2%) at 10 days interval are recommended. Spraying with Bordeaux mixture (5:5:50) or Blitox (0.2%) is also effective in checking the disease.

2. Viral diseases

Among the viral disease, papaya mosaic and papaya leaf curl diseases are common.

a. Papaya mosaic

This disease is of common occurrence in almost all parts of India. The affected plants become stunted in growth, show yellow mottling and distortion of leaves. Leaf petioles bend down and tendril like structures are formed from the leaves. All these development ultimately lead to the death of the plant. Diseased plants yield little or no crop. Several species of aphids act as vector in transmitting the disease.

Control

1. Thoroughly screen the nursery bed for the infected seedlings and rogue

them carefully so that others are not affected.

ii. Transplant only healthy seedlings.

iii. Remove the diseased plants in the mainfield.

iv. Spray 1% groundnut oil to inhibit the vector transmission.

b. Papaya leaf curl

Its causal organism is tobacco leaf curl virus. The leaves are severely affected and show symptoms of curling, crinkling and distortion of leaves accompanied by vein clearing and reduction in leaf size. The affected plants either do not flower or bear a few fruits only. The disease is transmitted through grafting and by white fly (*Bemisea tabaci*). In advanced stages, defoliation occurs and plant growth is arrested.

Control

i. Uproot and destroy the infected plants at the early stage of disease development.

ii. Collateral hosts of the virus such as tomato, tobacco and zinnia should not be grown in the vicinity of papaya plantation.

iii. Spraying with 0.1% Malathion or Metasystox at an interval of 10 to 12 days will control the insect vector.

B. Pest control

The major pests of papaya includes mites, aphids and white-flies. However, they are occasionally attached and damaged by grasshopper, fruit flies, mealybugs, scales, stem borer, leaf eating beetles and termites.

1. Mite

Mite is a serious pest of papaya in India. These mites suck the sap of the leaves and yellowish spots appear on the dorsal sides of the infested leaves which finally dry up and fall off prematurely.

Control

a. Spread of the mites can be prevented by removing the infested leaves and burying them.

b. Spray the plants with 0.4% Dicofol or 0.06% Dimethoate. If needed, repeat the spray once after 15 days.

2. Aphids

Aphids are known to transmit virus. They feed on leaves and suck the plant sap. Necrotic spots appear on the leaves, which later on turn into blistered patches of green tissues.

Control

a. Weeds should be removed which may act as an additional hosts.
b. Preventive spray of 0.03% Dimethoate or 0.04% Monocrotophos should be carried out in papaya plantation.

3. White flies

White flies are a common pest of papaya and are destructive/active during dry season. They suck the cell sap and are seen clustering between the veins on the ventral surface of the leaves. The leaves become yellowish, wrinkle and curl downwards. They also act as vectors in transmitting the virus.

Control

Preventive spray of 0.03% Dimethoate or 0.025% Methyl demeton or 0.04% Monocrotophos should be carried out.

4. Nematodes

The root knot nematode and reniform nematode cause severe damage to papaya.

Control

In the nursery they can be controlled by spraying granular insecticides (eg. Forate, Carbofuron) @ 0.6 g. per nursery polybag. In the main field, 25 g. of Furadan may be applied per plant.

C. Weed control

The weeds grow luxuriantly in the papaya orchard and exhaust most of the nutrients supplied. They also complete for light, air and water resulting in poor fruiting of papaya. These weeds can be controlled by two hand digging, one in the beginning of rainy season and other in January-February every year.

PROBLEMS OF UNFAVOURABLE CLIMATIC CONDITIONS

Papaya is very sensitive to frost and low temperature which restricts its cultivation in northern India. Under high humidity and rainfall, the fruit quality is said to be inferior and the plant becomes susceptible to collar rot disease. Temperature below 10°C retards the process of maturity and ripening of fruits and to a certain extent the growth and setting of fruits.

FLOWERING AND FRUITING

The papaya starts flowering and fruiting after about 6 months under normal conditions. It produces staminate (male), pistillate (female) and hermaphrodite flowers. Once the plant flowers, it is easy to distinguish the male, female and hermaphrodite flowers by their size, colour, flower stalk etc. Male flowers are small having 1 to 1.3 m. long stalk which hang out from the trunk, while female flowers are large, yellow in colour and about 2.5 cm. long borne singly or in a group of three in the leaf axils close to the trunk. The hermaphrodite flowers are similar to female flowers. They have a tubular base, cream or yellow in colour and are 3.8-4.4 cm. long. The fruits are borne on the trunk at the base of the leaves. For effective pollination, retaining about ten male plants for a group of about hundred female plants and bee keeping helps in good fruit setting.

MATURITY

The papaya tree matures and produces its first fruit in 10 to 14 months after transplanting. In north India, fruits mature throughout the spring and the summer, while in hills with cooler climate, fruits are available only from February-May and very little or no fruits mature in cold weather. In the milder climate like that of south India, fruits mature throughout the year mostly from July-February. Dry climate at the time of ripening is preferable. To avoid damage of fruits by the birds during ripening, it is better to cover the fruits with cloth or paper.

HARVESTING AND YIELD

Mature fruits which are still hard and green but turning yellow should be harvested. When the latex of the fruit becomes, watery, the fruit is considered ready for harvesting. The harvested fruits are wrapped in papers or in some other wrapping material for a few days to enhance the ripening of papaya fruits. The harvesting period extends over a period of 4-5 months. Fruits allowed to ripe on the tree have better fruit quality, but it is generally avoided to prevent the damage caused by birds. Fruits are harvested manually by hand by giving a careful twist, taking care of bruising of splitting of skin.

High yield is obtained in the first two years which gradually declines from the third year. The number of fruits harvested per tree in a year varies from 24 to 30, depending on soil, climate and cultural practices.

STORAGE AND RIPENING

Papaya being a highly perishable fruit cannot be store under room temperature. However, a temperature of about 20°C has been found optimum for both ripening and satisfactory storage. The post-harvest diseases of papaya are effectively controlled upto 14 days, when store at a temperature of 10°C and treated with Apendazole applied in wax formulation. The most common storage disease of papaya fruits caused by the fungus *Colletotrichum gloeosporioides* can be controlled by immersing the fruits in hot water (50°C) for 20 minutes.

Papaya can be artificially ripened by using growth regulators such as Ethephon 2000 ppm solution having few pellets of sodium hydroxide. This treatment will ripen the fruits within 24 hours.

Marketing

For local consumption, the harvested fruits can be stored in a single layer of straw and when turned yellow they can be sent to the market. For distant markets, the fruits should be packed in single layers in strong bamboo baskets and wooden crates, with straw paddings to avoid bruising during transporta

Intercrops

In the first year of planting, sufficient space is available in between two rows of papaya plantation, in which intercrops can be grown successfully. The crops selected should have no adverse effect on papaya. Keeping this in view, short duration vegetable crops such as cabbage, cauliflower, onion, chillies, radish, etc. should be grown. These crops will keep down the growth of weeds and give an extra income to the growers. The crops likely to be attacked by virus (eg., tomato, brinjal and okra) should not be grown as intercrops. Leguminous crops of low height like gram, green gram and black gram should be preferred which not only control the weeds but add nitrogen to the soil.

For obtaining a good crop of papaya, a suitable crop rotation is essential. Growing the same crop year after year, depletes the soil of some essential macro and micro nutrients, besides increasing the incidence of pests and diseases resulting in poor production of fruits. Intercropping leguminous crops after non-leguminous crops, and shallow rooted ones after deep rooted crops reduces this problem. A few suitable crop rotations are:

1. Papaya (October-May), maize (June-September), wheat (November-April), pigeon pea (June-April) and maize (June-September).
2. Maize (June-September), papaya (October-May), green manure crop (June-September), and wheat (November-April).
3. Sugarcane (February-February), green gram (March-June), maize (June-September), papaya (October-May), green manure crop (June-September) and potato (November-February)

USES

The ripe fresh fruits of papaya re eaten throughout the tropics. Papaya fruits are also used for preparation of jam, jelly, soft drinks, ice cream flavouring, pickles, crystallised fruits and are canned in syrup. The seeds are also used for their medicinal value. Unripe fruits are used as vegetables for cooking. Some other industrial and medicinal properties of papaya are described below.

1. Industrial importance

a. Several processed products such as papaya jam, jelly, candies, pickles, soft-drinks are slowly gaining economic importance in the market.

b. Papain, a dried powder obtained from the milky latex of immature papaya fruits is of great commercial significance. It is used in meat industry as tenderizer.

c. Papain is also used in preparation of chewing gum and cosmetics.

d. In textile industry for reducing shrinkage of certain types of wool and for degumming natural silk, papain is effectively used.

e. In beer industry for clarifying beer, papain is one of the best clarifying agents.

f. In tanning industry, papain is used for batting hides.

2. Medicinal value

a. Rich source of Vitamin A and Vitamin C.

b. Rich in enzyme papain, which helps in the digestion of proteins, thus being useful in pharmacy for preparing digestive medicines.

c. Papain (alkaloid obtained from the milky latex of papaya) is an effective heart stimulant and diuretic.

d. It is used to remove skin blemishes and scars.

e. Papain is also beneficial for the treatment of stomach ulcers, diptheria and even cancer.

f. The ripe fruit and seed have medicinal properties against disorders of live, spleen and digestive tract.

The composition and food value of ripe papaya fruits are given in table.

Composition and Fruit Value of Papaya Fruit

Sl.No.	Components	Amount
1.	Moisture	89.6%
2.	Protein	0.5%
3.	Fat	0.1%
4.	Carbohydrate	9.5%
5.	Calcium	0.01%
6.	Phosphorus	0.01%
7.	Vitamin A	2020 I.U./100 g.
8.	Vitamin B_1	0.04 mg./100 g.
9.	Vitamin C	40 mg/100 g.
10.	Micotinic acid	0.2 mg/100 g.
11.	Riboflavin	250 mg/100 g.

EXTRACTION OF PAPAIN

Papain, an alkaloid obtained from the milky latex of immature fruits of papaya is a very useful product and is a very useful product and is of great commercial significance. For papain extraction, the milky latex from the three-fourth mature fruits (70 to 90 days fruit set) are selected and lanced with an ordinary razor blade to a depth of 2-3 mm. The cuts are given length wise on the fruit 3 cm. apart, in the morning. The latex is collected in aluminium trays fixed to the trunk of the tree. Three days. For large scale production, drying can be done artifically at a temperature of 50 to 55°C. The dried latex is powdered and packed in polythene bags. A small quantity of potassium metabisulphite (350 ppm) should also be added to the liquid latex to enhance the storage life of papain. Nearly 200 to 250 kg of papain can be obtained from one hectare of papaya plantation in the first year. The yield reduces in the subsequent years.

ECONOMICS OF CULTIVATION

Papaya ia s profitable crop and provides and income next to bananas. It can be grown for plant material (seed-lings), fruits, seed and for papain extraction. Generally, a farmer can get Rs. 35,000 to 40,000 from one hectare of papaya plantation for fruits.

PLANT ECONOMICS OF PAPAYA CULTIVATION & PAPAIN MANUFACTURING

Rated Plant capacity = 75000.00 KG/annum PAPAIN FROM PAPAYA

LAND & BUILDING

Land area required 40 acres	Rs.	46,00,000.00

PLANT & MACHINERY

Tractor with all the accessories viz. DiscHaroow, Cultivator,Trailor, Plough etc.,Tube well with pumpset and overhead tank Slicing and Mincing machine,Aluminium/Wooden Trays,Scrapper, Sieving machine,Vacuum Shelfdries Grinder (Powdering machine) Stainless Steel Collecting tank Mixing tank with agitator & motor,Weighing machine,Laboratory testing,equipment,Automatic filling & sealing unit

TOTAL	**Rs.**	**9,00,000.00**

FIXED ASSETS

1. LAND & BUILDING	Rs.	46,00,000.00
2. PLANT & MACHINERY	Rs.	9,00,000.00
3. OTHER FIXED ASSETS	Rs.	3,13,000.00
TOTAL	**Rs.**	**58,13,000.00**

RAW MATERIALS

Papaya Seeds,Fertilizer
Preservatives Potassium
metabi- sulphite,Alcohol
Mic Chemical Pesticides

Packaging material

TOTAL	**Rs.**	**1,16,750.00**

TOTAL WORKING CAPITAL/MONTH

1. RAW MATERIAL	Rs.	1,16,750.00
2. SALARY & WAGES	Rs.	60,000.00
3. UTILITIES & OVERHEADS	Rs.	1,01,700.00
TOTAL	**Rs.**	**2,78,450.00**

COST OF PROJECT

TOTAL FIXED CAPITAL	Rs.	58,13,000.00
MARGIN MONEY	Rs.	2,08,837.50
TOTAL	**Rs.**	**60,21,837.50**

TOTAL CAPITAL INVESTMENT

TOTAL FIXED CAPITAL	Rs.	58,13,000.00
TOTAL WORKING CAPITAL FOR 3 MONTHS	Rs.	8,35,350.00
TOTAL	**Rs.**	**66,48,350.00**

TURN OVER/ANNUM

By sale of Papain 75000 kg. Rs. 1,08,75,000.00

PROFIT = RECEIPTS - COST OF PRODUCTION = 56,56,963.00

PROFIT SALES RATIO = Profit / Sales x 100 = 52.02 %

RATE OF RETURN = Operating profit / T.C.I x 100 = 85.09 %

BREAK EVEN POINT (B.E.P) = 31.92 %

PLANT ECONOMICS
PAPAYA CULTIVATION

Rated Plant capacity = 501.00 TON/annum

PAPAYA CULTIVATION (AVERAGE)

LAND & BUILDING

Land required 10 Acres	Rs.	10,00,000.00

PLANT & MACHINERY

Tractor,Cultivator,.Disc Harry ,
Disc Plough,Trailor,Shovel machine
Pump with motr,Seed & Fertilizer

TOTAL	**Rs.**	**3,15,500.00**

FIXED CAPITAL

1. LAND & BUILDING	Rs.	10,00,000.00
2. PLANT & MACHINERY	Rs.	3,15,500.00
3. OTHER FIXED ASSETS	Rs.	45,000.00
TOTAL	**Rs.**	**13,60,500.00**

RAW MATERIALS

Papaya seeds, Fertilizers	**Rs.**	**16,040.00**

TOTAL WORKING CAPITAL/ANNUM

1. RAW MATERIAL	Rs.	16,040.00
2. SALARY & WAGES	Rs.	7,05,000.00
3. UTILITIES & OVERHEADS	Rs.	41,000.00
TOTAL	**Rs.**	**7,62,040.00**

COST OF PROJECT

TOTAL FIXED CAPITAL	Rs.	13,60,500.00
MARGIN MONEY	Rs.	47,627.50
TOTAL	**Rs.**	**14,08,127.50**

TOTAL CAPITAL INVESTMENT

TOTAL FIXED CAPITAL	Rs.	13,60,500.00
TOTAL WORKING CAPITAL FOR 3 MONTHS	Rs.	1,90,510.00
TOTAL	**Rs.**	**15,51,010.00**

TURN OVER/ANNUM

By sale of 490 tons. Fruits Rs. 19,60,000.00

PROFIT = RECEIPTS - COST OF PRODUCTION = 7,33,862.80

PROFIT SALES RATIO = Profit / Sales x 100 = 37.44 %

RATE OF RETURN = Operating profit / T.C.I x 100 = 47.32 %

BREAK EVEN POINT (B.E.P) = 50.96 %

Chapter - 12

Piggery Farming

Terms Used in Pig Production

The knowledge of different terms used in pig production is important in order to describe the animals more clearly and easily. Certain general terms are commonly used when reference is made to describe animals of different ages, sexes, colour and types in the production and managemental practices. Important common terms which are widely used in connection with the breeding, feeding, housing and health of pigs are given below:

Pig:

Swine that are up to four months old or until they weigh about 60 kgs.

Hog:

Swine that are more than 60 kg in weight or more than four months old.

Gilt:

A female swine that has not produced a litter of piglings but is being prepared for breeding.

Boar:

Male swine that is used for breeding.

Sow:

The female swine that has produced a litter of piglings.

Boar Pig:

Young male pig designated to be the boar.

Sow Pig:

Young male pig designated to be the sow.

Litter:

A batch of piglings brought forth at the same time by a sow. It also means to give birth to a groupof piglings.

Farrowing:

Act of giving birth to piglets or piglings by a sow.

Pig lings:

Small swine up to the age of two months or 15,10,20 kg in weight.

Pre-starter:

Those piglings that are being introduced to feed. They are 7 to 21 days old and weight 2-5 kg.

Starter:

Those piglings that have started to eat and are 21-35 days old. They should be weighing 5 to 11 kg.

Pre-weaner:

Those piglings that are within 35-56 days old and weight 11 to 23 kg.

Weaner:

Piglings which are ready to be weaned or already weaned. They are two months old.

Grower or feeder:

Pigs that are fed abundantly and are in fast growing stage. They are 205 months old.

Finisher:

Swine which is five months old or that who has attained 60 kg weight and is being feed specially to fatten for marketing.

Fattener:

See finisher.

Barrow:

A male swine that is castrated before reaching sexual maturity.

Stage:

A male swine that is castrated after reaching sexual maturity.

Runt:

The smallest piglet of a litter.

Prolific sow:

Ability of a sow to produce and raise large litter size of healthy pigs.

Pork:

Flesh of swine which is unprocessed.

Hard:

The fat of swine.

Bacon:

Salted or smoked meat from upper part of swine leg.

Sausage:

Chopped up meat, fat, etc. of swine which is flavoured and stuffed into tube to skin or part of it.

CONSTRAINT OF PIG RAISING

***The following constraints are found in pig raising*:**

1. Consumption of pork is forbidden by certain religions and pig produc tion is not encouraged. Thus, it is not an universely accepted food.
2. Swine are easily susceptible to numerous diseases and parasites.
3. Since pigs have a single stomach and require only a small space, they are usually raised on a backyard scale in suburban communities.
4. One of the major disadvantages of raising hogs is the high expense of hog-tight fence.
5. As pigs consume large quantities of grain and are efficient converters of maize of sorghum into edible meat, there results a competition with people for foodgrains.

SYSTEMS OF PIG HOUSING

Depending on the economic resources, pig housing systems can be divided into three main groups:

(i) Open air system
(ii) Indoor system

(iii) Combination system.

The different categories of pigs need separate rooms in the same piggery and these are mentioned below.

1. *Breeding boars (on individual basis)*
2. *Pregnant sows (in batches)*
3. *Littering and lactating sows (each one)*
4. *Dry sows (and gilt selected for breeding in batches)*
5. *Growers in batches, and*
6. *Sick pigs (individual or group)*

There may be a number of pigs in each category. One might want to keep all the categories of pigs with optimum number in each category. While another may choose to maintain only the growers and still some may prefer to breed and sell the piglings only. The choice also depends on the availability of market.

In planning the housing, one has to fit these categories and number of pigs into a selected system. A detailed description of the common systems of pig housing given here will help one to select the system suited to his purpose.

(1) Open air system

Basically, open air means without a roof.

This is further divided into two types.

(i) **Permanently let loose**

In this system the pigs are left to roam around freely and fend forthemselves. Besides, they may be fed with household wastes. They may or may not be provided with a suitable night shelter during rainy and cold season.

(ii) **Enclosed open air**

When there are restrictions in letting loose the animals freely, theymay be kept in enclosed open air. Under this system pigs have to be handled almost entirely. Enclosed open air can be of two kinds namely permanently enclosed and rotationally enclosed.

a. Permanently enclosed

In this type of housing, the pigs are kept in a permanently enclosed area. The enclosure can be made of any king of fencing or wall provided with a door. A suitable night shelter can be provided to protect the pigs from rain and cold.

b. Rotationally enclosed

In this type of housing, the pigs are enclosed in different enclosures one after the other. This can be done in two ways: fixed fencing rotation and removable fencing rotation.

i. Fixed fencing rotation

A number of enclosed areas are maintained in this type of open air enclosure by fixed fencing or walls. The pigs are kept in each of these enclosures for a period of time and later they are shifted to the adjacent enclosures one offer the other and again brought back to the first one.

ii. Removable fencing

In this type, the fencing is made in segments which can be removed and refitted in another place to provide the necessary enclosed open air system.

iii. Advantages

1. Open air system is the cheapest method of raising pigs in terms of investment.
2. In the permanently let loose method, the only investment is on the makeshift night shelter.
3. Daily cleaning is not required.
4. Pigs get plenty of sunshine and exercise.

iv. Disadvantages

1. Unless given through feeding, the pigs will not get properly fed in any of the types of open air system.
2. Controlled breeding is not possible in the permanently let loose system. It may be possible in fixed enclosures if the boars and sows

are kept in separate enclosures.

3. The pigs will be exposed to insanitary conditions and diseases causing high mortality.
4. They will be exposed to adverse weather conditions and the growth rate will be less.
5. The pregnant and lactating sows and breeding boars will not get sufficient care which they need.
6. Large areas are required for enclosed open air system.
7. In the permanently let loose system the pigs are more of scavengers which is abominable.
8. In open air system pigs are more prone to the attack of internal and external parasites.
9. Good breeds of pigs cannot be maintained in this system.

2. Indoor system

As the term indicates, in indoor system the pigs are kept in well built and completely roofed system and they are entirely fed by hand. all other operations such as breeding, littering, weaning, growing, fattening, earning, treatment for sickness, cleaning, watering, etc are done inside the house. Each category of pigs are provided with separate rooms in the indoor system.

(i) Advantages

1. In indoor system every pig can be given care according to its own need.
2. Proper controlled breeding can be done to improved the herd.
3. Optimum sanitation can be maintained.
4. The diseases and parasites can be given to each animal according to its needs.
5. Properly balanced feed can be given to each animal according to its needs.
6. Various management practices can be done easily.
7. The animals can be protected from adverse climatic and environmental extremes like rain, cold and heat.
8. For commercial growing and breeding indoor system is suitable.

(ii) Disadvantages

1. Initially more capital is required to set the swine farm.
2. For the management of indoor system, scientific knowledge is required.
3. The house should be built carefully taking intoconsideration require ments of various categories of pigs.There should be proper arrange ments for drainage, light,ventilation, etc.
4. Indoor system is more labour intensive.

3. Combination system

As the term indicates, in this system the pigs will be kept partially indoor and partially in enclosed open air.

There will be some roofed area for each category of pigs. The open air area in combination system may be of two kinds i.e. common open air space and individual open air space.

(i) Common open air space

In this, open air space of the piggery is used commonly by all pigs together or in rotation. The control the pigs coming into the open space, doors are fitted between the roofed area and open space.

(ii) Individual open air space

In this type, each roofed room will have one open air space attached to it so that feeding, exercising and dunging are done in this area.

(iii) Advantages

1. It has all the advantages of indoor system.
2. In combination system, the roofed area is small and, therefore, it is cheaper than indoor system.
3. The pigs get enough sunlight and fresh air.
4. They get more area for exercising.

(iv) Disadvantages

All the disadvantages of indoor system will be present in the combination system.

CONSTRUCTION DETAILS

Piggery meant for rearing pigs on a permanent basis should be built strong and durable. Certain constructional details specific to piggery are described here:

1. Floor

The snout of a pig is said to be harder than a crowbar. It can dig up even the hardest surfaces and create pot holes. Therefore, the floor or the piggery should be made hard, unbreakable and rough. Materials such as reinforced concrete, stone slabs or hard cement files fixed with cement are suitable materials for constructing the floor of the piggery. A concrete floor laid on a hard and thick foundation with rough surface is the best. The floor should have proper slope from all sides towards the drainage.

2. Feeders and waterers

Pigs saliva is very corrosive and the feeders and waterers get easily pitted and holed. Under such situation hygienic feeding is impossible. To avoid the problem care should be taken while constructing the feeders and waterers. Reinforced concrete with a mixture of 1:1.5:3 Cement, sand and stone chips respectively would be the best material for a permanent feeders. This is topped with a thick coating of cement which is given a smooth and fine finish. There should be separate drainage facility from each feeders and waterers to outside. The corners of the feeders and waterers are made round and smooth. Stone, wood, brick and cement are other types of materials that can be used for the construction of feeders and waterers.

3. Walls

Walls for permanently built piggery may be made of brick and stone with cement and should be of nine inch thickness. The walls should be plastered and coated with fine cement upto a height of 4-5 ft. The corners and the place where the wall join the floor should be made smooth and round. The walls should be 4-5 ft. high from the floor. Rest of the portion, upto the roof could be made honeycomb like brick works or wire mesh.

4. Roof

The roof should be sufficiently high (about 10-12 ft.) to have enough air volume. The roof may be constructed conical or flat. The roof can be supported by pillars raised on walls. The following points should be kept in mind.

a. The roof should be all weather proof.

b. The roofing material should be such that it should not make the rooms too hot or too cold inside.

c. The roof should be higher in hot/warmer areas to provide larger air space in the pig house. There should be a minimum height of 8-10 ft. for the roof from the floor.

5. Doors

The doors should be built very strong and durable. any material may be used for the door. However, the best material for the door. However, the best material for the door is iron. Metal sheets fixed on an iron frame will serve the purpose. The door should be made strong and fitted close to the floor so that the pigs may not lift it up by putting the snout under it. The width of the door should be at least 3-4 ft.

6. Wallowing tank

In hot areas it is advisable to provide a wallowing tank in each room. It could be fitted best in the open space of combination system. On an average, a tank of 8 X 6 X 1 ft. would be sufficient. The size may be increased depending on the number of pigs in a room. The depth of the tank on one side could be upto 2 ft. and gradually decreasing towards the other side upto a depth of four inches. There should be an underground drainage to drain out the wallowing tank whenever needed.

7. Feeding passage

The feeders can be constructed in a row on one side of the feeding space of each room. All the room of the piggery can be constructed in such a way that the feeders come in one line. A feeding passage of about 3-4 ft. will be very convenient to move with feed stuff and feed to each pig. Feeding can be done over the half wall between feeders and the feeding passage or through the openings made on the half wall towards each feeder. For easy and convenient feeding, opening in the wall will be more suitable. These should be taken care of at the time of construction. Instead of a wall in between the feeders and feeding passage, strong wire mesh or iron frame can be fixed leaving sufficient space at the bottom for putting feed into each feeder. Wire or iron frame provides a good view of all the pigs in all the room in action while they are eating.

8. Cleaning passage

Similar to the feeding passage by the side of feeders, a cleaning passage on the opposite side of each room is very necessary. By the side of the cleaning passage and close to the outer wall the main drainage into which each room is drained out through a hole in the wall the main drainage into which each room is drained out through a hole in the wall. the door of each room opens to the cleaning passage. Moving on this passage one enters each room, remove dung and other wastes, wash and sweep, clean and drain out into the main drainage from each room. The same passage can be used to transfer pigs from one room to another for breeding, littering, weaning, etc.

9. Drainages

The drainages from each room and the main drainage should be constructed with sufficient slope (generally 1:100). The surface of these drainages should be made slopy and smooth so that cleaning becomes easy.

10. Sewage tank

In a very big piggery, a large quantity of sewage may be drained. Under such situation, it is highly advisable to have a separate collection tank for sewage collection. The sewage can be used for cultivating vegetables or other crops for human and animal consumption. Small quantities of sewage can be mixed with compost.

11. Compost pits

As already mentioned two pits are required side by side. They can be built with brick or stone with a mixture of cement and sand in 1:4 proportion No. plastering is required on the sides or on the floor at the bottom. If bricks are used, a coating of thick cement solution is recommended to preserve the brick from weathering.

The pits can be made downward or upward or half down and half up. Building upward is the best and cheap method. It is also very convenient for taking out the decomposed manure after 5-6 months. Constructing downward involves digging out the soil and building up of the sides with bricks or stones. Further, also much labour is required to take out the manure. Downward pits may lead to water stagnation.

In an upward constructed compost pits, one of the width side walls should be built with bricks or well cut stone blocks without cement so that this wall can be dismantled while taking out the decomposed manure and refit again. All the other side walls of the pits should be made permanent.

12. Room arrangement

The three section, namely eating space, resting space and dunging can be arranged in the following order.

1. The three sections are made together under the roof (indoor system).
2. Resting place under roof and eating and dunging space in the open air (combination system in less rainfall areas).
3. Resting place and eating place under the roof and dunging in the open air (combination system in more than average rainfall area).
4. Partitions:
   (a) no partitions between sections,
   (b) partitions between sections
   (c) partition separates dunging space from the other two
   (d) partition separates resting space from the other two.

14. Surroundings

The surroundings of the piggery should be maintained clean and weed free. There should be facilities for proper drainages from the surroundings of the piggery. Clean and dry surroundings reduce the occurrence of diseases and parasites.

CATEGORY-WISE HOUSING REQUIREMENTS

From the description of piggery housing systems and the general principles of construction details we come to the actual minimum requirement of space for each category of pigs. The table is a summary of the minimum space requirements in indoor system.

Table-1:

Minimum space requirements in indoor system (length & width, ft).

Category	Eating space	Resting space	Exercising and dunging space
Breeding boar (each one)	8'X6'	8'X6'	8'X8'
Littering	8'X6'	8'X6'	8'X8'
Lactating sows	8'X6'	8'X6'	8'X6'
Growers (batches eight)	13'X6'	13'X6'	13'X8'
Pregnant sows (batches of six)	10'X6'	10X6'	10'X8'
Young boars not yet bred (four)	8'X6'	8'X6'	8'X8'
Gilts (batches of six)	10'X6'	10'X6'	10'X8'
Sick and segregated	6'X6'	6'X6'	6'X8'
Store & office	20'X6'		
Wallowing tank	20'X8'		

Based on the dimensions given in the table a model plan for a piggery of one room each per category is given in Fig.

These are the requirements for large size pigs, for individuals and batches of optimum number. These specifications can be reduced if the pigs are of smaller size and one wants to keep lesser number in batches. It is highly recommended that more pigs than the number of feeders should not be kept in a single room.

In the breeding boar room, there should be two feeders and one waterer. Additional feeder is required for the sow introduced for breeding. In the lactating room one feeder for the mother pig and 10-12 smaller feeders for piglings and one waterer should be constructed. In the resting place or litering room there should be a guard railing fixed about 6" away from the wall and 6" above the floor. The guard rail should be made of steel pipes of 3" diameter or equally strong material. This is to protect the piglings from being crushed by the mother when they are born. In the littering box it is advisable to have a creep space of 2'X2'X2' to keep the piglings secure and to feed them with special feed. The creep space should have holes 6"X6" size to allow the piglings to come inside and to go out. Creep space may be constructed in any of the three sections provided it is protected from heat, sun, rain, cold etc. In every cold places heating arrangements similar to brooders for chicks are necessary for saving piglings. Similarly, for the grown up pigs straw or wooden plank or crates bedding should be provided. Wooden pannelling may also be provided if necessary.

Standard Grower Rations for Pigs

Ingredients	Parts	
	I	II
Ground Yellow maize	30	60
Wheat bran	20	10
Rice polish	20	—
Ground nut cake	20	10
Fish meal	8	8
Mineral mixture	2	2
Til oil cake	—	10
Total	100	100

Composition of Weaners and Growers Ratio

Ingredients	Growers ration (2-6 months age)	
	I	II
Maize	25	15
Wheat	—	—
Barley	—	—
Rice bran	50	36
Wheat bran	—	20
Molasses	—	5
Groundnut cake	19	18
Fish meal	4	4
Mineral mixture	2	2
Vitamins (g)	15	15
Antibiotics (g)	100	100

Composition of Finisher Ration

Ingredients	Finisher ration (7-8 months age)		
	I	II	III
Maize	—	—	—
Wheat	10	15	—
Barley	16	—	—
Rice bran	50	60	75
Wheat bran	—	—	—
Molasses	—	10	10
Groundnut cake	19	10	10
Fish meal	4	3	3
Mineral mixture	2	2	2
Vitamins (g)	15	15	15
Antibiotics (g)	100	100	10

IMPORTANT ADDRESSES

Mysore Feeds Limited
Regd. Office: 283/284, Old Tharagupet,
Bangalore - 560 053.
Tel : 2861471/2872215
Fax : 2874175
Factory : Nayandahalli, Mysore Road,
Bangalore-560 039.
Tel : 8600008/8600290
Fax : 8600840
(Pig Feeding)

PLANT ECONOMICS
PIGGERY FARM

Rated Plant capacity = 9920 Nos./Annum

LAND & BUILDING

(Land 20 Acres with half Land having a temporary fencing)	Rs.	9,75,000.00

PLANT & MACHINERY

1. Pots, buckets, Basinus, spades Daos etc.
2. Refrigerator 265 lits capacity with one stabliser
3. Miscellanewater and other water tubewells etc

FIXED CAPITAL

1.	LAND & BUILDING	Rs.	9,75,000.00
2.	PLANT & MACHINERY	Rs.	30,000.00
3.	OTHER FIXED ASSETS	Rs.	4,80,000.00
	TOTAL	**Rs.**	**14,85,000.00**

WORKING CAPITAL REQUIREMENT/ANNUM

LIST OF RAW MATERIALS

1. Feed concentrate for 630 gilts and 70 young boars at 2 Kgs.pig/day (700x2x365 = 511000 Kgs.)
2. Feed concentrate for piglets (0.5 Kgs./piglet) (out of 620 farrowed during the second yr.)
3. Medicines and vaccines

TOTAL WORKING CAPITAL/ANNUM

1.	RAW MATERIAL	Rs.	29,56,800.00
2.	SALARY & WAGES	Rs.	1,72,500.00
3.	UTILITIES & OVERHEADS	Rs.	28,000.00
	TOTAL	**Rs.**	**31,57,300.00**

TOTAL CAPITAL INVESTMENT

TOTAL FIXED CAPITAL	Rs.	14,85,000.00
TOTAL WORKING CAPITAL FOR 3 MONTHS	Rs.	7,89,325.00
TOTAL	**Rs.**	**22,74,325.00**

TURN OVER/ANNUM

1. By sale of piglets of the second batch (at age of 2 months)
2. By sale of piglets of the third batch (at the age of 2 months)
3. By sale of undamaged gunny bags 7700 Nos.
4. By sale of manure about 125 Tonnes

TOTAL **Rs. 49,95,600.00**

PROFIT SALES RATIO = Profit / Sales x 100 = 25.72 %

RATE OF RETURN = Operating profit / T.C.I x 100 = 56.50 %

BREAK EVEN POINT (B.E.P) = 33.02 %

Chapter - 13

POULTRY FARM

Poultry Farming is a specialized job and needs scientific knowledge. It requires a lot of money to start with for capital works and running cost and needs constant vigilance because you are dealing with live-stock. It is a seven day's work in week & No holiday. So before going into this business one must think seriously.

Some people start poultry farming as a side line business and in the course of time by investing their profit they expand the farm as a full time job. It is always a wise step that one should start to begin with on smaller scale, gain experience and expand the farm. For successful poultry farming the practical scientific knowledge plus practical experience is essential. Management plays a very important part in the success of a farm. So one must be thorough in management practices.

HOW TO START A POULTRY FARM

A for starting a poultry farm, the first thing to be considered is the choice of land and site.

The following points should be kept in mind while selecting the land.

1. Site:-

While selecting the site, you must see that it is not a low lying or water logging area. In such like places it becomes difficult to avoid dampness. So land must be free from flood & water logging and should be on higher level for good drainage and should also not be saline.

2. Proximity to Road or Approach Road :-

In a poultry farm the transportation of eggs, broilers, feed etc. are to be carried out through out the year. So it must be connected to a road passable in all seasons, In the farm, transportation of poultry products and feed etc is a regular feature. For example for every thousand birds and annual replacement on a unit, approximately 50 M. Ton feed, 900 culled birds and lakhs of eggs will have to be transported every year. Similarly, in case of broilers, every week, arrival and marketing of birds, and transport of feed is a regular feature. So there must be all seasonal passable passage.

3. Proximity to the Marketing and Feed Supply Centers :-

The greater the distance from the market the higher are the transport cost for eggs, broilers feed etc. Attempt should be made to have your farm near the town/city but the cost of land should also be kept in mind as near the cities/town the cost of land is always higher.

4. Water :-

An adequate water supply of reasonable good qualities is essential. Poultry consumes a lot of water. 1000 brids can drink 300-400 litter water daily. One must ensure before purchasing the land, the availability and quality of water, some times the underground water is not fit for drinking and when there is no water supply from out-side source (which is usually not available) It becomes extremely difficult to cope with the water supply. So the availability of water through handpump and bore-well water as the case may be is very important question while selecting the land. If you want to be more scientific, you can get the water tested in some water testing lab.

5. Electric Power :-

Electric power is a great help in the operation of the Poultry Farm for brooding etc. and In large commercial farms, for feed mixing plants, water pumping machine etc. Though given other facilities, a frm can be managed successfully without electricity but every efforts should be made to provide it.

6. Size and cost of land :-

It would be desirable tohave a reasonable priced land offering as many facilities as possible. Regarding size usually one acre land is sufficient for about 5000 layers or 10,000-12000 broilers farm depending upon the type of farming i.e. litter system or cage system. However in double storey sheds, the no. can be double.

7. Distance from Other Farm :-

To avoid infection the land should be far away from other farms as far as possible at least the drainage should never come from other farms to your farms.

Choice of breed

After selecting the site, the next question comes regarding choice of breed.

In Poultry, there are two types of farmings :-

1. Layer's farm for eggs production
2. Broiler farm for meat production

Layer's farm

In this kind of farming, one day old chicks are kept, they start laying after 5 months and kept for 1 year for laying. So total for 1.5 year and then culled & marketed, Because after that they are uneconomical to keep.

In the laying farm, initial investment is more & as they start laying after 5 months, income starts late but after that there is steady income & is very easy going job.

Broiler Farm

In this system, one day broiler chicks are kept, they are ready for marketing for meat purposes after 6-7 weeks of age. So in a broiler farming initial investment is less, return is quick but it is very laborious and time consuming work.

In poultry, there are different kind of breeds which are suitable to different type of farming i.e. layers farm or broiler. The breeds have been categorized according to their qualities as follows :-

1. Egg type.
2. Meat type.
3. Dual purpose.

Egg type:

Egg type breeds are those breeds which efficiently convert feed into eggs but are not good in meat production. They are light in weight, consume less feed, are non-broody and are used in laying farms.

The most important in this category is White Leg Horn (WLH) which is maintained through out the country. Characters of this breed are as follows :

It is a very hardy breed, chicks ar easy to rear, it has an early sexual maturity, consume less feed and can lay up to 280 eggs in a year.

Salient Points of White Leg Horn (W.L.H.)

1. Colour - White
2. Comb - Single
3. Earlobe-White
4. Shanks-Feather less
5. Egg shell Colour-White
6. Weight Adult hen-1.5 to 2 kg.

There are certain other light breeds also such as Black Minorca, Ancona etc. but these are not so good as white leg horn, so for laying farm White Leg Horn is the best proven breed. Now a days different commercial strain of WLH have been produced known by different names such as H.H. 260, Bab

Cock, hyline, Hysex Keystone etc which lay large number of eggs.

Meat Type breeds

- Meat type breeds are those breeds which convert the feed more efficiently into meat than eggs. They lay comparatively lesser number of eggs as compared to White Leg Horn but their body weight is much more. They consume more feed and are kept for broiler production. the important breeds in this category are No. 1. White Rock 2. White Cornish. Both these breeds and their crosses are excellent for meat production. In this type also very good commercial strains of heavy breeds with very good rate of growth of commercial chicks have been produced.

Character of White Rock and White Cornish

S.No.	Particular	White Rock	White Cornish
1.	Colour	White	White
2.	Comb	Single	Pea
3.	Earlobe	Red	Red
4.	Egg Shell Colour	Light Brown	Light Brown
5.	Weight (Adult hen)	3-4 kg	3-4 kg
	(Adult male)	4-5 kg	4-5 kg

For broiler production these breeds or their crosses are used. They lay about 180 eggs in a year. There are certain other breeds in this category but they are not so important for practical point of view. Now a days commercial breeds have been produced which produced high bred commercial broiler chicks which are sold by many reputed hatcheries in their own trade names.

Dual Purpose Breeds

Dual purpose breeds are those breeds which have got both the qualities i.e. moderate in egg production and meat production, In other words they are in between the white leg horn and heaby meat breeds. These breeds now a days ar rarely used in poultry farming except in cross breeding with white leg horn and sometimes crossing with meat type breeds.

Most common breeds under this category are :

1. Rhode Island Red (RIR)
2. New Hampshire (N.H.)
3. Australorpe (A.O.)

Character of Dual purpose breeds are :

Particular	R.I.R.	N.H.	A.O.
Colour	Dark Red	Golden	Black
Comb	Single	Single	Single
Ear lobe	Red	Red	Red
Egg shell colour	Brown	Brown	Brown
Weight Hen	2-2.5 kg	2-2.5 kg	2-2.5 kg
Cock	3-3.5 kg	3-3.5 kg	3-3.5 kg

These breeds start laying in about 6 and 6 1/2 months they can lay about 225-230 eggs in a year. R.I.R. is very hardy breed and very suitable for hilly areas. It was previously extensively used for crossing with White Leg Horne to produce cross bred commercial laying chicks. New Hamp. Is some times used for crossing with white rock and white Cronish for broiler production. Australope is used for crossing with white leg horn to produce excellent cross bred layers chicks.

To summarise the characters of important poultry breeds are :-

Light breed		Dual purpose			Heavy breed	
	W.L.H.	R.I.R.	N.H.	A.O.	W.R.	W.C.
Colour	White	Red	Golden	Black	White	White
Comb	Single	Single	Single	Single	Single	Pea
Earlobe	White	Red	Red	Red	Red	Red
Egg shell Colour	White	Brown	Brown	Brown	Brown	Brown
Weight Hen	1.5-2kg	2-2.5kg	2-2.5kg	2-2.5kg	3 kg	3 kg
Cock	2-2.5kg	3-3.5kg	3-3.5kg	3-3.5kg	4-5kg	4-5kg

Choice of the type of farm and its layout

After selecting the site and the breed now question comes as to what type of farm to be adopted and the layout of the farm.

As already discussed there are two types of commercial farming in poultry.

1. Broiler farms
2. Layers farms

Broiler Farms

In broiler farming, one day old chicks of meat breeds are kept for meat purpose. They belong to meat type breeds i.e. White rick, Cornish or their crosses. They are easily available from Hatcheries in different commercial names. The chicks are kept upto 6 to 8 weeks of age in which time they attain 1.25 to 1.75 kg body weight. Usually when they are about one kg live weight which they gain in about 6 week they are marketed.

For starting a broiler farm small investment is needed, return is quick as they are marketed after 6 to 7 weeks of age but it is a laborious and time consuming and needs maximum attention becuase the brooding which is the most difficult part of poultry farming is carried out through out the year.

In broiler farm there are two system:-

1. All in All-out
2. Batch system

1. All in all-out :

It means you bring all the chicks according to the capacity of your farm at a time, rear them and sell all of them at a time. Again bring chicks, sold them at a time and so on and so forth. You can have about seven crops in a year. it is suitable for small farmers.

2. **Batch System** :

Those who are having large commercial farms, the chicks are kept in batches and are brought either weekly or fortnightly according to the size of the farm. For example if the capacity of your farm is for six thousand broilers you should have partitions in your sheds and bring 1000 chicks every week and with in 6 weeks your sheds will be full and by the time you bring the 6th Batch, your first batch in the first compartment will be ready for marketing as is shown in the housing chapter. Next week, chicks of the second compartment will be ready and the cycle will go on and thus continue replacing the chicks in compartments after cleaning which have become empty. In this way you will have complete cycle. This is a very wise policy and working is easy and marketing is also suitable because if you take 6000 broiler at a time in the market, it may reflect on the prices. But it requires more attention due to regular brooding of the chicks.

Layer's Farm

In this type of farming one day old chicks of light breeds or commercial breeds, i.e. white leg horn (Its strain crosses) are kept, they start laying after five month and go on laying for one year so they are kept for about one and a half year in total. After that, they are disposed off for table purpose, as their economic life is for one year of laying. After that their laying capacity decreases by 20% and hance become uneconomical to keep.

In laying farm, initial investment is more and income starts late say after six month but it is very easy going work and needs lesser work then broiler farm as you have to brood the chicks only once in a year. Market of eggs is also more stable than broiler.

The best season in northern part of the country for starting a layers farms is from Februaru to April. Because if you start the farm say in February, they will start laying in July/August and will be laying at peak during winter season when the prices of the eggs are highest and in this way you will get maximum return. But if you start the farm in September/October they will start laying in March/April and the production will be at peak in the summer months when the prices are the lowest, so there will be less return.

In layers farm the replacement chicks are brought every year, the same month when you brought your first batch. For example you have brought your chicks in Feb, these chicks will start laying in July and will be culled in June next year. You should plain in such a way that when these birds after one year of laying are culled the replacement chicks starts laying. In this way there will be continuity of egg production and your sheds and equipments will be properly utilised.

Whether you start a broiler farm or a layers farm the fundamental things are the same. You must be acquinted with both type of farming. A time may come you may have to swith over from one type of farming to another according to the circumstances. You should have knowledge of both broiler as well as layers farming technique.

PLANNING AND LAYOUT OF POULTRY FARM

Layout of the farm depends upon the type of the farming you are going to adopt i.e. side line unit or a commercial farm.

You must know the cost involved in setting up the farm and should work out the requirements carefully especially the financial aspect. As the things stand today for setting up a 1000 layers farms an initial investment of more than Rupees one lakh is required for capital work and recurring cost of the chicks upto 6 months. Similarly in a broiler farm for 1000 birds about Rs. 60,000 are required for capital work and recurring expenditure for rearing of the chicks upto 6-7 weeks of age (First batch).

The running cost of layers chicks upto 6 months of age (excluding) capital works comes about Rupees 35 per bird and in case of broilers upto 6-7 weeks about 18 rupees per broiler. In a layers farm, additional houses for Brooding & rearing and rooms for Feed store, Eggs & general staore & office etc. are also to be constructed.

Side Line Unit

Side line unti means adopting poultry farming as a side business. You may carry out your usual occupation and have the poultry to supplement your income. it needs limited finance, housing can be made of local material. The family members can help you in carrying out the daily routine work. so when you have limited finance (to set up a Poultry Farm) or have a limited land for this purpose and want to supplement your income, may go in for side line unit. Usually upto 1000 layers or 2000 broilers can easily be maintained as side line business and you can earn upto rupees two thousand rupees per month in this way. For 500 layers or 1000 broilers can easily be maintained as a side line business and you can earn about 2 thousand broilers a shed of covered are of 1000 Sq. feet is sufficient and this house can be made by using the local material. After gaining experience and from the income earned from the side line unit one may expand ones unit into a commercial unit.

The Commercial Farm of Full Time Job

In setting up a commercial farm much capital is required Financial loan upt 75% of the total cost can be obtained from nationalised bank. One must know the technical and scientific requirement of poultry before adopting the commercial farming.

When the poultry farm is being planned, whether it is layers or broiler farm, certain basic principles as given below must be kept in mind. it will apply to small units as well as large one.

1. The ground plan of the farm must be prepared in which layout is properly balanced. The sheds should be set up in straight line which will make the working easy and give a good look, It should never be haphazardly planned. there must be scope for further expansion. In layers farm, Brooder sheds should be well separated from adult birds, it will help in controlling the disease and better rearing result.
2. With the planning of the farm, tree planting should also be carried out to cut the heat of the summer and as wind breaker. Fruit trees which are not very tall such as mulberry, Citrus trees are very useful.

Housing Principles and Construction

Poultry is housed for comfort, protection and efficient production. The maximum expenditure in the farm is on house construction. The house should be efficiently and economically built. The main criteria in house building is not the type of material but the main points are general dimension, good ventilation and handling facilities.

General Principle for Housing

Location of the Poultry House :

In planning a poultry house, one should provide space for expansion and additional building whenever required. Location of the house should be on ground higher enough to provide good drainage and protection against danger of food. The house should Be Accesible from road for delievery of feed, and transportion of other commodities and conveniently located for routine work. Poultry house should be so designed that it can be used for brooding, broiler rearing or laying frock. House should be kept in use for most of the time. it should be damp proof and rat proof.

Birds must be comfortably housed to produce well, they need adequate floor space, cross ventilation, moderate temperature and dry living.

Requirements of the Poultry House

1. Direction

It should face East west to safe-guard against heat waves in summer Loo and rains showers in Rainy season.

2. Width

The width of the shed should be about 30 ft. for better ventilations and economy in the cost. House moreb than 40 ft. wide are difficult to ventilate and 20 ft. or so wide will prove costly.

3. Length

Lemgth of the house can be extended according top the requirement. Usually 100 to 120 ft. length is more suitable. In broiloer farm, 1 sq. ft. floor space per shick and for layers (WLH) about 2-2.5 sq.ft. per birds is required.so in a house of 30x100 ft. (3000 sq. feet) covered area.you can keep 3000 broiler or 1200-1500 layers.

4. Floor

The floor should be pucca (concrete one) to avoid sippage of ground water and should be rat proof. It should be about 6-10 inches above the ground level. In low lying areas or where the water table is high, it is suggested that while making the floor put a layer of Jumuna sand (Retti) and over that spread the platic cloth then make it pucca with bricks and cement etc. By doing this there will be no sippage even in low lying areas and the floor will remain dry.

5. Walls

The side walls should be 2-2.5' ft. in deep litter system but in cages in walls should be avoided.

6. Wire netting

4.5 ft. wire netting are fixed above the side walls for cross ventilation. The netting should be strong and of about one inch mesh.

7. Roof :-

The main expenditure in housing is on roof. The roof may be of different type i.e. asbestos sheets or light roofing or may also be thatched one. The thatched roof are cheap, very good for summer as well as for winter and acts as an insulator but there is danger of fire, rats and needs replacement after every 2-3 years. Asbestos sheets are ideal in gable type houses but a bit costly. In gable type houses the central height of the roof should be about 13-14 feet. The Iron sheets are not good for roofing for poultry houses as during summer period there will be danger of heat stroke and temperature will not be controlled.

In shds, flat roofs may also be given especially where double storey houses are constructed. In this case (slabs) (Turkies) are used. The height is kept about 8-8 1/2 ft. In double storeyd houses there is saving of land, cost is also reduced, because as in the second storey there is no need for foundation and floor is antomatically ready due to flat roof. The height of the second storey is kept about 6 1/2 ft. only.

8. Over-hang :

Every type of house whether it is single or double storey must have an overhang on both the sides to protect the house from rain showers. The over-hangs should project about 3 5 ft on sides. This is very essential to avoid rains showers.figure

9. Partitions :

For better management it is advised to have partitions in the sheds to divide it into pens. it is always good to keep the birds in small groups in pens instead in large number in a shed. The management becomes more efficient, birds of different ages and sources can be put in different pens in the same shed. The shed should be partitioned insuch a way that about five hundred adult birds or 500-1000 broiler can be kept in one partition. In a shed of 30 x 100 ft. 3 or 4 partitions are given to have 4 to 5 pens. The partition can be done by giving 2 ft. wall and above that 4-5 ft. wire netting or by providing portable partitions.

10. The Distance from house to house should be about 30 feet for circulation of air.

Note:

In areas where there is too much cold i.e. hilly areas like HP, J & K the house may be of flat roof, The front wall 8 ft. high and rear wall 6 ft. but in the side wall instead of wire netting it is better to have windows with shutters for controlling the temperature, in gable type house, on the roof there should be ridge ventilation to eliminate the foul air.

Additional Requirement for layers houses :

In addition to the main house, there should be brooding-cum-rearing house to keep the replacement stock. (As the replacement stock will have to be kept 5 months earlier before disposing off the old stock). This is done to keep the regular egg production in the farm.

The rotation of the laying farms will be as follows :-

Suppose you start the farm in Feb. '89. then the chain will be :

1st batch Feb. 89	Laying Starts August 89	Culled & marketted July 90
2nd batch (replacement)	Feb. 90 (Shifted to laying shed which has becomesvacant after disposal of the old stock)	August 90

Additional Requirement for Broiler Farm:

For large farms, you should construct one small separate nursery room, say 15 x 20 ft. to keep 1000 chicks for first week only and then transfer them to the main shed. The advantage of this nursery room will be:

1. In case you are not able to market your ready chicks in time due to some or the other reasons for a few days, you are not under pressure to dispose these chicks immediately because your replacement chicks are in the nursery room for a week.
2. In the nursery room you can pay more attention and the work of paper on the floor guards etc will also be over in the nursery stage of 7 days. so when you shift your chicks to the main sheds, only heating arrangement will be required. the root of the nursery room may be flat, height may be 6-7 ft. and windows, instead of wirenetting, may be provided for easy temperature control. But this nursery room is not very essential you may or may not have it.

In addition to the poultry sheds, a feed store, egg collection room and general store and office etc should also be constructed at convenient place. the feed store must be Rat proof.

In a large poultry farm, an incinerator should also be conveniently located for disposal of the dead birds, In small farms a pit of 6 x 6 ft. may be made with one feet mouth opening for disposal of the dead birds.

House for cages are like deep litter houses except that there is no need for side-walls and the height of the roof is a bit more.

IMPORTANT ADDRESSES

Arora Poultary Products Ltd.
119, Patel Nagar, Regal School,
Lucknow - 226 005
Tel : 52425
Fax : 4098536
(Wholeseller and Dealer of Eggs)

Bhajan Lal Laxmi Narain
2717, Gali Patewali,
Naya Bazar,
Delhi - 110 006.
Tel : 29290347
(Cattle Feed)

Dayal Polutry Appliances
wz-16, Lazwanti Garden,
New Delhi - 110 046.
Tel : 5555091
(Incubators)

Dera Farms
D - 429, Defence Colony,
New Delhi - 110 024
Tel : 4626864
(Poultry Products)

Gold Feeds
894/8, Mehrauli,
New Delhi - 110 030
Tel : 6864231.
(Manufacturing of Cattle feed)

North Star Agro Ind. Pvt. Ltd.
408, Lakshmi Bhawan,
72, Nehru Place,
New Delhi - 110 019
Tel : 6430517
(Poultry Feed)

R.P.Pal
1802, Bhagirath Palace, Chandni Chowk,
Delhi - 110 006.
Tel : 2966751
(Poultry Equipments)

Top Farm Industries
15, Tilak Nagar Indl. Area,
New Delhi - 110 018.
Tel : 5438108
(Manufacturer of Chikpik Brand Feeder Drinker, Specially Designed for Easy Handling)

National Poultry and Cattle Feed
E-100, Shastri Nagar, Delhi - 110 052
Tel : 7512978/7534744/7293411
(National Feed Mill)

Santokh Ram Narinder Nath
Old Grains Market, Phagwara (Punjab)
Tel : 01824-60281,65593
Fax : 91-01824-65593
(Cattle Feed, Poultry Feed and Molasses)

PLANT ECONOMICS OF POULTRY & BROILER (HATCHERY) FARMING

Rated Plant capacity = 110100.00 NOS/annum BROILER CHICKENS

LAND & BUILDING

Land Area Required 500 sq.mts. **Rs. 14,12,500.00**

PLANT & MACHINERY

Cages (3tiers) for 12,000 Birds
with automatic feeding systems.
Blowers & Exhaust Fans 4 mm
Complete with a HP motor , Electric Heaters
Eggs storing Racks, Food feeder

with suitable, Distribution system Cap
Automatic vaccination, Watering devices
Laying cages with capacity of
Belt conveyor, Three-wheel manure
cleaning machine, Diesel engine operated
dumpers, Manure handling drum-type dryer
Tube wells of 4", Diesel Generating set
Lighting system, Black lamps candler
Egg packing table on rails, Water and
temperature Control Equipments,
Depolluting equipments, miscellaneous

TOTAL	**Rs.**	**16,29,700.00**

FIXED CAPITAL

1. LAND & BUILDING	Rs.	14,12,500.00
2. PLANT & MACHINERY	Rs.	16,29,700.00
3. OTHER FIXED ASSETS	Rs.	2,64,000.00
TOTAL	**Rs.**	**33,06,200.00**

RAW MATERIALS

Alfa meal dehydrated
Medicines, feed supplements
for nutrition Packing Materials
e.g. Carboard cartons, Egg trays etc.

TOTAL	**Rs.**	**1,15,500.00**

TOTAL WORKING CAPITAL/MONTH

1. RAW MATERIAL	Rs.	1,15,500.00
2. SALARY & WAGES	Rs.	55,625.00
3. UTILITIES & OVERHEADS	Rs.	34,500.00
TOTAL	**Rs.**	**2,05,625.00**

COST OF PROJECT

TOTAL FIXED CAPITAL	Rs.	33,06,200.00
MARGIN MONEY	Rs.	1,54,218.75
TOTAL	**Rs.**	**34,60,418.75**

TOTAL CAPITAL INVESTMENT

TOTAL FIXED CAPITAL	Rs.	33,06,200.00
TOTAL WORKING CAPITAL FOR 3 MONTHS	Rs.	6,16,875.00
TOTAL	**Rs.**	**39,23,075.00**

TURN OVER/ANNUM

By sale of Egg 30,00000 Nos.
Broilers 1,10,000 Nos.
Chicks (one day old) 90,000 Nos
Culled chickens, 20,000 Nos.
Parent Birds 1000 Nos
Recovering by sales of poultry

TOTAL **Rs. 49,82,700.00**

PROFIT = RECEIPTS - COST OF PRODUCTION = 11,62,386.00

PROFIT SALES RATIO = Profit / Sales x 100 = 23.33 %

RATE OF RETURN = Operating profit / T.C.I x 100 = 29.63 %

BREAK EVEN POINT (B.E.P) = 60.57 %

PLANT ECONOMICS
POULTRY & BROILER FARMING

Rated Plant capacity = 720000.00 NOS/annum
POULTRY & BROILERS FARMING

LAND & BUILDING

Land Area required 10500 sq. mts. **Rs. 1,03,50,000.00**

PLANT & MACHINERY

Cages (4 tiers)
Blowers & Exhaust Fans
Electric Heaters
Room type incubator with
sophisticated controls to maintain optimum
conditions for hatchability.
Eggs storing racks
Food feeder with suitable
Automatic Vaccination system.
Watering devices for keeping water
Laying cages with capacity
Belt conveyor for egg collection
Three-wheel manure cleaning machine
Diesel engine operated dumpers
Manure handling drum-type dryer
Tube wells ,Diesel Generator set
Lighting system, Black lamps candler
Egg packing table on rails
Water and temperature control
Miscellaneous expenses
Angithee Bukhari

TOTAL **Rs. 29,12,700.00**

FIXED CAPITAL

1. LAND & BUILDING	Rs.	1,03,50,000.00
2. PLANT & MACHINERY	Rs.	29,12,700.00
3. OTHER FIXED ASSETS	Rs.	25,35,000.00
TOTAL	**Rs.**	**1,57,97,700.00**

WORKING CAPITAL REQUIREMENT/MONTH

RAW MATERIALS

Poultry feed
Medicines and Vaccines
Egg Trays for packings

TOTAL	**Rs.**	**18,20,000.00**

TOTAL WORKING CAPITAL/MONTH

1. RAW MATERIAL	Rs.	18,20,000.00
2. SALARY & WAGES	Rs.	1,07,250.00
3. UTILITIES & OVERHEADS	Rs.	74,500.00
TOTAL	**Rs.**	**20,01,750.00**

COST OF PROJECT

TOTAL FIXED CAPITAL	Rs.	1,57,97,700.00
MARGIN MONEY	Rs.	15,01,312.50
TOTAL	**Rs.**	**1,72,99,012.50**

TOTAL CAPITAL INVESTMENT

TOTAL FIXED CAPITAL	Rs.	1,57,97,700.00
TOTAL WORKING CAPITAL FOR 3 MONTHS	Rs.	60,05,250.00
TOTAL	**Rs.**	**2,18,02,950.00**

PROFIT = RECEIPTS - COST OF PRODUCTION = 1,35,34,794.00

PROFIT SALES RATIO = Profit / Sales x 100 = 31.81 %

RATE OF RETURN = Operating profit / T.C.I x 100 = 62.08 %

BREAK EVEN POINT (B.E.P) = 30.24 %

Chapter - 14

Rabbit Farm

INTRODUCTION

The importance of the domestic rabbit as a source of meat for human consumption is widely recognized throughout the world. The popularity of rabbit in India also is on the increase. The domestication of the major livestock species like cattle, sheep, pigs and poultry is lost in the dawn of prehistoru, but rabbit domestication is of more recent origin. The wild areas of Southern Europe and North Africa are believed to be the original places for rabbit. However, rabbit is not found widely in the wild state in India, but the domesticated breeds are common in all parts. Various races of rabbit have been produced by breeders. They may be pure white, pure black or white with brown or black patches.

Besides being highly prolific, rabbits are also herbivores with efficient feed conversion. They can turn 20% of the protein they eat into edible meat. Rabbit meat is more economical in terms of feed energy than beef. Rabbits can also easily convert the available proteins in cellulose rich plants better than chicken and tukeys. The traditional grains and soyacakes fed to these domestic poultry put them in direct competipluses, rabbit meat production is, thus, of special importance.

Physiology and Habitat

The zoological name of the typical rabbit is Orytolagus cuniculus. It belongs to the family Leporida and class Mammalia

A. Habbit

Rabbits are rodents by nature. They are relatively quiet on rest during the day. At night they wander about eating both greens and dry leaves.

The rabbit is sociable and terrestrial in habit. It lives for eight years becoming mature at six months. Itis also a fast multiplier. It breeds four times a year producing 6-10 young ones in each litter. The young ones are fed on milk once a day. This mostly occurs at early morning or late evening. The bunnies (young ones) are born blind,naked (without hair) and to deaf. In 11 days their eyes will open and they begin to grow fur. After 14 days they venture out of the burrow. At 11-21 days they start to eat grass.

The natural enemies of rabbit are wolf, jackal, fox and wild cat.

B. Exteranal features

The body length of an adult rabbit varies from 16 to 18 inches.It consists of a head, neck, trunk and tail. The trunk is divisible into thorax and abdomen. It has liong hond limbs and feet, large eyes, a short tail and soft pelage (fur)

1. Head

The upper lip has a cleft in the middle exposing the long front teeth known as incisors. Immediately above the mouth are two oblique nostrils which lead through nosal passages into the pharynx. From the upper lip, thick tactile hairs project outwards. These are highly sensitive mechano-receptors and recpond to contact, pressure and movements of air.

On the sides of the head are eyes, each having movable upperand lower eyelids with a few eyelashes,and a separate small third eyelid or nictitating membrane in the inner corner of the eye which is movable and used for cleaning the cornea. Ontop of the head is a pair of large, movable externawl ears of pinnae.

2. Neck

The head is joined to the trunk by a distinct neck on which the head is freely movable in all direction.

3. Trunk and tail

On the ventral side of the thorax and abdomen are four or five pairs of teats or nipples in both sexes. However,these are functional only in the female. At the posterior end of the trunk is an anus. In front of the anus is a urogenital aperture which in the female lies within a slit like vulva and in the male at the tip of a cylindrical skin-covered penis. At the side of the penis the adult male has scrotal sacs into which the testes have descended from the abdominal cavity. On each side of the anus, in both sexes, is a hairless depression into which the duck of a perineasl gland opens. The secretion of perennial gland produces the peculiar odour of the rabbit.

At the end of the trunk is a short bushy tail. The rabbit raises its tail to give a warning signal to other rabbit when danger approaches.

4. Limbs

There are two pairs of pentadactyle (with five fingers) limbs. The forelimbs are short and are held rigid to take the shock at the end of a leap. They are also used for digging,each has a proximal upper arm which is directed backwards, below which is the fore-arm directed for wards. At the end is the hand having a wrist, metacarpals and five digits with claws.

The hind limbs are longer than the fore limbs, each has a proximal thigh directed forwards, a shank directed backwards, then a foot directed forwards. The foot has an ankle and four claws. When the hind limbs are suddenly straightend a powerful forward thrust results in jumping.

Locomotion is accomplished not by walking but by a series of jumps.

C. Anatomy

Anatomy of the rabbit consists of skeletal system, circulatory system, digestive system, urinogenital system, nervous system,endocrine system, muscular system and epithelial system. However, only the first four system mentioned above are discussed here.

1. Skeletal system

This system consists of the bony structure which provides the rabbit its structure and shape. The main parts of the skeletal system are skull, vertebral column, appendicular skeleton, pectoral girdle, pelvic girdle and bones of the limbs.

2. Circulatory system

The circuklatory system is responsible for the purification of blood and its circulation in the rabbits body. This system consists mainly of heart, lungs, arteries and veins.

3. Digestive system

Rabbits, being herbivorous have a longer digestive system than the carnivoruous. The main parts of the digestive system are month,oesophagus, stomach, liver, pancreas, small intestine, restumand anus. They ingest the food and chew thoroughly before it is swallowed and passed on to the stomach.

The dentition of a rabbit is as follows.

a.	Incisors :	(1)	Upper jaw	4
		(ii)	Lower jaw	2.
b.	Canines are absent in rabbit.			
c.	Pre-molars :	(i)	Upperjaw	6
		(ii)	Lower jaw	6
	Total tereth			28

The feed in the stomach is broken down to simpler organic compounds which are absorbed into the body.The caecum is the home of various kinds of symbiotic bacteria which digest the cellulose and hemicellulose of the rabbit feed. The undigested materials are excreted through the anus.

4. Urino-genital system

Like in all other mammals, in rabbits too the urinary and genital system are considered together. The urinary system comprises of kidneys, ureter, bladders and urinary aperture. The genital system in male rabbits consists of a pair of testes, vas deferens, seminal vesciles, prostrategland, cowpears glands and penis with urogenital opening. Sperms are produced in the testes.

Advantages of Rabbit Rearing

India needs to produce more meat in order to supply its rising population with animal protein. Rabbit has several points nin its favour as a meat producer.

1. The feed can be very cheap. Rabbits can be fed on a great variety of locally available foods, weeds, some green leaves and kitchen vegetable scraps, at almost no cost. However,these have to be aupplimented with concentrate or grains.
2. Rabbits can breed and grow quickly. Thus they can form a regular source of income instead of a large amount at once.
3. Initial capital outlay is minimal. Houses can be built from pieces of wood and bamboo, and no special materials or equipments needs to be bought for the backyard ravbbitary, if the financial conditions do not permit it.
4. To start a rabbit business one does not need a large initial investment. A few does with a buck is enough to start. Once the kindling begins the herd rapidly increases in size and very soon one can slaughter the young males.
5. If one start a rabbit business with borrowed animals,within half a year the initial credit can be returned as live animals.
6. Animals often serve as a saving account. When a small amount of money is needed (for school,medicines,etc) it is easier to sell a small animal like rabbit than for example a cattle or buffalo.
7. The meat is tasty, of good quality and similar to chicken meat.
8. The quantity of meat provided by the rabbit is big enough for a small dish (compared to size of chicken). On the other hand a rabbit is small enough to eat all the meat at once without the need for refrigeration or other conservation.
9. Except for Jews and certain Hindu sects (vergetarian culture), there is no religious taboos on eating rabbit meat.
10. Rabbit can be attended by women and children and, unlike bigger

animal need no force to be restrained.

11. The rabbit manure can be used for growing vegetables.
12. The rabbit does not smell too much, neither does the rabbit make much noise.

Problems of Rabbit Rearing

In spite of many advantages of rabbit raising, there are certain practical difficulties which are of ten encountered by the rabbit farmers. Some of these are discussed here.

1. The most important problem is that often people are reluctant to accept something new. Moreover in India, the market is more and more organised for chicken. This reduces potential money income, but it should not be a problem where the intention is to raise rabbits as a family enterprise, mainly to provide protein rich meat.
2. Diseases are common and unlike chicken, specific rabbit medicines for rabbit are not easily available. On the other hand with good hygiene and knowledge one should not have too many worries about diseases.
3. Rabbit are more easily stolen or attacked by predators. They need to be protected form these predators by fences and other barriers.
4. Rabbit need protection against extreme of climate. They are especially sensitive to heat and sun, and must always have access to shade.
5. Large number of rabbits require a lot of labour, particularly if they are kept in individual hutches. Each hutch has to be cleaned out daily. Each rabbit needs to be fed and given water daily at least three times.
6. Keeping rabbits is time consuming too. Time required depends on the number of animal one keeps, the housing system and the way one obtain the rabbit feedstuff. For example, keeping five rabbits will take about 1 to 2 hours a day.

Rabbit Production Systems

The exact way in which people keep differs from place to place, but there are three main systems of production.

1. The backyard rabbitry

In this system rabbit keeping is on a small, family scale. A few does and one or two bucks may be kept in a home built rabbitry just next to the house. The rabbits are fed on greens, wweeds and vegetable kitchen scraps. Production form this type of rabbitary is low, but it provides enough meat to supplements the family diet. It is a very useful way of keeping rabbits, especially in the poorer parts of the community and provides a valuable supply of meat. Backyard rabbit production should be encouraged and improved. The incidence of diseases can be reduced through better hygiene and production is increased by better feeding and the introduction of improved strains of rabbit. Improvement often depends on the following possibilities or questions.

a. What can the small rabbit afford to buy in the way of housing materials, feed and livestock ?
b. What materials are available locally for low cost housing ?
c. What cheap feeding stuffs are available for feeding the animals throughout the year ?

As a result of improvement, some bachyard rabbit keepers may be able to increase their productivity, so that they have some surplus rabbit which they can sell to their neighbours or at local markets. The cash received will help to raise their owner's standard of living.

2. The small commercial rabbitry

This system may have 10 to 50 breeding does in a properly built rabbitry. The aim of this type of rabbitry is to sell rabbit meat for a profit. The rabbit are usually fed on concentrates as well as bulky food which cost money. In order to obtain a good profit, one must consider matters such as sources and prices of rabbit feed, management techniques and markets. It would be unwise for anyone to start a commercial rabbit farming, even on a small scale unless good preparations are made and al the details taken into account. New rabbit farmers should be advised to start with three does and a buck to build up gradually. In such a way they gain valuable experience without taking any risk.

3. The large commercial rabbitry

This type of rabbitry is not common in India. To support such type of rabbitries it is necessary to have a reliable market outlet for the carcasses,a source of good quality commercial feed, and expert veterinary services. In addition to meat they provide, these commercial rabbitries also serve a useful purpose in the multiplication of breeding stock for distribution, the investigation of some of the problems concerning rabbit keeping in hot countries, and in training the local people in improved rabbit husbandry techniques.

Rabbit By-products and Their Use

The rabbit has a number of uses. Some of are mentioned here.

1. The dressed meat may be used fresh or made into ham and preserved for later use.
2. The bones may be converted into bone-meal for preparing mineral mixture.
3. The head may be used as food for animals like dogs and the brain is consumed as food or may be used in the laboratory for preparing vaccines.
4. The blood can be collected separately and coverted into blood meal which is a high protein feed for animals.
5. Skin and pelts are very valuable by-products of rabbit and they can be easily prepared at home. Well-tanned pelts are used in manufacturing garments, bedding, gloves, furniture, upholstery, single piece decoratives footwears, bags and toys.
6. The cured paws and tail can be changed into beautiful trinklets and charms.
7. The processed leather can be used for manufacturing bags, footwears, etc.
8. The loose wool is a good stuffing material and can be spun into threads which again can be weaved into warm clothing.
9. The faces and urine are good raw material for cooking gas production. The residual mixture after the gas extraction is an excellent manure.
10. The fresh rabbit excreta is an excellent raw material to grow chlorells, a high protein algae. It may be composted along with other waste materials and used directly in the field as munure.

Breeds of Rabbit

There are nearly 30 breeds and 80 varieties of rabbits, varying in colour, type and size, found all over the world. The breeds may be suitable for meat, fur, laboratory and fancy purposes. For practical purposes, the breeds are grouped into two categories, namely

(1) Fancy and fur breeds
(2) Meat breeds.

1. Fancy and fur breeds

Fancy and fur breeds differ from meat breeds in such a way that the fancy types are not necessarily good meat producers. Also they do not produce large litters and are quite susceptible to diseases. They, however, have nice skin and colours.

One of these types which deserves attention is the Angora. Its hair can become very long and provides a very valuable fibre for spinning and we aving. Its hair seems to grow better in colder climates which might reduce the value of Angora in the tropical lowlands. There are several grades of hairs identified by length, type of animal and cleanliness.

2. Meat breeds

These breeds are good producers of meat, either by fast growth rate or large and frequent litters. It is necessary to make further distinction here in weight.

a. Light breeds (up to 2-3 kg adult weight)
b. Medium breeds (3-5 kg)
c. Heavy breeds (more than 5kg)

Some of the common breeds found all over the world and the specific purposes they are suited to are given in table 1.

Table 1: Common breeds and varieties of rabbit

S. No	Breed	Country of origin	Type	Colour	Average weight (kg)
1	2	3	4	5	6
1.	Flemish Giant	Britain	Fancy	Steel grey	4.9-9.0
2.	British Giant	Britain	Fancy	White,grey brown, blueblack	4,9-6.8
3.	American Chinchilla	America	Fur	Grey	5.5-6.0

4.	Blane de Bouseat	France	Fur	White	4.9-6.8
5.	New Zealand	New Zeeland	Meat	White,red black	4.0-5.5
6.	Californian	America	Meat &fur	White,with coloured nose ears, feed & tail	3.5-5.0
7.	Blanc de Jermonde	Belgium	fur	white	3.6-4.5
8.	Belgium Hare	Unknown	Fancy	Tan chestnut	3.6-4.5
9.	Beeveren	Belgium	Fur	White,blue black,brown	3.1-3.6
10.	Argente Champagne	France	Fur	various colours	3.1-3.6
11.	Alaska	Germany	Fur	Brown,black	3.1-3.6
12.	English Spot	Britain	Meat	White,with various colours	2.5-3.5
13.	Chinchilla	France	Fur	Blue	2.2-3.1
14.	Chinchilla Giganta	France	Fur	Blue	4.5-50
15.	French Lop	France	Fancy	White	4.9-5.4
16.	Harieguim	France	Fancy	White	2.7-4.6
17.	English Lop	Britain	Fancy	Dark brown and white	2.7-3.1
18.	Dutch	Netherlands	Fancy	various colours	1.8-2.7
19	Havens	Netherlands	Fancy	Chocolate	2.2-2.7
20.	Lilac	Britain	Fur	Grey	2.2-2.7
21.	Himalayan	East	Fancy	various colours	1.8-2.2
22.	Satin	USA	Satin	various colours	2.7-3.6
23.	Rhinelander	Germany	Fur	White,with motted ears	2.7-4.0
24.	Rex	France	Fancy	Several colours	2.7-3.6
25.	Thuringer	Germany	Fur	Light and dark brown	2.7-3.6
26.	Smoke Pearl	Britain	Fur	Siamese	2.2-2.7
27.	Silver	Britain	Fur	Grey,fawn	2.2-2.7
28.	Tan	Britain	Fancy	Black tan	1.3-2.2
29.	Sable	Unknown	Fur	Various colours	2.2-3.1
30.	Siberian	Britain	Fur	Black, Brown blue	2.2-3.1
31.	Angora	Unknown	Fancy	White	2.7
32.	Polish	Unknown	Fancy	White	0.9-1.3

Conclusion

It is worthwhile to mention here that scientific rabbit rearing is still a new venture in India. A Rabbit is not reared like a chicken, so rural producers have to betrained likewise. They also need tobe assisted with the technical problems that can crop up periodically, viz. health, reproduction problems etc.

To make good use of the advantages offered by the rabbit, it requires a better knowledge of the animal: knowledge of its requirements vis-a-vis the environments,knowledge of rearing techniques, knowledges of its by-products, etc. It also needs a motivated labour force.

PLANT ECONOMICS OF RABBIT FARMING

Rated Plant capacity = 39900.00 NOS/annum RABBIT & RABBIT DOE

LAND & BUILDING

Open Land 500 sq.mt
Built up Area 300 sq.mt

TOTAL Rs. 1,90,000.00

PLANT & MACHINERY

Nesting boxes
Cages of galvanized wire
Lightening arrangement
Feed pot for rabbit
Hand pot (L.S.)
Hand water pump 5 Nos.
Electric cooling fans
Water sprinkler system with pipe

TOTAL Rs. 48,500.00

FIXED CAPITAL

1.	LAND & BUILDING	Rs	1,90,000.00
2.	PLANT & MACHINERY	Rs.	48,500.00
3.	OTHER FIXED ASSETS	Rs.	7,000.00
	TOTAL	**Rs.**	**2,45,500.00**

RAW MATERIALS

Rabbit of young breed
Feed 100 M.T.
Miscellaneous like vaccination,
Packaging

TOTAL	**Rs.**	**1,27,500.00**

TOTAL WORKING CAPITAL/ANNUM

1.	RAW MATERIAL	Rs.	1,27,500.00
2.	SALARY & WAGES	Rs.	36,000.00
3.	UTILITIES & OVERHEADS	Rs.	2,680.00
	TOTAL	**Rs.**	**1,66,180.00**

COST OF PROJECT

TOTAL FIXED CAPITAL	Rs.	2,45,500.00
MARGIN MONEY	Rs.	10,386.25
TOTAL	**Rs.**	**2,55,886.25**

TOTAL CAPITAL INVESTMENT

TOTAL FIXED CAPITAL	Rs.	2,45,500.00
TOTAL WORKING CAPITAL FOR 3 MONTHS	Rs.	41,545.00
TOTAL	**Rs.**	**2,87,045.00**

TURN OVER/ANNUM

By sale of 20,000 rabbit
By sale of 20,000 rabbit (doe)

TOTAL **Rs. 5,00,000.00**

PROFIT = RECEIPTS - COST OF PRODUCTION = 2,65,857.58

PROFIT SALES RATIO = Profit / Sales x 100 = 53.17 %

RATE OF RETURN = Operating profit / T.C.I x 100 = 92.62 %

BREAK EVEN POINT (B.E.P) = 23.89 %

PLANT ECONOMICS OF ANGORA RABBIT

Rated Plant capacity = 6000.00 KG/annum ANGORA RABBIT WOOL

LAND & BUILDING

OPEN LAND 4000 SQ MTS.
SHADED AREA 2500 SQ.MTS.
OFFICE BUILDING 50 SQ.MTS.
BOUNDARY WALL WITH GATE.

TOTAL **Rs. 16,55,000.00**

PLANT & MACHINERY

NESTING BOXES
CAGES OF GALVANISED WIRE
LIGHTENING ARRANGEMENT
OF BULB OF FEED POT FOR
RABBIT MADE OF CLAY
HAND POT (L.S)
HAND WATER PUMP.
ELECTRIC COOLING FANS
WATER SPRINKLING SYSTEM
WITH PIPE PREPARATION OF
FEED MIX. MIXERS.PALLETING
MACHINE. GROOMING AND
SHEARING TABLES.
BRUSH, SCISSORS ETC.
DIESEL GENERATING SET.
PERSONAL COMPUTER WITH PRINTER.
RABBIT OF YOUNG BREED (DOE).

TOTAL **Rs. 4,59,000.00**

FIXED CAPITAL

1.	LAND & BUILDING	Rs.	16,55,000.00
2.	PLANT & MACHINERY	Rs.	4,59,000.00
3.	OTHER FIXED ASSETS	Rs.	10,000.00
	TOTAL	**Rs.**	**21,24,000.00**

WORKING CAPITAL REQUIREMENT/MONTH

RAW MATERIALS

HAY
OTHER NUTRIENTS
MISCELLANEOUS
PACKING CHARGES.

TOTAL	**Rs.**	**44,750.00**

TOTAL WORKING CAPITAL/MONTH

1.	RAW MATERIAL	Rs.	44,750.00
2.	SALARY & WAGES	Rs.	1,09,375.00
3.	UTILITIES & OVERHEADS	Rs.	40,000.00
	TOTAL	**Rs.**	**1,94,125.00**

COST OF PROJECT

TOTAL FIXED CAPITAL	Rs.	21,24,000.00
MARGIN MONEY	Rs.	1,45,593.75
TOTAL	**Rs.**	**22,69,593.75**

TOTAL CAPITAL INVESTMENT

TOTAL FIXED CAPITAL	Rs. 21,24,000.00
TOTAL WORKING CAPITAL FOR 3 MONTHS	Rs. 5,82,375.00
TOTAL	**Rs. 27,06,375.00**

TURN OVER/ANNUM

BY SALE OF 6000 KG. OF ANGORA RABBIT **Rs. 37,20,000.00**

PROFIT = RECEIPTS - COST OF PRODUCTION = 6,23,772.50

PROFIT SALES RATIO = Profit / Sales x 100 = 16.77 %

RATE OF RETURN = Operating profit / T.C.I x 100 = 23.05 %

BREAK EVEN POINT (B.E.P) = 70.40 %

Chapter - 15

Sheep Farming

Introduction

India is the sixth largest country in sheep population of the world having more than 48 millions of them. This number can further be increased, because sheep require low cost feed, is well adapted to arid environmentes and suited to the small low-capital family, as an additional source of income and mutton for domestic use.

However the production efficiency of sheep india is much lower. The level of flock management, breed improvements and disease control technuques are largging far behind. These are the challenges facing sheep industry in India.

Meat production is on a continuous decline and production other food stuffs is not keepign up with the population growth. Per capita cereal production is also levelling off and is likely to decline until farm prices increase dastically . Under such situations the sheep, the most efficient converters of low quality feed maaterial to high quilty efficiency to provide an adequate supply of low cost meat for every one.

Origin and Distribution

There are verious opinions regarding the origin of sheep. A study of bone-remains and cave paintings revealed that before 10,000 B.C. sheep was not domesticated. The present studies show that sheep are goat must have been domesticated before 7,000 B.C. There are some investigation which indicate that sheep may have originated from a sudden mutation or gentic change in goats. Sheep's association with man started when he was a nomadic hunter. Sheep herds were also nomadic and man learned to follow the herds. He killed sheep to satisfy his needs and in return protected the sheep flock from wolves and other carnivores. India, with 48 million sheep population contributes 4.2% of the world's sheep population and produces about 1.1% of the world's total wool. The state-wise population is given

Table -1: Statewise distribution of sheep population in India (in million) as per 1982 livestock census

S.No.	State	Crossbred	Indigenous	Total
1.	Andhra Pradesh	93	7426	7519
2.	Assam	2	44	46
3.	Bihar	34	1288	1322
4.	Gujrat	28	2329	2357
5.	Haryana	64	694	758
6.	Himachal Pardesh	54	1037	1091
7.	Jammu & Kashmir	485	1424	1909
8.	Karnataka	132	4660	4792
9.	Kerala	-	7	7
10.	Madhya Pradesh	6	953	959
11.	Maharashtra	38	2671	-
12.	Manipur	-	14	14
13.	Nagaland	-	-	-
14.	Orissa	62	1938	2000
15.	Punjab	-	11	611
17.	Rajasthan	33	1339	1372
18.	Sikkim	1	10	11
19.	Tamil Nadu	282	5255	5537
20.	Tripura	-	5	5
21.	Uttar Pradesh	178	2129	2307
22.	West Bengal	34	1331	1365
23.	Other States	1	14	15
	All India	**1522**	**35172**	**36694**

Sheep Characteristics

Successful sheep rearing is posible only when sheep keepers properly understand sheep habits and charateristics. Some of sheep characteristics are described here.

1. Gregarious habit

Sheep tend to flock together or follow the leadre, when they move from one location to another. If this gregarious habit is understood properly and applied to sheep to sheep flock, they can be handled easily.

2. Timed and unaggressive

Sheep have limited means of self protrection and are usually timid and unggressive. They tend to run away from danger and are easy prey for predators. Therefore, due proection must be offered to sheep from predators and climatic like heat and clod.

3. Clean eating habits

Sheep are very particular in their eating habits. They refuse to eat or drink from dirty or contaminated feed troughs or water containers.They have a high requirements for salt, which should be supplied daily along with plenty of fresh water. They prefer slowly moving streams rather than stagnant pool.They avoid wet, marshy ground and mud and are reluctant to enter into water.

4. Efficient nutilisation of grasses

Sheep are superior to cattle in utilising grasses and other forages and canmeet 80 to 90%of their total nutrient requirement from forages alone. For this reason they must be given limited amount of cereal grains and other concentrates. Excessive consumption of concentrates results in enterotoxaemia, diarrhea and bloat, which can be fatal in many cases.

Sheep prefer to graze in the early moring and late evening. They consume the shorter grasses, so pastures with more than 15-20 cm of growth are unpalatable to them. They will destroy 90% of the weeds with which they come into contact. They prefer to graze on higher ground, which may be beneficial in spreading manure on less fertile areas. Sheep manure has a higher fertilizing velue than that of any other farm animal's excreta poultry.

5. Readly susceptible to parasites

Most of the area subjected to infestation by internal parasites which have a secondry life cycle on pastures. Without an adequate programme of parasite control, sheep may become heavily parasitized on pastures. This can result in reduction weight, anaemia, diarrahiea and death.

6. Require simple shelter

Sheep can spend a large part of the year on pastures. Housing will be necessary during the lambing period, but need not be expensive. Protection against severe storms, snow and wind should be provided for young lambs or nely born sheep during winter months.

7. Live on very cold climate

Sheep rearing is successfully done in cold weather conditions. Critical temperature, below which the sheep must speed up its metabolic rate to maintain a constant body temperature of 102.3F is 28 F and for the newly born is 50 F

8. Lambs grow better

It is advantageous to rear lambs for fattening on sheep farms. This covers the risk of diseases, over-grazing, tiredness and provides a balanced food to achieve a regular weight gain. One can grow more number of sheep on a given piece of land than other animal.

9. Requires timely management

Every sheep has a massage to give. It is the best observation of the shepherd that can get the time arrangement of operatins to minimize the loss. Any delay causes poor productivity. For example, delay in breeding, delay in deworming, delay in weaning, vaccination, etc. Each sheep producer should develop a management calendar for each month of the year to be sure that each job is completed on time and not overlooked.

Sheep Breeds of India

Sheep is found all over India. The breeds of sheep differ in their characters which largely depend on the geographical conditions of the region. India can be viewed through three sheep growing regions, namely 1) cold himalayan region,2) dry western rehion and 3) southern region.The breeds of sheep are very specific in each region and produce either wool or meat and have adjusted to the climate, feed and fodder availability in the region. At present various indigenous breeds, exotic rams for breeding, crossed strains and synthetic breeds for fine wool and mutton are found in various regions of the country. One can get the information of latest breds for his locality from the sheep breeding station in that region. Table-2 gives an over view of some important breeds in our country.

Recent Developments

The control and manipulation of the sheep reproductive system is one of the main objective of sheep breeding. The sheep has gestation period of about five months, and can produce more than one off-spring per pregnancy. Therefore,reasonable control over its interbreeding period,ensurance on fertilization,the shedding of ovules and rate surival rate bcan increase its reproductive rate.

Table -2: Sheep beeds of india

S.No.	Region	Name of the breed
1.	Synthetic breeds for fine wool	Nali-Synthetic, Chokla Synthetic
2.	Synthetic breeds for muton	New-Synthetic Mandya-Synthetic Nellore-synthetic
3.	Clod Himalayan region	Gureze,Karanah,Bhakarwal, Guddi. Rampur Bushair
4.	Dry western region	Lohi, Bikaneri, Marwari, Kutchi, Kathiawari,
5.	Southern region	Deccani, Nellore, Bellary, Mandya, Bandur,
6.	Exotic breeds	Rambouillet, Leicester, Corriendale, Merinos, Lincoln Cheviot.

Recent advances in synchronization of oestrus during breeding season by use of vaginal progestagen pessaries or progesterone implants or prostagalandin injection have not only shortened the lambing period but have also allowed the off season breeding at more freuent rate. futher, use of lambs at younger age of 7-8 months in breeding have resulted in genetic advances in fecundity or fertility. Similarly, develpment of tecurition for testing pregnancy and induction of premature parturition have revolutionized the reproductive rate of the sheep. Immunization against steroid hormones have increased ovulation rate and production of twins and triplets.

Sheep Husbandry in India

Sheep in India are useally samll flocks with a few large sheep flacks in Gujarat, Rajasthan, Himachal Pradesh and Jammu & Kashmir. Sheep are generally grazed on common land pastures, alone the canal side or roadside pasture or on the slopes of hills during summer. The housing of sheep during parturition, fattening lambs or diseaed animals is pittiable. Management lavel of the sheep floks is very low.

Constraints in Sheep Production in India

Various factors like price level, trade, capital and labour always come in the way of increasing efficiency of sheep production. These constrainsts are dicussed one by one.

1. Wool price

Though India is famous for quality wool fabric production,the prices of indigenous raw wool paid to the sheppherds are ridiculously low. There are many reason for this, which have been discussed in the booklet no 221 on Marketing of Indigenous Wool. Import of fine wool for blending 20-30% to prepare a superior lustrous quality fabric is not the real cause of low prices of wool. The predominance of middlemen in wool trade, which allow a nominal price of wool for shepherd, seem to be the real cause of poor income and constraints in sheep production.

2. Poor management

The low production rate of sheep because of sheep flock management is a serious restriction. This gives low return to investment. Sheep are not inherntly poor producer. In Fact, their biological potenmtial is higher than cattle. Still sheep producers are not able to make the best use of sheep's potential. Therefore, it is through prudent management that one can get higher production and sell it at a favourable price.

3. Cheap food policies

The Goverment of India because of high inflation rates, intervenes in food market by establishing price control. These cheep food policies do not promote production orattract new producers or to invest more on sheep rearing.

4. Grazing problems

In regions where a large population of the sheep is located, there is difference in the amount of grazing, feed available in rainy season and dry season. During the dry season due to feed shortages the sheep producers are forced to reduce the number of sheep by forced sale. This creates an excess supply which in turn, cause a decrease in price. To counteract these seasonal variations, management at the farm level needs to be improved by introducing some alternative feed supplements during the drought. Howerver, the cost of supplements limits their use unless credit or some other type of support is available.

5. Trade

Other constraints on increase of sheep production are international wool and meat trade bottlenecks and limitations imposed by the shortage of foreign exchange.India exports sheep meat to Arabian countries. The international mutton price is subjected to erratic changes which drastically affect the sheep trade.

6. International restrictions

Import and export policies on sheep products limit the supply by several factors and thereby influencing the sheep production. These factors are enumerated here.

a. Health and sanitation restriction,
b. Anticipated increases in domestic demand,

c. Influence of international market price,

d. Seasonal fluctuations in supply create problems in shipping and coordination with trading countries, and

e. lack of international grading and packing system.

7. Capital

Capital investment is a most for making any improvement in sheep production. In India mostly landless and poor prople are induced in sheep rearing. They hardly get any financial support from the government.

8. Nomadic production system

The nomadic nature of sheep flocks in India is anther problem which limits sheep production. Sheep owners are poor, ignorant and wander on forest lands and seldom represent in local administration. They are nearly powerless and depend upon the mercy of others who have predominant role in product marketing. Therefore, they cannot afford to get sufficient training and income for improving productivity of the sheep flock.

9. Risk as constraint

Sheep are living in harsh environment conditions. Adverse weather conditions, diseases, etc. Cause death or forced selling of sheep at cheaper rates.

10. Skilled labour

The recent advances in synchronization of oestrus with breeding season, increasing ovulation for twins and triplets production and get more lambing form off-season breeding require a highly skilled labour for feeding, breeding, housing, fattening lambs and disease control. As the production system becomes more sophisticated, so does the management skills. This is one of the major constrainys to achieve higher sheep flockproductivity.

11. Poor administration

Poor administraton in forest range pastures, common panchyat land or canal and roadside pastures, harassments and illegal hindrances discourage sheep owners. They are compelled indirectly to abandon their sheep flocks. They are fored to pay much more than official requriemants for grazing in common pasture lands.

Prospects for Increasing Sheep rearing enterprise are excellent, because sheep produce mutton and wool at relatively low quality feed material which often cannot be used in any period, high prolificacy, rapid growth rate and good marketaability to give return within one yea. Sheep do not complete with people, pigs, poultry, goats or cattle for food, and concentrates. Sheep production can be started with very little investment. Waste land pasture can be profitably used to supply enough food for sheep grazing.

PLANT ECONOMICS OF CHICKEN/MUTTON (SHEEP MEAT) PROCESSING

Rated Plant capacity = ***CHICKEN/MUTTON/SHEAT MEAT***
5000x12x25 KG MUTTON (ANNUM)
2000x12x25 KG CHICKEN PRODUCTS
500x12x12 KG EDIBLE OFFALS
2500x12x25 KG EDIBLE OFFALS

LAND & BUILDING
(Land required 3000 sq.mt) **Rs. 23,50,000.00**

PLANT & MACHINERY

Cutters & Choppers
Disintegrator Capable of producing homogenization of meat & mincer
Deep freezers with all accessories
Mincer S.S. complete with motor & starter Rs. 40,000.00
Preparation table
Jacketed kettle (S.S.)
Vessels of Aluminium & stainless
Weighing Plate form
Exhaust Box
Retort with thermometer & Pressure

Plastic crates
Baby Boiler
Tanks for curing, blanching etc.

TOTAL	**Rs.**	**9,57,000.00**

FIXED CAPITAL

1. LAND & BUILDING	Rs.	23,50,000.00
2. PLANT & MACHINERY	Rs.	9,57,000.00
3. OTHER FIXED ASSETS	Rs.	9,40,000.00
TOTAL	**Rs.**	**42,47,000.00**

RAW MATERIALS

Sheep 7500 x 25 kg
Broiler 3000 x 25 kg
Preservative & salt (10%)

TOTAL	**Rs.**	**56,27,000.00**

TOTAL WORKING CAPITAL/MONTH

1. RAW MATERIAL	Rs.	56,27,000.00
2. SALARY & WAGES	Rs.	33,600.00
3. UTILITIES & OVERHEADS	Rs.	19,850.00
TOTAL	**Rs.**	**56,80,450.00**

COST OF PROJECT

TOTAL FIXED CAPITAL	Rs.	42,47,000.00
MARGIN MONEY	Rs.	42,60,337.50
TOTAL	**Rs.**	**85,07,337.50**

TOTAL CAPITAL INVESTMENT

TOTAL FIXED CAPITAL	Rs.	42,47,000.00
TOTAL WORKING CAPITAL	Rs.	1,70,41,350.00
TOTAL	**Rs.**	**2,12,88,350.00**

TURN OVER/ANNUM

By sale of 5000x12x25 kg of Mutton
By sale of 2000x12x25 kg of Chicken
By sale of edible offals of
By sale of non-edible offals of

TOTAL **Rs. 8,50,50,000.00**

PROFIT = RECEIPTS - COST OF PRODUCTION = 1,29,78,054.15 =15.26%

RATE OF RETURN = Operating profit / T.C.I x 100 = 60.96 %

BREAK EVEN POINT (B.E.P) = 24.29 %

PLANT ECONOMICS OF GOAT AND SHEEP FARMING

Rated Plant capacity = 120000 LT.GOAT MILK/YEAR
1250 EIGHT,MONTHS,GOAT/YEAR
1250 NINE MONTHS SHEEP/YEAR.
1875 GOATS/Y.1875 SHEEPS/YEAR

LAND & BUILDING

Open land 2000 sq.mts.
Closed Aera 300 sq.mts.
Store, Office, Feed stock store 100 sq.mts.

TOTAL	**Rs.**	**8,90,000.00**

PLANT & MACHINERY

Milk tank (300 L Cap) made of S.S.
Milk Cans (Made of Aluminium)
First Aid isntruments
Laboratory & Testing Equipments
Ordinary Filter
Feeding Equipments Viz. Hay racks &

TOTAL	**Rs.**	**2,10,000.00**

FIXED CAPITAL

1. LAND & BUILDING	Rs.	8,90,000.00
2. PLANT & MACHINERY	Rs.	2,10,000.00
3. OTHER FIXED ASSETS	Rs.	10,44,000.00
TOTAL	**Rs.**	**21,44,000.00**

WORKING CAPITAL REQUIREMENT/MONTH

RAW MATERIALS

Cattle Feed Green Fodder Concentrate.
Health Expenses medicines etc.

TOTAL	**Rs.**	**1,00,000.00**

TOTAL WORKING CAPITAL/MONTH

1. RAW MATERIAL	Rs.	1,00,000.00
2. SALARY & WAGES	Rs.	41,880.00
3. UTILITIES & OVERHEADS	Rs.	34,500.00
TOTAL	**Rs.**	**1,76,380.00**

COST OF PROJECT

TOTAL FIXED CAPITAL	Rs.	21,44,000.00
MARGIN MONEY	Rs.	1,32,285.00
TOTAL	**Rs.**	**22,76,285.00**

GOAT AND SHEEP FARMING

TOTAL CAPITAL INVESTMENT

TOTAL FIXED CAPITAL	Rs.	21,44,000.00
TOTAL WORKING CAPITAL	Rs.	5,29,140.00
TOTAL	**Rs.**	**26,73,140.00**

TURN OVER/ANNUM

Receipt by sale of 1,20,000 litre.
By sale of 1,250 goat in a year
By sale of 1875 Goats in a year
By sale of 1,250 Nine mouths sheep
By sale of 1875 sheep in a year

TOTAL **Rs. 50,95,000.00**

PROFIT = RECEIPTS - COST OF PRODUCTION

PROFIT SALES RATIO = Profit / Sales x 100 = 47.26 %

RATE OF RETURN = Operating profit / T.C.I x 100 = 90.08 %

BREAK EVEN POINT (B.E.P) = 28.02 %

Chapter - 16

Tea Plantation/Cultivation

INTRODUCTION

Tea (Camellia spp) is an important beverage which is liked world wide more than any other drink. It is made from the tender or young leaves and unopened buds of the evergreen tea plant, which is popularly known as a 'health herb'. Two distinct varieties of tea plant generally recognised are the small-leaved China (Sinensis) and the large leaved Assam (assamica) which have been raised to a specific rank by a well known tea botanist.

The tea plant in its natural state grows into a small or medium sized tree, but in commercial plantation it is pruned and trained to from a multi-branched low bush and is encouraged to produce vigorous vegetative growth by adopting an appropriate schedule of fertilizer application.

The probable centre of origin of tea is near the sources of the Irrawaddy river and from there it spread to South-east China, Indo-China and Assam. The important tea growing countries are India. Sri Lanka, East Africa, Japan and Indonesia. In India, the crop is grown in Assam, West Bengal, Kerala, Karnataka and Tamil Nadu and to some extent in Tripura and Himachal Pradesh. The total area under tea in our country is about 4,28,000 hectare and over 682 million kg of product is obtained annually. Over one million workers are employed by the tea industry. Besides, it earns a considerable amount of foreign exchange to the country.

CLIMATE

Tea is grown on a plantation scale in many areas where the climate is moist and warm. These range from 43° N to 27° S latitude. It si grown from almost the sea level to about 2,460 meter. A well-distributed rainfall is essential for its satisfactory cultivation, although it is grown in many marginal rainfall areas also. The rainfall varies from about 125 to 750 cm in the tea growing areas in this country. Suitable temperature for the crop is in the range 10 to 27°C for optimum growth. However, the China tea are more tolerant to cold than the Assam types.

SOIL

Tea is planted on soils of widely different geological origin and actually it is grown on soils of almost all physical types. However, a well drained, deep and friable loam or forest land rich in organic matter is considered ideal. Tea soils are generally acidic (pH4 to 6) in nature, low in calcium and rich in iron and manganese. A soil depth of at least 1.8 m is normally required. Calcarious soils are unsuitable for tea cultivation.Sandy loam texture with sufficient moisture content is optimum for rooting.

The two main forms of cultivated tea are the China and Assam tea. The China type is fairly flow growing, dwarf trees with dark green, erect, toothed and narrow leaves. This normally grows to a height of about 4.5 metres. This type is relatively resistant to low temperatures but it is rather low yielding.

The Assam tea have a faster rate of growth and their leaves are large and dropping. They are tolerant to tropical temperatures and generally grow taller than the China type, often reaching a height of 9 to 10 m if unpruned.

Some hybrids and vegetatively propagated clones have been developed by UPASI Krishi Vigyan Kendra and other research institutions. Name of the important varieties and their qualities (given in bracket) are: UPASI-1 (hardy), UPASI-2 (hardy), UPASI-3 (yield & quality), UPASI-6 (hardy), UPASI-8 (yield), UPASI-9 (yield), UPASI-9 (yield), UPASI-10 (hardy), UPASI-24 (hardy), UPASI-25 (yield), UPASI-26 (hardy), UPASI-27 (yield), TRI-2024 (yield), TRI-2025 (hardy), CR-6017 (quality), W-35 (hardy),

C-1 (hardy), ATK-1 (hardy), 7/7/36 (hardy), SA-6 (hardy), etc.

PROPAGATION

Tea may be propagated by seed but it is now more customary to plant root cuttings. Cuttings are selected from high yielding clones, to avoid variation in vigour, maturity and quality which may result from seed propagations.

1. Seed propagation

Seeds are obtained from high yielding selected trees, preferably propagated from cuttings, which are grown in special seed gardens. These trees begin to produce seeds at about eight years of age. The seed capsules which fall to the ground are collected and graded. Due to their short period of viability, they should be sown in sand loam within four days at a depth of about 2.5 cm. The seeds are spaced at about 12 to 15 cm. apart. Germination may be improved by soaking them in water at about 12°C for 30 minutes. This treatment will also kill the larvae of the cover beetle.

The seeds should be protected from excessive sun and wind. On germination the seedlings should be transferred to polythene bags or 'sleeves' measuring 7.5 to 10 cm in diameter and 20 to 23 c in length. These are filled with soil containing organic matter and sand. Alternatively the seeds may be sown be in nursery beds.

Whatever the methods used, the seedlings requires regular watering and shading until they are hardened. It is customary to erect similar shading structures over seedlings to protect them from excessive radiation from the sun.

2. Vegetative propagation

Propagation by cuttings is becoming popular, due to the increased yield and improved vigour which can be obtained from selected clones.

Cuttings with one node and a leaf attached are generally used. They are obtained from green or moderately mature shoots. Special propagation beds are used. They should consist of a well drained subsoil. These beds are well watered and shaded. Polythene sheets, stretched over wire roof, are used for shading. Root cuttings are normally transferred to polythene bags and transplanted to nursery beds. About six to ten months time is required for the cuttings to root and grow to approximately 45 cm height when they are ready for planting out.

NURSERY MANAGEMENT

The tea are initially raised in nurseries. Careful attention is paid to the seedlings in the nursery to produce healthy plants. Depending upon the weather and region, one to one and half year old nursery seedlings are used for planting in the field.

1. Common maladies in tea nursery

In the tea nursery bed some problems may arise and they should be controlled periodically otherwise they will affect the yield of the tea significantly. Common maladies found in tea nursery and preventive measures are explained in table

2. Manuring of nursery plants

Composition of tea mixture can be prepared with following components.

Ammonium phosphate (20:20)	35 parts
Potassium sulphate	15 parts
Muriate of potash	12 parts
Magnesium sulphate	15 parts
Zinc sulphate	3 parts

Dissolve 3 kg of the mixture in 10 litres of water. Take 100 ml. and dilute to 10 litres (0.3 per cent). Apply with rose can over 4 sq. m (900 plants) at weekly interval.

LAND PREPARATION

In India, tea is grown on relatively steep sloping sites although undulating land is more widely used crops have not previously been grown. The forest, secondary bush or grass land should be cleared and all stumps and roots be removed, preferably by burning. On steep slopping sites, contour terracing will be essential and in valley drainage may be required. All weed cover should be removed and burned, particularly in areas where perennial weed grasses occur since these can compete seriously with new planted tea.

COMMON MALADIES IN TEA NURSERY

Sl. No.	Problems	Reasons	Preventive/curative measures
1.	Bitten off roots (in seedling)	High soil pH	Check pH of the medium before use.
2.	Club callusing	High soil pH, clay or sandy texture of soil	Check the soil pH and texture before use
3.	Mother leaf fall	Loose planting, deep planting, delayed planting excess shade, over watering in clayey soils	Put cuttings properly soon after collection and regulated watering
4.	Surface rooting moss growth	Clayey soil	Check soil texture and before use
5.	Early shoot growth	Excess light inside the nursery	Increase the shade
6.	Chlorosis and stunted growth	Manganese toxicity due to over heating	Avoid over heating of soil of soil
7.	Stunted growth, with vague chlorosis	Zinc deficiency with manganese &	Spray 2% zinc sulphate boron Check quality of cutting and put out in time. leach out excess salt with water
8.	Rooting of cutting	Tender cuttings loose planting delayed planting high electric conductivity	- do -

Adequate steps should be taken to prevent soil erosion in sloppy areas. Planting lines are drained and pits of a convenient size (generally 30-45 cm deep and 24 cm wide) are dug. The normal accepted spacing is 120 X 75 cm, accommodating about 10,000 plants in a hectare. The soil is heavily mulched during the initial one or two years.

TRANSPLANTING

Seedlings grown in polythene bags are transplanted to well prepared planting holes when they are of 40 to 50 cm height. This height may be attained when the seedlings are about 18 to 24 months old. Those grown in nursery beds should be planted with a ball of earth around the roots. If allowed to remain in the nursery up to three years, the seedlings can be cut back and transplanted as base-root plants. Planting holes should be prepared well in advance and should be at least 30 to 40 cm across and 45 to 50 cm deep. These should be half filled with top soil, to which about 15 to 25 g of double superphosphate or potassium sulphate should be well watered before being transported to the planting site. Care should be taken to disturb the root system as little as possible while transplanting, particularly if the plants have been grown in nursery and are lifted with a ball earth attached.

Newly planted tea should be regularly watered during the first four months to ensure good root development and should be shaded from the sun by leaves or fronds cut from the nearest trees.

SHADE TREES AND THEIR MANAGEMENT

In most of the tea growing areas in country, a system of shading the tea plants is practiced and experience has proved it to be a useful practice.

1. Advantage of shade

Advantages of shading are given here.

1. It regulates the temperature and increases humidity at bush level.
2. It minimizes loss of water through evaporation and tranpiration.
3. It serves as wind breaks.
4. It helps in the circulation of nutrients.
5. It reduces incidence of pests mites.
6. It generates additional income by way of timber and fuel.

7. It increase soil fertility by addition of 8-10 tonnes of organic matter/hectare/year.
8. It minimises soil erosion.
9. It helps in recharging of ground water.
10. Shading also maintains the ecological equilibrium.

2. Characters of good shade trees

1. Shading tree should be evergreen and should not defoliate during summer months.
2. It should be easy to propagate, quick growing and deep rooted.
3. It should be able to provide filtered shade.
4. It should withstand frequent looping, coupled with faster regeneration.
5. It should be tolerant to wind and frost.
6. It should have commercial timber value and should be less susceptible to pests and diseases.

In southern India, the silver oak (*Gravellea robusta*) is the best shade tree of choice (planted 600 X 600 cm later thinned to 600 X 1200 cm or 1260 X 1200 cm, as required). Other trees which are used for shading are *Ethyrina lithosperma* (dudap), species of *Acacia* and *Albizia*. Trees of *Albizia* species are most commonly used in tea plantations in North India. The shade provided by these is carefully regulated by pollarching (the practice of cutting the main stem with the object of developing lateral branches) the tree, wherever possible, and thinning out the branches, as required.

SPACING

The usual spacing for both seedlings and rooted cuttings is 75 cm apart in rows which are 1.2 or 1.5 m apart. This method of row planting which gives a plant density of 8000 plants/has is now widely used since it provides adequate access for the pickers and permits mechanical harvesting too.

MANURES AND FERTILIZERS

A systematic manuring schedule is followed right from the nursery stage up to maturity. The doses of fertilizers applied varies according to the type of tea, its performance, soil fertility and the yield potential of the crop.

The dosage of fertilizer according to the pH and age of the plant is given in the tables.

1. For soil with pH below 4.5

Composition	:	60:90:10::N:P:MgO
Ammonium sulphate	:	300 parts
Muriate of potash	:	150 parts
Magnesium sulphate	:	60 parts

Rate of Application

Age of plant	Kg/ha/annum N:P:Mgo	No. of applications	Qty. applied per plant (q.)
1st year	180:270:30	5	24
2nd year	240:360:40	6	26
3rd year onwards upto 1st pruning	300:450:50	6	33

Apply phosphorus at 90 kg per hectare every year in one application.

2. For soils with pH between 4.5 and 5.5

Composition	:	60:90::N:K
Ammonium sulphate (AS)	:	300 parts
Muriate of potash	:	150 parts
	or	
Urea	:	132 parts
Muriate of potash	:	150 parts

Rate of Application

Age of Plant	Amount kg/ha/yr N K$_2$O	No. of Appl.	Qty. applied/plant in grams cation	
			AS based	Urea based
1st year	180:270	5	21	13
2nd year	240:360	6	23	15
3rd year onwards upto 1st pruning	300:450	6	29	18

Apply phosphorus at 90 kg/ha every year in one application.

3. **For soils with pH above 5.5**

Composition with water soluble phosphate	:	3:1:3::N:P:K mixture
Ammonium sulphate	:	100 parts
Ammophos (20:20)	:	50 parts
Muriate of potash	:	50 parts

Rates of application

Age of plants	Amount kg/ha/yr N:P$_2$O$_5$:K$_2$O	Number of application	Qty. applied plant (g)
1st year	180:60:180	5	19
2nd year	240:80:240	6	21
3rd year onwards upto 1st pruning	300:100:300	6	27

Apply the recommended quantity of mixtures along the drip circle of plants when there is adequate soil moisture and when the fields are free from weeds. Punch holes of 15-22 cm depth in the soil in either side of the plants and place the rock phosphate.

MULCHING

Freshly planted tea plantations should be heavily mulched with dried grass, cereal straws or maize stalks to conserve soil moisture. Care is taken not to place the much too close to the base of the newly planted bushes. Mature tea plantation can be mulched with the pruning, when it is necessary to reduce the height of the plucking table.

TRAINING AND PRUNING

The tea plant is initially trained into a small bush by 'centering' low within a few months of planting or at the nursery stage itself, by removing the central leader stem in order to encourage a quick development of the lateral branches. The lateral branches are cut to a convenient length of 40 to 50 cm, and their growth above this length is periodically plucked.

In southern India, the pruning cycle extends over a period of 4-5 or 6 years depending on the elevation and growth. In some instances a 'skiff' is given at a convenient height and the pruning cycle is extended for a further 2 or 3 years. Pruning and skiffing are done periodically to keep the height of the bush at convenient level for the pluckers to operate and to encourage vegetative growth.

IRRIGATION AND WATER MANAGEMENT

Majority of tea growing areas in South india receive adequate rains for crop production. Yet due to the seasonal pattern of rainfall, most of the districts are exposed to drought of varying degrees. The obvious solution is efficient water management measures. These include proper soil and water management practices in the field. The following irrigation systems are practiced in tea plantations.

1. Subsoil irrigation

Subsoil irrigation is specifically recommended for young tea plants. Water is delivered to the plants at about 15 cm. depth through tubes or by subsoil injectors. This method helps in the development of deep root system in young plants.

2. Sprinkler irrigation

This is the most popular system of irrigation in tea plantations. The advantages of sprinkler irrigations are:

(a) It can be employed in all the terrains
(b) The required quality of water is uniformly distributed
(c) Water can be applied to the soil at slightly lesser than infiltration rate thereby preventing run-off and deep percolation loses.

3. Drip irrigations

In this micro-irrigation system, water is applied through a network of plastic tubing with drippers which are suitably spaced to deliver water to the soil surface near the root of the plants. Consequently there is less water loss through evaporation or percolation. Drip irrigation @ 2 mm per week gives desired results. However, the major constraint in this system is the larger initial investment which cost about Rs.50,000.

If the monsoon comes early, its effect may be extended by a month by giving three to four inches of water in two applications at about 15 days interval. Similarly, if summer showers are not received in time, irrigation may be resumed by late March. It is necessary to expose the plants to certain length of drought so as to harden them in the field. Water requirement of tea is given in the table.

Water Requirement of Tea (cm)

Yield kg/ha /month	Soil water	Transpiration per annum	Evaporation loss/annum	Minimum water required per month
1000	36	17.5	60	6.46
2000	36	35.00	55	7.52
4000	36	70.00	50	10.04
6000	36	140.00	45	15.49

WEED CONTROL

Herbicides can be used to control most weeds but some weeds are resistant to them and may require removal by hand. Cock grass (Digitaria scalarum) is a serious weed of tea, and it should be controlled at an early stage. The use of hoes in weeding is likely to damage the surface feeding roots.

DISEASES AND PESTS

All the tea plantations in India are susceptible to diseases and pests. The major diseases and pest of tea and their control measures are mentioned here.

A. Diseases

The main pathogen which attacks the tea plant are fungi. They mainly attack roots and leaves of the plant and reduce the yield significantly. some of the important diseases are explained here.

1. Root diseases

The roots of tea plant is affected severely by diseases. They are classified as:

(a) Primary root disease
(b) Secondary root diseases.

a. Primary root diseases

Under this the fungi attacks the roots of the plants. There are about five primary root diseases which are explained here.

i. Black root diseases

This disease is caused by fungus *Rosellinia arcuata*. This is the first identified disease in tea plant. The main symptoms of this disease are black, woolly mycelium growth on root surface and at collar regions. There is also white and star shaped mycelium between bark and wood. Black red-shot like bodies (perithecia) are seen occasionally, Mycelium of the fungus grows freely through surface soil and organic matter.

Control

1. Remove surface mulch from 10 meters area.
2. Drench the soil with Dithane M-45 or Captan 30 g per 10 litres of water.

ii. Red root disease

This disease is cause by the fungus *Puria hypolateritia*. The main symptoms of this disease are, mycelium becomes white, which later on turn red and in advanced stages it may appear black. It is inter woven with adhering soil, on washing the soil blood red mycelium is seen. Frutification plate like structure with spores at collar region is seen. Slowly the wood becomes spongy.

Control

1. Isolate the infested area.
2. Uproot and burn the infected branches.
3. Rehabilitate soil with Guatemala grass.
4. In the month of April/May or November/December punch hole of 30 cm depth, Drench these holes with the chemicals such as Methane sodium 8 ml/hole and Carbon disulphate 16 ml/hole and fill with the soil. After filling the holes, provide light watering.

iii. Brown root disease

This disease is caused by the fungus *Fomes noxium*. This is a common disease wherever tea garden is at low elevation. the major symptoms of this disease are not the colour of fungal mycelium turns brown and the wood turns soft and spongy. Honey comb like reticulations are found on the wood and the fruitification seen on stumps are irregular and hard.

Control

The control measures of this disease are same as that of red root diseases.

iv. Root splitting disease

This disease is caused by the fungus *Armillaria melllea.* Under the attack of this disease longitudinal cracks are seen on the root bark. Mycelium growth is seen as white and compact which grows in between bark and wood with strong mushroom smell. There is also presence of rhizomorphs resembling shoe lace and is dark brown in colour.

Control

The control measures of this disease is also same as that of red root disease.

v. Xylaria root disease

The disease is caused by the fungus *Xylaria spp.* which occurs in isolated patches. The root surface of the plant is covered by black ribbon like hyphae, mycelium is superficial and confined to bark which is seen on collar regions. Extensive necrosis is seen on feeder roots.

Control

Control measures are same as for red root disease.

b. Secondary root disease

In this case the fungus is of secondary importance, because some predisposing factors like drought, waterlogging, lightning, malnutrition, etc. are responsible for th infection. There are three types of secondary root disease, which are explained here.

1. Charcoal stump rot

This disease is caused by *Ustulina zonata.* The predisposing factor of the disease is lightning. The symptoms are sudden death of bushes. White fan shaped mycelium between bark and wood, and charcoal like encrustation is seen on the bark in advanced stages.

Control

1. Uproot the lightning affected bushes immediately.
2. Fork and loosen the soil one year prior to planting.
3. Make 60 X 60 X 60 cm. pits with 1% copper oxychloride suspension
4. Avoid application of nitrogen in the first year of planting.

ii. Diplodia root disease

This disease is caused by *Botryodiplodia thebromae* which is commonly seen in low and mid elevations. The predisposing factors of the diseases are bard and continuous plucking, prolonged drought and damage due to pest and diseases. The main symptoms of this disease are: weak appearance of frame and presence of unhealthy leaves; failure of bushes to recover after pruning; die-back of new shoots developed after planting; and presence of white spots with black centers on roots.

Control

1. Carry out pruning at the right time.
2. Adopt proper plucking standards.
3. Adequate manuring and timely plant protection.

iii. Violet root rot

This disease is caused by *Sphaerostilbe repens*. The predisposing factor of the disease is waterlogging. Due to the attack of this disease leaves turn yellow and droop. There is also gradual death of bushes. Roots become inky black/violet and there is presence of elongate lenticels on root bark. Due to this there is development of rancid odour-vinegar smell. The mycelium of the fungus is white which later on turns to purple colour and is seen on wood.

Control

1. Avoid planting in waterlogged areas.
2. Improves drainage.

2. Collar canker

This disease is caused by *phomposis thene*. It is mostly seen n young tea garden. The pathogen invades stem mostly through open wound. The predisposing factors are deep planting, planting in gravelly soils, mulching closer to collar, wound caused by weeding implements, fertilizer application closer to collar pegging, low moisture status in bark and surface watering during dry weather. The main symptoms of this disease are chlorosis, cessation of growth, profuse flowering and formation of canker on stem.

Control

1. Avoid plating susceptible cones in gravelly soils and drought prone area.
2. Avoid other predisposing factors.
3. Remove affected portion by pruning to the healthy wood.
4. Apply copper fungicides to cut ends.

B. Pests

Every part of tea plant is subjected to the attack of pests and it is estimated that more than 1000 species of pests including mites, insects, nematodes and rodents feed on tea. The important insect pests which attack tea plants are described here alongwith their control measures.

1. Red spider mite (*Oligorychus coffeae*)

It is an important pest of North-eastern India which is the largest of all mites of tea and can be seen with naked eyes. This is generally wide-spread pest of tea. Due to mites feeding the upper surface of the leaves darken and then turn brown.

Control

Apply Quinalphos 25 EC or Monocrotophos @ 1 litres per hectare.

2. Thrips (*Scirtothrips bispinosus*)

Thrips are major pest in all tea growing countries. They are small in size but large in number. Warm and humid condition is favourable for their growth. Due to heavy feeding leaf surface becomes uneven, curled and matty. Feeding marks in buds appear as parallel lines on either side of mid rib when the leaf unfolds Yellowing along leaf margin also occurs.

Control

To control the insects apply Phosalene 35 EC @ 750 ml per hectare.

3. **Red coffee borer** (*Zeuzera coffeae*)

This insect is mostly seen in new clearing and occur in batches. Eggs are laid in strings. Larva is of 3 cm in size with reddish brown colour. The larva bores young stems and moves downwards which also makes holes at intervals to eject excreta and wood particles. Excreta, etc. are seen around the plants.

Control

1. Cut the affected stem from healthy plant.
2. Pour Aldrin/Heptachlor using ink filler.
3. Plug the holes with clay paste.

4. **Tea mosquito bug** (*Helopeltis theivora*)

This insect is a serious problem in the tea plantation area of Kerala. Adult insects are black in colour with red thorax. Eggs are whitish with two long filaments. The insect sucks the sap from buds, young leaves and tender stem. Leaves curl up, become gradually deformed and remain small.

Control

Apply Endosulfan 35 EC @ 750 ml/hectare controls the insects.

HARVESTING

The leaves are plucked and harvested at regular intervals depending on the growth. In hand plucking, two leaves and a bud are removed by twisting the shoots between the thumb and forefinger. Harvesting usually begins after four years for bushes propagated from seed, but vegetatively propagated plants comes to maturity earlier. The rate of growth is dependent on climatic and soil conditions. Therefore the growth rate of both seedlings and vegetatively propagated plants may be somewhat variable.

Due to maturity variations and rate of growth of many lateral branches, it is generally possible to harvest tea every 5 to 10 days at low elevations. At higher elevations, this period may extend to 14 days. The rate of plucking varies from 25 to 40 kg per person per day.

YIELD

It has been calculated that at an average moisture content of 75 to 80%, 2.5 kg. of harvested shoots will produce 10.5 kg of dried tea, and one hectare of tea plantation will produce 800 to 1000 kg of processed tea. However, yield may vary considerably due to environmental factors. Under good management, plantations which have good soil and climatic conditions may produce yields of more than twice this amount.

In north India the economical life of the tea bush is generally 40 to 50 years and, therefore, 2 to 2.5% of the area is uprooted and replanted every year. In south India, such regular uprooting and replanting are not practiced, because economic yields are obtained from sections which are 80 years or even older.

PROCESSING

The shoots may be prepared in several ways to produce either 'blade' or 'green' tea. To make the former, the leaf is usually withered and rolled or distorted, by rolling in the conventional tea rollers, or is passed through tea machines. Of latter origin, the 'rotorvane' and C.T.C. rollers which exert drastic pressure on the withered leaves (for unconventional methods of manufacture). The juice of the leaf cells is exposed to air for oxidation (fermentation in tea parlance) when important chemical changes takes place. When the optimum state in the chemical change is reached, the action of the enzyme is arrested by drying the fermented leaves in a current hot air in suitable tea dryers. In the production of 'green' tea the shoots are steamed as soon as possible after plucking and the leaf oxidiase is destroyed so that fermentation does not take place on rolling.

The processed tea is passed through a series of meshes, thus sorting out leaf grades and dust. By this method of tea leaves are sorted into different grades.

PLANT ECONOMICS OF TEA PLANTATION

Plant capacity = 12231.00 KGS/day

LAND & BUILDING

(Land area required 1500 acres) Rs. 3,20,50,000.00

PLANT & MACHINERY

Tractors, Kudalis, Belcha, Axes, Sprayers, Ridge plough and other Agricultural implements unspecified

TOTAL Rs. 5,75,000.00

OTHER FIXED ASSETS

TOTAL Rs. 1,30,000.00

FIXED CAPITAL

1.	LAND & BUILDING	Rs.	3,20,50,000.00
2.	PLANT & MACHINERY	Rs.	5,75,000.00
3.	OTHER FIXED ASSETS	Rs.	1,30,000.00
	TOTAL	**Rs.**	**3,27,55,000.00**

WORKING CAPITAL REQUIREMENT/ANNUM

RAW MATERIALS

(Tea seeds/cuttings Land preparation for plantation of the plants from nursery to main garden,as cultivation,digging, Plantation expenses, Manuring, Weedicides, pesticides

TOTAL Rs. 88,00,000.00

TOTAL WORKING CAPITAL/ANNUM

1.	RAW MATERIAL	Rs.	88,00,000.00
2.	SALARY & WAGES	Rs.	21,62,160.00
3.	UTILITIES & OVERHEADS	Rs.	41,12,000.00
	TOTAL	**Rs.**	**1,50,74,160.00**

COST OF PROJECT **Rs. 3,36,97,135.00**

TOTAL CAPITAL INVESTMENT **Rs. 3,65,23,540.00**

COST OF PRODUCTION/ANNUM **Rs. 2,18,72,044.10**

TURN OVER/ANNUM

1. By sale of 3669300 Kgs. of tea

TOTAL **Rs. 2,93,54,400.00**

PROFIT SALES RATIO = Profit / Sales x 100 = 25.49 %

RATE OF RETURN = Operating profit / T.C.I x 100 = 20.49 %

BREAK EVEN POINT (B.E.P) = 55.44 %

IMPORTERS OF TEA

Agio Chai and Beverages Ltd.
119870, Zuhovsky Boul,
22/39, Moscow.
Tel : 246 - 7600
Fax : 245 - 3027

C.B. International
117393, Vlasova Arkhitektora Ul.51,
Moscow.
Tel : 128 - 9666/9621
Fax : 128 - 9666

Mil Ford
129100, Krasnogvardeysky 1st proezd 12,
Moscow.
Tel : 253 - 9275, 205 - 6054
Fax : 205 - 6054

United World Limited
Yushunskaya bol. Ui. 1A.
Kor.4, # 904
Tel : 318-5853
Fax : 3185853

Wayport Developments
129099, Smolenskaya Ul.8,
Belgrade Hotel.
Tel : 248 - 7021/2521/9685
Fax : 248 - 7017/2303

M.K. Shah Export Ltd.
121248, Kutuzovsky prosp. 5/3,
Moscow
Tel : 243 - 4603/1854
Fax : 243 - 1854

Chapter - 17

TEAK TREE PLANTATION

Time table of Plantation Work

It is essential to work out a suitable time table in each region for carrying out different items of plantation work and adhere to it strictly. The arrangements commence often as long as 2-3 years before the actual planting and success of the plantation depends largely on timely execution of these operations. If any one of the operations concerned is delayed, the success of the whole plantation is jeopardized. For instance, if the preliminary burn is delayed due to non completion of felling and extraction within the specified date, an early shower will make a clean burn impossible. Similarly, if planting is delayed the plants get a relatively late start, greatly increasing casualties as well as weed problems. even to the extent of making the plantation more or less failure. Inordinate delay may necessitate change in the method of stocking e.g., entire planting in place of stumps.

A typical time table for rising a regular teak plantation by stump planting without toungya is South coimbatore division, Tamil Nadu is given below.

Table

Time table for Regular teak plantation raised from stumps

	Nature of work	Last Date For completion
1.	Timber Felling	31st October
2.	Rubbish felling	15th January
3.	Preliminary Burning	15th February
4.	Piling Reburning	15th March
5.	Alignment and Staking	1st April
6.	Stump Planting	10th April (Started by 10th April)
7.	Enumeration	1st June
8.	Replacement of casualties	15th June
9.	1st weeding	May or early June
10.	Subsequent weedings	About 5 more weeding are done as weed growth is very heavy.

A typical time table for raising teak plantation as commercial venture is part of bori and Sukhtawa range of Hoshangabad forest division , Madhya Pradesh with stemp and pre sprouted stump planting is given below.

Table

Time Table For Raising Commercial Teak Plantation

	Nature of Work	Period
(a)	Exploitation, Logging	1st September to 31st March With haulage upto 30th april
(b)	Nursery operations for raising of Planting Stock	
	(i) Collection of Seed	1st February to 31st March
	(ii) Weathering and storage	15th June to 16th September
	(iii) Preparation Of bed	1st Dec. to 23rd Feb.
	(iv) Sowing in bed	1 March to 31 March
	(v) Watering, weeding	1st March to 30th June and 1st Sep. to 15th June.
	(vi) Digging out and preparation of stumps	15th June to 7th July.

(c) **Planting Operation**

(1) Disposal of slash/debris	1st March to 31st March
(2) Burning and Reburning	15th April to 30st April
(3) Staking at 2 m X 2 m	1st May to.31st May
(4) Planting operations	15th June to 15th July
(5) Weeding (3 weedings in the first year, 2 in the 2nd Year and one in the 3rd Year)	1st Aug to 15th Oct.
(6) Soil working, mulching and application of fertilizers	1st September to 15th Sep. and 1st May to 31st May

Note:- The time schedule indicated above for various operations envisages that the spill-over work is to be extended to a week only, and not beyond and planting is to be done after 5 cm of cumulative rain has occurred with the break of monsoon. The soil working is done, one in october with 3rd weeding and the other in May. Proper doses fertilizer are to be applied twice in a year, one in september and the other in May.

It will be seen that the two planting time tables are largely conditioned by the likely date of break of monsoon in South Coimbatore and Hoshangabad division. In the former, this date is in the middle of April, but in the latter, in the middle of June. Time tables for various regions are dictated by the expected dates of break of monsoon in those regions.

Problems of pure teak plantation and remedial measures

Most of the teak plantations in the past have been done due to its very high value and great hardiness. Attempts at raising mixed crops have been few and rarely successful. As with other monocultures, strong objections have been raised to the growing of pure even aged teak plantations. The chief amongst these are : their rate of growth slackens after 20 years; they cause deterioration in the soil and lower the site quality; they accelerate soil erosion resulting in loss of increment and volume production; the crops, in course of time, develop excessively fluted boles and epicormic shoots, depreciating timber quality; pure teak crops have greater exposure to epidemics and damage by insects and other pests; and pure teak crops create conditions wherein second rotation regeneration is difficult, Attention has also been repeatedly drawn to the fact that teak is not naturally gregarious but is found singly or in relatively small groups, in complex mixtures unless the forests have been much altered by fire and grazing. Thus, it is argued that, as the natural mode of occurrence is in mixtures, attempts to raise pure crops are against nature. A conservative approach to follow nature and retain the mixed type as far as possible has thus been urged upon.

The available evidence with regard to the ill - effects attributed to the purity in teak plantations was sifted and weighed carefully. They found lack of satisfactory statistical evidence to support the alleged disadvantages mentioned above. These alleged disadvantages are discussed and the conclusions reached by an auther are listed below:

(1) Falling off in rate of growth vigour :-

The young teak plantations which started full of promise in Burma and elsewhere often became disappointing after reaching about 20 years of age or even earlier. These observations were, however, contradicted by the observations made in West Bengal. Kerala. Tamil Nadu The normal pattern of growth of a uniform crop is faster to start with, and slower later on, as compared to that in an irregular corp. A very rapid height growth in early youth, falling off gradually in later years, is a characteristic of teak when grown in a uniform crop. This may give a wrong impression of a falling off from early promise. The study of the height/age curves in the teak plantation yield tables for India further showed no unnatural falling off in growth rate. The normal fall in rate of growth in middle age is not of much importance when considered in relation to total increment. On the other hand, in natural mixed forest, the growth to begin with is almost certainly slower and rises later when the plant shoots up above the level of its competitors.

(2) Deterioration of soil lowering of the site quality-

The difficulties experienced in generating the oldest plantation in Nilambur after the first rotation between the years 1917 and 1928 and the poor growth put on by some second rotation crops in comparison to the original first rotation crop were apparently responsible for the widely expressed view that soil had deteriorated under the pure first rotation crop. Studies were made in the forest soils of Nilambur division , Kerala to determine the extent to which soil characteristic were affected by deforestation followed by a pure plantation of teak. Examination of soil profiles both from natural forests and teak plantation of age 1,15,30,60 and 120 years showed that morphological features of the soils had been altered by silvicultural operations. A surface layer of decomposing organic matter was seen only in natural forest and the 120 years old teak plantation . The study further indicated that with the variation in the age of the teak plantation the organic matter content of soil ft. different depths also varied. The surface oils of young aged teak plantation showed higher values for apparent density absolute specific gravity and relatively lower values for pore space water holding capacity and percentage volume expansion indicating that physical condition of soil are markedly altered due to deforestation and planting to teak. These values are well pronounced upto a period of 30 years after planting. The physical properties o soils from the 120 years old plantation were found comparable to those of the natural forests.

Subsequent studies also indicated no apparent inferiority in second rotation crops and ascribed the past failures mainly to faulty methods of stocking, or faulty selection of site. No serious permanent deterioration in soil had become apparent, though temporary adverse conditions, such as hardening of soil and appearance of coarse grasses and climbers, had been caused hindering regeneration. These could, however, be got over by soil working and suitable modifications in plantation technique. Soil moisture relations did appear to have somewhat changed adversely under pure teak crops, possibly due to soil having developed low permeability. Occasionally, such areas turned swampy after clearfelling.

There is no definite evidence of deterioration of soil under pure teak plantations, though it is believed to occur to some extent in dry types of teak forest owing to exposure of soil when teak is leafless and also on the slopes in moist regions. The available information is still too scanty to permit any decisive conclusions regarding the alleged soil deterioration under pure teak crops. There has been no general agreement among different workers and much more research work is still needed to prove or disprove the hypothesis and provide an exact knowledge of the soil changes.

(3) Soil erosion:-

Pure plantations of teak with sparse undergrowth, of without any, commonly have exposed roots as the top soil is easily washed off. It is believed by certain workers that degenetation of pure teak forests is correlated with this kind of sheet erosion, which may be more serious if the ground is further exposed by burning. On the contrary, where an undergrowth is maintained and plantations are fire protected, erosion is not sufficient to cause any notable damage and erosion is not greater than under natural mixed forest. Therefore, the concensus of opinion is that erosion under pure teak can be effectively preventend by proper management practices which can create or promote undergrowth under the teak canopy .

(4) Fluting and general branchiness : -

These deformities were believed by some workers to be worse in plantations, who held that trees in pure plantations exhibited more fluting than trees growing in the natural forest. There is no statiscaly evidence for this alleged increased amount of fluting and branchiness to be due to crop purity. Fluting and branchiness are now regardind largely hereditary characters with seed origin.

(5) Epicormic shoots:-

The development of epicormic shoots is now regarded as the result of injuries and unfavourable conditions, particularly fires, defoliation and overcrowding. There is no proof to correlate it directly with purity of the crop. Moreover, as they do not usually persist, they are of little practical significance.

(6) Damage by insects and other pests:-

Indications are that damage to the timber by the beehole borer is somewhat worse in plantations than in natural forest, but factors like growth, vigour and rainfall are more important in controlling its incidence than the degree purity of the crops. The introduction of mixtures of undergrowth into teak plantation is believed to have a negligible effect on borer incidence.

Defoliation appears to be heavier and more common and epidemic attacks are more serious in pure plantations, especially where undergrowth is inadequate or lacking and this may cause considerable loss in increment.

The attacks of longicorn teak canker grub, Dihammus cervinus, in young plantations are more severe in pure crops than in mixed teak forests, though the damage done is not serious. The trees usually outgrow the vulnerable stage without serious loss. The same applies to Hypophassus attack in south India. Loranthus attack is also probably more severe in pure plantations than in mixed crops, but does not cause sufficient damage to warrant dilution of a valuable teak crops with less valuable species in mixtures.

(7) Difficulty in regenerating pure teak plantations- :

There is no evidence to show that purity of teak crop in the first rotation will cause difficulty in regenerating such crops artificially. The previously experienced difficulties in regenerating second rotation plantations on sites formerly occupied by pure teak are taken to be caused due to lack of material for a good burn, superficial changes in soil conditions and aggressive weed conditions. These are no longer taken to be significant, having been overcome by adopting suitable planting and weeding techniques.

(8) Inferiority of timber quality in plantations - The alleged inferiority of plantation grown teak timber due to paler colour, knottiness and a slightly greater tendency to split at the ends as compared to that from natural teak forests is believed to be primarily due to too rapid a growth. No data is available to correlate it with purity of the crop. Tests on strength properties have shown that these properties are independent of the origin of timber, irrespective of whether from plantations or from natural forest, as long as the rate of growth is satisfactory.

Thus most of the alleged disadvantages can not be attributed directly to species purity. For the few that can be traced back to pure planting, slight dilution of the teak crop with other species is not likely to bring a sufficiently great beneficial influence to counter balance the loss from introducing species of inferior value in the crop. However, it is of interest to examine the mixtures that grow, or have been introduced from time to time, in teak crops.

Mixtures:-

The associated species of the mixtures can form exclusively a cover crop, being of shrubby nature, or they can form an understorey beneath teak or penetrate the lower portion of the canopy, or grow between the crowns, or even go further above and tend to suppress teak. In addition, mixtures with teak can even be aged or uneven-aged, and may be further differentiated into natural or artificial. It may be mentioned here that the same mixture often changes its nature during the life even aged mixture of teak and Dabbergia latifola providing an example. The latter species starts as an undergrowth develops progressively to an under wood then to a crown mixtures and finally may become an overawed of wolf trees. Similarly the underplanting of teak by a younger species may later on acquire the appearance as an even aged mixture of teak and that species.

The advantages considered to result from crown mixture are based chiefly on theoretical conceptions, concerning optimum conditions of the growth of teak. Greater total volume production, improvement of soil with richer quality of humus matter and less vulnerability to insects and disease are some of these advantages. These advantages have in no case been practically demonstrated, and appear to be largely illusory. In India, teak is far more valuable than other species that might be mixed with it, and even if an increase in total volume production could be obtained from a mixture taking all species together, the value of such a crop would almost certainly be considerably less than that of pure teak plantation on the same site, though teak may be comparatively poorly grown. On the other hand, there is clear evidence that the competition of the intermixed species usually react unfavourably on the rate of growth of teak and on its branching; trials to raise several species in mixture led to wider spacing, which resulted in poorer stem and crown form in addition to a lower number per unit areas in teak, and often it was suppressed by the intermixed species and lost its straight stem. The mixtures also presented difficulties in silvicultural treatments.

On account of very rapid growth of teak in early stages, most of mixed species remain behind to start with; the spacing of teak, therefore, has per force to be increased for the development of mixture. Some species afterwards makes up with teak and then out strip it. Competition in the crown canopy and roots is a most unfavourable and decisive factor ultimately reducing the increment of teak. The stage at which the influence of root competition become active has not been determined, and even when the second species remains altogether below teak, its growth is checked.

Observation shows that the soil quality is not significantly raised under mixtures. Neither the greater shade nor the different humus formation, nor the more intensive exploitation of soil by the roots, influence of growth of teak one way or the other. Strip and group mixtures do not appreciably reduce borer damage and other attacks by insects or parasites. Crown mixtures, either natural or artificial, on the whole, are therefore, not considered as palliatives for the disadvantages attributed to pure plantations.

Early efforts in rising mixtures were made both with species which grow in height alongwith teak and with those that remain behind as underwood. Attempts were made to raise Artocarpus hirsuta and Artocarpus heterophyllus in alternative lines in some of the old teak plantations of Kerala and Karnataka. Planting of teak in sal lines in the toungyas of West Bengal; planting of Bambax ceiba and Mysore gum at wide spacing with teak in Kerala and Orissa; sowing of Dalbergia latifolia with teak in parts of Karnataka, Tamil Nadu and Madhya Pradesh; sowing of Albizia Lebback, Albizia procera, Clistanthus collinus, Dalbergia sissoo, Ougeinia oojenensis with teak in Uttar Pradesh and Madhya Pradesh; broadcast sowing of adina cordifolia, Anogeissus acuminata and Mitraguna parvifolia in teak taungyas; sowing of Pterocarpus Marsupium with teak in Karnataka and Madhya Pradesh and sowing of Lagerstroemia speciosa and Toona Ciliata with teak in West Bengal are example of attempts to raise mixed crop of teak, which have not met much success. Sowing of teak and Pterocarpus dalbergiodes 1.2 m part in alternate lines 2.7 m apart in Andamans, resulted in failure, as the latter was outstripped and suppressed by teak. Similarly, Gmelina Arborea in Assam, Madhya Pradesh, Maharahshtra, West Bengal and Orissa as well as Grewia tiliifolia in Kerala and Dalbergia latifolia in Karnataka and Kerala, overstripped and outgrew teak due to rapid growth. Trials with Swietenia macrophylla for a mixed crop in Kerala showed no true mixture, as teak suppressed the species on good soil and on laterite it suppressed teak. Among other species tried which produced a successful mixture to some extent, mention may be made of sowings of Acacia Catechu in Rabs in Maharashtra; sowing in Dalbergia Latiifolia in north Dhulia, Maharashtra, and North Kanara, Karnataka; dibbling of Terminalia Alate in ploughed lines in Teak pole areas of North Kanara, Karnataka and mixed plantations of Teak and Eucalyptus spp. in the sub Himalyan Montane region to provide protection of teak plants from frost in early years in Uttar Pradesh. Other species tried in mixture with teak are various bamboos, Ailanthus spp., Michelia Champaca etc. Mixed plantations of teak and Eucalyptus spp., raised in Yellapur and Dandeli division of Karnataka by intimate mixtures as well as by mixtures in patches and alternating strips with several planting patterns, indicated that the species can not be grown together without loss of increment and damage of the teak stems. The expectation that teak would not be suppressed by the lighter foliaged. Eucalyptus was found to be misplaced. Not only teak was suppressed by Eucalyptus, its stem become branchier and, in many cases, its leading shoots died. Not a single species has been found to form a satisfactory crown mixture; indeed most are harmful apart from posing difficulties for tending. The alleged disadvantages of pure teak plantations are, therefore, unlikely to be alleviated by growing mixed crops with only a moderate proportion of the subsidiary species.

Experience has shown that the raising and tending of mixed plantation requires far more experience and knowledge of the relative rates of growth and varying light as well as space requirement of the constituent species under different conditions than is at present available. Experiments in Java indicate that all mixtures in teak plantations result in a loss of increment of the teak, much exceeding, in value, the increment of subsidiary species so that they benefit likely to be reaped from the mixture must be derived from the maintenance of the soil in good condition for future rotations. The experience at Nilambur was that without an adequate soil cover deterioration may take place on the poorer sites but not on the better sites. The deterioration can be prevented by promoting a suitable undergrowth, the technique having been modified to encourage its natural re-growth.

The beneficial effects of mixtures by underwood or undergrowth in teak plantations are believed to be prevention of erosion and soil deterioration, control of defoliators and other insect pests, and provision of material for a suitable burn when regenerating pure plantations. Another benefit witch may occasionally be looked for is that it should be of economic value. The harmful effects: are reduction in the rate of growth of teak through root competition, increasing insect attack and damage by other pests through creating favourable conditions for the pests, lowering the soil quality by impoverishing it, and increasing the fire hazard.

Teak is not a good soil improver and it would often be silviculturally desirable to introduce an underwood artificially where a natural underwood of bamboos and wood species does not make its appearance, choosing a useful species, where possible, whose cultivation would be desirable. Undergrowth is desirable for preventing soil erosin under pure teak as well as to control defoilation and maintain soil fertility. Practically no attempts have been made to raise an underplanted crop with truly undergrowth species except for raising of mulberry at Nilambur, Kerala, perhaps on grounds of cost. The more usual practice is to encourage the existing natural undergrowth to come up. In Maharashtra, the undergrowth is often induced by adopting a proper sequence of regular thinining ending at half the rotation period and then carrying out selective cutting in the second half of rotation .

Although various species have been tried in the understorey in mixture with teak one ofthe two has almost failed being outgrown or suppressed by the other. Some underwoods of even age with teak but of doubtful value as soil improver have shown promise. A useful understroy has been successfully raised in Tamil Nadu, Kerela and West Bengal by underplanting teak with bamboos like Cephalostachyum pergracile, Thysortachys olivery, Bambusa Polymorpha, Dernrocalamus Longispthus, Bambusa arundinacea, Bambusa tulda nd Melocanna baccifera. But the rresulting benefit to teak or to soil is not very certain. It is however believed that introduction of bamboo might be helpful as teak with a bamboo understroay is a frequent assocition in natural forests where teak is usually very clean and well grown.

Studies made in Java showed that shallow rooted bamboos may be harmful to teak where competitions for moisture is severe but may be useful in the more moist forests types.

It has been possible to introduce an understorey in teak by underplanting immediately after thinning using several tree species. Undercrops of Hopea parviflora, Hydnocarpus weghtiana, Mesua ferrea Kingiodendron pinnaum and Artocarpus hirsutus etc. had been successfully raised in some earlier attempts in Kerala and Tamil Nadu while trails with Erythrina spp, Dalberiga letifoila xylia xylocarpa, dysoxylim malabricum toona Cilita and Sweitenia macrophylla did not meet much success. Similarly in west Bengal Palyquam polyanthum Dalbergia lotifoila and Artocarpus Choplasha dnin Madhya Pradesh and Maharashtra Erythrina spp. were tried but without success.

Opinion is devided as to when underplanting is best done. Some favour the idea of planting after the first thinning while other argue that as teak canopy closesagain too rapidly at this stage the work is much more likely to succeed it done at later stage. The balance of opinion favour the later stage owing to the dense cover drop and probably other factors considerable difficulty is experience in introducing an understroey perhaps for non existent benefits. It would be preferable to employ a shade bearer whenever a soil protection species or accessory species is to be introduced thinning teak more heavily than would be the case otherwise.

Underplanting involves cutting of lines through the undergrowth and the lower canopy. putting strong transplants along them and then removing the overhead cover gradually as the plants become established and the crowns become fully free. Underplanting is attempted only when the canopy has been lifted sufficiently to let in enough diffused light of permit the growth of the new planting and fairly heavy opinion is usually necesser. This is always a more difficult operation than the original planting the reduction of weed growth and competition being more than counter balanced by slow growth in the relatively weak light. In Java teak crops had to be opened out to 250 stempts per hectare at the age of 15 years before the underplanting was successfully accomplished. The operation resulted in a loss of increment to the teak. Therefore it was not considered to be an economics proposition. In Tamil Nadu it is now usual to underplant teak after the penultimate thinning with Evodia spp. Mesua spp. and Swietenia spp. at 3.3 m X 10 m using pot plant

Rauvolfia serpentna was cultivation as an intercop in teak plantation in Thana district of Maharashtra and was reported to have given encouraging results. In North west Bengal tumeric was planted in 2 years old plantation and harvesting after 2 years it improved the growth of teak apart from providing a substantial source of revenue.

In Maharahstra Ocimum kilimandscharicum after in teak plantation on rabs and also in teak nursery lines. It was found to adersely effects the growth of teak. Teak leaves were observed to have silted discoloured and shed earlier and the growth was almost stagnant. In the area not interplanting with ocimum teak plants were healthy taller and with full foliage. The adverse effects were ascribed to the close promixity of the aromatic shrub.

Leucanea leaucephala Tephrosia candida ingigorera spicata Indigofera Tinctora, Indigofera glegoides, Cajanus cajan and Crotalaria Juncea have tried as cover crops with teak for weed suppression and soil improement in Kerala and Karnataka. None of the species proved really efficient as nurse and cover crops. Similar results were obtained from experiments carred out at Dehra Dun.Such cover crops were found to retard the growth of teak without conferring any benefit. These however could often help in controlling grass which becomes a serious problem in many areas by arresting the growth of teak plants and increasing the fire hazard Leucaena leucoceptala one of the longest lived cover crops under teak was found to be better than any other species tried so far.

On the basis of available information a underplanting teak species should have the following attributes:

(1) The species must be a shade bearer preferably an evergreen or nearly so capable of withstanding drip and persisting throughout the life of the plantation bearing leaves and shading the soil while teak is leafless.

(2) It should be either a species that comes in or a species which can be easily introduced and can be retained with little tending.

(3) The species must be deep-rooted feeding in the soil layers below the teak roots.

(4) It should be capable of growing under teak without interference in the top canopy and should hvae minimum adverse effect on the increment of teak.

(5) It should be effective in checking soil erosion and also be a soil improver or at least be effective in maintaining the soil condition as far as possible.

(6) It should be effective as a parasite reserve against defoliators and other pests.

(7) It should not create serious fire hazars and be preferabley a fire hardy species.

(8) The species should have some economic value if possible.

The species having dense surface root systems which compare with teak and those with characteristics opposite to those mentioned above are to be avoided. No single species is likely to have all or even many of those properties. Perhaps maintaining a mixed undergrowth of selected species alongwith selective removal of undesirable species may be effective.

Plantation Method of Teak

The area to be planted with teak is clearfelled and the site is given a good burn. The areas teaken up for raising teak plantation are mostly South Indian moist ecidous forests in moist teak (3b/Clb) and slightly moist teak (3b/Cls) forests and Southern tropical dry deciduous forests in dry teak forests (5A/Clb). Teak is the most important species in these moist and dry mixed deciduous forests with **Terminala alata, Lagerstroemia parviflora, Pterocarpus Marsupium, Anogeissus latifoila, Chloroxylon Swietenia, Hardwickia Binata, Xylia Xylocarpa, etc as important association. Understorey is mostly of Dendrocalamus strictus, Mallotus phillippensis, Diospyrus spp. Grewia spp. etc**. These areas, among others, also include degraded teak forests.

Although various methods have been tried in the past e.g. dibbling seeds at different especements planting seedlings and planting stumps in pits and crow bar holes. the technique adopted now is mostly stumps planting of pre sprouted stumps is also practised to a limited extent. Of late, teak seeds collected from seed production areas in the state containing trees of good form and well developed crowns selected exclusively for the seed collection purpose are used for raising nursery stock. Permanent of semi permanent nurseries with watering facitlities especially in dry localaties are used with sunden of level nursery beds of size 1.3 m X 1.3 m . It has been found that the stups obtained from nurseries are usually of poor quality. Hence small dry nurseries are occawionally used if unavoidable only for augmenting the planting stock produced from the wet nurseries. The seeds are suitably pre treatment before sowing in the nursery beds. The method commonly used for pretreatment is pit treatment by spreading cowdung and farmyard refuse in a layer of 15cm depth inside a conveniently sized pit. A layer of teak seeds 15cm thick is spread over the bottom layer again 7.5 cm of cowdung and farmyard refuse is spread over the seeds. This layering operation is repeated till the pit is full. It is than covered with grass and leaf litter and watered for a week. The seeds are then taken out the sown in beds. Alternate soaking in water and drying for 24 hours repeating the operation for a week and than sowing in the beds is also sometimes followed.

For producing stumps, sowing of seeds in usually done in April and the seeds are sometimes covered with straw to aid germination. The beds are watered profusely until germination starts and thereafter moderately till the onset of monsoon, In the drier parts of the st.:te the beds are shaded to protect the seedlings from insolation during the whole or part of the hot wheather especially where pre-monsoon showers are delayed after germintion the shading is removed is removed after occurrence of pre-monsson showers. Pricking out of seedlings to remove congestion in the beds is usually not done.

Stums are made out of one year old seedlings raised in wet nurseries. Stump planting is done in crow bar holes at an espacement of 1.8 m X 1.8m with the first shower in the monsoon and where the soil is hard as in parts of Adilabad district. Planting is done in 30 cm cube pits. The best planting time in Telengana region is middle of May whereas in Andhara region best region best result are obtained by planting about 3 weeks before the break of monsoon . Inextermely dry areas planting of pre-sprouted teak stumps are done though failures due to dying back after prsproutingin field becouse of lack of development of roots, are not uncommon. *Taungya*method for raising teak plantation is practised on a smaller scale. Casualties are replaced in the second year both in regular and taungya plantation. Two to three weeding are done be weed cutting of weed pulling round the plant in the first year. Rigorous and repeated cutting back of bamboo regrowth is also done in areas where it possess serious problem. Lantana is equally serious in some plantation areas by reapperaing and retarding the growth of teak plants and needs to be controlled effectively in the second year, one or two weedings are done.

Important Adresses

M/s. Parasrampuria Plantations Ltd.,
Mittal Tower,
A-Wing,
Nariman Point,
Mumbai - 400 021.

M/s Sterling Tree Magnum (INDIA) Ltd.,
Appavoo Appts.",
1/5, Venus Colony
2nd Street,
Alwarpet,
Chennai - 600 018
Tel : 456456
Fax : 453277

M/s Khaitan Agro Industries Ltd.,
65, M.G.Road, Ist Floor,
Flora Fountain,
Mumbai - 400 023.
Tel : 275127/277796.

Anubhav Plantations
Anubhav Centre, 11,
Somasundaram Street,
T.Nagar,
Madras-600 017.
Te l: 823 5029, 8254155, 8282629, 8282833, 8283316.
Fax : 8284967.

Perutek Services Ltd.
M-4, Chiranjiv Tower,
43, Nehru Place,
New Delhi - 110 019
Fax : 91 - 11 - 6223958

Shri Chakra Agro Farms and Finvest Pvt. Ltd.
2nd Floor,
Ratna Devi Complex,
Dwaraka Nagar,
Ist Lane, Vishakapatnam - 16 (A.P.)
Tel : 0891 - 595249/556703

Balhara Inds. Ltd.
105, Freedom Fighters Enclave,
Nab Sarai,
New Delhi - 68
Fax : 91 - 11 - 6862288

PLANT ECONOMICS OF TEAK TREE PLANTATION

Rated Plant capacity = 67,450 Trees/20 Years.
TEAK TREE PLANTATION

LAND & BUILDING
Total land in 200 Acres **Rs. 2,21,46,000.00**

PLANT & MACHINERY

Tubewell with overhead tanks, Water Tanks Pneumatic seed sowing machine,Seedspaning drill, Pipe Line System, Wood Cutting Saws

TOTAL **Rs. 32,50,000.00**

FIXED CAPITAL

1.	LAND & BUILDING	Rs.	2,21,46,000.00
2.	PLANT & MACHINERY	Rs.	32,50,000.00
3.	OTHER FIXED ASSETS	Rs.	78,38,490.01
	TOTAL	**Rs.**	**3,32,34,490.01**

WORKING CAPITAL REQUIREMENT/MONTH

RAW MATERIALS

Manuring,Pesticides,Miscellaneous

TOTAL	**Rs.**	**18,000.00**

TOTAL WORKING CAPITAL/MONTH

1.	RAW MATERIAL	Rs.	18,000.00
2.	SALARY & WAGES	Rs.	59,375.00
3.	UTILITIES & OVERHEADS	Rs.	62,16,000.00
	TOTAL	**Rs.**	**62,93,375.00**

COST OF PROJECT

TOTAL FIXED CAPITAL	Rs.	3,32,34,490.01
MARGIN MONEY	Rs.	47,20,031.25
TOTAL	**Rs.**	**3,79,54,521.26**

TOTAL CAPITAL INVESTMENT

TOTAL FIXED CAPITAL	Rs.	3,32,34,490.01
TOTAL WORKING CAPITAL FOR 3 MONTHS	Rs.	1,88,80,125.00
TOTAL	**Rs.**	**5,21,14,615.00**

TURN OVER/ANNUM

By sale of 67450 Trees **Rs. 67,45,00,000.00**

PROFIT = RECEIPTS -COST OF PRODUCTION= 59,64,53,120.17

PROFIT SALES RATIO = Profit / Sales x 100 = 88.43 %

RATE OF RETURN = Operating profit / T.C.I x 100 = 1,144.50 %

BREAK EVEN POINT (B.E.P) = 5.19 %

PLANT ECONOMICS OF TEAK TREE PLANTATION

After the Age = 20 Years, the tree gets the
Average diameter = 27.2 Cm. and
Average height = 23.17 m
When the no. trees per hectare = 252
So the final yield of stem timber/ha. (m^3) is 68.223.
Let the teak plantation is done in 990 Acres.

LAND & BUILDING

1.	*Land 990 Acres (4074 square metres).*	Rs.	2,97,00,000.00
2.	*Miscellaneous construction, Boundry walls, Gate & Other construction*	Rs.	5,00,000.00
	Total	**Rs.**	**3,02,00,000.00**

PLANT AND MACHINERY

1.	Pump Set	Rs.	1,50,000.00
2.	Miscellaneous equipments for planting the trees	Rs.	10,000.00
	TOTAL	**Rs.**	**1,60,000.00**

OTHER FIXED ASSETS

Office equipments & Furniture	Rs.	12,000.00

FIXED CAPITAL

1.	Land and Building	Rs.	3,02,00,000.00
2.	Plant & Machinery	Rs.	1,60,000.00
3.	Other fixed assets	Rs.	12,000.00
	Total	**Rs.**	**3,03,72,000.00**

RAW MATERIAL

SEEDS OF TEAK

1 Hectare	=	10,000 m^2
We have 4033260 m^2 of land.		
So Land	=	403.326 hectare.
In 1 Hectare	=	No. of trees are 252
Total No. of trees	=	1,01,638 trees.
In 1 Kg. of seeds	=	No. of seeds are 1000
So quantity of seeds required	=	$\frac{1,01,638}{1000}$
	=	101.638 Kg. seed
Seed required	=	105 Kg.
Cost of seeds	=	105 x 25
	=	2625.00
Seed Required 105 Kg.	=	Rs. 2,625.00

TOTAL WORKING CAPITAL/MONTH

1)	Raw Material	Rs.	2,625.00
2)	Salary & Wages	Rs.	36,960.00
3)	Utilities & Overheads	Rs.	6,300.00
	Total	**Rs.**	**45,885.00**

TOTAL CAPITAL INVESTMENT

Total Fixed Capital	Rs.	3,03,72,000.00
Total working Capital for 3 months	Rs.	1,37,655.00
Total	**Rs.**	**3,04,09,655.00**

COST OF PRODUCTION / 20 YEARS

1.	Working Capital for 1 year	Rs.	45,185.00
2.	Interest	Rs.	55,21,321.60
	Total	**Rs.**	**55,67,306.60**

20 Years = 55,67,306.60 x 20 = 1.11 x 10^8

TURN OVER AFTER 20 YEARS

1.	By sale of 1,01,638 trees	Rs.	9.147 x 10^8

Profit = Receipts - Cost of Production = 9.147 x 10^8 - 1.11 x 10^8,

= Rs. 8.034 x 10^8

Profit/Sales Ratio = 87 %

Chapter - 18

Tissue Culture

Most plant species produce seeds which retain their viability for several years at normal temperatures. The viability of these seeds can be further extended by storing them in sealed containers at low or sometimes sub-zero temperatures keeping the moisture content between 5 and 7%. This is the most economical; means of germplasm preservation. However, there are many seed-bearing plants, belonging to the aquatic species, some tree species, some tropical fruit trees, perennial crops like coconut, rubber, etc, which lose their viability within a relatively short time, and for which alternative methods of germplasm preservation are important. In addition, there are some plants which do not produce seed, the only method for storing them being in their vegetative form as tubers, roots, cuttings, etc. This is a costly process involving labour for field collection and a proper arrangement for storing the propagules to prevent attack by pests, pathogens or by climatic or natural disorders.

Recent advances in agriculture with the development of selected high-genetic base. This has created a situation in which there has been a gradual disappearance of valuable germplasm resources which are an integral part of any plant-breeding programme. According to a recent report (Swaminathan, 1983), it has been estimated that tree formations are being lost at the rate of million hectares every year. Estimates also indicate that so far only 1 in 6 tropical plants have ever been given a scientific name, which means that with the destruction of the forests we may not be knowing what plants are being lost (Swaminathan, 1983).

Steps to preserve these genetic resources, now listed under 5 distinct types, were taken only during the 1960's. These groups of plants considered for conservation have been given in the International Biological Programme Handbook (Franknel and Bennet, 1970) (IBP) and include (i) cultivars in current use, (ii) obsolete cultivars, (iii) special genetic stocks, genetic and cytogenetic material, induced mutants, etc, (iv) primitive varieties or land races, and (v) wild and weedy species related to the cultivated species. Under the fifth type, wild species can be included which could be exploited but have not been cultivated and whose importance has not been assessed. Commercially important cell lines developed by tissue culture can also be added to this group.

This chapter deals with some of the current information on the application of tissue culture methods for storage and protection of such cultures. Tissue culture techniques using shoot tips have been extensively used for the clonel propagation of many economically important plant species. This method is preferred since plantlets regenerated from protoplasts, disorganised callus cells, etc are known to result, in many instances into genetic instability.

There are 2 main methods by which they can be preserved. The first aims at developing suitable procedures by which one could extent the interval between subcultures, and the latter for storage over long periods under very low temperature (cryopreservatio).

I. Requirements

a. Equipment

Laminar air-flow cabinet or sterile room
Sterile forceps, scalpel
Environmental growth cabinet
Microscopic slides
Pasteur pipettes
Binocular research microscope
Gyratory shakers

Stainless-steel sieves 60-70 um pore-size
Beakers (50, 100, and 500 ml)
Parafilm[R]
Cryopreservation equipment (as shown in figure)
Dewar vessel
Screw-cap bottles, petri dishes
Leather gloves, protective goggles and other apparel for handling liquid nitrogen
Water bath at 40°C
Low temperature deep freeze

b. Culture media, washing solutions, sterilizing agents
1 M DMSO
1 M glycerol
2 M L-proline
2 M sucrose
Evan's Blue 0.025% w/v
Fluorescein diacetate 0.5% w/v

c. Source tissue
Protoplasts isolated from various tissues grown in vitro or leaves, shoot apical meristems of plants, callus cultures, zygotic and somatic embryos

II. Procedure

a. Short-term preservation

It would be more advantageous to store either a callus or a cell suspension, which at the required time can be induced to undergo somatic embryogenesis or adventitious shoot formation generating the desired number of plants. In actual practice, however, this approach is not applicable to many plant systems. Moreover the morphogenetic potential of several unorganized tisue cultures declines when grown under in vitro conditions for an extended period of time. Another factor is their genetic instability in several cases. In general, the preferrec choice of starting material for germplasm storage are samples, derived from apical meristems for which methods of clonal propagation are developed.

However, it is often necessary, particularly when dealing with germplast preservation, to grown the callus, suspension shoot or root cultures under conditions which allow growth to take place only at a slow rate, so that periods between subcultures can be reduced. By manipulating the physical or chemical changes in the existing medium such controls can be regulated.

1. The composition or the concentrations of the nutrients of the culture medium can be altered to a subnormal level, or some of the essential growth hormones or regulators can be omitted or their concentration may be reduced
2. More recent research has shown that the growth rates can also be reduced by adding growth retardants like abscisic acid, maleid hydrazide, cycocel or compounds which induces an osmotic stress like mannitol, sorbitol, etc to the medium. The concentrations of these chemicals have to be determined in each case
3. Overlaying cultures with mineral oil (Caplin, 1959) can also reduce the growth rate of tissue cultures substantially. The depth of the oil layer varying from 5 to 40 mm is an important factor and has to be tested for each plant tissue
4. Changes in the incubation can also help in increasing the interval between subcultures. One of the methods by which this can be done, is by incubating the cultures in a refrigerator or maintaining them at 0° to 20°C depending upon the plant species being temperate or tropical. Temperate crop species like grapes, apples, strawberries and beets etc have generally been stored successfully at temperatures from 0° to 10°C and the tropical plants like cassava, potato, sweet interval, the growth at subopmital temperatures may not always be satisfactory (Rose and Martin, 1975). In some cases a combination of lowering the temperature to about 10°C with the addition of low levels of ABA or high sucrose concentrations has been found useful for prolonging the intervals from 6 months to over a year (Kartha et al., 1981).
5. A lowering of the oxygen tension of the medium has also been found to reduce the growth rate of some cultures. A similar result could be obtained by covering the culture vessels with a permeable polypropylene film (Westcott et al., 1977).

b. Long-term storage of cultures-cryopreservation

The methods discussed so far suffer from some drawbacks-although the meristems, buds, etc can be stored undisturbed for a few weeks or months, complete suspension of the metabolism of the plant material is not obtained.

However, in cryogenic storage of cells and tissues mainly at temperatures below-140°C or at the temperature of liquid nitrogen (-196°C), complete the cessation of the metabolism of the living material (plant or microbes).

For this method to prove satisfactory, the cultures must have the ability to grow after freezing and thawing. It is now known that depending upon the type of plant material used, the concentration of the cryoprotectant and the rate of freezing and thawing is decided.

Cryogenic equipments are now available commercially wherein the freezing rates of biological specimens can be precisely and linearly programmed by carefully monitoring the temperatures of the coolant and the specimens.

The details regarding the construction of the apparatus and the main protocol for cryopreservation is discussed. The procedures, however, have to be standardized for each species.

Protocol for cryopreservation

1. Cells or tissues in the exponential phase, pregrown in standard culture medium containing 6% w/v mannitol, are dispersed into sterile flasks cooled on ice
2. A cryoprotectant is required in all cases when a period of cold acclimitization is used. The more common cryoprotectant solutions used are either 1M dimethylsulfoxide (DMSO) + 1 M glycerol + 2 M L-proline or 1 M DMSO + 1 M glycerol + 2 M sucrose prepared in the culture medium, adjusted to pH 6.0, filter sterilized and chilled on ice. A 1-M DMSO solution has been found to be most suitable for preservation of protoplasts, meristems, callus pieces, zygotic and somatic embryos. An equal volume of the desired viscous cryoprotectant solution is then added to the previously cooled plant tissues and thoroughly mixed for an hour. Aliquots of the suspension containing the plant material are then dispensed in ampoules which are closed tightly and engraved
3. The ampoules are then transferred to an improvised freezing unit (Withers and King, 1980) and the cooling applied to lower the temperature at the rate of 1°-2°C per min. The rate of cooling has to be carefully studied if the rates given above do not prove good. As an altenative, the ampoules can be placed inside an insulated container and kept in a low-temperature deep freeze (-90°C or -10°C) (Sugawara

and Sakai, 1974). The specimens ar then kept at an intermediate sub-zero temperature of -30° to 40°C for about 40 min or to any determined length of time found suitable. The cooling is provided to the chosen temperature in the freezing unit at a reproducible rate and maintained at the desired temperature. They are then rapidly transferred to a Dewar vessel containing liquid nitrogen which serves as a suitable vessel for storage.

4. Some frozen specimens may then be thawed slowly in air at room temperature without loss of viability (Withers, 1984). However the majority of specimens require rapid thawing, because of the presence of freezable water which usually remains in the cells. Samples frozen in ampoules must be agitated in asterile warm water-bath at about 40°C until the ice in the mdium has melted

5. The protective agents are inhibitory to growth of plant tissue cultures and are removed by several washings with fresh medium. The time for each washing and the volume of the wash-medium is an important factor which has to be carefully studied. After this treatment cells are cultured on the respective media.

c. Viability assays

The viability of the tissues is determined at this stage using vital stains such as fluorescein diacetate (Nag and Street, 1975) or Evan's Blue.However, the viability of the tissues as determined by this procedure is no indication of the ability of the cultures to grow after freezing and thawing.

The conditions for conducting the viability tests using the stains are described (Withers, 1980) henceforth.

1. Fluorescein diacetate (FDA) staining

The 0.1 ml of an 0.5% w/v stock solution of FDA in acetone is added to 5 ml of a fresh culture medium. Once drop of this is mixed with one drop of the cell suspension culture and observed in a microscope under UV illumination where the viable cells fluoresce.

2. Evan's blue staining

One drop of a 0.025% w/v solution of Evan's Blue in culture medium is added to one drop of the cell suspension and observed in a light microscope. Viable cells remain unstained. This method of staining should be complementary to the FDA method.

The survival and growth of the tissues when transferred to the fresh culture medium after freezing and thawing and washing of the cryoprotectant, is also dependant on the correct stage in the growth curve at which cells are taken for freezing and thawing. Tisues taken from the late-lag to the mid-exponential phases gave the best regrowth (Sugawara and Sakai, 1974). the excised shoot-tips from Dianthus caryophyllus plants grown at 4°C and in an 8 hr light/day for 3 days, when subjected to freezing and thawing showed 6 to 7 times better performance than the shoot-tips from untreated plants (Seibert and Wetherbee, 1977).

CONCLUSIONS

The present state of our knowledge shows that although, the tissue culture methods have a potential application in genetic conservation, but we still lack the knowledge to decipher the structual and physiological changes that occur in *in vitro* cell-lines or the plants regenerated from them, as a result of freezing and thawing. This problem still requires extensive scientific research efforts before freeze-preservation methods form a practical solution for conservation of plant species, now endangered.

IMPORTANT ADRESSES

Chowgule Industries Limited
No.2, Unity Bldg.2nd Floor,
Tower Block, Mission Road.
Bangalore-560002.
Tel : 2224171-2235583
Fax : 2226217
[Range of horticulture/tissue culture products & cocopeat (Organic Manure), Range of products, recomended for Horticultural Activities].

Central Research Institute For Dry Land Agriculture
Santosh Nagar, Saida Bad P.O.,
Hydearbad-500 059.(A.P.)
Tel : 4530177
Fax : 453802

(Tissue Culture of Neem & Teak,Farm Implements, Agricultural Equipments & Machinery)

Indo-Australian Bio-Tech Services Private Limited
No.7, 7th Cross,
Lakashmi Road, Shanthi Nagar,
Bangalore-560 027.
Tel : 2224134-2232747
Fax : 2234223
(Indo-Austrilian Bio-Tech Services Pvt. Ltd. (IABS) is commited to produce eco-frinedly items useful for plant cultivation. It has come out with substitutes for chemical fertilizers and plastic con tainers. Organic manure manufactured have shown excellent results in reclaiming and conditioning soil and providing the plants with nutrients. They improve the taste, flavourm and shelf life of the produce and are economical. Bio-degradable bio-pots make the transport and transplant easier. the pots keep the root system suitably moist, promots growth and allow the roots to easily pierce through the wall. It degrades into compost in about four months after use. The plant can be transplanted along with the pot. it is a very useful innovation for hardening tissue cul tured plantlets. Bio-degradable bio-pellets serve the function of medium and the container as it retains shape for about four months after use.

Jain Irrigation Systems Limited
Jain fields , N.H.No.6,
Ramrhori,
Jalgaon-425 001.(M.S.)
Tel : 0257-220011
Fax : 0257-221122
(Drip Irrigation, Sprinkler Irrigation, Pipes, Tissue Culture, Green Houses, Liquid Fertilizers, Solar Energy)

Khadi & Village Industries Centre
65/B Zakir Nagar,
P.C.Colony , Kankarbagh,
Patna-800 020
Tel : 351935
Fax : 0612-350127-558857

(Manufacturers of Organic Liquid Fertilizer "Bio-Fert-M". It covers the field of Agriculture ,Horticulture, Floriculture, Sericulture, PIsciculture Mushroom, Tissueculture and Hydro ponics)

Kumar Gentech & Tissue cultures Co.
783,Bhavani Peth, Opp.- Nishat Theater,
Pune-411 042.
Collaboration: Flamingo International B.V.Holland,
Florist - De - Kwakel Holland,
Hilverda B.V. Holland.
Tel : 0212-650065-651165(Pune)
011-4645451 (New Delhi)
080-2241459 (Bangalore)
Fax : 0212-653365 (Pune)
011-4645169 (New Delhi)
(Production Displayed: Cut Flowers-Gerberas,Cladiolus, Liliums, Carnations , Tissue Culture Products & Company Profile.
Product Manufactured/ Services Offered: Gerbera, Banana Tis sue Culture Plants, Gladiolus, Lilium, Tulips etc. Flower Bulbs, Carnation Rooted Cuttings & Technical Services.
Products/Services Exported : Export of Gerbera, Banana & Ornamental Plants.

Micro plantae Ltd.
407, Dalamal Chambers,
29, New Marine Lines,
Mumbai- 400 020
Tel : 2080611-8351741
Fax : 2015248-8351753.
(Tissue Cultured Fruit, Flower & Ornamental)

S.R.Electronics
No. 87, Old Post Office Road,
T.Nagar,
Bangalore-560 028.
Tel : 6605354
Fax : 080-66004403/603302,.
(Manufacturers of Tissue Culture , Labs Equipments and Medical Equipments)

SIV Industries
" Viscose Towers ", 1078, Avinashi Road,
Coimbatore-641 018.
Tel : 0422-218020-29
Fax : 0422-218030
(Main Activity is to a manufacture Man-made Fibre. sister Concern Bhavani Seeds & Agro Products Limited, Agro Forestry Division, Tissue culture, Mico Farm Chemicals Ltd., Sterling Oil Division.)

Yamko JKM Engineering Limited
11,Peenya Industrial Area,
Phase-II,
Bangalore-560 058.
Tel : 8394933.
Fax : 8394936
[Greenhouses and its components, Floriculture (Rose Plants & Tissue Cultured Plants, Carnations, Ornamentals)]

Doulatram Agro-Tech Pvt. Ltd.
L.R.E.W., 'Empire House ', 3rd Floor,
214, A.K.Nayak Marg,Fort,
Mumbai-400 001.
Tel : 022-2063228.
Fax : 022- 2069709.
(Agro Shade Net For Plant protection, Floriculture Shading, Aplications : Tissue culture)

So Vitro Trading & Services
Flat No. 208-209, Cover Dale C,
South Main Road, Koregaon Park Extension,
Pune-411 001.
Tel & Fax : 0212 63 93 97.
(Undertakes Tissue Culture Projects)

Serwell Instruments Inc.
#149, First "R" Block, Rajajinagar,
Bangalore- 560 010
Tel : 3320209, 3325697.
Fax : 091-080-3325697

E-Mail: Serwell.blr@elnet.ems.vsnl.net.in

(Leading Suppliers of Complete Laboratory Analytical Instruments Such as: pH Metres, EC Meter, Lux Meter, Rotary Shakers, Imported Balances, Humudity/ Growth Chambers, Persitaltic Pumps & Laminar Flow Cabinets etc. for Tissue Culture)

Rajdeep Enterprises
3229/1,Ranjit Nagar,
New Delhi-110 008
Tel : 5748881, 5768881.
Fax : 91-11-5749991

(Specialist in: Timer and Tissue Culture Racks)

PLANT ECONOMICS
TISSUE CULTURES (100% E.O.U)

Rated Plant capacity = ***150000000.00 /annum TISSUE CULTURE***

LAND & BUILDING

Total land area required 1 Acre. Rs. 69,50,000.00

PLANT & MACHINERY

Tube well ,Pipe and fittings
Incubator ,Incubator shakers
Autoclave ,Inoculation Hoods,
Deep Freeze Refreigerator,
Plastic Carboys Weighing Balance
Hot Plate cum magnetic stirrer,
Benches of the height suitable to
work standing metallic wire racks,
PH meter, Aspirator to facilitate
filter sterilization, Vacuum Pump,
Steamer for melting agar, Glass Test Tubes
Wide mouthed, Glass culture vials &
other lab equipments, Disposable plastic

culture vials, Screw-cap glass bottles
Culture tubes and flasks, beakers,
traditional cottong plugs, wrapper
in cheese cloth.
Plastic kin laps
D. G. Set.
Boiler
Distilled water perparation Unit
Spectrophotometer

TOTAL **Rs. 64,55,000.00**

FIXED CAPITAL

1.	LAND & BUILDING	Rs.	69,50,000.00
2.	PLANT & MACHINERY	Rs.	64,55,000.00
3.	OTHER FIXED ASSETS	Rs.	29,00,000.00
	TOTAL	**Rs.**	**1,63,05,000.00**

WORKING CAPITAL REQUIREMENT/ANNUM

RAW MATERIALS

Seeds for Potato, Onion, Tomato,
Cauliflower, Cabbage, Ladies finger
Other types of beam, flower seeds
Ethanol (25%) & 70% Isopropyl
Alcohol for sterilization,Stock solution
Enzyme solutions,Coconut milk (cm),
corn milk yeast extreat eassence
Hydrolysate, amino
acids malt extract (ME).
Chromic acid,Sulphuric Acid
Banana, Potatos and Bamboo seeds
Miscellaneous Viz/sucrose, urea,
vitamins, detergents.

TOTAL **Rs. 14,50,000.00**

TOTAL WORKING CAPITAL/ANNUM

1.	RAW MATERIAL	Rs.	14,50,000.00
2.	SALARY & WAGES	Rs.	10,77,000.00
3.	UTILITIES & OVERHEADS	Rs.	12,08,000.00
	TOTAL	**Rs.**	**37,35,000.00**

COST OF PROJECT

TOTAL FIXED CAPITAL	Rs.	1,63,05,000.00
MARGIN MONEY	Rs.	2,33,437.50
TOTAL	**Rs.**	**1,65,38,437.50**

TOTAL CAPITAL INVESTMENT

TOTAL FIXED CAPITAL	Rs.	1,63,05,000.00
TOTAL WORKING CAPITAL FOR 3 MONTHS	Rs.	9,33,750.00
TOTAL	**Rs.**	**1,72,38,750.00**

TURN OVER/ANNUM

By sale of Tissue Culture of
Banana, Potato & Bamboo 5 lacs No. **Rs. 1,50,00,000.00**

PROFIT = RECEIPTS - COST OF PRODUCTION = 53,79,975.00

PROFIT SALES RATIO = Profit / Sales x 100 = 35.87 %

RATE OF RETURN = Operating profit / T.C.I x 100 = 31.21 %

BREAK EVEN POINT (B.E.P) = 55.83 %

Chapter - 19

Addresses of Agricultural Equipment & Implements

Ajay Kumar & Co.
C-149, Moti Nagar,
New Delhi-110 015
Tel : 5100776,535404,5441949
Fax : 011-5441950
Product : Specialist in Environment Controlled Green Houses, Glass Houses, Agro Shading Nets, Nylon Nets, Tissue Culture Racks, Plastic Pots, Temperature Controllers & Timers.

Anand Mech Works Pvt. Ltd.
A-103/8, Wazirpur Indl. Area,
Delhi- 110 052
Tel: 7232902
Product : Tractor parts & Agricultural Parts.

Advance Industries
Khandsa Rd., Gurgaon.
Tel : 32 0006

Agricultural Engg. Co
Ajay Bijli Mkt. 2865/66,
G.B. Road, Shahganj, Delhi-110 006
Tel: 52 5907

Ambica Drip Irrigation System
202,2nd FLoor, Kedia Arcade
Infantry Road-560 001
Tel: 559 3815

Aekam Industries
Dherbarbhad Roa (South),Rajkot
Tel: 82461
Product : Tractor Trailor, Water Tanker, Power Press

Ambika Agro Industries
Gondal Road, Rajkot.
Works : Dhebarbhai Road, Rajkot.
Tel : 82461 Fax : 0281- 81069
Product : Mfr. of Machine Tools and Agriculture Equipments.

Automark Traffic Systems Pvt. Ltd.
16, Benham Hall Lane,
Dr. D.D. Sathe Marg,
Mumbai - 400 004.
Works :
A-43, M.I.D.C.,
Lohra-445001
Tel : 3869103, 3827484
Fax : 022 - 8941352
Product : Mfr. of Sugar Cane Planter, Harvestor & Agricultural Farm machine

Balwinder Singh Pritam Singh
Link Road,
Mansa-151 505.
Product : Mfr. of Combine Reaper

Bharat Engg. Work
Budhvari Bus Stand,
Ujjain, M.P.
Product : Mfr. of Lipcup Making Machine, Disposable Plates Making Machines, Potatochips Making Machines, Agricultural Machinery.

Bhuller Sheller Mfrs.
Taran Taran Road,
Off, 1-02,
East Mohan Nagar,
Amritsar-143 001.
Tel : 231281
Product : Mfr. of Rice Sheller, Paddy Dryer, Modern Parbolling Plants & Drying Plants.

Banwari Lal Radha Kishan
3631,GI Piaowali,
Chawri Bazar,
Delhi - 110 006
Tel : 326 2551

Creative Plastics
Gala Compd, Hazi Bapu Rd.,
Opp. Post Office,
Malad (East),
Mumbai.- 400097
Tel: 022 - 8409368,
Fax: 843 - 1209
Products : U.V. Stablized, Poly Film & Grippers.

Dandekar Brothers
1113, Factory Area,
Shivaji Nagar,
Sangli - 416 416.
Tel : 72758, 72757
Product : Mfr. of Groundnut Decorticator, Maize Sheller, Grinding Mill, Plano Knife grinding Machine, Plough & Agricultural Implements & Industrial Machine & Equip.

Dashmesh Agriculture
Near Bus Stand,
Dhanaula - 148 105
Product : Mfr. of Reapers

Dashmesh Engg. Works
Samadh Road,
Khanna - 141 401, Punjab.
Tel : 21515
Product : Mfr. of Cattle Feed Plant and Ice Cream Plant.

Dayal Poultry Appliances
C-160,Mayapuri, Phase-II,
New Delhi-110 064.
Tel : 5401793
Fax : 011 - 5405615
Product : Poultry Equipments.

Deccan Farm Equipment Pvt. Ltd.
F-10/2, MIDC, Shiroli,
Kolhapur - 416 122
Works:
C-35,MIDC, Shiroli,
Kohlapur - 416 122
Tel : 468665,469903,468904(W)
Fax : 0232-468905
Product : Mfr. of Agricultural Machines

Delux Kuthali Works (Regd.)
G.T.Road, Batala - 413 505
Tel : 42638
Product : Mfr. of Agricultural Implements,Tube Well Accessories, Machine Tools, C.I.Pulleys,Threshers & Engine Parts, Sugar Mill Machinery Parts & Husk Furnace for Rice Plant Dryer & Polishers & Reflex Walls Etc.

Dev Raj & Co.
Industrial Area , Ferozpur-152 001.
Tel : 2468
Product : Mfr. of Mini Rice Mill Machinery & Automatic Rice Plants.

Dewan Engg. Works
G.T.Road,
Sirhind - 140 406.
Tel : 427
Product : Mfr. of Tractor Driven & Self Propelled Harvesting Combines.

Dhanalakshmi Industries
204,Suramanglam Road,
Pallapatty Salem-636 009.
Tel : 50674
Product : Mfr. of Oil Mills, Rice Mills Machinery.

Dhiraj Lal & Bros.
54 Sarang Street -3,
Mumbai.
Tel: 342 8343

Doulatram Agro-Tech Pvt. Ltd.
40 B, Mittal Est. 5, Marol Naka,
Andheri East , Mumbai.
Tel : 850 0707

Doulatram Agro-Tech Pvt. Ltd.
L.R.E.W., "Empire House",
3rd Flr., 214 A K Nayak Marg,
Fort,
Mumbai - 400 001.
Tel : 022 - 2063228,
Fax : 022 - 2069709
Product : Knitted Shade Cloth For Plant Protection Nurseries From Excessive Sunlight, Hail,Wind & Birds.

Eicher Goodearth Limited
12, Commercial Complex,
Masjit Moth,
Greater Kailash.-II,
New Delhi.
Tel : 6445521,6445523
Fax : 6431612,6431929.
Product : Mfr. of Agricultural Machinery.

Elgi Equipments Ltd.
India House,
Trichy Road,
Coimbatore-641 018.
Works:
Elgi Indl. Complex-III,
Trichy Road, Signallur,
Coimbatore.

Tel : 0422 - 210155
Fax : 0422 - 214344
Product : Mfr. of Reciprocating Air Compressers, Rotary Screw Compressers, Service Station Equipment, Drip Irrigation Systems, Pasteurizer Plants, Bottle Washing machines, Air Craft Refuullers, Bogie & Wheelset Cleaning Plants, Mobile Workshops, Fuel Bonser & Auto Accessories

Essar Industries
53, Naresh Park Extn.,
Nangloi, Delhi - 110 041.
Tel : 5473927
Product :Tawa, Tasla & Agricultural Goods.

Farm Implements (India) Pvt. Ltd.
10 Kumarappa Street,
Nugambakkam-600 034 (Chennai)
Tel : 826 1676
Product : Rotavators & Agro-Fores Machines.

Garden Aids
1099/13, Hari Singh Nalwa Street,
Karol Bagh, New Delhi- 110 005
Tel : 011- 5724554, 6521529
Products : Flower Seeds - Bulk Quantity, Small Pictorial Packets Flowering Bulbs - Chincherinchee, Gladiolus, Garden Accessories, Manures, Goat-Sheep Compost.

G.S. Agro Inds.
Nabha Road,
Bhadson-147 202
Product: Mfr. of Harvestor Combines

H.M.T. Limited
Agri Implements Complex,
Madfhya Marg, Sec7C, Chandigarh.
Product : Mfr. of HMT Tractors

Harvel Irrigation Pvt. Ltd.
301-304, Meghdoot, 94 Nehruplace,
New Delhi-110 019.
Tel: 6413370,642802,6485365
Fax: 91-11-6464819.
Product: Wide Range of World Class Irrigation Equipments - landscape, Farmhouses, Hotel & Resorts, Green Houses, Plantations, Orchards, Nurseries, Golf Courses.

Hymatic Argo Equipment Pvt. Ltd.
301,Kanchan House,
Comm. Complex, Karampura,
New Delhi-110 015.
Tel : 5415868.
Fax : 91-11-5458097
Product : Mfrs. of All Types of Pesticides Spray Equipment

Industrial Consultants
35-A, Yashodham Film City Road,
Goregaon East, Mumbai - 400063.
Tel : 840 0333
Product : Distrs. of Japenese & Amrican Agri & Horti Machines.

IAG Marketing (P) Ltd.
Swatantra Nagar, Gali - 7, Narela,
Delhi-110 040

Irrigation Engineering Co. Ltd.
D-47,South Extn., Part-1,
New Delhi-110 049
Tel: 4618796

Jain Group of Industries
Sadhna Rayon House, D.N. Road,
Fort - 400 001.
Tel : 0222610011, 2620011 ,
2670011(Mumbai)
Fax: 022 - 2621177, 2641177(Mumbai)
Tel : 0116210660, 6210816,
6416902, 6449770(Delhi)
Fax : 011-644815
Product : Drip Irrigation Systems, Sprinkler Irrigation Systems, Green House Structures & Roofing Material, Water Soluble Fertilizers, Liquid Fertilizers, HDPE and PVC Pipes & Fittings,Plastic Valves, Turn-Key Projects

Kailash Plastic
5/31,Kirti Nagar Indl. Area-110 064.
Tel : 511 8110

Kappor Engg. Works
B-56,Mayapuri Indl. Area-110 064.
Tel : 513 7765

Kesri Sales & Engg Corpn.
Loha Mandi, Phagwara- 144 401.(PB)
Tel : 65377,62039
Fax : 01824-65377.
Product : Mfrs. of Agrl. Sprayers & Parts

Kumar Gentech & Tissue Culture Co.
Head Office : 783,Bhawani Peth,
Pune - 411 042.
Tel : 0212-650065. (INDIA)
Fax : 0212-653365.(INDIA)
Product : Florist Gerbera Hilverda Carnation Flamingo Flower Bulbs Green Houses.

Multan Iron Manufacturing Works
F-33/4, Okhla Indl. Area,
Phase -II,
New Delhi - 110 020
Tel : 6912733
Product : Agricultural Implements

Mantag Irrigation Systems (P) ltd.
B-4, Ashok Bhawan,
93 Nehru Place - 110 019.
Tel : 641 0599

Market Share Consultants
25/A, Latif House,
Sant Tukaram
Marg Masjid Bunder - 400 009.
(Mumbai)
Tel : 3415611

Pee Dee Stream Lines
B - 220, Nariana Indl. Area,
Phase - 1,
New Delhi - 110 028
Tel : 5798825,5500863
Product : Mechanized Irrigation Thru'U/G Sprinkler/Drip System

Phoel Industries
G-8, Kirpal Bhawan,
Model Town - III,
Delhi - 110 009.
Tel : 7116973
Fax : 7436974
Product : Mfrs. Of Sprinkler Irrigation System (Micro, Pop Up), And Drip Irrigation System. Special Irrigation System Available For Green Houses/FarmHouses. Also Mfrs. of ISI Marked HDPE Pipes for Water Supply Etc.

Power Mobiles Private Limited
Plot-9,Mugalivakkam Road,
Porur - 600 116 (Chennai)
Tel : 234 2543

Quality Disc Manufacturers (P) Ltd.
MIE. Tikri Border,
Bahadurgarh - Harayana
Tel : 8310480
Fax : 3794057,831809
Product : Mfrs/Exptrs of Harrow Discs, Cutting Edges Endblts, G.R.Blades.

R S Products (P) Ltd.
A-220 Okhla Phase-1,
New Delhi - 110 020
Tel : 6813189,6810413
Product : Israeli Irrigation System From : Pan - Israeli Floriculture, Horiculture, Green House Nurseries Lawns & Golf Courses.

RajDeep Enterprises
3229/1, Ranjit Nagar,
New Delhi -110 008.
Tel : 5768881, 5749991,5748881.
Product : Environment Controlled GREEN HOUSES

Rajico
357, Johnapur,
Mehrauli,
New Delhi - 110 030.
Tel : 6801345,6802243
Fax : 6801243.
Product : Export & Import Agricultural Equipment - ploughs, Harrows, Cultivators Trailers, Lawn Movers,Rotary Tillers

Sonalika Agriculture Industries
704, Nirmal Tower,
Barakhamba Road,
New Delhi - 110 001.
Tel : 3318911
Fax : 3714768
Product : Multi Crop,Thershers, Submresible Pumps, Agri, Implement

Standard Agri Engg Co
842,Industrial Area,'B',
Ludhiana - 141 003.
Tel : 531888
Product : Mfr. of Agri Implement & Multicrop Thresher.

Shah Irrigation Systems
111/113,
Vithalwadi'K' Devi - 2 (mumbai)
Tel : 2018174
Product : Distr. of Rain Bird (America) Drip & Sprinkler Systems For Garden, Landscape, Golf & Agriculture

Shivagrico Implements Ltd.
405,Adinath Apt.,
281 Tardeo Rd. - 7,
Mumbai.
Tel : 201 8174,389 3022.
Fax : 91-22-388 2678
Product : Mfrs & Exptrs. of Agricultural Implements. LION Brand & Re-Roller

Stichwell Qualitex Private Limited
G-58, Sector-6,
Noida - 201 301.
Tel : 8 52 1982

Union Tractor Workshop
B-8, Mayapuri Indl. Area,
Phase-II,
New Delhi - 110 064
Tel : 5404615
Product : Agricultural Implements

Vishkarma Engg. Works
A-6, Mayapuri Indl. Area,
Phase-II,
New Delhi -110 064
Tel : 5402815, 5400321
Fax : 01 - 11- 5132815.
Product : Trailor

Avance Industries
Khandsa Rd., Gurgaon.
Tel : 8-320006
Product : Agricultural Implements & Fabricators Jobs

Escorts Class Ltd.
15/3, Mathura Rd.,
Faridabad - 121 003.
Tel : 8-270660
Product : Combine Harvester

Girish Agro Industries
Opp. Durga Shakti Mandir,
Basai Rd., Gurgaon (Haryana)
Tel: 8-321593
Product : Agricultural Implements & Poultry Feed Machinery

Jagson Agricultural Implements
A-14, Nehruground, NIT,
Faridabad.
Product: Agricultural Implements, Tractors Mudguard, Sheet & Harrow Tractor.

Jukie Electro Machine Pvt. Ltd.
79, Udyog Vihar,
Phase-I,
Gurgaon.
Tel : 8 - 341628, 340192
Fax : 011- 6896454
Product : Seed Processing Machine

Kapursons
1/41A, DLF Indl. Estate,
14th Milestone,
Faridabad - 03 (Haryana)
Tel : 8 - 27688
Fax : 0129 - 274365
Product : Tractor Drawn Agriculture Implements

Mahalakshmi Ispat Private Limited
Daultabad Rd.,
Gurgaon (Haryana)
Tel : 8 - 321801, 322274, 320413
Product : Agricultural Implements, Light Machinery & Steel Equipments.

Milan Shah
2, Kamdar Colony,
Jamnagar-6,
Gujarat
Tel : 552900,551497/8
Fax : 91 - 288 - 556075
Product : Grower, Processer & Supplier of All Types of Dried Rose Petals.

Modern Farm Aids
A-5C,M.I.E.,
Bahadurgarh - 124 507.
Tel : 310292
Product : Agricultural Discs

Nice Steel Industries
Khandsa Road, Gurgaon.
Tel : 322006
Product : Agricultural Implements & Automobile components.

Prakash Agro Engg. Works
Nr. Gas Godown,
Basai Rd., Gurgaon.
Tel : 8-33277
Product : Harrow, Lift Harrow, Cultivators, Trolley, Water Tanks & Agricultural Implements.

Premier irrigation Equipments Ltd.
1/3, Milestone, Khandsa Rd.,
Gurgaon.
Tel : 8-321212
Product : Alm. Stroke Sets & Drip System

Quality Disk Manufacturers (P) Ltd.
Modern Indl. Estate,
Bahadurgarh - 124 507.
Tel : 310779,310809.
Product : Agricultural Implements

S.L. Sharma Trading & Engg. Work
1A/270, Nr. Police Post,
Nellam Bata Rd., Faridabad.
Product : Grass Cutters, Lawn Movers & Other Accessories.

Sikander Agro Engineering
H-611,RIICO Indl. Area,
Bhiwadi - 301 019
Tel : 20424
Products : Agri Implements,Engg. Job,Special Machine,Dies,Heat Exchanger & Fabrication Works.

Dates Discs (P) Ltd.
8/9, Mile Stone G.T. Road,
Mohan Nagar,
Sahibabad, Ghaziabad
Tel : 766640,767830.
Product : Agricultural Disk (Cultivation Purposes)

Saraswati Udyog
C-210, Site-1,Indl. Area,
Bulandshahar Road,
Ghaziabzd.
Tel : 733267, 731889, 722563.
Product : Oil Engines, Oil Expellers, Filter Presses C.I. Moulds, Agricultural Implements, Machine Tools & Their Spare Parts.

Siya Ram Alloys & Steel Pvt. Ltd.
8 KM. Mile Stone,
Meerut Road, Gaziabad.
Tel : 723726
Product : Agricultural Implements Discs, Harrow Cultivator.

Westend Marketing Co.
(Best Of Holland Flowers & Floritech Co.)
219, First Floor, 4th Cross,
Lal Bagh Road,
Bangalore - 569 927
Tel : 080 - 2225746, 2239708.
Fax : 080 - 2225746, 2215888.
Product : IMPORTERS of Planting Material- Gladiolus, Lilium, Iris -Bulbs,Carnation, Chrysenthimum Cuttings.
EXPORTERS & INDENTORS OF: Auction Houses for Roses & Other Cut Flowers.

LIST OF AVAILABLE "DETAILED PROJECT REPORTS"

1. AAC & ACSR ALUMINIUM CONDUCTORS
2. ABRASIVE EMERY
3. ABRASIVE PAPER
4. ABRASIVE
5. A.B.S. GARNUELS
6. ACETIC ACID
7. ACETIC ANHUDRIDE
8. ACETIC ACID FROM ETHANOL
9. ACETIC ACID FROM MOLASSES
10. ACETATE DYES
11. ACETYLENE GAS
12. ACID SLURRY
13. ACRYLIC ADHESIVES
14. ACRYLIC SHEETS
15. ACRYLIC LATEX
16. ACRYLIC FIBRES
17. ACRYLIC YARN
18. ACRYLIC MIRROR (GOLDEN, PINK, BLACK & SILVER)
19. ACRYLIC & COTTON YARN SPINDLES
20. ACRYLIC EMULSION PAINT
21. ACTIVATED CARBON FROM SAW DUST, RICE HUSK & COCONUT SHELL
22. ACTIVATED CARBON FROM RICE HUSK
23. ACTIVATED CARBON FROM WOOD
24. ACTIVATED CARBON FROM COCONUT SHELL
25. ACTIVATED BLEACHING EARTH
26. ACTIVATED FULLERS EARTH
27. ACTIVATED ALUMINA BALLS
28. ACTIVATED CALCIUM CARBONATE
29. ACETYLENE BLACK (CARBON BLACK)
30. ADHESIVE (FEVICOL TYPE)
31. ADHESIVE (DIFFERENT TYPES)
32. ADHESIVE (ALL TYPES)
33. ADHESIVE INDUSTRY (LAMINATED, FEVICOL, STICKER, DDL & OTHER TYPES OF ADHESIVES)
34. ADHESIVE MAKING FOR JOINING HDPE PIPES/JOINTS
35. ADHESIVE BASED ON POLYURETHANE
36. ADHESIVE FOR TWO/THREE WHEELER CLUTCH PLATES
37. ADHESIVE FOR CORRU-GATION (DRY POWDER)
38. ADHESIVE FOR RUBBER TO RUBBER, THREAD RUBBER TUBE PUNC-TURE & LATEX RUBBER BASED
39. ADHESIVE FOR STICKER
40. ADHESIVE TAPES FOR HOSPITAL USED
41. ADHESIVE POWDER FOR ELECTRIC LAMPS
42. ADHESIVE FOR CORRUGA-TION DRY POWDER/PASTE
43. ADHESIVE TAPES (PRESSURE SENSITIVE)
44. ADHESIVE (FOR PHOTO ALBUM)

45. ADVERTISING AGENCY
46. AEROSOL SPRAY
47. AFTER SHAVE LOTION
48. AGRICULTURAL & GARDENING HOSE PIPE
49. AGRICULTURAL IMPLEMENT
50. AGRICULTURAL EQUIPMENT
51. AGARBATTIES (INSENCE STICK)
52. AIR BUBBLE PACKAGING
53. AIR CONDITIONERS (WINDOW TYPES)
54. AIR FRESHNERS (ROOM)
55. AIR FRESHNER (ODONIL TYPES)
56. AIR CONDITIONERS (CAR & ROOM) SERVICE
57. AIR CONDITIONING (CENTRALIZED)
58. AIR TAXI (12 SEATERS) [ON RENTAL BASIS OF TWO]
59. AIR FRESHNERS & AIR PURI-FIERS (BLOCK RING TYPE)
60. AIR FILTERS (FOR SCOOTER, CAR & EXCAVATORS ETC.)
61. AIR COOLER
62. ALUMINIUM ROLLING MILL & ALUMINIUM UTENSILS BASED ON ALUMINIUM SCRAP
63. ALKYD RESIN
64. ALTERNATORS
65. ALKALINE CELLS
66. ALUMINIUM ELECTROLYTIC CAPACITORS
67. ALUM (FERRIC)
68. ALUMINIUM COLLAPSIBLE TUBES
69. ALCOHOL BY RICE STRAW
70. ALUMINIUM & ALUMINIUM ALLOYS From Aluminium Scraps to Make Utensils
71. ALUMINIUM SLUGS (For Collapsible Tube Containers)
72. ALUM (NON FERRIC)
73. ALUMINIUM BEVERAGES CANS
74. ALUMINIUM CANS FOR CAPACITORS
75. ALUMINIUM UTENSILS, SCHOOL BOXES FOR BOOK CARRYING
76. ALUMINIUM/STAINLESS STEEL PRESSURE COOKER & WATER FILTER
77. ALUMINIUM SILICATE
78. ALUMINIUM UTENSILS
79. ALUMINIUM EXTRUSION
80. ALL PURPOSE ADHESIVES
81. ALUMINIUM CHANNELS, BEEDINGS & PIPE
82. ALLOY STEEL PLANT
83. ALKYLATED PHENOL
84. ALLOY STEEL PLANT
85. ALKYLATED PHENOL
86. ALUMINIUM RE-ROLLING
87. ALUMINIUM SHEET CIRCLES/UTENSILS
88. ALUMINIUM BOTTLES (Cold Extrusion of Aluminium)
89. ALCOHOL FROM POTATOES (From Non Molasses Based)
90. ALUMINIUM ALLOY CONDUCTORS
91. ALUMINIUM POWDER (ATOMIZED)
92. ALUMINIUM DOOR, WINDOW AND FITTINGS
93. ALUMINIUM/COPPER CABLE LUGS
94. ALCOHOL BY GRAINS
95. ALUMINIUM KNOBE (for Domestic Electric Appliances)
96. ALUMINIUM CIRCLE
97. ALUMINIUM ROLLING MILL (SHEET & CIRCLES)
98. ALUMINIUM ROLLING MILL & ALUMINIUM UTENSILS BASED ON ALUMINIUM SCRAPS
99. ALUMINIUM HYDROXIDE
100. ALUM FOR WATER TREATMENT
101. ALUMINIUM PRINTING PLATES FOR OFFSET PRINTING MACHINE
102. ALCOHOL INDUSTRIES BASED ON TAPIOCS STARCH
103. ALUM FOR WATER TREATMENT
104. ALUMINIUM PAINT

Price Rs. 2500/- for each ``Detailed Project Report'' Payable in advance through Draft/Cash/M.O. in favour of ``ENGINEERS INDIA RESEARCH INSTITUTE". Or Ask by V.P.P. PH.: 291 8117, 291 6431, 292 0361 Fax: 91-11-291 6431 (24 Hrs.)

105. ALUMINIUM HYDROXIDE GEL
106. ALUMINIUM INGOTS FROM BAUXITE
107. AMLA PLANTATION
108. AMPICILLIN TRIHYDRATE IN CAPSULES WITH STRIP PACKING
109. AMMONIUM CHLORIDE TABLETS
110. AMMONIUM DI-CHROMAT
111. AMMONIUM SULPHATE
112. AMMONIA GAS
113. AMMONIA PAPER
114. AMMONIUM NITRATE
115. AMUSEMENT PARK
116. AMMONIUM CHLORIDE BLOCK
117. AMMONIA LIQUOR
118. AMINO ACID FOR POULTRY FEED
119. AMINES & ALLIED PRODUCT
120. ANODIC ALUMINIUM LABEL
121. ANGORA RABBIT WOOL
122. ANTI CORROSION LUBRICANTS (No Costing)
123. ANTI SCALE COMPOUND for Adding Sugar Juice Boiling
124. ANTHRAQUINONE
125. ANTIMONY TRI-OXIDE
126. ANTI STATIC POLYTHENE BAGS
127. ANHYDROUS CALCIUM CHLORIDE
128. ANTIMONY
129. APPLE JUICE CONCENTRATE & DEHYDRATED FRUITS & VEG. MANUFACTURING
130. APPLE POMACE PECTIN
131. APPLE JUICES
132. AQUA CULTURE SHRIMP FARM (EOU)
133. AQUA CULTURE PRAWN FARMING (100% EOU)
134. ARTIST COLOURS
135. ARTIFICIAL FLOWERS
136. ARTIFICIAL FISH MEAL for Poultry Feed
137. ARMOURED CABLES
138. ASBESTOS CEMENT PIPE & FITTING FOR BUILDING SEWARAGE & DRAINAGE
139. ASBESTOS RIDES & ROOFING SHEET
140. ASBESTOS CEMENT PIPES AND FITTING FOR BULDING SEWIRAGE & DRAINAGE
141. ASPHALTIC ROOFING SHEET
142. ASH TRAYS FOR MARUTI CARS
143. ASBESTOS FIBRE MOULDED PRODUCTS
144. ASBESTOS GASKET SHEET
145. ASPIRIN
146. ASAFOETIDA (HING)
147. ATRAZIN PESTICIDE
148. AUTO CLUTCH PLATE
149. AUTO TUBES (ALL TYPES)
150. AUTO BULBS (HEAD & TAIL)
151. AUTO FLAPS
152. AUTO PISTON & PISTON RING (Piston Assembly - Aluminium Alloy)
153. AUTO SPOKES
154. AUTO TYRE, TUBE & FLAPS
155. ATTA (MINI FLOUR MILL)
156. AUTOMATIC BISCUIT PLANT
157. AUTOMATIC BREAD PLANT
158. AUTOMATIC BREAD & BISCUIT MAKING PLANT

159. AUTO CABLES
160. AUTO PINS
161. AUTO LEAF SPRING
162. AUTO TELEPHONE RECORDING & ANSWERING M/C.
163. AUTO GEARS
164. AUTO PART (RUBBER)
165. AUTO FLOUR MILL
166. AUTO INJECTION MOULDED PLASTIC COMPONENTS
167. AUTO WIRES FOR 2/3 WHEELERS, CLUTCH WIRES, BRAKE WIRES, SPEEDO METER WIRE & GEAR WIRES
168. AUTO VOLTAGE STABILIZERS
169. AUTOMOBILE FILTER
170. AUTOMOBILE BUSHES
171. AUTOMATIC BRICK PLANT
172. AUROMINE - O
173. AUTOMOBILE PAINTS
174. AUDIO CASSETTE ASSEMBLY AND RECORDING
175. AUDIO & VIDEO CASSETTES
176. AUTOMATIC BOOK BINDING
177. AUTOBODY BUILDING
178. AUTOMOBILE REFRIGERATORS
179. AUTOMOBILE RADIATORS
180. AUTOMATIC VOLTAGE STABILIZER
181. AUTOMOBILE BRAKE SHOES
182. AUDIO MAGNETIC TAPES
183. AUTOMOBILE WORKSHOP & SERVICE CENTER
184. AUTOMOBILE PISTON RINGS
185. AUTOMOBILE PISTONS
186. AUTOMOBILE CYLINDERS
187. AUTOMOBILE WIRES FOR TWO/THREE WHEELERS, CLUTCH WIRE, BRAKE WIRE, SPEEDO METERS WIRE & GEAR WIRES
188. AUTOMATIC PLANT FOR TOFFEE/CANDY
189. AUTOMATIC CANDLE UNIT
190. AUTOMATIC VENDING MACHINE FOR HOT & COLD BEVERAGES
191. AUTOMOBILE POLISH
192. AUTOMOBILE BLINKERS
193. AUTOMOBILE GASKET
194. AUTOMOBILE PARTS FOR MARUTY VEHICLE
195. AUTOMOBILE GARAGE WORKSHOP FOR TRUCKS (12-15 TRUCKS)
196. AUTOMOBILE PARTS
197. AUTOMOBILE RUBBER PART
198. AUDIO CASSETTE SCREW
199. AYURVEDIC MEDICINES
200. AYURVEDIC SHARBAT
201. AYURVEDIC PAIN BALM OINTMENT
202. AZO-DYE STUFFS
203. BABY DIAPERS
204. BACTERICIDA FOR CANE JUICE
205. BADMINTON RACKETS
206. BADMINTON SHUTTLE COCKS
207. BAKELITE MOULDED PRODUCTS
208. BAKERS YEAST
209. BAKELITE SHEETS (PHENOLIC SHEETS) ELECTRICAL GRADE
210. BAKELITE ELECTRICAL ACCESSORIES
211. BAKERY UNIT
212. BAKING POWDER
213. BALL POINT PEN REFILLS
214. BALL POINT PEN REFILLS AND INKS
215. BALL BEARING
216. BALLOONS (ALL TYPES)
217. BAMBOO STICKS FOR AGARBATTIES

Price Rs. 2500/- for each "Detailed Project Report" Payable in advance through Draft/Cash/M.O. in favour of "ENGINEERS INDIA RESEARCH INSTITUTE". Or Ask by V.P.P. PH.: 291 8117, 291 6431, 292 0361 Fax: 91-11-291 6431 (24 Hrs.)

218. BANANA & ITS BYE PRODUCTS
219. BANANA POWDER
220. BANQUET HALL
221. BAND SAW BLADES
222. BANANA PUREE
223. BARBED WIRE
224. BARIUM CARBONATE
225. BARIUM COMPOUND
226. BARIYAN & PAPPAD
227. BASMATI RICE TRADING
228. BATTERY PLATE
229. BATTERY CONTAINER
230. BAYGON SPRAY
231. BESAN PLANT
232. BED SHEET, BED COVERS, FURNISHING, ETC.
233. BEER PLANT
234. BEES WAX REFINING AND BLEACHING
235. BEES WAX
236. BENEFICATION OF CHROMITE ORE PROCESSING CHARGE CHROME
237. BENZENE
238. BENZENE HEXA CHLORIDE
239. BENZYL BENZOATE
240. BENZYL PEROXIDE
241. BETA NAPHTHOLS
242. BI-METAL BUSHES
243. BI-CHROMATES OF SODIUM POTASSIUM & AMMONIUM
244. BINDIA & SINDUR
245. BITUMINIZED COMPOUND FOR WATER PROOFING
246. BITUMINOUS ROAD EMULSION
247. BI-CYCLE MANUFACTURE AND ITS PARTS
248. BI-CYCLE PARTS
249. BIO COAL FROM AGRO WASTE
250. BITUMEN
251. BLANKETS
252. BLACK & WHITE T.V. PICTURE TUBE
253. BLEACHING DYEING, PRINTING/FINISHING OF CLOTH
254. BLEACHING POWDER
255. BLEACHING & REFINING OF BEES WAX
256. BLEACHING & MORDANT DYEING OF YARN
257. BLACK & WHITE T.V. PICTURE TUBE
258. BLACK PEPPER
259. BLISTER FILM PVC
260. BLOCK BOARD
261. BLOCK BOARD
262. BLOOD BAGS
263. BLOW MOULDED PLASTIC CONTAINER
264. BLACK & GALVANIZED STEEL CONDUIT PIPES
265. BLEACHING LIQUOR (CALCIUM HYPO CHLORATE LIQUOR)
266. BLOWING AGENT
267. BLUE DETERGENT POWDER
268. BOILER DE-SCALING COMPOUNDS
269. BOOT/SHOE POLISH
270. BORIC ACID
271. BONE MILL
272. BOPP FILMS
273. BOPP TAPES

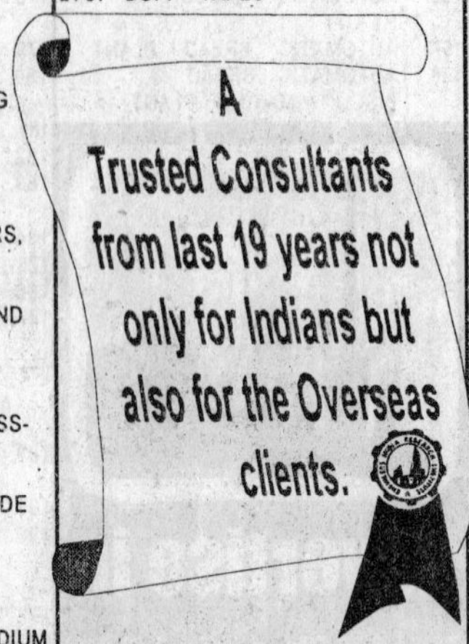

274. BORAX
275. BOARD MILL BASED ON RICE STRAW
276. BONE CRUSHING
277. BOLTS (MILD STEEL)
278. BOTTLING PLANT
279. B.P. HARD COKE
280. BRAKE LININGS
281. BRAKE OIL, COOLANT AND PACKING OF LUBE OIL AND GREASE
282. BRAKE OIL
283. BRASS/COPPER SHEET CIRCLES & UTENSILS
284. BRA & PANTY (HOSIERY)
285. BREAD PLANT
286. BRICK PLANT
287. BRASS HOLDERS
288. BRASS & COPPER TUBES
289. BRANDY
290. BRIQUETTED FUEL FROM AGRO WASTE
291. BRASS UTENSILS
292. BRASS SHEET ROLLING
293. BRASS PIPES
294. BRASS WARES
295. BROILER CHICKEN
296. BRASS STAIRCASE AND WROUGHT IRON, RODS, RAILING, GATE & GRILL
297. BULK DRUGS
298. BUTTON FROM HOOVES AND HORNS
299. BUILDING HARDWARE OF ALUMINIUM
300. BUTT HINGES OF BRASS SHEET
301. BUFFING & POLISHING COMPOUNDS
302. BUS TRANSPORT
303. BUBBLE GUM & CHEWING GUM
304. BUFFALO MEAT PROCESSING
305. BUTTONS (PLASTIC) FROM POLYESTER SHEETS & RODS
306. BUSINESS CENTRE (JOB WORK)
307. BUS AND TRUCK BODY BUILDING
308. CABLE JELLY COMPOUND
309. CASSETTE RECORDER PLAYER (STEREO)
310. CAMPHOR
311. CATTLE & POULTRY FEED
312. CARBON DIOXIDE
313. CARBON BRUSHES
314. CARBON ZINC CELL
315. CARBON - ACTIVATED
316. CARBON - ONE TIME
317. CARBON - HIGH FERRO
318. CARBON BLACK
319. CARBON BLACK FROM NATURAL GAS
320. CARBON ELECTRODE
321. CARBON BLACK FROM NATURAL GAS
322. CARBON POTENTIO METERS
323. CARBON MONO-OXIDE FOR WATER GAS
324. CARBON SEAL
325. CARBON POWDER
326. CARBON PAPER
327. CARBON PLATES GRAPHITE
328. CARBON/METAL FILM RESISTORS
329. CARBON - (CINE-ARC)
330. CARD BOARD SLATE
331. CAPACITORS
332. CALCIUM CARBIDE
333. CALCIUM SILICATE BLOCKS
334. CARBONATED BEVERAGES
335. CAR BURGLAR ALARM
336. CAUSTIC SODA
337. CALCIUM CARBONATES
338. CAR AIR FRESHNER
339. CAR SHAMPOO
340. CASTOR OIL
341. CATTLE FEED
342. CATTLE & POULTRY FEEDS
343. CAST STEEL PANS FOR MELTING FURNACE
344. CAST IRON PIPES & FITTINGS (VERTICAL) FOR DOUBLE FLANGED PIPES
345. CALCINING OF MANGANESE & DEAD BURNT MANGANESE
346. CALCIUM CARBONATE BASED ON STEAM COAL
347. CASING UNIT OF SAUSAGE FOOD (100% EOU)
348. CARPET WOOL YARN SPINNING
349. CANNING OF MANGO PULP AND MANGO SLICES
350. CAFFEINE BY TEA WASTE

351. CALCINED PETROLEUM COKE
352. CALCIUM CARBONATE, MAGNASIUM CARBONATE & METAL FROM DOLOMITE
353. CALCIUM CASEINATE & SODIUM CASEINATE
354. CAMERA (35 M.M.)
355. CARTONS FOR DISTILLERY
356. CASHEWNUT SHELL LIQUID & KERNELS (CNSL)
357. CARPET WOOLLEN YARN DYEING
358. CASTOR OIL HYDRO-GENATION
359. CASTOR OIL REFINING
360. CANDLE (Semi Automatic)
361. CAST IRON POWDER
362. CASEIN BASED PIGMENTS USED IN SPORT INDUSTRY
363. CASHEWNUT (Dried & Fried)
364. CARD/GREY BOARD
365. CANDLE (NON DRIP)
366. CATTLE FEED BY TAPIOCA
367. CAUSTIC SODA/CHLORINE PLANT MEMBRANE CELL
368. CARBOXY METHYL CELLULOSE
369. CANNING & PRESERVATION OF FRUIT & VEGETABLE
370. CANNING & PRESERVATION OF FRUITS & VEGETABLE WITH COLD STORAGE & RAISIN (KISHMISH MAKING)
371. CASSETTE TAPES (COVER)
372. CANVAS SHOES, JUNGLE BOOT, RUBBER KNEES & BOOT, COMBAT
373. CALCIUM SILICATE
374. CALCIUM GLUCONATE
375. CANVAS SHOES
376. CASTOR OIL EMULSIFIER
377. CASEIN FROM MILK
378. CARPET WEAVING
379. CARPET FOR CABLE NETWORK
380. CABLE (FLAT/RIBBEN)
381. CABLES FOR AUTOMOBILE
382. CABLES (PVC WIRE)
383. CABLES-ARMOURED
384. CABLES-TEFLON COATED
385. CABLES-TELEPHONE
386. CABLES-XLPE/PVC
387. CABLES-WELDING
388. CABLES-OPTICAL FIBRE
389. CANNING OF ROSGULLAS IN METAL CANS
390. CALCIUM NITRATE
391. CATIONIC SOFTENER
392. CANNING & BOTTLING OF FRUITS AND VEGETABLE PRODUCTS
393. CATECHU (KATTHA)
394. CATTLE BREEDING
395. CARPET DRY CLEANING
396. CAR AIR CONDITIONERS
397. CARBOXY METHYL CELLULOSE (C.M.C.)
398. CARD BOARD MATCH BOXES
399. CARDINAL FROM C.N.S.L.
400. CAPACITOR DISCHARGE IGNITION (CIDI UNIT)
401. CASHEWNUT KERNEL EX-TRACTION FROM CASHEW-NUT FRUIT
402. CARBON ZINC CELL (DRY CELL)
403. CASHEW FENI (WINE DISTILLATION FROM FRUITS & CASHEWNUT)
404. CANDY HARD BOILED
405. CARD BOARD BOXES & CARTONS *SYSTEM PACK)
406. CAR PAINTS
407. CAR POLISHES
408. CASTOR OIL DERIVATIVE OLEORESINS
409. CANNED FRUITS AND VEGETABLES
410. CANNED VEGETABLES
411. CANNED FRUITS
412. CERAMIC INSULATOR
413. CERAMIC CORES & TUBES
414. CEMENT PLANT
415. CHEESE (Processed)
416. CEMENT ROOFING TILES
417. CERAMIC TILES (GLAZED)
418. CELLULOSE ACETATE
419. CEMENT WATER PROOF COMPOUND
420. CEMENT PAINT
421. CEMENT PLANT (800 TPD)
422. CEMENT COLOUR/LIME COLOUR (SYNTHETIC RED IRON OXIDE) USED FOR FLOORING
423. CEMENT FROM RICE HUSK
424. CEMENT (CLINKER)
425. CEMENT FROM FLY ASH AND LIME
426. CEILING FAN
427. CENTRIFUGAL PUMP
428. CELLULOSE POWDER & MICRO CRYSTALLINE
429. CELLULOSE ACETATE MOULDING POWDER
430. CERAMIC NOVELTIES
431. CERAMIC TRANSFERS (FOR PRINTING ON CERAMICS)
432. CERAMIC COATED ALUMINIUM THREAD GUIDE
433. CERAMIC THREAD GUIDE
434. CERAMIC FIRING DECORATIVE TILES
435. CEMENT POLE, JALLIE & TILE
436. CHEMICAL LABORATORY
437. CERAMIC CROCKERY WARE (Bone China-Hitkari)
438. CHEMICAL RESISTANT IRON AND STEEL
439. CERAMIC GLAZED TILES
440. CEMENT GRINDING
441. CEMENT OXIDE
442. CERAMIC MAGNET
443. CEMENT TILES (LAYING OVER RCC ROOFS)
444. CHINA CLAY
445. CHOKES, TRANSFORMERS & ELIMINATORS
446. CHOLORINATED PARAFFIN WAX
447. CHICKEN/MUTTON (SHEEP MEAT) PROCESSING
448. CHICKEN/MEAT PROCESSING & PACKAGING
449. CHROME PLATED (C.P.) BATH ROOM FITTINGS
450. CHAIN LINK FENCING OUT OF PVC COATED WIRE

451. CHOKES & PATTIES
452. CHEWING TOBACCO
453. CHROMIC ACID
454. CHINESE SOYA SAUCE
455. CHROMIC ACID
456. CHEWING GUM
457. CHLORAM PHENICOL
458. CHELATED ZIND (Zn-EDTA)
459. CHILLI POWDER
460. CHOCOLATE
461. CHEWING GINGER & AMLOKI
462. CHROME PLATING
463. CHOKE & STARTER
464. CHOKE OF FLUROSCENT TUBES
465. CHEMICAL ETCHING OF STAINLESS STEEL
466. CHEMICAL LAMINATION OF PHOTO
467. CHLORINATED RUBBER BASED PLANT
468. CITRONELLS OIL
469. CINEMA HALL
470. CIGARETTES
471. CIGARETTES-HERBAL
472. CINNAMON BARK OIL
473. CINE-ARC-CARBON
474. C.I. CASTING (FOUNDRY)
475. CITRIC ACID BY MOLASSSES
476. CIGARETTE & BIDI
477. CIDER PLANT (APPLE WINE)
478. CITRONELLA OIL
479. C.I. POWDER BY GRINDING PROCESS
480. CLOVE OIL
481. CLOTH (COTTON PROCESSING & FINISHING OF CLOTH)
482. CLUTCH WIRE FROM DRAWN WIRE
483. CLEANING OF COOLING SYSTEM & BOILER
484. CLAY PLATES FOR ELECTRIC HEATERS
485. CLUTCH PLATE FOR 4 (FOUR) WHEELERS
486. CLUTCH PLATE FOR 3 (THREE) WHEELERS
487. CLEANING POWDER (VIM)
488. CLUTCH FACING AND BRAKE LINING
489. CLEAR TRANSSPARENT LACQUOR FOR COATING ON BRASS BANGLES TO MAKE IT WEATHER
490. CLINICAL THERMOMETER
491. C.N.S.L. BASED RESIN IN LIQUID & Powder Form
492. COPPER WIRE DRAWING & ENAMELING
493. CORDLESS PHONE
494. COPPER & BRASS TUBES
495. CONCENTRATION OF MANGANESE ORE
496. CORRUGATED SHEET BOARD AND BOXES
497. COPPER BOTTOM STAINLESS STEEL UTENSILS
498. COOLING COILS FOR AIR CONDITIONERS
499. COLOUR LAB (QSS-PHOTO)
500. COMPUTER CONTINUOUS STATIONERY
501. COMPUTER ASSEMBLY
502. COMPUTER MONITOR
503. COMPUTER RIBBON
504. COMPUTER RIBBON REFILLING & REINKING
505. COMPUTER MONITOR TUBE & T.V. PICTURE TUBE (B/W)
506. COMPUTER SOFTWARE (100% EOU)
507. COMPUTER FORMS AND SECURITY PRINTING PRESS
508. COMPUTER JOB WORK

509. COMPUTER FORM (COMPUTER STATIONERY)
510. COMPUTER ATTENDANCE REGISTER
511. COMPUTER PRINTER
512. COMPUTER KEYBOARD
513. COMPUTER EDUCTION INSTITUTE
514. COMPUTER (MINI PERSONAL)
515. COMPUTER-LAPTOP
516. COMPUTER PERIPHERALS
517. COMPUTER STATIONERY AND IMPORTED HARDWARE PARTS
518. COOLANT ENGINE
519. COLLEGE
520. COLD DRINKS
521. COLD PROCESSED TYRE RETREADING
522. COLD STORAGE
523. COLD STORAGE & ICE
524. COLD ROLLING MILL
525. COLD PROCESSSED TREAD RUBBER
526. COLD CREAMS
527. COLD ROLLING OF STEEL STRIPS
528. COLD ROLLED PRESSED STEEL DOORS, WINDOW FRAMES
529. COTTON ADHESIVE TAPES & PLASTER OF PARISS BANDAGES for HOSPITAL
530. COLOUR & B/W T.V.
531. COLOUR TELEVISION
532. COSTUME JEWELLERY
533. COTTON SEED OIL
534. COTTON YARN
535. CONDUIT IRON PIPES (C.I. PIPES)
536. CONDENSED MILK SWEETENED
537. COIR FOAM (RUBBERIZED COIR) CUSHION & MAT ETC.
538. CONCRETE HOLLOW BRICK BLOCKSS
539. CONDENSED MILK
540. COCONUT OIL
541. COFFEE PLANTATION
542. COBLAT OCTOATE
543. COIR PITH
544. COPPER NITRATE
545. CONCENTRATE OF TOMATO (TOMATO PASTE
546. CONFERENCE BAG, FOLDERS ETC. (PLASTIC)
547. CORN FLAKES
548. COATING ON PLASTICS
549. COPPER OXY-CHLORIDES
550. COPPER PHTHALOCYNINE BLUE AND GREEN
551. COATED PAPER & BOARD
552. CONVERTER
553. COPPER CLAD LAMINATES FOR PCB'S (PAPER & FABRIC BASED)
554. COPPER RODS BY SCRAPS
555. COLLECTION OF MILK & PACKAGING IN POLYTHENE POUCHES (MILK CHILLING)
556. COURIER SERVICES
557. CONFECTIONERY
558. CONFECTIONERY INDUSTRY - SEMI AUTOMATIC PLANT (TOFFEE & CANDY MANUFACTURING)
559. COAL BRIQUETTING FROM COAL
560. COAL BRIQUETTES FROM AGRO WASTE
561. COUNTRY LIQUOR
562. COPPER STRIPS COILS
563. CONCAST STEEL BAR
564. COATING & PRINTING OF LAMINATED PAPER POUCH
565. COATING & LAMINATION ON PAPER (HOT MELT FILM LAMINATION METHOD)
566. COUNTRY LIQUOR FROM MOLASSES
567. COSMETIC UNIT
568. COPPER BERYLLIUM ALLOY SPRING

569. COMPOSITE CONTAINER
570. COLOUR MASTER BATCH FOR VARIOUS PLASTICS
571. COMPACT DISC PLAYER
572. COMPACT DISC (CD)
573. COTTON FINISHING
574. CONSTANT VOLTAGE TRANSFORMER (C.V.T.)
575. CORROSION CONTROLLING CHEMICAL (PIPE LINE)
576. COPPER FOIL
577. COMPRESSOR (HERMETIC) FOR AIR CONDITIONER
578. COATING ON PLASTICSS & GLASS
579. COATING OF CLEAR TRNAPARENT LACQUER ON BRASS BANGLESS TO MAKE IT WEATHER RESISTANT

602. COSTUME/IMITATION ARTIFICIAL JEWELLERY (CHAINS & BANGLES)
603. CONCENTRATE OF ROSE, JASMINE & LILLY EXTRACT
604. COPPER WINDING FOR SUBMERSIBLE PUMP AND MOTOR
605. COMPACT FLUORESCENT TUBES
606. CONE FOR SOFTY ICE CREAM
607. CORRUGATION OF PLAIN GALVANIZED SHEET
608. CORN FLAKES
609. COTTON GINNING & PRESSING
610. COMPUTER PERIPHERALS
611. COMPUTER HARDWARE
612. COMPACT DISC PLAYER (AUDIO/VIDEO)
613. CO_2 WELDING WIRE

638. DAIRY PRODUCTS
639. DAIRY PRODUCTS & MILK
640. DALL/PULSE MILL
641. DAIRY FARM AND MILK PRODUCTS
642. DAIRY PLANT
643. DETERGENT POWDER
644. DETERGENT CAKE AND POWDER
645. DECORATIVE LAMINATED SHEET (SUNMICA)
646. DESK TOP PUBLISHING (DTP)
647. DEHYDRATED ONIONS & ONION POWDER
648. DTP CUM OFFSET PRESSS
649. DISPOSABLE SYRINGES
650. DHOOP BATTI
651. DEHYDRATION OF FRUITS AND VEGETABLES
652. DEXTROSE SALINE

580. COPPER & BRASS INGOTS
581. COCONUT PLANTATION
582. COCONUT PRODUCTS AND BYE PRODUCTS
583. CONVEYER BELTS
584. COPPER SULPHATE
585. COIR INDUSTRY
586. COSMETIC (HERBAL AND SYNTHETIC)
587. COTTON & ACRYLIC YARN SPINDLES
588. CO-EXTRUSION MULTI-LAYER FILM
589. COLOURED FLAME CANDLE
590. COMMUTATOR FOR ELECTRIC MOTOR
591. COTTON BUDS/SWABS
592. COATING ON METALLIZED POLYESTER FILM METALLIZED PAPER ALUMINIUM FOILS
593. COOLER BODY & TRUNK (FABRICATION UNIT)
594. COSSMETIC, DETERGENT POWDER & PERFUMERY COMPOUND
595. COLOUR MASTER BATCHES FOR VARIOUSS PLASTICS
596. COUNTRY LIQUOR
597. COBALT OCTOATE
598. CONDENSER FOR MOTOR
599. COAL GRINDING
600. COCOA POWDER
601. COTTON ROLLS

614. COPPER POWDER
615. COPPER EXTRACTION FROM PCB WASTES
616. CRYSTAL TABLEWARE
617. CRUCIBLE BY FIRE CLAY
618. CRACKING OF MERNELS (DESHLLING/DECORTICATING)
619. CRICKET BAT/BALL
620. CROCKERY WARES
621. CRAYON WAX
622. CRITICAL AUTO BODY SHEET METAL PARTS
623. CREPE BANDAGES
624. CUBICAL ELECTRICAL PANEL BOARD (SWITCH BOARD)
625. CUSHION COMPOUND, THREAD & VULCANIZING SOLUTION, FORMULATION AND MANUFACTURE
626. CUTLERY (STAINLES STEEL)
627. CUTLERY & SILVER JEWELLERY (GOLD PLATED)
628. CURRY POWDER
629. CUTTING OIL
630. CYCLE & RIKSHAW FRAMES
631. CYANIDE ZINC BRIGHTENER
632. CYCLE TYRE & TUBES
633. CYLINDER LINERS FOR AUTOMOBILES
634. CYCLE HANDLE BAR GRIPS
635. CYCLE SPOKES
636. DAIRY FARM & PRODUCTS
637. DAIRY FARM AND DAIRY (MILK) PRODUCTS

653. DEXTROSE FROM POTATO
654. DEHYDRATED GARLIC FLAKES
655. DEXTRIN & STARCH BASED ADHESIVE
656. DEXTRIN
657. DEXTROSE 5%
658. DEXTROSE (ANHYDROUS) FROM STARCH
659. DESICATED COCONUT POWDER
660. DEXTROSE POWDER FROM STARCH
661. DEAD BURNT DOLOMITE
662. DETERGENT CAKE
663. DEXTROSE SALINE (I.V. FLUID) IN PLASTIC BOTTLES
664. DETERGENT WASHING POWDER (ARIEL TYPE)
665. DEHYDRATED CASTOR OIL
666. DENIM JEANS & JACKETS
667. DENIM CLOTH (INTEGRATED UNIT WITH BLEACHING, DYEING & PRINTING)
668. DETTOL TYPE ANTISEPTIC LOTION
669. DEPARTMENTAL STORE
670. DEHYDRATION OF VEGETABLES
671. DENIM CLOTH
672. DEHYDRATION AND CANNING OF FRUITS & VEGETABLES
673. D.G. SET

674. DEHYDRATION OF FRUITS VEGETABLES & NON VEGETABLE PRODUCTS
675. DE-HULLING OF JAUN FOR BEER INDUSTRY
676. DHOOP BATTI STICK
677. DISPOSABLE PLASTIC SYRINGES (STERILIZED)
678. DISSPOSABLE PLASTIC CUPS, GLASSES, ETC.
679. DISTILLED WATER AMPOULES
680. DI-OCTYL PHTHALATE (DOP)
681. DISTRIBUTION TRANS-FORMER
682. DIRECT COTTON DYE (NO COST ESTIMATION)
683. DAIRY EQUIPMENT
684. DIAZO COATING LUMINESCENT PIGMENT
685. DISTILLED WATER
686. DISPOSABLE DIGARETTE GAS LIGHTER
687. DISPOSABLE NEEDLES
688. DIE MAKING FOR SHEET METAL WORKING
689. DIAMOND TOOLS FOR CUTTING/DRILLING & POLISHING
690. DIRECT BLACK DYE
691. DISH ANTEENA
692. DI-CALCIUM PHOSPHATE FROM ROCK PHOSPHATE
693. DI-CALCIUM PHOSPHATE FROM ANIMAL BONES
694. DIGITAL ELECTRONIC WATCHES
695. DISTILLATION OF ROSIN AND TURPENTINE
696. DIAMOND IMPREGNATED SEGMENTS (METAL BONDED) FOR MARBLE SAWING
697. DI-NITRO CHLORO BENZENE (D.N.C.B.)
698. DI-ETHYL PHTHALATE (DEP)
699. DISH ANTEENA & SATELLITE EQUIPMENTS
700. DIAMOND CUTTING AND EXPORT
701. DI-ETHYL OXALATE
702. DISPOSABLE BABY DIAPER
703. DIAGANOSTIC CENTRE
704. DIESEL GENERATOR SETS
705. 4,4-DIAMINO STILBENE 2,2 DISULPHONIC ACID
706. DOOR BELL
707. DOOR LOCK/PAD LOCKS
708. DODECYCLE BENZENE
709. DOUGH MOULDING COMPOUND
710. DRY ICE
711. DRY DISTEMPER & LIME COLOURS
712. DRY GINGER
713. DRY CELL
714. DRYING OF RED CHILLIES, HALDI, DHANIA, PEAS, AND GREEN PEAS
715. DRIP IRRIGATION
716. DROSS LEAD SCRAP, LEAD POWDER
717. DRY CELLS & STORAGE BATTERIESS
718. DRUM CLOSURES
719. DRY FRUIT ROASTING & PACKING
720. D.T.P. & OFFSET PRESS
721. D.T.P. CUM TABLE OFFSET
722. DUPLICATING INK
723. DUPLICATING INK (BLACK) FOR GESTENER DUPLI-CATOR
724. DUPLICATING STENCIL PAPER
725. DUPLEXFILE BOARD
726. DYE STUFFS

727. DYE INTERMEDIATE
728. DYE FIXING AGENTS
729. DYEING OF HANK YARN FOR POWER LOOM
730. EAF BASED STEEL
731. EARTH LEAKAGE CIRCUIT BREAKERS (ELCB)
732. EASTER GUM (NOCOSTING)
733. E.C.G./E.E.G. PAPER
734. EDIBLE & NON EDIBLE OIL
735. EDTA AND ITS SALT
736. EDIBLE OIL (MUSTARD OIL)
737. EGG POWDER
738. EGG POWDER (100% EOU AUTOMATIC IMPORTED PLANT)
739. EGG TRAY
740. EHT TRANSFORMER
741. ELECTRICALS GLS LAMP
742. ELECTRIC FANS
743. ELECTRONIC SERVICE CENTRE
744. ELECTRONIC CHOKE
745. ELECTRICAL APPLIANCES
746. ELECTRONIC FLASHER FOR AUTOMOBILES
747. ELECTRONIC TOYS
748. ELECTRONIC GAS LIGHTER (MULTI SPARK)
749. ELECTRONIC TIMER
750. ELECTRONIC ENERGY METER
751. ELECTRIC IRON
752. ELECTRICAL INSULATION TAPES (USING BOPP FILM)
753. ELECTRONIC BALLAST (CHOK)
754. ELECTRICAL LAMP (GLS)
755. ELECTRONIC QUARTZ CLOCK/WALL CLOCK
756. ELECTRICAL STAMPING
757. ELECTRONIC TELEPHONESS
758. ELECTRONIC INDICATOR
759. ELECTRO MAGNETICRELAY
760. ELECTROPLATING ON GOLD AND THEIR CHEMICAL TREATMENT IN GOLDEN COLOUR & SULVER THREAD
761. ELECTROPLATING SCHEME PLANT
762. ELECTROPLATING OF SILVER & SILVER
763. ELECTRICAL INSULATION TAPE (USING BOPP FILM)
764. ELECTRICAL LAMP (INCANDESSCENT LAMP)
765. ELECTRICAL REPAIR
766. ELECTRICAL HORN FOR AUTOMOBILE
767. ELECTROPLATING BRIGHTENER
768. ELECTROLYTIC CAPACITOR (MOTOR START)
769. ELECTRIC HEATER CLAY PLATES
770. ELECTRIC LAMP ADHESIVE POWDER
771. ELECTRONIC FAN REGULATOR
772. ELECTRICAL ACCESSORIES (SWITCH, SOCKET, PLUG)
773. ELECTRO CARDIOGRAM MACHINE (ECG. MACHINE)
774. ELECTRIC PORTABLE TOOL
775. ELECTRO POLISHING OF STEEL
776. ELECTRO PLATING
777. ELECTRIC MIXER
778. ELECTRIC CABLES (POWER AND CONTROL CABLES, MINING CABLES, FRLS CABLES, INSTRUMENTATION CABLES, SCREENED CABLES, SUBMERSIBLE PUMP CABLES ETC.)
779. ELECTRONIC SECURITY
780. ELECTRONIC T.V. TUNER
781. ELECTRONIC TEST & MEASURING INSTRUMENT
782. ELECTRONIC TELEPHONES
783. ELECTRONIC TIMER (PROCESSED CONTROL)
784. ELECTRO REFINING OF ZINC
785. ELECTRONIC FLASH GUN

Price Rs. 2500/- for each "Detailed Project Report" Payable in advance through Draft/Cash/M.O. in favour of "ENGINEERS INDIA RESEARCH INSTITUTE". Or Ask by V.P.P. PH.: 291 8117, 291 6431, 292 0361 Fax: 91-11-291 6431 (24 Hrs.)

786. ELECTRONIC MAIL (E-MAIL)
787. ELECTRICAL AND ELECTRONIC PANEL METER (ANALOGUE, DIGITAL, VOLTMETER ETC.)
788. ELECTRICAL MOTOR STARTER
789. ELECTRONIC FIRE ALARM
790. ELECTRIC SWITCHES & OTHER ACCESSORIESS
791. ELECTRIC WATER HEATER
792. ELECTRIC MOTOR WINDING (FOR FAN, MIXIES ETC.)
793. ELASTIC & RIGID TAPESS
794. ELECTROPLATING BRIGHTENER FOR NICKEL
795. ELECTRICAL FIXTURES (CHOKESS & STARTER, PATTIES LIGHTENING FIXTURES ETC.)
796. ELECTROPLATING UNIT
797. ELASTIC THREADS & TWINE
798. ELECTRIC GENERATORS
799. ELECTRIC MOTOR
800. EMERGENCY LIGHT
801. EMBOSSING POWDER OR RESIN COMPOUND
802. EMERY POWDER
803. EMPTY AMPOULES
804. EMULSIFIER FOR PESTICIDE
805. EMPTY GELATIN CAPSULES
806. EMERY PAPER CLOTH
807. EMULSIFIER FOR CUTTING OIL
808. EMULSION PAINTS
809. EMPIRE SLEEVINGS
810. ENAMELING OF COPPER WIRE
811. ENGINEERING WORKSHOP
812. ENAMEL WARE
813. ENDOSULFAN
814. ENGINE VALVE
815. EPABX/EPAX SYSTEM
816. EPOXY RESIN & METAL FILLING COMPOUND
817. EPOXY RESIN BASED PRIMER (PUTTY)
818. EPOXY TRANSFORMER (CURRENT & POTENTIAL)
819. EPOXY RESIN
820. ERW STEEL CONDUIT PIPE
821. E.R.W. PIPES
822. ERW TUBES
823. ESSENTIAL OILS
824. ESSENCE & SOFT DRINK CONCENTRATE
825. ETHYL ALCOHOL FROM MOLASSES
826. ETHYL ACETO ACETATE FROM ALCOHOL
827. ETHYL HEXANOL FROM ETHYL ALCOHOL
828. ETHYLENE GLYCOL MONO STEARATE ETHYLENE GLYCOL DI-STEARATE
829. ETHYL ACETATE
830. ETHYL ACETATE
831. ETCHING OF BRASS
832. ETCHING PROCESS
833. EUCALYPTUS OIL
834. EUCALYPTUS TREE PLANTATION
835. EXERCISE NOT BOOK AND REGISTER
836. EXPANDED POLYSTYRENE MOULDING
837. EXTRACTION OF OIL (CARDAMOM, JEERA ETC.)
838. EXTRACTION OF GLUE POWDER
839. EXPANDED POLYSTYRENE EXTRUSION PROFILE USED FOR MATCH BOX MAKING
840. EXTRACTION OF ALKALOID FROM SOLANIUM KHASIANUM
841. EXTRACTION OF GOLD, SILVER & COPPER
842. EXTRACTION OF ESSENTIAL OIL AND PACKING OF GROUND SPICES (100% EOU)

843. EXTRACTION OF EDIBLE OIL FROM OIL SEEDS (EXPANDER-EXTRUSION COOKING PROCESS)
844. EXTRACTION OF ACID OIL FROM SOAP STOCK
845. EXHAUST FAN
846. EXTRACTION OF OIL FROM WAX, GENERATED AS A BYE PRODUCT FOR PETRO CHEMICALS
847. EXTRACTION OF JASMINE ESSENCE
848. EXTRACTION OF ALKALOIDS FROM VINCA ROSEA
849. EXTRACTION OF CHEMICAL FROM D.M.O.
850. EXTRACTION OF SOYBEAN OIL FROM SOYABEAN
851. EXTRACTION AND FILTRATION OF EDIBLE OIL
852. EXTRACTION & FILTRATION UNIT FOR EDIBLE OIL
853. EXTRUDED ALUMINIUM SECTION
854. EXTRACTION & REFINING OF VEGETABLE OIL
855. FABRICATION , WORKSHOP TO MANUFACTURE TRUSSES & TANKS (PRESSURE VESSELS)
856. FABRICATION OF STORAGE TANKS AND M.S. DRUMS
857. FAT LIQUOR
858. FAST FOOD PARLOR
859. FACSIMILE/FAX MACHINE
860. FABRICATION INDUSTRIES (WORKS) FOR S.S. & M.S. VESSELS WITH LECTRO-PLATING UNIT (TOOLROOM)
861. FATTY ACID
862. FAST COLOUR
863. FATTY ACID FROM WASTE VEGETABLE
864. FASTENERS (NUTS, BOLT, RIVET & WASHERS)
865. FERRO ALLOYS
866. FERRIC ALUM
867. FERRO CEMENT
868. FERROUS SILICATE
869. FERRO MANGANESE ON ALUMINA THERMIC PROCESS
870. FERRO SILICON
871. FERRITE COURSE
872. FERRIC CHLORIDE
873. FEED MILLS (CATTLE & POULTRY FEED)
874. FERRO ALLOYS (OF NIOBIUM, MOLYBDENUM, TITANIUM, TUNGSTEN & VANADIUM)
875. FIBRE BASED BITUMINOUS WATER PROOF FELT
876. FROZEN FOODS, FRUITS & VEGETABLE PROCESSING WITH BACKWARD LINKAGES (100% EOU)
877. FERRITE MAGNETS
878. FERROUS SULPHATE
879. FERRITE CORE TRANSFORMERS
880. FERRO SILICON
881. F.H.P. MOTOR
882. FILE/DUPLEX BOARD
883. FILTERS FOR ALL VEHICLES
884. FIBRE REINFORCED PLASTIC
885. FISH FARMING
886. FISH CANNING & POUCHING
887. FISH OILS
888. FIRE BRICKS
889. FIBRE GLASS
890. FIRE WORKS & PYRO TECHNIQUE
891. FILM STUDIO
892. FISH (PRAWN & OTHERS) & MARINE PRODUCTS
893. FISH MEAL
894. FISH NET
895. FIRE EXTINGUISHER
896. FLAT/RIBBON CABLES
897. FLUSH DOORS
898. FLOCK PRINTING
899. FLAVOURED MILK
900. FLIP TOP CANS
901. FLEXO GRAPHIC & ROTO GRAVURE PRINTING INK
902. FLOURSPER BRIQUETTES
903. FLUSHING CISTERN
904. FLOPPY DISKETTES

905. FLORICULTURE (CUT-FLOWER)-100% EOU
906. FLORICULTURE (CUT FLOWER) WITH GREEN HOUSE TECHNOLOGY
907. FLOURESCENT TUBE
908. FLY ASH BRICKS
909. FLOOR POLISH
910. FLUORESCENT TUBES & GLS LAMPS
911. FLUSH DOOR, CHIP BOARDS, INSULATING BOARDS AND HARD BOARD
912. FLOAT GLASS
913. FLOOR COVERING SHEET
914. FLOUR MILL (ROLLER)
915. FLOUR MILL (GRINDER/ PULVERIZED)
916. FLUORESCENT TUBE & CHOKE
917. FLUORESCENT POWDER FOR FLURESCENT TUBES
918. FLEXOGRAPHIC & ROTOGRAVURE PRINTING
919. FLEXOGRAPHIC PRINTING INKS
920. FOAM AND ITS PRODUCTS ANS MATTRESSES (CUSHION, PILLOWSHEET)
921. FORMALDEHYDE
922. FOOD COLOUR
923. FORGING (NON FERROUS)
936. FRUIT JUICES, SQUASHES, KETCHUP ETC.
937. FRUIT JUICE MAKING AND PACKING IN PLASTIC CONTAINERS (POUCHES)
938. FROZEN FRUITS & VEGETABLES
939. FRUIT DRINKS IN TETRA PACKS (FROOTI TYPE)
940. FRUIT JUICE MAKING & PACKING
941. FRP PRODUCTS
942. FRICTION DUST (LIQUID & POWDER) FROM CNSL
943. FRIED & ROASTED GROUNDNUT, GRAM, PEA, ETC IN POUCHES
944. FRUIT PULP & JUICE CONCENTRATE (i.e., MANGO AND PINEAPPLE PULP & CONCENTRATE)
945. FRENCH POLISH
946. FRUIT JUICES BOTTLING
947. FRUITS & VEGETABLES DRYING BY FREEZE DRYING METHOD
948. FRUIT JUICES, PICKLE PROCESSING & CANNING
949. FRUIT FLAVOURS (WHISKY, VODKA, GRAPE, BUTTER SCOTCH & RUN)
950. FROZEN FINGER CHIP
951. FURFURAL FROM RICE HUL
969. GATE, GRILL, WROUGHT IRON & BRASS STAIRCASE RODS & RAILING
970. GENERATOR SET (PORTABLE)
971. GEMS & JEWELERY
972. GEMS MANUFACTURE
973. GEM CLIPS, PAPER PINS & STAPLE
974. GELATIN & OSSEIN FROM BONE
975. GEOMETRY BOX (MATHEMATICAL INSTRUMENTS)
976. GELATIN
977. GENERATOR (MUSICAL SOUND)
978. GENERATOR (D.G. SET)
979. GELATIN CAPSULES (HARD)
980. GRINDING UNIT (CEMENT)
981. G.I. WIRES
982. GINGER POWDER
983. GINGER OIL, SANDAL WOOD OIL, NAGARMUTHA OIL
984. G.I. PIPES
985. G.I. PIPE FITTINGS
986. GLAZED CERAMIC TILES
987. GLS LAMPS & FLUORESCENT TUBE
988. GLASS SILVERING (MIROR)
989. GLACIAL ACETIC ACID
990. GLASS SHEET (AUTOMATIC PLANT)

924. FORGING PLANT (FOR MANUFACTURING OIL/GAS PIPE FITTINGS)
925. FOUNDRY & MACHINING JOB WORK UNIT
926. FORMIC ACID
927. FOOD GRADE CALCIUM CHLORIDE
928. FOOD DEHYDRATION
929. FORMAL DEHYDRATION
930. FORMULATION FOR DDT, BHC, MELETHION
931. FORGING PLANT (FOR MANUFACTURING OIL/GAS PIPE FITTINGS)
932. FOUNDRY/C.I. CASTING
933. FOAM BOOSTERS
934. FRACTIONAL DISTILLATION OF D.M.Q.
935. FRACTIONAL DISTILLATION OF ESSENTIAL OIL & MEDICINAL PLANT EXTRACTS
952. FURNISHING FABRICS ON POWER LOOM
953. FUEL OIL
954. FUEL BRIQUTTES FROM AGRO WASTE
955. FUEL BRIQUETTES FROM JUTE CADDIES (BIO COAL FROM AGRO WASTE)
956. FURNACE OIL
957. GARLIC FLAKES
958. GAS PIPE (LPG)
959. GARLIC POWDER
960. GALVANIZED ERW PIPES
961. GAS LIGHTER
962. GALION THREAD
963. GAS FILLING OF LPG CYLINDER (LPG GAS BOTTLING PLANT)
964. GALVANIZING PLANT
965. GARLIC OIL & POWDER
966. GAS MANTLES
967. GAS DETECTOR FOR L.P.G.
968. GASKET SHEET
991. GLASS BOTTLE BY SCRAPS
992. GLASS WIRE
993. **GLASS TUBE**
994. GLOW SIGNS
995. GLASS BOTTLES
996. GLS LAMP/BULBS
997. GLASS WOOL
998. GLUE FROM LEATHER WASTE
999. GLASS SHEET FOR WINDOW PANELS
1000. GLUE EXTRACTION & GLUE WHITE POWDER
1001. GLUCOSE & GLUCOSE SALINE
1002. GLASS MARBLES
1003. GLUE & GELATIN
1004. GLYCERIN PURIFICATION
1005. GLYCERIN EXTRACTION PLANT FROM COCONUT OIL
1006. GLASS FLOORING TILES
1007. GLASS SYRINGES
1008. GOAT FARMING

1009. GLUE POWDER FOR TECHNICAL GLUE FLAKES
1010. GOSSY POL (POLY PHENOL) FROM COTTON SEED OIL
1011. GOAT SLAUGHTERING & BREEDING FARM
1012. GOLD EXTRACTION USING CYANIDE SOLUTION & ACID
1013. GOBAR GAS (BIO GAS)
1014. GOLDEN COLOUR SHADE
1015. GOLD ELECTROPLATING
1016. GOLD PLATING ON GLASS
1017. GOAT & SHEEP FARMING
1018. GOLF COURSE
1019. GOLD JEWELLERY
1020. GOLD ELECTROPLATING OR METALLIC JEWELLERY ARTICLE INCLUDING METALLIC WATCH STRAPS
1028. GOLD CYANIDE POWDER
1029. GRAPE DEHYDRATION
1030. GRAPE WINE
1031. GRINDING OF SPICES (TURMERIC, RED CHILLIES, MASALA)
1032. GRANITE SLAB/TILE
1033. GRAPHITE POWDER FROM GRAPHITE ORE
1034. GRANITE MONUMENT
1035. GRANITE CUTTING & POLISHING UNIT
1036. GREEN HOUSE, PLANT MICRO PROPAGATION
1037. GRANULES FROM RESIN
1038. GRANULES (PLASTIC) FROM WASTE
1054. GRAPHITE ORE
1055. GRADED & M.I. CASTING
1056. GRADES OF GUAR GUM
1057. GRIPE WATER
1058. GRANULATED MIXED FERTILIZER
1059. GRAVURE PRINTING CYLINDER
1060. GUM FROM TAMARIND SEED POWDER
1061. GUAR GUM
1062. GUAR GUM POWDER
1063. GUNNY BAGS
1064. GUM FOR PASTING LABELS/ OFFICE PASTE (GUM)
1065. GUAR GUM POWDER (FOOD GRADE)
1066. HAZMOLA TYPE AYURVEDIC TABLET

HELLO

Many Entrepreneurs have gained from 'EIRI' and it is still going on;

Are you one of them ?

if not, contact Today

'EIRI'

1021. GOLD, ROLLED GOLD AND SILVER JEWELLERY
1022. GOLD & SILVER PLATING ON PVC & NYLON
1023. GOLD SALT
1024. GOLD PLATED SILVER JEWELLERY
1025. GOLD PLATED SILVER JEWELLERY AND CUTLERY
1026. GOLD COLOUR (POWER) FOR MORE BRIGHTNESS PROCESS AND FORMULATION FOR OBTAINING MORE BRIGHTNESS FOR PRECIPITATED GOLD POWDER
1027. GOLD COLOUR ELECTROPLATING ON CHEAPER ORNAMENTS WITHOUT USING GOLD
1039. GROUND NUT OIL MILL
1040. GROUND NUT OIL REFINING
1041. GREASES MANUFACTURE
1042. GRANITE & MARBLE TILES
1043. GRAPHITE CARBON PLATES
1044. GREETING CARD BY OFFSET PRINTING PRESS
1045. GRAPHIC DEVELOPER FOR GRAPHIC ART FILM AND GUM SOLUTION FOR PRINTING
1046. GHEE, BUTTER & PANEER
1047. GREASES FROM CASTOR OIL
1048. GRINDING WHEELSS
1049. GRINDING MEDIA BALLS
1050. GRANITE CRUSHING
1051. GRAM DALS & FLOUR MILLS
1052. GRAM DALL/PULSE MILL
1053. GREEN PEAS PROCESSING & CANNING
1067. HAWAI CHAPPAL (RUBBER)
1068. HARD RUBBER BATTERY CONTAINER
1069. HATCHERY FARMING (BROILER)
1070. HAND BLODK PRINTING
1071. HAND TOOLS
1072. HAIR SHAMPOOS
1073. HAIR DYE IN CREAM FORM
1074. HAMMERS
1075. HAIR FIXER
1076. HALOGEN LAMPS
1077. HAIR DYE POWDER
1078. HARD CHROMIUM & NICKEL CHROMIUM PLATING
1079. HANDKERCHIEF
1080. HANDICRAFTS
1081. HARD GREASE
1082. HAIR DYE IN HAIR OIL FORM
1083. HARD & SOFT FERRITES

Price Rs. 2500/- for each "Detailed Project Report" Payable in advance through Draft/Cash/M.O. in favour of "ENGINEERS INDIA RESEARCH INSTITUTE". Or Ask by V.P.P. PH.: 291 8117, 291 6431, 292 0361 Fax: 91-11-291 6431 (24 Hrs.)

1084. HARD GELATIN CAPSULES (EMPTY)
1085. HANK YARN DYEING FOR POWER LOOM
1086. HAMMER TONE PAINTS
1087. HARD COKE
1088. HARD CHROMIUM PLATING
1089. HAND MADE PAPER
1090. HAND LOOM PRODUCTS KHES, BED SHEET, BED COVERS, FURNISHING
1091. HARD BOARD FROM RICE HUSK
1092. HARD BOARD FROM BAGASSE
1093. HAWAN SAMAGRI
1094. HACK SAW BLADE
1095. HYDRATED LIME
1096. HDPE/LDPE MANUFACTURING FROM ETHYL ALCOHOL
1097. HOLIDAY RESORTS
1098. HOSPITALS
1099. HOSPITAL (Rs. 100 cr. Project)
1100. HOSPITAL/NURSING HOME
1101. HOLLOW CONCRETE BLOCK/BRICK
1102. HDPE FILM/SHEET
1103. HOTEL (*** STAR)
1104. HOTEL (***** STAR)
1105. HOTEL (NO STAR)
1106. HOT ROLLING MILL
1107. HOSE PIPE (RUBBER)
1108. HING (ASAFOETIDA)
1109. HOT DIP GALVANIZING
1110. HYDROGEN GALVANIZING
1111. HDPE/LDPE PIPES
1112. HIGH VOLTAGE WIRE
1113. HOSIERY INDUSTRY (GENTS)
1114. HOSEIRY INDUSTRY (LADIES)
1115. HOSPITAL RUBBER GOODS AND SHEETS
1116. HDPE/PP WOVEN SACKS
1117. HDPE PIPE & FITTING
1118. HDPE & LDPE PIPE FITTING
1119. HDPE TARPAULINS
1120. HDPE BOX STRAPPINGS
1121. HDPE/LDPE PIPES AND FITTINGS
1122. HDPE PIPE
1123. HERBAL KUM-KUM ROLI
1124. HEAT TRANSFER LABEL FOR RUBBER
1125. HEXAMINE FROM FORMALDEHYDE
1126. HEAT TRANSFER LABEL BY SCREEN PROCESS
1127. HEAT TREATMENT OF LEAF SPRING
1128. HELICAL SPRING (COIL SPRINGS)
1129. HELMET
1130. HEALTH CENTRE
1131. HERBAL MEDICATED CIGARETTES
1132. HERBAL COSMETICS
1133. HERBAL TOOTH PASTE AND TOOTH POWDER
1134. HESSIAN BAGS (LAMI-NATED) WITH PRINTING
1135. HESSIAN CLOTH
1136. HEPTAL DEHYDE
1137. HERBAL SHAMPOO/CREAM
1138. HEALTH CLUB CUM BEAUTY PARLOUR WITH HAIR SALOOR & SONA BATH
1139. HELMET FOR COAL MINES
1140. HEAT CHAMBER PAINTING
1141. HINGES (PIANO TYPE)
1142. HINGES (M.S.)
1143. HIGH ALUMINA CERAMICS
1144. HIGH RUPTURING CAPACITY (HRC) FUSES
1145. HIGH TENSILE FASTENERS
1146. H.M. BAGS
1147. HOMOEOPATHIC MEDICINE
1148. HOSIERY PRODUCTS LIKE CHILDREN KNITWEAR, T-SHIRTS & ACRYLIC FIBRE
1149. HOT DIP GALVANIZING
1150. HOSIERY & TAILORS LABELS
1151. HOMEO & BIO MEDICINES WITH MOTHER TINCTURE
1152. HOT ROLLED (HR) COILS
1153. HOSIERY MERCERIZING
1154. HOSIERY CLOTH (COTTON) PROCESSING-BLEACHING, DYEING & FINISHING OF CLOTH
1155. HOIST & CRANES (MATERIAL HANDLING EQPT.)
1156. HOOKS & CLIPS (METAL)
1157. HOT MIX PLANT
1158. H-ACID
1159. H.T. & M.V. INDUSTRIAL CUBICAL SWITCH BOARDS
1160. HUME PIPES
1161. HURRICANE LANTERN/STOVE
1162. HYDROGENATION OF CASTOR OIL
1163. HYDROCHLORIC ACID (HCL)
1164. HYDROGEN PEROXIDE BY AUTO OXIDATION PROCESS
1165. HYDRAULIC BRAKE CYLINDER
1166. HYDROFLUORIC ACID
1167. HYDRAULIC DOOR CLOSER
1168. HYBRIC SEED
1169. HYDRATED CALCIUM SILICATE BRICKS
1170. HYPODERMIC NEEDLES FOR DISPOSABLE SYRINGES
1171. HYDRAULIC LIFTING DEVICES (FOR AUTOMOBILE SERVICING & REPAIR)
1172. HYDROGENATED CASTOR OIL
1173. HYDROGEN GAS PLANT (HYDROGEN & OXYGEN)
1174. IBUPROFIN
1175. ICE MAKING PLANT
1176. ICE CUBE PLANT
1177. ICE CREAM OF DIFFERENT FLAVOURS
1178. ICE CREAM STABILIZERS
1179. ICE CREAM & ICE CANDY
1180. ICE CREAM
1181. ICE CREAM CUPS OF PLASTIC
1182. ICE & COLD STORAGE
1183. IDLER ROLLERS FOR CONVEYERS (PLAIN & RUBBER COVERED)
1184. IF/RF COILS
1185. IGNITION CONDENSERS
1186. IGNITION CONDENSER
1187. IMMERSION HEATER
1188. IMITATION JEWELLERY
1189. INDUCTION WATER & SALINE
1190. STAINLESS STEEL PATTA
1191. INJECTION WATER & SALINE
1192. INSULATING VARNISH
1193. INJECTION MOULDED PLASTIC ARTICLES
1194. INDUSTRIAL REFRIGERATION
1195. INJECTION & BLOW MOULDED PLASTIC PRODUCTS
1196. INJECTION MOULDED HOUSE HOLD ITEMS
1197. INSECTICIDES FROM NEEM OIL, LEAVES & NEEM SEEDS
1198. INJECTION MOULDED PLASTIC COMPONENTS
1199. INSTANT FOODS (IDLI MIX, SAMBER MIX, VADA MIX, GULAB JAMUN, TOMATO SOUP MIX ETC.)
1200. INDUCTION FURNACE BASED C.I. CASTING
1201. INDUCTION HARDENING OF MACHINE COMPOUNDS
1202. INFORMATION MOVING DISPLAY
1203. INJECTION MOULDED PLASTIC COMPONENTS FOR ELECTRICAL/ELECTRONICS INDUSTRIAL
1204. INSULATING VARNISH (POLY VINYL BUTYRAL BASED FFC GRADE)
1205. INDUSTRIAL OXYGEN GAS
1206. INTRAVENOUS (I.V.) SET
1207. INDIAN PICKLE
1208. INDIAN MADE FOREIGN LIQUOR (IMFL)
1209. INDUCTION FURNACE
1210. INSULATING VARNISH (DRY TYPE)
1211. INTERNAL COMBUSTION ENGINE (FOR AGRI-CULTURAL EQUIPMENTS)
1212. INTEGRATED COMPLEX OF EASTERS & ALLIED PRODUCTS (DOP, DBP, ETHYL ACETATE, BUTYL ACETATE, WIRE ENAMEL JELLY CBLE COMPOUNDS
1213. INSULATING VARNISH & WIRE ENAMEL
1214. INDUSTRIAL KNIFE
1215. INDIGO BLUE
1216. INVESTMENT CASTINGS
1217. INVESTMENT CASTINGS OF BRASS
1218. INVERTER
1219. INDUSTRIAL HARD OIL USED IN SOAP MAKING
1220. INDUSTRIAL GLOVES

1221. INVERTER & CONVERTER
1222. INSTANT ICE CREAM MIX
1223. INTEGRATED CIRCUITS
1224. INDUSTRIAL ALCOHOL FROM MOLASSES
1225. INVESTMENT CASTINGS FOR SS & HIGHER ALLOYS
1226. INDUSTRIAL ALCOHOL FROM ETHYLENE
1227. INSTANT TEA & COFFEE
1228. INJECTABLE FOR PHARMACEUTICALS
1229. INSTANT SOUP
1230. INSTANT NOODLES
1231. INSULATING LAGGING OF BOILERS & STEAM TUBES
1232. INTIMATE SCENT, CHEMICALS ETC. FROM ALL TYPES OF FLOWERS
1233. IONES FROM LEMON GRASS OIL
1234. IODIZED SALT
1235. IODIZED SALT (MOISTURELESS-FREE)
1236. IRON POWDER FROM MILL SCALE SCRAP ARISING FROM IRON & STEEL REROLLING MILL
1237. IRON TAWA
1238. IRON & STEEL WIRE & NETTING
1239. IRON OXIDE PIGMENT
1240. IRON (WROUGHT) & BRASS STAIRCASE, RODS, RAILING, GATE AND GRILL
1241. ISO PROPANOL (ISO PROPYLALCOHOL)
1242. ISOPRENE & NEOPRENE BASED RUBBER ADHESIVE
1243. I.V. CANNULA
1244. I.V. FLUID
1245. I.V. SET
1246. I.V. PLASTIC BOTTLES
1247. JAM & JELLY
1248. JAM, CHUTNEY, PICKLE AND SQUASHES
1249. J-ACID
1250. JASMINE & LILY FLOWER OIL
1251. JACQUARD FABRICS
1252. JAUN DEHULLING FOR BEER INDUSTRY
1253. JEANS & JACKETS (DENIM)
1254. JEAN DYEING & FIXING BY INDIGO BLUE (JIGGER DYE & DIP DYE)
1255. JELLY FILLED CABLES
1256. JELLY & JAM
1257. JEWELLERY (GOLD AND SILVER)
1258. JEWELLERY (GOLD)
1259. JOB WORK
1260. JUTE TAR FELT
1261. JUTE BAGS
1262. JUTE BATCHING OIL
1263. JUTE WASTE PRODUCTS
1264. JUTE PROCESSING TWIN & GUNNY BAGS
1265. JUTE TWIN INCLUDING COTTON & COIR
1266. JUTE BAGS BY RAW JUTE
1267. JUTE, COIR, GRASS, ROPE SUTLI MAKING
1268. JUICES (FRUIT)
1269. KATECHU (KATTHA)
1270. KALI MEHANDI (HAIR DYE)
1271. KATTHA & CLUTCH
1272. KATTHA
1273. KANTHAL/NICHRO-ME FURNACE HEATING WIRE
1274. KERNAL (CASHEW NUT KERNAL EXTRACT)
1275. KHANDSARI SUGAR
1276. KIMAM MANUFACTURE
1277. KITCHEN SINK (S.S.)
1278. KNITTING FABRICS
1279. KNITTED CLOTH
1280. KRAFT PAPER (FROM WASTE PAPER)
1281. KRAFT PAPER AND MILL BOARD
1282. KRAFT PAPER & SPECIAL PAPER
1283. KRAFT PAPER FROM WASTE CARTON BOXES
1284. LAMINATED OF PAPER WARE (CARDS) WITH GLOSSY PP (POLYESTER FILM)
1285. LAUNDRY & DRY CLEANER
1286. LACTIC ACID
1287. LACTIC ACID FROM WHITE SUGAR (BY FERMENTATION PROCESS)
1288. LATEX RUBBER THREAD
1289. LAMINATED SAFETY GLASS
1290. LAMINATED SAFETY & TOUGHENED GLASS
1291. LAMINATED PARTICLE BOARD & HARD BOARD
1292. LATEX RUBBER ADHESIVE
1293. LAUNDRY & WASHING SOAP
1294. LAUNDRY SOAP
1295. LAMINATED HESSIAN BAG
1296. LAMINATED SPRAY BRASS ARTICLES/BADGES
1297. LAMP CAPS
1298. LAMINATED JUTE BAGS
1299. LABORATORY CHEMICAL UNIT
1300. LATEX RUBBER CONDOM
1301. LATHER SHAVING CREAM
1302. LAPTOP COMPUTERS
1303. LAMP FILAMENT
1304. LATEX FOAM PRODUCTS
1305. LADDU
1306. LACTOSE & BYE PRODUCTS PROCESSING FROM MILK
1307. LAMINATION OF CO-EXTRUSION, THREE LAYER FILM WITH LAMINATION & PRINTING
1308. LAMINATION OF CO-EXTRUSION MULTI LAYER FILM IN ROLL FORM
1309. LAUNDRY FOR '5' STAR HOTEL
1310. LDPE/HDPE FROM ETHYL ALCOHOL
1311. LDPE/HDPE PLANT
1312. LDPE/HDPE PIPES
1313. LEATHER GARMENTS
1314. LEAD CRYSTAL
1315. LEMON GRASS OIL BASED IONES
1316. LEATHER GOODS
1317. LEATHER TANNING & COLOURING
1318. LEATHER SHOE & CHAPPAL
1319. LEATHER BINDER
1320. LEVELING & DISPERSING AGENT
1321. LEATHER STRAPS FOR WRIST WATCHES
1322. LEATHER SHOES
1323. LEATHER BOARD
1324. LECITHIN (SOYA BASED)
1325. LEATHER TANNING
1326. LEATHER GOODS
1327. LETTER PRESS PRINTING
1328. LEATHER AUXILIARIES AND CHEMICAL
1329. LEATHER TANNING & LEATHER GARMENTS
1330. LEATHER DYES
1331. LEASING BUSINESS
1332. LEASING & HIRE PURCHASE
1333. LEAD STEARATE
1334. LEMON GRASS OIL
1335. LEAD REFINING USING LEAD DROSS, LEAD SCRAP, LEAD POWDER,
1336. LEAD NITRATE
1337. LEATHER GARMENTS, SHOES & CHAPPALS
1338. LEATHER WASHERS
1339. LEAD MONOXIDE
1340. LEATHER SUIT-CASES, BRIEF CASES & TRAVELING BAGS
1341. LEAD EXTRACTION FROM SCRAP BATTERIES
1342. LEAD BATTERY PLATES & BATTERY ASSEMBLY
1343. LEAD PENCILS
1344. LEAD SMELTING
1345. LEAD OXIDE (A) LEAD MONOXIDE (B) REA LEAD (LEAD TETROXIDE) (C) GREY LEAD OXIDE
1346. LEAD EXTRACTION (SECONDARY) FROM SCRAPS (A) BATTERY PLATE (B) PIPES (C) SHEET
1347. LIQUID BINDI & SINDUR
1348. LIQUID GLUCOSE & ITS BYE PRODUCTS FROM MAIZE
1349. LIQUID SOAP
1350. LIQUID DETERGENTS
1351. LIQUID SHOE POLISH PUFF
1352. LITHOPONE
1353. LIQUID GLUCOSE FROM POTATOES
1354. LIQUID OXYGEN BOTTLING
1355. LIGHTNING ARRESTER AND ISOLATOR
1356. LIGHT LIQUID PARAFFIN
1357. LILLY FLOWER & JASMINE
1358. LIQUID SOAP BY PINE OIL
1359. LITMUS PAPER
1360. LIGHT EMITING DIODE (LED)
1361. LIME STONE, DOLOMITE CHIPS & POWDER

1362. LINK CHAIN
1363. LIME STONE CRUSHING, GRINDING & PULVERISING
1364. LIQUID DETERGENTS
1365. LIME COLOUR/CEMENT COLOUR/SYNTHETIC RED IRON OXIDE USED FOR FLOORING
1366. LIMIT SWITCHES & METAL PLUG SOCKETS
1367. LIQUID DETERGENT
1368. LIPSTICKS
1369. LINSEED OIL
1370. LICHEN (JHYAU) (CHARILA)
1371. LIQUID GLUCOSE
1372. LIST OF 100% EOU/EOU UNIT
1373. LINING MATERIAL FOR FLUID FLOWING PIPE (LIQUID PETROLEUM)
1374. LOW PRESSURE CELLULOSE LIQUID
1375. LOUDSPEAKER
1376. LOOM OIL
1377. LOW TENSILE TRANSFORMERS (L.T.) upto 400 KVA.
1378. LPG STOVE
1379. LPG CYLINDER TESTING CENTER
1380. LPG CYLINDER
1381. LPG GAS REGULATOR
1382. LPG GAS BOTTLING PLANT
1383. LPG GAS STOVE
1384. LPG GAS PIPE
1385. LPG GAS DETECTOR
1386. L.T. TRANSFORMER REPAIRING (400 KVA)
1387. LUBE OIL FROM CNSL TO REDUCE FRICTION
1388. LUBE OIL & GREASES
1389. LUBE OIL RECLAMATION
1390. LUBE OIL BLENDING
1391. LUBRICATING OIL & GREASES (BLENDING OF LUBRICATURE OF GREASE)
1392. LUBRICANT VISCOSITY INDEX IMPROVERS
1393. LUBRICANT-WIREDRAWING
1394. MACARONI & VERMICELLI
1395. MANUFACTURE OF T-SHIRTS WITH KNITTING FABRICS
1396. MANGO PEEL BASED PECTIN
1397. MASALA/SPICES
1398. MATCH BOS MAKING UNIT
1399. MARBLE & GRANITE TILES
1400. MANGANESE ORE CONCENTRATION
1401. MAGNESIUM CARBONATE, MAGNESIUM METAL, CALCIUM CARBONATE FROM DOLOMITE
1402. MAGNESIUM SILICATE (TALC)
1403. MAIZE/CORN STARCH
1404. MALTED MILK FOOD
1405. MARINE CONTAINERS
1406. MANILA ROPES
1407. MALACHITE GREEN
1408. MANGO PULP & MANGO SLICES CANNING
1409. MAIZE STARCH
1410. MAGNESIUM HYDROXIDE POWDER
1411. MAGNESIUM SULPHATE
1412. MAGNESIUM TRI-SILICATE
1413. MAIZE/CORN OIL
1414. MALEIC ANHYDRIDE
1415. MALTING PLANT
1416. MARKING INK
1417. MACARONI
1418. MANGALORE TILES/BRICKS
1419. MAN POWER EXPORT
1420. MACHINE SCREWS & SELF TAPPING SCREWS
1421. MANGO POWDER
1422. MANGO JUICE
1423. MANGO KERNEL POWDER
1424. MAGNET

Ask for other Detailed project Reports apart from this list. (Ready 15000 Project Reports)

1425. MAGNESIUM CARBONATE & BI-CARBONATE
1426. MAGAZINE
1427. MATCH SPLINTERS & INNER BOX MAKING PLANT FROM POPULAR WOOD
1428. MATERIAL HANDLING EQUIPMENTS
1429. MANUFACTURING OF PHARMACEUTICALS, TABLETS, CAPSULES ETC.,
1430. MANGO PROCESSING & CANNING (MANGO PULP)
1431. MANGO PRODUCTS, MANGO JUICE, PICKLES, ETC.
1432. METAL CUTTING DIE DESIGN
1433. MEASURING TAPES (STEEL, METALLIC & PLASTIC)
1434. MENTHOL CRYSTAL & OTHER CHEMICALS
1435. METHANE GAS
1436. METAL SPECTACLE FRAME
1437. MELAMINE CRYSTALS
1438. METTOL FROM HYDRO QUINENE & METHYL AMINE
1439. MEDICAL X-RAY FILM, SLITTING & REPACKING
1440. MEDICAL PLANT EXTRACT
1441. METAL FINISHING
1442. MENTHOL & D.M.O.
1443. MELAMINE CROCKERY
1444. METHYL METHA CRYLATE
1445. MELAMINE FORMALDEHYDE POWDER
1446. METAL HARDENING
1447. METAL FITTINGS FOR LEATHER GOODS & GARMENT
1448. METAL CONTAINER
1449. MECHANICAL TOY
1450. MENTHOL CRYSTAL
1451. METAL BONDED DIAMOND IMPREGNATED SEGMENT FOR MARBLE SAWING
1452. METHYLATED SURGICAL SPIRIT
1453. METALLIZED POLYPROPYLENE FILM
1454. METAL NAPHTHANATE
1455. METALLIC GASKET (SPIRAL WOUND)
1456. METAL PRE-TREATMENT CHEMICALS
1457. MENTHA OIL
1458. METALLIC ACID
1459. MERCURIC OXIDE
1460. METHYL METHACRYLATE MONOMER & VARIOUS CHEMICAL ADDITIVES FOR PLASTIC BANGLES
1461. METAL POLISH SOAP
1462. METAL HOOKS & CLIP
1463. METALLIC STEARATES
1464. METHYLINE GLUE
1465. METHYL SALICYLATE
1466. MEAT PROCESSING (BUFFALLO)
1467. METAL POLISHING BAR
1468. METHYL ETHYL KETONE
1469. M.G. KRAFT PAPER FROM WASTE PAPER
1470. MICRO SCALE STEEL
1471. MICRO WAVE OVEN
1472. MINI CEMENT PLANT (BY ROTARY KILN PROCESS 800 TPD)
1473. MILK PRESERVATION & MARKETING TO WHOLESALERS (IN POUCHS)
1474. MILK/DAIRY PRODUCTS
1475. MINI RE-ROLLING MILL
1476. MINI PAPER PLANT FORM JUTE STICK & WHEAT HUSK/RICE HUSK
1477. MILK/DAIRY PRODUCTS
1478. MILK CHOCOLATE
1479. MINI STEEL PLANT BY INDUCTION FURNACE
1480. MINI CEMENT PLANT
1481. MICA PAPER FOR ELECTRICAL INSULATION
1482. MINI SUGAR PLANT
1483. MICRO CRYSTALLINE WAX
1484. MINIATURE CIRCUIT BREAKER (MCB)
1485. MINI FLOUR MILL (ROLLER)
1486. MINI FLOUR MILL (PULVERISED)
1487. MINI PAPER PLANT (KRAFT PAPER)
1488. MINI PAPER PLANT FROM SISAL WOOD

1489. MITHAI/NAMKEEN
1490. MICRO CRYSTALLINE WAX FROM SLUDGE OF PETRO CHEMICAL REFFINERY
1491. MINIATURE WATCH BATTERY
1492. MICRO NUTRIENT MIXTURE (SOLID)
1493. MISHRI PEARL SUGAR CANDY
1494. MINI PAPER PLANT FROM EUCALYPTUS WOOD
1495. MILL & KRAFT PAPER FROM WASTE CARTON BOXES
1496. MINI PAPER PLANT (WHITE WRITING & PRINTING)
1497. MINERAL WATER IN POUCHES
1498. MINERAL WATER IN POUCHES & PLASTIC BOTTLES
1499. MIRIT SANJEEVNI SURA
1500. MINI STEEL PLANT
1501. MILK PRESERVATION & MARKETING (MILK CHILLING PLANT)
1502. MICRO NUTRIENTS MIXTURES
1503. MICRO WAVE TUBES USED IN MICRO WAVE OVEN
1504. MILK POWDER
1505. MILD STEEL BOLT
1506. MILD STEEL NUTS
1507. MINI (PERSONAL) COMPUTER
1508. MINIATURE TRANSFORMER
1509. MINI PAPER PLANT USING BAGASSE
1510. MILK POWDER, GHEE & SPICES
1511. MICRO PAPER
1512. MIRROR (GOLDEN, SILVER AND PINK)
1513. MICROVEE & ABSOLUTE FILTER
1514. MICRO MOTORS
1515. MIXERS/GRINDERS (MIXIE)
1516. MILK POWDER & GHEE
1517. MICRO CELLULAR SHEET FOR SHOE SOLE
1518. MILK TOFFEE
1519. MILK CHILLING PLANT & PACKING IN POUCHES
1520. MODERN COSMETIC INDUSTRY
1521. MOSQUITO COILS & MATS
1522. MOULDED CASE CIRCUIT BREAKER (MCCB)
1523. MOTHER BOARD
1524. MONOCHROME MONITOR FOR COMPUTER
1525. MOULDED LUGGAGE
1526. MOULDED LUGGAGE (V.I.P. TYPE)
1527. MOULDED LUGGAGE (CHEAP QUALITY)
1528. MOSQUITO REPELLENT MAT
1529. MOTHER TINCTURE & BIO-CHEMIC MEDICINES
1530. MOTEL/SMALL HOTEL
1531. MOSQUITO COILS
1532. MODERN RICE MILL
1533. MOSAIC TILES
1534. MOTOR START ELECTROLYTIC CAPACITORS
1535. MOSQUITO MAT RECHARGER

1536. MONO CHLORO ACETIC ACID
1537. MOBILE CATERING VAN
1538. MODERN VEHICLE WORKSHOP
1539. MODERN BREAD AND BAKERY UNIT
1540. MONOCHROTOPHOS (TECHNICAL)
1541. MOSQUITO REPELLENT OIL
1542. MOTEL/SMALL HOTEL, BANQUET HALL WITH RESTAURANT
1543. MOSQUITO COILS USING EUCALYPTUS LEAVES
1544. MODERN ADVERTISING AGENCY WITH DTP & FILM STUDIO
1545. M.S. INGOTS (INDUCTION FURNACE)
1546. M.S. WIRE DRAWING PLANT & ANNEALING
1547. M.S. HINGES
1548. M.S. INGOTS & H.R. STEEL STRUCTURES
1549. M.S. WELDING ELECTRODES
1550. M.S. DRUM & FABRICATION OF STORAGE TANK
1551. MUSTARD OIL (EDIBLE OIL)
1552. MULTI PURPOSE SPRAY DRIER
1553. MUSICAL DOOR BELL
1554. MUSHROOM CULTIVATION
1555. MUSHROOM CULTIVATION & PROCESSING WITH CANNING
1556. MULTI LAYER PRINTED CIRCUIT BOARD (PCB)
1557. MULTI PURPOSE COLD STORAGE FOR MEDICINES, FRUITS &VEGETABLES
1558. MULTIPLE RELAY FOR LOW VOLTAGE APPLICATION
1559. MUSHROOM(EOU) CULTIVATION & PROCESSING UNIT (DEHYDRATION & PICKLING OF OYSTER & PADDY STRAW MUSHROOM)
1560. MUTTON TALLOW FOR INDUSTRIAL USE
1561. MUFFLERS & SILENCERS FOR TWO WHEELERS
1562. MUFFLER & SILENCER PIPES FOR FOUR WHEELER
1563. MUSHROOM & PROCESSED FOOD
1564. MUSICAL SOUND GENERATOR
1565. MULTI LAYER FILM
1566. MULTI STOREY COMMERCIAL COMPLEX ALONGWITH RESIDENTIAL & DELUXE FLATS FOR FOREIGN TOURISTS & REVOLVING RESTAURANT
1567. MUSTARD OIL EXTRACTION & REFINING
1568. MURABBA
1569. MULTI LAYER CO-EXTRUSION, THREE LAYERS-FILM WITH LAMINATION PRINTING
1570. NAPHTHALENE BALLS
1571. NAMKEEN & SWEETS
1572. NAIL ENAMEL (NAIL POLISH)
1573. NAMKEEN INDUSTRY
1574. NAPHTHALENE BALLS
1575. NAPHTHA BASED THINNER
1576. NAIL CUTTER WITH FILER & MANICURE
1577. N-ACETYL, L-TYROSINE
1578. N.C. PUTTY
1579. N.C. THINNER USED IN AUTO PARTS
1580. N.C. SENDING SEALERS
1581. NEWS PRINT PAPER FROM RICE STRAW/BAGASSE
1582. NEWS PAPER
1583. NEOPRENE BASED ADHESIVES
1584. NEON SIGN
1585. NEON BULB
1586. NEEM OIL FROM SEEDS
1587. NEON LAMP INDICATORS
1588. NEON INDICATOR
1589. NEEM SEEDS INSECTICIDES
1590. NEEDLE ROLLERS FOR BEARING
1591. NEROL LAUNDRY SOAP
1592. NEWS PAPER FOR CHILDREN (DAILY)-EVENING NEWS PAPER

1593. NITRO CELLULOSE (LACQUER)
1594. NICHROME WIRE
1595. NICHROME/KANTHAL FURNACE HEATING WIRE
1596. NICKEL PLATING BRIGHTNER (PRIMARY OR CARRIER BRIGHTNER AND SECONDARY)
1597. NICKEL SALT
1598. NICKEL/CADMIUM BATTERY
1599. NICKEL PLATING
1600. NICKEL PLATING BRIGTNER
1601. NICKEL LINED SCREENS
1602. NICKEL SULPHATE
1603. NICKEL CATALYST
1604. NICKEL CATALYST FOR HYDROGENETION OF VEGETABLE OIL
1605. NICKEL ELECTROPLATING SALTS (ONLY MARKET SURVEY)
1606. NICKEL CHROMIUM PLATING & HARD CHROMIUM
1607. NICKEL RECLAMATION FROM SPENT CATALYST OF VANASPATI INDUSTRY
1608. NITROGEN & OXYGEN UNIT
1609. NILGIRI OIL
1610. NICOTINIC ACID
1611. NIRMA TYPE DETERGENT POWDER
1612. NITRO CELLULOSE
1613. NITRO MUSK
1614. NICOTINE SULPHATE FROM TOBACCO WASTE
1615. NON-STICK KITCHEN WARES (TEFLON COATED UTENSILS)
1616. NON-FERROUS SCRAP MELTING ROD CASTING & WIRE DRAWING
1617. NON-IONIC SURFACTANTS WETTING AGENTS
1618. NOODLES
1619. NON-BASMATI RICE FROM PADDY
1620. NON-IONIC LIQUID DETERGENT
1621. NON-ALCOHOLIC FLAVOUR
1622. NON-CARBONATED SOFT DRINK
1623. NON-FERROUS METAL ALLOY
1624. NON-FERROUS FORGING
1625. NON-EDIBLE & EDIBLE OIL MILL
1626. NOTE BOOK, REGISTER & FILES
1627. NON-WOVEN CARPETS (WADDED WITH POLYESTER FIBER)
1628. NUMBER COMBINATION AUTO LOCKS FOR LUGGAGES
1629. NUT, BOLTS, RIVETS/WASHER
1630. NURSING HOME
1631. NURSERY SCHO-OL (PRE-NURSERY & NURSERY)
1632. NYLON YARN CRIMPING DOUBL-ING, BLEACHING, DYEING ETC.
1633. NYLON POLYESTER & P.P. ROPE MAKING
1634. NYLON ZIP FASTENERS
1635. NYLON SOCKS
1636. OCTYL ALCOHOL
1637. OFFSET PRINTING PRESS
1638. OFFSET SECURITY PRINTING PRESS
1639. OFFSET COLOUR & TREADLE TYPE PRINTING PRESS
1640. OFFSET PRINTING INK
1641. OIL (COTTON SEED)
1642. OIL (MUSTARD)
1643. OIL (GROUND NUT)
1644. OIL MILL
1645. OIL SEALS
1646. OIL (CASTOR)

1647. OIL (RICE BRAN)
1648. OIL (ESSENTIAL)
1649. OIL BOND DISTEMPER PAINT
1650. OLEORESIN OF SPICES
1651. OLEORESIN FROM CHILLY
1652. ONE TIME CARBON PAPER
1653. ONION POWDER
1654. ONION & POTATO POWDER
1655. OPTICAL GLASS GRINDING
1656. OPTICAL FIBER CABLE
1657. OPTICAL WHITENER
1658. OPEN END SPINNING PLANT
1659. OPTICAL WHITENER
1660. ORTHO BORIC ACID
1661. ORGANIC SOLVENT PURIFICATION PLANT
1662. ORTHO TOLUENE SOLVENT
1663. ORGANIC MANURE
1664. OSSEIN & GELATIN
1665. OSSEIN FROM ANIMAL BONES
1666. OXYGEN GAS
1667. OXALIC ACID
1668. OXALIC ACID FROM WASTE VEGETABLES
1669. OXYGEN & NITROGEN PLANT
1670. OXALIC ACID FROM SAW DUST
1671. OXIDISED WAX
1672. OYSTER MUSHROOMS (CULTIVATION & PROCESSING UNIT)
1673. PAINT INDUSTRY
1674. PACKAGING OF NAMKEEN, BHUJIA, DALMOTH ETC. IN FLEXIBLE POUCHES
1675. PARAFFIN WAX FROM SLACK WAX
1676. PAINT BRUSHES
1677. PAPER BAGS
1678. PALM OIL
1679. PARACETAMOL
1680. PAPPAD PLANT
1681. PAN MASALA IN POUCHES & TIN PACKS
1682. PAPER FROM BAMBOO
1683. PAPER FROM WASTE PAPER (KRAFT PAPER)
1684. PAPER FROM WASTE PAPER (WRITING & PRINTING PAPER)
1685. PAPER FROM BAGASSE
1686. PAPER FROM RICE STRAW
1687. PAPER CONES & TUBES
1688. PAPER & PULP
1689. PAPER FROM EUCALYPTUS
1690. PAPER ENVELOPS
1691. PAPER FROM RICE HUSK & WHEAT HUSK
1692. PAPER FROM PAPYRUS GRASS
1693. PAPER (HAND MADE PAPER)
1694. PAPER CUPS
1695. PAPER PLANT FROM TREE BARK & EUCALYPTUS WOOD
1696. PAPER BASED PHENOLIC SHEET (FOR ELECTRICAL APPLIANCES)
1697. PAPER WASTE RECYCLING
1698. PAPER & PAPER BOARD
1699. PAPER PRODUCTS
1700. PAPAIN
1701. PAPAIN FROM PAPAYA
1702. PAPAYA CULTIVATION
1703. PAPAYA & TOMATO CULTIVATION
1704. PAPAYA CULTIVATION & PAPAIN MANUFACTURE
1705. PARTICLE BOARD
1706. PAPER COATED ALUMINIUM & COPPER WIRES
1707. PANEL, FLUSH DOOR, WINDOWS, OFFICE FURNITURE & HOUSE HOLD FURNITURE
1708. PANEER
1709. PAPER PLATES
1710. PAINT & VARNISH
1711. PARACETAMOL BY PNCB
1712. PARAAMINO BENZOIC ACID

1713. PAINT INDUSTRY (LIME COLOUR, DRY DISTEMPER, OIL BOUND DISTEMPER, ENAMEL PAINT, RED OXIDE PRIMER/RESIN, MICA BASED PAINT)
1714. PAN MASALA & POUCH MAKING PLANT
1715. PARA CHLORO NITRO BENZENE
1716. PASTEURIZATION OF MILK (FLAVOURED MILK)
1717. PARTICLE BOARD FROM RICE HUSK
1718. PAN MASALA, TOBACCO, ZARDA & KIMAM
1719. PAINT-BITUMINOUS BASED CORROSION RESISTANT
1720. PAINT REMOVERS
1721. PALM OIL CRUSHING UNIT
1722. PAPER VARNISH
1723. PAPER FROM AKRA
1724. PARTICLE BOARD WOOD CHIPS
1725. PARTICLE BOARD & BLOCK BOARD WITH SENDING & LAMINATION OF PARTICLE BOARD
1726. PAPER CONES FOR LOUDSPEAKER
1727. PATCHES (TUBE REPAIR MATERIAL)
1728. PAINT INDUSTRY (PRIMER)
1729. PAPER PLANT (KRAFT & WHITE WRITING & PRINTING PAPER)
1730. PAPAIN FROM PAPAYA (PAPAYA LATEX)
1731. PCB SHEETS
1732. PCC ELECTRIC POLES
1733. PCC/RCC PIPES
1734. PEPSI COLA IN POLY TUBES
1735. PETROMAX CONTAINER
1736. PERFUMERY COMPOUND
1737. PERFUMERY COMPOUND, COSMETICS ETC.
1738. PERFUMED PHENYL (PINE OIL DISINFECTANT)
1739. PERFUMERY COMPOUNDS (AROMATIC)
1740. PERFUME (SPRAY)
1741. PERFUMERY COMPOUND (SYNTHETIC AGARBATTI)
1742. PERFUMES (SCENT) FROM LEMON GRASS OIL AND JASMINE OIL
1743. PET BOTTLE/CONTAINERS
1744. PERSONAL COMPUTER
1745. PECTIN BY RAW PAPAYA
1746. PECTIN FROM APPLE POMACE
1747. PECTIN FROM CITRUS, LEMON & ORANGES
1748. PECTIN BY MANGO PEELS
1749. PECTIN FROM ORANGE/ LIME PEELS
1750. PERFUME FOR SOAP, DETERGENT & AGARBATTI (YARA YARA)
1751. PERFUME & SCENTS
1752. PERFUMED PHENYL (THICK)
1753. PETROLEUM COKE
1754. PESTICIDE FORMULATIONS
1755. PETROLEUM JELLY
1756. PESTICIDES (MELATHION, MANCOZEV, COPPER OXY-CHLORIDE, WATTABLE SULPHUR, ZINC PHOSPHIDE)

1757. PEANUT COATING (SPICES, HONEY, CHEESE, CHOCOLATE, SALT)
1758. PENCIL (LEAD)
1759. PELLETIZER PLANT (FOR CATTLE FEED, POULTRY FEED, SHEEP FEED, PIG & OTHER FEED)
1760. PETHA PACKAGING
1761. PEPPERMINT OIL
1762. PHARMACEUTICAL
1763. ALCOHOL FROM NON-MOLASSES BASED
1764. POWER LOOM
1765. POWDER COATING (CHAMBER TYPE)
1766. POUCH FILLING for SAUNF, SUPARI & ELAICHI ETC.
1767. PUBLISHING & PRINTING UNIT
1768. POTATO STARCH
1769. POLYTHENE BAGS & AUTOMATIC PRINTING
1770. PVC FABRIC YARN ON POWER LOOM (TERRYCOT)
1771. PVC CONDUIT PIPE
1772. PVC PIPE & FITTINGS
1773. PHARMACEUTICAL UNITS (TABLETS, CAPSULES, SYRUPS, LOTION, OINTMENT, POWDER INJECTABLE, EYE DROPS & EYE OINTMENT ETC.)
1774. PHENACETIN
1775. PHTHALOCYNINE BLUE & GREEN
1776. PHOTO POLYMER COATING FOR PLATE & BLOCK MAKING
1777. PHOTO GRAVURE & FLEXO GRAPHIC PRINTING INK FOR PLASTIC FILM PRINTING
1778. PHOSPHORIC ACID FOR POLLUTION CONTROL
1779. PHOTO ALBUM ADHESIVES
1780. PHENOLIC RESIN
1781. PHENOLIC FORMALDEHYDE RESIN (PF RESIN)
1782. PHOTO GRAPHIC DEVELOPERS & FIXERS
1783. PHENYL ACETIC ACID
1784. PHOTO DEVELOPER & FIXER
1785. PHENOL
1786 PHOTO ETCHING OF STAINLESS STEEL PLATES
1787. PHOTO TYPE SETTING
1788. PHENYL (BROWN & WHITE)
1789. PHENYL (BLACK) IN LIQUID FORM
1790. PHOSPHORIC ACID FROM ROCK PHOSPHATE
1791. PHOTO COLOUR LAB (QSS)
1792. PHOTO EMULSION FOR ROTARY SCREEN PRINTING
1793. PHOSPHORIC ACID (Purification) FROM CRUDE
1794. PILFER PROOF CAPS & CROWN CAPS
1795. PILFER PROOF CAPS (P.P. CAPS)
1796. PIG IRON
1797. PICKLES, MURABBAS, SAUCES ETC. (VEGETARIAN & NONVEG.PICKLES)
1798. P.I.D. CONTROLLER
1799. PIGMENTS (DYE PIGMENTS)
1800. PISTON ASSEMBLY (ALUMINIUM ALLOY)

1801. PISTON ASSEMBLY (ALUMINIUM ALLOY)
1802. PIGGERY/MEAT/CHICKEN PROCESSING
1803. PINEAPPLE JUICE & CANING
1804. PINE APPLE SLICE CANNING
1805. PIGMENT DYE & DYE INTERMEDIATES
1806. PICKLE & SAUCES
1807. PIGMENT BINDER FOR TEXTILE PRINTING
1808. PIGGERY FARM
1809. PICKLES
1810. PICTURE VARNISH
1811. PLASTIC MOULDED T.V CABINETS
1812. PLASTIC INJECTION MOULDED AUTO COMPONENTS
1813. PLASTIC PRODUCT-AUDIO, VIDEO CASSETTE SHELL)
1814. PLASTIC BUCKETS & DOLI
1815. PLASTIC DRINKING STRAW
1816. PLASTIC FILM CAPACITOR
1817. PLAIN PAPER COPIER
1818. PLASTIC GRANULES (HDPE, LDPE, PP) FROM PLASTIC SCRAPS/WASTE
1819. PLATINUM LABORATORY APPARATUS
1820. PLASTIC SPRAY LAMINATED BRASS ARTICLES/BADGES
1821. PLASTIC TOOTH PICK
1822. PLASTIC I.V. BOTTLES
1823. PLASTIC FILM & SHEETS WITH PRINTING (FLEXO & ROTO) LDPE/HDPE/PP/HM/PVC
1824. PLASTIC CORRUGATED SHEET & BOXES
1825. PLASTIC BUTTONS FROM POLYESTER SHEET & RODS
1826. PLASTIC ADVERTISEMENT BALLOONS
1827. PLASTIC CONTAINER (BLOW MOULDED)
1828. PLASTIC INJECTION MOULDING PROJECTS
1829. PLASTIC SHEET FROM PLASTIC SCRAPS
1830. PLASTIC CANES
1831. PLASTIC SYRINGE (DISPOSABLE)
1832. PLASTER OF PARIS BANDAGES
1833. PLASTER OF PARIS
1834. PLASTER OF PARIS BANDAGES & COTTON ADHESIVE TAPE
1835. PLASTIC BUTTONS
1836. PLASTIC CONFERENCE BAGS, FOLDERS ETC.
1837. PLASTIC MOULDED FURNITURE
1838. PLASTIC WASTE REPROCESSING
1839. PLASTIC SUTLI
1840. PLANT PROTECTION EQUIPMENTS

EIRI

Areas of Expertise

IDENTIFICATION OR PRODUCT

CONDUCTING MARKET SURVEY

PREPARATION OF PROJECT PROFILES & FEASIBILITY STUDIES

PREPARATION OF TECHNOECONOMIC FEASIBILITY STUDIES

PREPARATION OF FINANCING SCHEME & LOAN APPLICATION

GUIDANCE OF PROCEDURES FOR GOVERNMENT CLEARANCE

TURNKEY SERVICES

TECHNOLOGY TRANSFER

1841. PLASTIC COLLAPSIBLE TUBES
1842. PLASTIC TANKS (WATER STORAGE SINTEX TYPE TANKS)
1843. PLASTIC MOULDED TOYS
1844. PLASTIC WARES
1845. PLASTIC SPRAY LAMINATED ARTICLES
1846. PLASTIC MOULDED ARTICLES
1847. PLY WOOD & PLY BOARD
1848. PLY WOOD
1849. PLY WOOD BOARD
1850. PLY WOOD & PLY BOARD (PHENOL BONDED, BOILING WATER PROOF, TERMITE, RESISTANCE, LAMINATED & COMMERCIAL PLY WOOD & PLY BOARD)
1851. PLASTIC STRIPPABLE COATING MATERIAL
1852. PLASTER OF PARIS (CALCIUM SULPHATE)
1853. POLYSTYRENE MOULDING (EXPANDED)
1854. POTATO POWDER
1855. POLYESTER RESIN
1856. POULTRY & CATTLE FEED
1857. POULTRY FEED
1858. POLYESTER YARN
1859. POUCH PACKING FOR MILK
1860. POWER PLANT
1861. PORK PROCESSING & FARMING
1862. POUCHES FOR OIL & GHEE PACKING
1863. POLYPROPYLENE BOX STRAPPING
1864. POWER SUPPLY (LINER&SWITCHMODE)
1865. POWER TRANSFORMER
1866. POLYURETHANE FOAM FLEXIBLE & RIGID
1867. POTATO CHIPS/WAFERS
1868. POWER SUPPLY (SWITCH MODE)
1869. POTATO GRANULE
1870. PROCESSED FRUITS
1871. POLYPROPYLENE/HDPE BOX STRAPPING
1872. POULTRY & BROILER FARMING
1873. POULTRY & HATCHERY FARMING
1874. POULTRY FARM
1875. POTABLE ALCOHOL FROM GRAINS & ROTTEN FRUITS
1876. POTASSIUM SILICATE
1877. POLY VINYL ALCOHOL
1878. POLY BUTENS FROM CAREFFINATES
1879. POLYESTER HOSIERY LABELS & PATCHES
1880. POLYURETHANE FOAM (P.U. FOAM)
1881. POLYPROPYLENE SPINNING FILAMENT YARN

Price Rs. 2500/- for each "Detailed Project Report" Payable in advance through Draft/Cash/M.O. in favour of "ENGINEERS INDIA RESEARCH INSTITUTE". Or Ask by V.P.P. PH.: 291 8117, 291 6431, 292 0361 Fax: 91-11-291 6431 (24 Hrs.)

1882. PORTABLE TELEVISION
1883. POLYSTER YARN FROM WASTE
1884. POLYSTER BEADING
1885. POUCH MAKING & GRAVURE PRINTING
1886. POWDER COATING
1887. POLY VINYL ACETATE
1888. POLYTHENE PRINTING BAG (P.P & H.M. FLEXIBLE FOUR COLOURS ROTO GRAVURE PRINT)
1889. POWER TRANSFORMERS UPTO 600 KVA
1890. POLYTHENE BAGS & TUBES
1891. POLYESTER RESIN FOR WIRE ENAMEL
1892. PORTABLE GENERATOR SET
1893. POTASSIUM NITRATE
1894. POTASSIUM PERMANGANATE (IN SOLUTION FORM)
1895. POWER COATING PAINT (EPOXY, ACRYLIC & POLYESTER BASIS)
1896. POTATO & ONION POWDER
1897. POTATO CHIPS WITH IMPORTED MACHINERY
1898. POLYURETHANE RIGID FROM MOULDING
1899. POLYURETHANE SOLE
1900. POLYURETHANE FOAM & ITS PRODUCTS
1901. POUCH PACKING FOR MILK
1902. POWER PLANT
1903. PORK PROCESSING & FARMING
1904. POTASSIUM IODIDE
1905. POTATO POWDER AUTOMATIC IMPORTED PLANT
1906. POTABLE LIQUOR
1907. POLYESTER YARN
1908. POLISH (WAX)
1909. POLISH (CAR)
1910. POTASSIUM DI-CHROMATE/BI-CHROMATE
1911. POWER INVERTER
1912. POLYPROPYLENE & MULTI-FILAMENT SPINNING YARN
1913. POLYESTER MICRO FIBER
1914. POWER PLANT (HYDRO BASED)
1915. POLYETHENE POUCHES FOR GHEE, BUTTER, OIL, MILK ETC.
1916. POLYTHENE BOTTLES FOR MINERAL WATER, I.V. FLUIDS ETC.
1917. POPLAR PLANTATION
1918. PRINTED TIN CONTAINERS
1919. PRINTING INKS
1920. PRINTING INKS (FLEXO GRAPHIC)
1921. PRINTED CIRCUIT BOARD
1922. PROCESSING OF FRUIT & VEGETABLE
1923. PRINTING PLATE FOR OFFSET PRINTING MACHINE
1924. PRUSSIAN BLUE
1925. PROCESSED FOOD
1926 PRECIPITATED CALCIUM CARBONATE
1927. PROCESSED CHEESE
1928. PRE STRESSED CONCRETE RAILWAY SLEEPER
1929. PRINTING (LETTER) PRESS
1930. PRINTING PRESS (OFFSET)
1931. PRESSURE DIE CASTING

ALUMINIUM
1932. PROTEIN -BASED PRODUCT
1933. PRECIOUS METAL PLATING & MANUFACTURE OF THEIR SALTS
1934. PRESSURE COOK-ER & ALUMINIUM UTENSILS
1935. PRESSURE COOKER (ALUMINIUM/STAINLESS STEEL) & WATER FILTER
1936. PRESSURE SENSITIVE ADHESIVE TAPES
1937. PRESSURE SENSITIVE ADHESIVE FOR BOPP TAPES (ACRYLIC BASED)
1938. PRECIPITATED CALCIUM CARBONATE FROM BYE-PRODUCTS LIME SLURRY & CARBON DIOXIDE
1939. PRINTING INK (ROTO GRAVURE & FLEXO GRAPHIC)
1940. PRINTING INK (OFFSET)
1941. PROCESSED FOOD & MARINE PRODUCTS
1942. PRINTING INDUSTRY (DTP & OFFSET)
1943. PRESSURE COOKER
1944. PRESSURE COOKER (ALUMINIUM & STAINLESS STEEL)
1945. PRECIPITATED SILICA
1946. PRODUCTS BASED ON INDUSTRIAL WASTE (COVERING TEN PROJECT PROFILES)
1947. PROCESSED FOOD & SPICES
1948. PROCESSED CONTROL TIMER (Electronic Timer)
1949. PRAWN FISH FARMING
1950. P.U. (POLYURETHANE) RIGID FOAM
1951. PUMIC WHITE ABRASIVE CAKE/STICK
1952. PULVERIZED FLOUR MILL
1953. PULSE MILL (DAL MILL)
1954. PULP FROM WOOD, BAMBOO OR GRASS
1955. PULP FROM BAMBOO & WOOD
1956. PUTTY (METAL CASEMENT PUTTY)-ASIAN PAINT TYPE
1957. PUTTY & WATER PROOFING PLANT
1958. PURIFICATION OF CASEIN
1959. PVC INSULATION TAPES
1960. PVC WIRES & CABLES
1961. PVC WIRES/TWIN FLAT CABLE
1962. PVC PIPES & FITTINGS
1963. PVC GRANULES/ COMPOUNDS BY CHEMICAL PROCESS
1964. PVC GRANULES FROM PVC SCRAPS (POLLUTION CONTROL)
1965. PVC GRANULES/ COMPOUNDS BY PLASTIC WASTE
1966. PVC RIGID PIPE
1967. PVC INSULATED CABLES
1968. PVC PROFILES (DOOR & WINDOW)
1969. PVC FOOTWEAR

1970. PVC SOLES FOR LEATHER SHOE UPPERS
1971. PVC STABILIZERS
1972. PVC/XLPE (ARMOURED) CABLES
1973. PVC WIRE & CABLES/PIPES & FITTINGS
1974. PVC CASING CAPING MATERIAL FOR ELECTRICAL FITTING
1975. PVC/PLASTIC/SOFT/RIGID/ FILM SHEETS
1976. PVC LEATHER CLOTH
1977. PVC CABLES
1978. PVC FLOOR TILES
1979. PVC ELECTRICAL INSULATION TAPE WITH PRINTING (STEEL GRIP TYPE)
1980. PVC COATING ON LEATHER SHEETS
1981. PVC BATTERY SEPARATOR
1982. PVC PIPES & FITTINGS (RIGID PIPE, FLEXIBLE PIPE, CONDUIT PIPE, ELBOW FITTING, T-JOINTS ETC.)
1983. PVC RULLER
1984. PVC SOLVENT CEMENT
1985. PVC SUCTION HOSES
1986. PVC FLEXIBLE PIPES
1987. PVA BASED ADHESIVES
1988. PVC ON G.I. WIRE
1989. PVC ROOFING SHEET
1990. PVC FILM
1991. QSS COLOUR PHOTO LAB
1992. QUICK LIME
1993. RAILWAY SLEEPERS (PRE STRESSED CONCRETE)
1994. RAISING COMPOUNDS OR EMBOSSING POWDER
1995. RABBIT FARMING
1996. RAINBOW COLOUR ON PVC FILM & SHEET
1997. RAINBOW COLOUR ON METALS
1998. RAZOR BLADE
1999. RCC SPUN PIPES
2000. REACTIVE DYES
2001. READY MADE PROCESSED FOOD
2002. RECTIFIED SPIRIT FROM MOLASSES & MAHUA FLOWER
2003. REROLLING OF SARIYA (TOR)
2004. RESTAURANT
2005. REFINED OILS (COTTON SEEDS, GROUNDNUT, SUNFLOWER ETC.)
2006. RESIN BASED LEATHER BINDER
2007. REROLLING OF STEEL
2008. RECOVERY OF LEAD FROM DISPOSED LEAD ACID BATTERY
2009. REFRIGERATOR & MINI REFRIGERATOR
2010. RESIN CORED SOFT SOLDERING WIRE
2011. RECLAMATION OF TRANSFORMER OIL
2012. RED IRON OXIDE
2013. RE-ROLLING MILL (ALUMINIUM) & UTENSILS
2014. REFINED SUNFLOWER SEED OIL
2015. RESIDENTIAL APARTMENT
2016. RESIDENTIAL & DELUXE FLATS
2017. RECLAMATION OF USED ENGINE OIL
2018. RECLAMATION OF WAX SLUDGES FOR MANUFACTURING OF MICROCRYSTALINE WAX
2019. READY MADE GARMENTS

2020. READY MADE GARMENTS AND HOSIERY
2021. REFINING OF GROUNDNUT OIL
2022. RECONDITIONING OF EMPTY CEMENT JUTE BAG
2023. RED OXIDE PRIMER
2024. REFINING OF CASTOR OIL
2025. RECHARGEABLE TORCHES
2026. READY MADE GARMENTS MERCHANDISE PLANT
2027. RECOVERY OF SILVER NITRATE FROM PHOTO GRAPHIC WASTE FIXERS
2028. REMOTE CONTROL SYSTEMS (FOR STARTING DOOR, OPEN & CLOSE HEADLIGHT ON & OFF FOR CAR)
2029. RECOVERY OF SILVER FROM WASTE FIXTURE BLEACH OBTAINED FROM PHOTO COLOUR LAB BY SULPHIDE PROCESS
2030. RECYCLING OF WASTE CELLULOSE ACETATE INTO CELLULOSE ACETATE SHEETS
2031. RED OXIDE PIGMENTS FROM IRON PICKLING PLANT WASTE
2032. REFRACTORIES
2033. REFINED OIL & GROUNDNUT OIL
2034. REROLLING OF STEEL CUTTING
2035. RED MUD PVC PIPES & FITTINGS
2036. REXINE CLOTH & ALIKE PRODUCTS
2037. RECONDITIONING OF T.V PICTURE TUBE
2038. RECONDITIONING OF FLUORESCENT TUBE
2039. RECTIFIED SPIRIT FOR POTABLE ALCOHOL, INDUSTRIAL ALCOHOL & MEDICAL ALCOHOL
2040. RE-REFINING OF USED LUBRICANT
2041. RECTIFIED SPIRIT FROM RICEPADDY STRAW
2042. RED OXIDE PRIMER (ANTI CORROSIVE)
2043. READY MADE GARMENTS (100% EOU)-STITCHING, WASHING, DYEING, PRINTING & FINISHING ETC.)
2044. REFINED VEGETABLE OILS
2045. REROLLING OF STEEL SECTIONS
2046. REFINING OF MUSTARD OILS
2047. REPACKING OF MEDICINES
2048. READY MADE SALWAR SUITS
2049. RED OXIDE PIGMENTS
2050. RECLAMATION OF HYDRAULIC OIL
2051. RED MIRROR BY ELECTROLESS DIPPING METHOD
2052. REACTIVE DYE M5B DYE
2053. RIGID PVC PIPES & FITTINGS (RIGID PIPES, PIPE FITTINGS LIKE ELBOW FITTINGS, T-JOINTS ETC.)
2054. RE-WINDING OF BURNT ELECTRIC MOTOR
2055. RECLAMATION OF NICKEL FROM SPENT CATALYST OF VANASPATI INDUSTRY
2056. RECLAMATION OF SPENT BLEACHING EARTH
2057. REFRIGERANT ALFA-R134
2058. RESISTORS (WIRE WOUND)
2059. RESIN CORED SOFT SOLDERING WIRE
2060. RESIN COATED SAND (SHELL MOULDING SAND)
2061. RED PHOSPHORUS
2062. RICE HUSK BASED CEMENT
2063. RICE&CORNFLAKE
2064. RICE MILL
2065. RICE FLAKES (CHUDA)
2066. RICE POLISHING AND PACKAGING IN POUCHES
2067. RIGID PVC PIPES
2068. RIGID PVC PIPES & FITTINGS
2069. RICE BRAN OIL
2070. RICE TRADING (BASMATI)
2071. RICE POLISHERS
2072. RIVETS
2073. ROLLING BEARING FORGING OF OUTER/INNER RINGS
2074. ROLLER FLOUR MILL

2075. ROLLING MILL
2076. ROLLING OF STAINLESS STEEL SHEET (PATTA)
2077. ROTARY PRINTING & DYEING ON COTTON/ SYNTHETIC TEXTILE
2078. ROOFING TILES (CEMENT)
2079. ROSIN & TERPENTINE DISTILLATION
2080. ROSE CRYSTALS
2081. ROSE PLANTATION & ROSE OIL EXTRACTION
2082. ROLLER FLOUR MILL & MUSTARD OIL MILL
2083. ROTO GRAVURE PRINTING
2084. ROASTED & FRIED DRY FRUITS, GROUNDNUTS/ PEANUTS WITH PACKAGING
2085. ROUND GLASS MARBLES
2086. ROASTED/SALTED/COATED CASHEWNUT, PEANUT, ALMOND (IMPORTEDAUTOMATIC)
2086A. RIGID & ELASTIC TAPES
2087. RUBBER BALLOONS (DECORATIVE, TOYS & INDUSTRIAL BALOONS)
2088. RUBBER HAWAI CHAPPALS
2089. RUBBER ADHESIVES
2090. RUBBER CHAPPALS & GENTS LEATHER SHOES
2091. RUBBERISED CORK SHEETS
2092. RUBBER SHEET & ALLIED HOSPITAL GOODS
2093. RUBBERIZED COIR FOAM
2094. RUBBER FOAM MATTRESS
2095. RUBBER SHEET FROM USED TYRE
2096. RUBBER SHEET FOR SHOE SOLE
2097. RUBBER LATEX FOAM PRODUCT
2098. RUBBER CONDOM
2099. RUBBER SOLUTION
2100. RUBBER AUTO PARTS
2101. RUBBER LINING
2102. RUBBER GOODS FROM WASTE RUBBER
2103. RUBBING COMPOUND FOR AUTOMOBILE
2104. RUBBER BANDS
2105. RUM FLAVOUR
2106. RUBBER TOYS
2107. RUBBER PLASTIC STAMP & PAD (AUTOMATIC)
2108. RUBBER HOT WATER BOTTLES
2109. RUBBER COTS & APRONS
2110. RUBBERIZED CLOTH
2111. RUST PREVENTIVE (PETROLEUM)
2112. RUBBER COMPOUND TOYS (USING PLASTER OF PARIS)
2113. RUBBER BUSHING
2114. RUBBER HOSE PIPES & RUBBER GLAZING
2115. RUBBER PLANTATION
2116. RUBBER MOULDING & LINING OF RUBBER SHEETING
2117. RUBBER ADHESIVE (All PURPOSE)-NEOPRENE & ISOPRENE BASED
2118. RUBBER ADHESIVE
2119. RUBBER ROLLERS
2120. RUBBER ROLLER FOR PRINTING , MACHINE
2121. RUBBER ROLLER FOR RICE MILL

2122. RUBBER CONVEYOR BELT
2123. RUBBER HOSE PIPE
2124. RUBBER RECLAMING
2125. RUBBER CAPS FOR PHARMACEUTICAL USE
2126. RUBBER ROLLERS FOR TEXTILE MILLS & PAPER INDUSTRIES
2127. RUBBER ROLLER& EBONITE ROLLER
2128. RUBBER (LATEX) LINED JUTE MATS
2129. RUBBER PROCESS OIL
2130. RUBBER BELTING (FAN/V BELT)
2131. RUBBER (FIELD) CONVERTED TO THE 60% LATEX RUBBER
2132. RUBBER ERASERS (SCHOOL RUBBER)
2133. RUBBER AUTO GASKET
2134. RUBBERISED CANVAS SHOES
2135. RUBBER (SYNTHETIC)
2136. RUBBER HOSES FOR AUTOMOBILE
2137. SAFETY GLASS
2138. SANITARY WARE & WALL TILE/FLOOR TILE
2139. SALINE & INJECTION WATER
2140. SANITARY NAPKIN
2141. SANITARY NAPKIN & DISPOSABLE BABY DIAPERS
2142. SAW MILLS
2143. SAFETY MATCHES (MATCH BOX)
2144. SAND PAPER (ABRASIVE PAPER)
2145. SALT GLAZED STONE WARE PIPES & FITTINGS
2146. SAND LIME BRICKS
2147. SAGOL
2148. SAUSAGED FOOD CASING (100%EOU)
2150. SAFETY PINS
2151. SALINE & INJECTION WATER
2152. SALTED GROUNDNUT
2153. SAGO SEED FROM POTATO & SWEET POTATO (SABOO DANA)
2154. SAFETY MATCH & FIREBOX
2155. SALT LICKS FOR CATTLES
2156. SANITARY NAPKINS (TAB ENDED-TUBE FILLED)
2157. SAFETY BELT
2158. SABOO DANA
2159. SCOOTER TYRE & TUBE
2160. SCREEN PRINTING INKS
2161. SCREEN PRINTING ON PAPER/CARDS
2162. SCREEN PRINTING
2163. SCREEN EMULSION
2164. SCREWS FOR AUDIO CASSETTE
2165. SCENT & PERFUME FOR AGARBATTI
2166. SCENTS/PERFUME
2267. SCENT BY LEMON GRASS OIL & JASMINE OIL
2168. SCENTED SUPARI
2169. SCENT (INTIMATED SCENT, CHEMICALS ETC.)

2170 SCREEN PRINTING ON TEXTILES
2171. SCHOOL
2172. SCOOTER RIMS
2173. SECURITY SYSTEM
2174. SECONDARY LEAD EXTRACTION FROM SCRAPS (A) BATTERY PLATE (B) PIPES (C) SHEETS
2175. SNACK FOOD (CRAX TYPE-ROLL & BALL TYPE)
2176. SNUFF FACTORY
2177. SELF TAPPING STEEL SCREWS
2178. SEWING NEEDLES (FOR USED WITH DOMESTIC/ INDUSTRIAL SEWING MACHINE)
2179. SECURITY OFFSET PRINTING PRESS
2180. SEWING THREADS, REELS & BALLS
2181. SEMI CONDUCTORS FOR TRANSISTORS & DIODE
2182. SEMI CONDUCTOR DEVICES
2183. SESAME OIL FROM SESAME SEEDS
2184. SERVO CONTROLLED STABILIZERS (1-100 KVA)
2185. SEWING MACHINE (PARTS MACHINING & ASSEMBLY)
2186. SEMI AUTOMATIC BRICKS PLANT
2187. SEMI AUTOMATIC CONFECTIONERY PLANT
2188. SEAMLESS M.S. TUBES
2189. SEALING MATERIAL COMPATIBLE TO CERAMIC & NICHROME WIRE
2190. S.G. IRON & MALLEABLE IRON CASTING
2191. S.G. IRON & ALLOY STEEL CASTINGS
2192. SHEET GLASS
2193. SHAMPOOS
2194. SHOE POLISH PUFF
2195. SHOVELS
2196. SHOCK ABSORBERS
2197. SHAMPOOS FOR DOGS
2198. SHAMPOO & CREAM (COLD CREAM, ALL PURPOSE & VARNISHING CREAM)
2199. SHUTTLE LESS LOOM
2200. SHAVING CREAM & SHAVING SOAP
2201. SHAWLS (POWER LOOM)
2202. SHOE UPPER
2203. SHOE POLISH (BOOT POLISH)
2204. SHEET METAL PRODUCTS (FERROUS/NON-FERROUS)
2205. SHIP CONTAINERS
2206. SHEEP & GOAT FARMING
2207. SHOE LACES
2208. SHOES, CANVAS AS WELL AS BOOT, RUBBER KNEES, JUNGLE BOOT COMBAT, RUBBER LINED
2209. SHAVING CREAM (LATHER)
2210. SHERBAT
2211. SHOTS & GRITS OF HIGH CARBON STEELS
2212. SHUTTLE COCKS FOR BADMINTON
2213. SHOE TACKS
2214. SHEHNAZ HUSSAIN'S INSTITUTE FOR SKIN, HEALTH & HAIR CARE (HEALTH CLUB CUM BEAUTY PARLOUR TRAINING INSTITUTE)
2215. SILK COCOON CULTIVATION (GROWING OF SILK COCOON FROM SILK WORM)
2216. SILICA GEL
2217. SINGLE SUPER PHOSPHATE (S.S.P)
2218. SILICON COMPOUND
2219. SILICON EMULSION (MOULD RELEASING AGENTS)
2220. SILK SCREEN PRINTING ON SAREES (BLOCK & SCREEN PROCESS)

2221. SILK WASTE PROCESSING & SPINNING
2222. SILK REELING UNIT
2223. SILICA SAND
2224. SILICON RELEASE PAPER
2225. SILVER NITRATE
2226. SILVER DIP (CLEANING SOLUTION)
2227. SIZING OF YARN
2228. SINTERED BUSHES
2229. SINTERED BUSHES (SELF LUBRICATED)
2230. SINTERED METAL PRODUCTS
2231. SHISHAM PLANTATION
2232. SILICON RUBBER NIPPLE/ TEAT
2233. SILENCERS FOR TWO/ THREE WHEELERS
2234. SINGLE CORE TWIN FLAT CABLE
2235. SILICON EMULSION
2236. SILVER EXTRACTION FROM WASTE HYPO SOLUTION BY CHEMICAL PROCESS
2237. SILVER EXTRACTION BY WASTE HYPO SOLUTION, X-RAY FILM
2238. SILVER JEWELLERY & CUTLERY (GOLD PLATED)
2239. SILVER & GOLD JEWELLERY
2240. SINGLE SUPER PHOSPHATE (S.S.P) & SULPHURIC ACID
2241. SILVER & GOLD PLATING ON PVC & NYLON
2242. SILICON
2243. SINDHUR
2244. SILVER DIP (CLEANING SOLUTION)
2245. SILVER PLATED UTENSILS
2246. SINTERED BEARINGS
2247. SILVER JEWELLERY
2248. SILVER BRAZING FOIL
2249. SILK FABRICS (POWER LOOM)
2250. SILICON FROM RICE HUSK
2251. SKIMMED MILK (LIQUID)
2252. SKIMMED MILK POWDER
2253. SKYLATED PHENOL
2254. SKY BAGS
2255. SKIMMED MILK POWDER & GHEE
2256. SMOKE LESS COAL
2257. SOFT DRINKS (NON CARBONATED)
2258. SODIUM DICHROMATE & SODIUM SULPHATE
2259. SOLVENT EXTRACTION & REFINING OF SOYA BEAN
2260. SORBITOL
2261. SODIUM TRI-POLY PHOSPHATE
2262. SODIUM THIO-SULPHATE FROM SODIUM SULPHATE
2263. SODIUM SULPHATE
2264. SOLID FUEL CAKE
2265. SODIUM HEXA META PHOSPHATE
2266. SODIUM SULPHIDE FROM AMMONIUM SULPHITE & SODIUM CHLORIDE
2267. SOFT DRINK CONCENTRAT (SACCHARINE BASED)
2268. SOAP COATED PAPER
2269. SODIUM BENZOATE
2270. SOLVENT EXTRACTION PLANT
2271. SOCKS KNITTING
2272. SODA ASH
2273. SODA LIME
2274. SOLAR CELL
2275. SOLAR COOKER
2276. SOLAR PHOTO VOLTAGE MODULES (SOLAR ELECTRICAL CELLS & PANEL)
2277. SOLAR PHOTO VOLTAIC SYSTEM
2278. SOLAR PUMP
2279. SOLAR ELECTRICAL CELLS & PANELS
2280. SOLAR PUMP
2281. SOLAR ENERGY WATER HEATER (GEYSER)
2282. SOLAR POWER EQUIPMENTS